➤ 2021–2023 ◄

A COMPLETE GUIDE TO GUN LAW IN TEXAS

TEXAS GUN LAW
Armed And Educated

Copyright © 2021 Stanley Marie, LLC
All rights reserved.
No part of this book may be reproduced in any form or by any means without permission in writing from the publisher.

Written by Kirk Evans, Edwin Walker, Emily Taylor, and Richard Hayes and published in the United States of America.

Texas Law Shield, LLC
ISBN 978-1-7333432-7-5

To order additional books by phone or
for wholesale orders call (877) 448-6839.

TABLE OF CONTENTS

PREFACE vi

CHAPTER ONE 1
Brief Legal History Of The Right To Bear Arms And The Laws Regulating Firearms
I. Introduction And Overview 1
II. Do I Have A Constitutional Right As An Individual To Keep And Bear Arms? 2
III. Major Firearms Statutes Every Gun Owner Needs To Know 9
IV. Do Texans Have A Right To Keep And Bear Arms In The Texas Constitution? 12

CHAPTER TWO 17
Know Your Rights: Part I
The Fourth Amendment: Understanding Police Power
Some Basic Legal Concepts
I. Introduction And Overview 17
II. What Is The Fourth Amendment? 18
III. Legal Levels Of Proof 19
IV. What Is A Search? 22
V. What Is A Seizure? 23
VI. Police Power 23
VII. Encounters With The Police 25
VIII. The Fifth Amendment 28
IX. What Happens If The Police Violate My Rights? 30

CHAPTER THREE 33
Know Your Rights: Part II
The Fourth Amendment: Understanding
The Warrant Requirement In Texas
I. Introduction And Overview 33
II. What Is The Warrant Requirement? 34

CHAPTER FOUR..................................41
Know Your Rights: Part III
The Fourth Amendment: Exceptions To The Warrant Requirement
   I. Introduction And Overview 41
   II. When Can The Police Search Or Arrest Me Without A Warrant? .. 42
   III. When Can The Police Search My Home Without A Warrant?..... 45
   IV. When Can The Police Search My Vehicle Without A Warrant?.... 48
   V. Other Search Issues...................................... 53

CHAPTER FIVE...................................59
Legal Definitions And Classifications Of Firearms: What Is Legal?
   I. Introduction And Overview 59
   II. Ammunition And The Law............................... 70

CHAPTER SIX....................................79
Purchasing, Transferring, And Possessing Firearms
   I. Laws Of Purchasing And Possessing: The Basics 79
   II. Federal Law Disqualifications For Purchasing And Possessing Firearms 86
   III. Texas Law Disqualifications: Who Cannot Buy A Firearm Under Texas Law?..................................... 101
   IV. Understanding "Private Sales" Laws 108
   V. Buying, Selling, And Transferring Through An FFL 113
   VI. What If I'm Denied The Right To Purchase A Firearm?......... 119
   VII. Additional Considerations In Firearms Purchasing And Possession Law.................................. 120
   VIII. Ammunition: The Law Of Purchasing And Possession 125

CHAPTER SEVEN..................................129
When Can I Legally Use My Gun: Part I
Understanding The Law Of Justification
Some Basic Legal Concepts
   I. Ignorance Of The Law Is No Excuse!...................... 129
   II. Gun Owners Need To Know Chapter 9 Of The Texas Penal Code. . 130
   III. To Legally Use Force Or Deadly Force, You Must Be "Justified." What Is Legal Justification? 130
   IV. Categories Of Force For Justification Under Chapter 9 132

    V. What Does It Mean To "Reasonably Believe Force Is
       Immediately Necessary"?................................. 142
    VI. The Burden Of Proof In Criminal Cases..................... 147

CHAPTER EIGHT 149
When Can I Legally Use My Gun: Part II
Self-Defense And Defense Of Others
Understanding When Force And Deadly Force
Can Be Legally Used Against Another Person
    I. Introduction And Overview 149
    II. Defending People With Force Or Deadly Force.............. 150
    III. Do I Have A Legal Responsibility To Defend Another Person?... 184
    IV. The Use Of Force In Preventing Suicide 187

CHAPTER NINE 189
When Can I Legally Use My Gun: Part III
Understanding When Deadly Force Can Be Used Against Animals
    I. Can I Legally Use Deadly Force Against Animals?............ 189

CHAPTER TEN....................................199
When Can I Legally Use My Gun: Part IV
Understanding When Deadly Force Can Be Used To Protect Property
    I. Overview And Location Of The Law To Protect Property....... 199
    II. When Is Someone Legally Justified To Use Force But Not Deadly
       Force To Protect Their Own Property?...................... 200
    III. When Is Someone Legally Justified In Using Deadly Force
       To Protect Or Recover Their Own Property? 208
    IV. Can I Protect Another Person's Property?.................... 213
    V. How Are The Crimes Associated With Defending Property
       Defined Under Texas Law?............................... 215
    VI. How Can I Assist Law Enforcement?....................... 218

CHAPTER ELEVEN...............................223
What Crimes Can I Be Charged With When My Use Of Deadly
Force Is Not Justified?
    I. Introduction And Overview 223
    II. Crimes Against Persons 224
    III. Crimes Against Society................................. 226
    IV. The Aftermath.. 230

CHAPTER TWELVE **233**
Law Of Handgun Carry: Part I
Qualifications To Carry A Handgun
    I. The Evolution Of The Texas Handgun Carry Law 234
    II. Qualifications For And Steps To Get An LTC 235
    III. The LTC Application And Process 247
    IV. Benefits Of Having An LTC 249
    V. Qualifications For Texas Constitutional Carry 256

CHAPTER THIRTEEN **259**
Law Of Handgun Carry: Part II
Methods And Notice For Legally Carrying In Texas
    I. How To Carry A Handgun 261
    II. What Signs Apply To Me? 265

CHAPTER FOURTEEN **283**
Law Of Handgun Carry: Part III
Where A Non-Prohibited Person Can Legally Carry
    I. Introduction 284
    II. Federal Property 284
    III. General Preemption Laws For Texas 292
    IV. Texas Penal Code Section 46.03: Places People Should Not Carry . 294
    V. Texas Penal Code Section 46.15: The Non-Applicability Statute... 316
    VI. Generally Non-Prohibited Places A Non-Prohibited Person May
        Carry Without Notice 318
    VII. Understanding Gun-Free School Zones Laws 350
    VIII. How LTC Holders And Constitutional Carriers Should Interact
        With Law Enforcement While Carrying 355
    IX. Law Concerning Long Guns 361
    X. Traveling Across State Lines With Firearms 363
    XI. Air Travel With A Firearm 366

CHAPTER FIFTEEN **373**
Restoration Of Firearms Rights:
The Law Of Pardons And Expunctions
    I. Is It Possible To Restore A Person's Right To Bear Arms? 373
    II. Federal Law 375
    III. Texas Law 380

CHAPTER SIXTEEN **387**
I'm Being Sued For What?
Civil Liability If You Have Used Your Gun
    I. What Does It Mean To Be Sued? 387
    II. What Might You Be Sued For? Gun-Related Claims In Civil Courts 395
    III. What Can The Plaintiff Recover? 403
    IV. How Good Are Texas Civil Immunity Laws For Gun Owners?... 406
    V. What About Third Parties? 411
    VI. Will Insurance Cover It If I Shoot Someone? 413
    VII. What Civil Liability Does A Person Face If Their Children Access Their Firearms? 415

CHAPTER SEVENTEEN **421**
Beyond Firearms: Knives, Clubs, And Tasers
    I. Introduction And Overview 421
    II. Absolutely Prohibited Weapons 423
    III. Generally Prohibited Weapons 428
    IV. Tasers 438
    V. Traps And Spring Guns 439

CHAPTER EIGHTEEN **441**
What Is The National Firearms Act?
Silencers, Short-Barreled Weapons, And Machine Guns
    I. Introduction And Overview 442
    II. What Firearms Does The NFA Regulate? 443
    III. Process And Procedure For Obtaining NFA Firearms 459

APPENDICES **469**
    Appendix A: Selected Texas Statutes 469
    Appendix B: Selected Federal Forms 475

ABOUT THE ATTORNEY AUTHORS **479**

PREFACE

U.S. & Texas LawShield would like to thank its members and others who made previous editions of *Texas Gun Law: Armed And Educated* an overwhelming success. As many Texans know, the 87th Texas Legislature created, amended, and repealed several laws that impact the Second Amendment rights of gun owners. In order to keep Texans up to date on the law, U.S. & Texas LawShield has prepared this revised 5th Edition of *Texas Gun Law: Armed And Educated*.

As lawyers with years of representing law-abiding gun owners in cases all over the State of Texas, we have seen how well-intended folks exercising their rights get mixed up in the legal system because they simply didn't understand the law. Through this revised edition, we are continuing with our commitment to produce the best one-volume resource that provides any gun owner with a base level of knowledge about laws that they need to know.

The law can be complicated, overlapping, hard to understand, and in some cases, completely arbitrary to the point of confusion. Laws are often written by lawyers for lawyers or are the result of political compromises generating confusing laws that the courts are left to interpret. After years of legal work in the arena of firearms law, we found there did not exist a resource that explained gun law in a manner that was easy for everyone to understand—because understanding the law goes far beyond just reading statutes or regulations. If you do not know either the process by which the law is being administered or how the courts are interpreting the meaning of the law, then you don't understand the full legal story.

That is why we wrote and will continue to revise *Texas Gun Law: Armed And Educated*. It is a one-volume guide to the minimum law every gun owner needs to know to stay on the right side of the law. Whenever appropriate, we tried to present useful analysis and real-world applications. Our goal was to explain the "law" so gun owners could inform and educate themselves. Thousands of attorney hours have gone into producing this resource, always with the goal in mind of education. Our collective legal experience has taught us that anyone can become ensnared in the legal system. Many people firmly believe that "it" can't happen to them. Even people who have never been in trouble before find themselves in the world of statutes, court, prosecutors, and law enforcement through ignorance of the law.

We are committed to helping protect Second Amendment rights for all legal gun owners. It is our passion and our mission. We want people to know the law, because only through eternal vigilance will we protect our cherished right to bear arms. If you own a gun, the laws concerning firearms and their use apply to you. Ignorance of the law is not a valid legal excuse. Therefore, if you want to stay legal, know the law. We hope you enjoy reading this book as much as we enjoyed writing it!

➤ CHAPTER ONE ◄

BRIEF LEGAL HISTORY OF
THE RIGHT TO BEAR ARMS
And The Laws Regulating Firearms

I. INTRODUCTION AND OVERVIEW

To fully understand gun rights today in Texas or the United States, one should start first at the beginning: the formation document for our federal government, the United States Constitution. The Constitution was originally written without any enumerated guaranteed individual rights. The Founding Fathers thought it obvious and apparent that individuals had rights; therefore, there was no reason to elucidate them in a document that was supposed to control the government. James Madison also thought that by naming certain rights, it would imply that those were the only rights an individual possessed. After much discussion, and a complete change of opinion by Madison, the lack of enumerated rights was remedied in the First Congressional session and the state ratification process. When the dust settled, 10 amendments were added to the Constitution; these 10 amendments are the Bill of Rights. It is the Second Amendment that concerns firearms specifically, though throughout this book, we will reference many others, including the Fourth and Fifth Amendments that both affect your right to bear arms and fundamental rights for us all.

II. DO I HAVE A CONSTITUTIONAL RIGHT AS AN INDIVIDUAL TO KEEP AND BEAR ARMS?

Yes. The United States Supreme Court has decided that an individual has a constitutional right to keep and bear arms. This right is recognized by the Second Amendment, which simply states:

> A well-regulated Militia, being necessary to the security of a free State, the right of the people to keep and bear Arms, shall not be infringed.

From a plain reading, there are two important parts to this amendment. First, the prefatory clause, which is an introduction explaining why the right is necessary; and second, the operative clause, which states what the right is. The prefatory clause of the Second Amendment explains that a well-regulated militia is necessary to the security of a free state. The operative clause states that the individual right to bear arms belongs to the people. For years, before the issue was decided, anti-gun activists have tried to argue that the Second Amendment only applied to "militias" and not individuals. Luckily, this argument is not the law. Despite Supreme Court rulings stating otherwise, this myth seems to persist. What do these parts of the Second Amendment mean? Are they the same, or are they different?

A. What is a "well-regulated militia"?

As we discussed earlier, the first part of the Second Amendment references a "well-regulated militia." What is a well-regulated militia? The U.S. Supreme Court has made rulings as to what this phrase does and does not mean. In 1939, in the case of *United States v. Miller*, 307 U.S. 174 (1939) (ironically, a ruling that upheld federal firearms regulations), the Court defined a "militia" as comprising "all males physically capable of acting in concert for the common defense." Based on how the Amendment was drafted, the Court stated, it was clear that the militia predated Article I of the Constitution, because unlike armies and navies, it did not have to be created by Congress. What then is "well-regulated" per the Court? It is exactly what it sounds like: the imposition of discipline and training. So, is this just the National Guard? No.

In the case of *D.C. v. Heller*, 554 U.S. 570 (2008), the U.S. Supreme Court stated that the well-regulated militia is not the state's military forces, but a separate entity altogether. The Supreme Court explained that the word "militia" referred to the body of the people, and they— the people—were required to keep a centralized government in check. The Supreme Court considered and rejected the position that the National Guard is the current militia under the Second Amendment.

B. How has the phrase "right to keep and bear arms" been interpreted by the courts?

One of the first cases to directly deal with the Second Amendment was *United States v. Miller*. In *Miller*, the Supreme Court found that the National Firearms Act ("NFA"), which imposed registration requirements on machine guns, short-barreled weapons, destructive devices, and other similarly unique firearms, did not violate the Second Amendment. The Court used the reasoning that possession of weapons regulated by the NFA did not reasonably relate to the preservation or efficiency of a well-regulated militia; therefore, the NFA was upheld as constitutional.

> **UNITED STATES v. MILLER, 307 U.S. 174 (1939)**
>
> **THE FACTS**
> Defendants, Miller and Layton, transported a double-barrel 12-gauge shotgun with a barrel length of less than 18 inches from Oklahoma to Arkansas and were being prosecuted under the National Firearms Act (which required certain types of firearms to be registered and a tax to be paid). Defendants challenged the NFA as an unconstitutional violation of the Second Amendment.
>
> **THE LEGAL HOLDING**
> Upheld the National Firearms Act as constitutional and not a violation of the Second Amendment.

An interesting quirk of history in the *Miller* case (and not a shining moment for the legal system) is that Miller's attorney never appeared at the arguments before the U.S. Supreme Court because he was court-appointed and had not been paid. There was no written brief and no legal representation at oral arguments by the party arguing that the law was unconstitutional. The Court only heard the government's side. To make matters worse, Miller was shot to death before the decision was rendered.

C. 69 years later, the U.S. Supreme Court interprets the Second Amendment again: *D.C. v. Heller*

It would be 69 years after *Miller* until the U.S. Supreme Court addressed the Second Amendment directly again, except this time, the Court would hear both the government's and the defendant's arguments. Fortunately, freedom and Second Amendment rights prevailed in court that day. The Court held that individuals have a right to keep and bear arms.

DISTRICT OF COLUMBIA v. HELLER, 554 U.S. 570 (2008)

THE FACTS

Heller applied for a handgun ownership permit and was denied; additionally, D.C. required that all firearms (including rifles and shotguns) be kept unloaded and disassembled, or bound by a trigger lock, even in a person's own home.

THE LEGAL HOLDING

1. The Supreme Court found that the Second Amendment protects an individual right of firearms ownership for the purpose of self-defense and is not connected with any militia or military purposes; it further elaborated that individual self-defense is "the central component" of the Second Amendment. Further, handguns are the primary defensive weapon of choice and are protected by the Second Amendment.
2. A well-regulated militia is not the state's military force.
3. The Court also discussed what the phrase "bear arms" meant: "wear, bear, or carry...upon the person or in clothing or in a pocket, for the purpose...of being armed and ready for offensive or defensive action in a case of conflict with another person."
4. The D.C. regulations were held to be unconstitutional.
5. The Court concluded that, like other rights, the right to bear arms is not completely absolute. Reasonable provisions and restrictions have been upheld.

Keep in mind *D.C. v. Heller* was a split 5-4 decision; only one Justice away from a completely different outcome, where the Second Amendment (according to the dissent) had "outlived its usefulness and should be ignored."

D. Can states ignore the Second Amendment? *McDonald v. City of Chicago*

D.C. v. Heller was fantastic, but there was a slight quirk: the District of Columbia is under the exclusive jurisdiction of Congress and is not part of any state. Therefore, the case shed no light on the question of what states can do when it comes to regulating or banning firearms. How do state constitutions interact with the Second Amendment? Can states ban guns outright? Two years after *Heller*, *McDonald v. City of Chicago* sought to answer these important questions.

> **McDONALD v. CITY OF CHICAGO, 561 U.S. 742 (2010)**
>
> **THE FACTS**
>
> A Chicago city ordinance banned handgun possession (among other gun regulations). McDonald was a 76-year-old retired maintenance engineer who wanted a handgun for self-defense. Chicago required that all handguns had to be registered, but refused all handgun registration after a 1982 citywide ban.
>
> **THE LEGAL HOLDING**
>
> The Supreme Court held that the Second Amendment is fully applicable to the states and that individual self-defense is "the central component" of the Second Amendment. Therefore, the Second Amendment prohibits states from enacting bans on handguns for self-protection in the home.

E. Legal limitations of the right to keep and bear arms

The U.S. Supreme Court has stated: "Of course the right [to keep and bear arms] was not unlimited, just as the First Amendment's right of free speech was not." *D.C. v. Heller*, 554 U.S. 570 (2008). Courts may have struggled over the years with what the Second Amendment means, but they have been resolute that there is an element of self-defense. The *Heller* Court stated that, "we do not read the Second Amendment to protect the right of citizens to carry arms for any sort of confrontation," focusing their decision on self-defense. Further, the *Miller* Court stated that the weapons protected were those "in common use at the time" of the decision. This is supported by historical traditions of prohibiting the carry of "dangerous and unusual weapons" that are commonly used by criminals offensively, as opposed to by law-abiding citizens for defensive purposes.

The Second Amendment does not protect against legislative prohibitions on firearm possession by felons and the mentally ill. *Heller* made this point in its decision, and many circuit court cases such as *U.S. v. Everist*, 368 F.3d 517, 519 (5th Cir. 2004), which had previously used the same reasoning prior to *Heller*. The Fifth Circuit Court of Appeals in *U.S. v. Everist* stated that the Second Amendment is subject to "limited narrowly tailored specific exceptions or restrictions for particular cases that are reasonable; it is clear that felons, infants and those of unsound mind may be prohibited from possessing firearms." Along this same train of thought, the U.S. Supreme Court did not want to eliminate laws that imposed conditions and qualifications on the commercial sale of firearms.

It also does not mean that the Second Amendment includes the right to carry anywhere a person wants. The *Heller* Court stated that their opinion was not meant to allow the carrying of firearms in sensitive places, such as schools and certain government buildings.

PRACTICAL LEGAL TIP

Currently, the two most important court decisions fortifying our gun rights are *Heller* and *McDonald*. But those cases were very, very close to going the other way! Both were decided by a 5-4 majority, meaning that if only one other Supreme Court Justice had decided differently, our individual right to possess and carry firearms could have been severely limited. −Edwin

F. The future of the Second Amendment

How will the Second Amendment be treated going forward? With the passing of Supreme Court Justice Antonin Scalia, one of the key supporters and author of the 5—4 decision that was *Heller,* the split-down-the-middle Supreme Court truly seemed poised to either continue protecting firearms rights or backslide to the position that the Second Amendment only applied to militia activity. When the dust settled, Justice Scalia's empty seat ended up going to Neil Gorsuch. Additionally, the Court's newest Justices, Brett Kavanaugh and Amy Coney Barrett, are presumptive supporters of the right to bear arms. Oddly, since the appointments of these two Justices, the Court has continued its hesitancy to hear Second Amendment cases. Despite this hesitancy, their position on the bench bodes well for the future of the Second Amendment.

Although Justice Scalia's opinion in *Heller* affirmed the right for individuals to bear arms, it includes the famous caveat: "Like most rights, the right secured by the Second Amendment is not unlimited." *D.C. v. Heller,* 554 U.S. at 626. That sentence left open the possibility that some gun regulations could pass muster without spelling out the criteria for constitutionality. Overall, these regulations can be generalized into three major archetypes: those that impose registration requirements on firearms or their owners, those that ban certain types of firearms or firearm accessories, and those that prohibit the carrying of firearms in public (be it through impossible-to-obtain licensing schemes, or piecemeal prohibition).

The sheer volume of such cases allowing the erosion of the Second Amendment is alarming, but not as alarming as how many are denied certiorari.

In the years since *McDonald,* there have been more than 75 U.S. Circuit Court opinions upholding state restrictions on the Second Amendment that the U.S. Supreme Court has refused to review. These restrictions include requiring the registration of firearms, prohibiting "large capacity" magazines, banning certain firearms as "assault rifles," and creating classes of individuals who are restricted from owning firearms. In 2021, the Supreme Court refused to hear almost all Second Amendment challenges to state and local gun laws. However, the Court agreed to review New York State's restrictions on issuing handgun carry permits in *New York State Rifle & Pistol Association Inc. v. Bruen*, Docket No. 20-843, argued November 3, 2021. The decision in the New York case could have wide-reaching implications with "may issue" licensing states; stay tuned.

III. MAJOR FIREARMS STATUTES EVERY GUN OWNER NEEDS TO KNOW

At the federal level, there are plenty of laws and regulations that concern firearms, but this section will focus on some of the more major legislative actions that all gun owners need to know.

A. Gun Control Act of 1968

The Gun Control Act of 1968 ("GCA") was enacted by Congress to "provide for better control of the interstate traffic of firearms." This law is primarily focused on regulating interstate commerce in firearms by generally prohibiting interstate firearms transfers except among licensed manufacturers, dealers, and importers; however, interstate commerce has been held by the courts to include nearly everything. It also contains classes of individuals to whom firearms should not be sold. For the specifics of who can and can't purchase a firearm, please refer to Chapter 6. Among other things, the GCA created the Federal Firearms License ("FFL") system, imposed importation restrictions on military surplus rifles (adding a "sporting purpose test" and a "points system" for handguns), and marking requirements.

B. The Brady Handgun Violence Prevention Act

The Brady Handgun Violence Prevention Act, commonly referred to as the Brady Law, instituted federal background checks (the National Instant Criminal Background Check System, or "NICS") for firearm purchasers in the United States. It also prohibited certain persons from purchasing firearms. *See* Chapter 6 for more information on who can and can't purchase a firearm.

C. The Firearm Owners' Protection Act

The Firearm Owners' Protection Act ("FOPA") revised many provisions of the original Gun Control Act, including "reforms" on the inspection of FFLs. This same Act updated the list of individuals prohibited from purchasing firearms that was originally introduced by the GCA. The FOPA also banned the ownership by civilians of any machine gun that was not registered under the NFA as of May 19, 1986. FOPA also created what is called a "safe passage" provision of the law, which allows for traveling across states with a firearm. Finally, FOPA prohibited a registry for non-NFA items that directly linked firearms to their owners.

D. The Public Safety and Recreational Firearms Use Protection Act

The Public Safety and Recreational Firearms Use Protection Act, commonly referred to as the Federal Assault Weapons Ban, was a subsection of the Violent Crime Control and Law Enforcement Act of 1994. It banned outright the manufacture and transfer of certain semi-automatic firearms and magazines. This ban grandfathered-in previously legally owned weapons, but no prohibited firearm could be acquired or manufactured after September 13, 1994. With great foresight, the drafters of this law included a so-called "sunset provision," which stated that the ban would expire 10 years later unless renewed. The ban expired in 2004, and all attempts to renew it have been unsuccessful.

E. The National Firearms Act

The National Firearms Act ("NFA") regulates and imposes a statutory excise tax on the manufacture and transfer of certain types of firearms and weapons: machine guns, short-barreled weapons, suppressors, explosive devices, and "any other weapons" ("AOWs"). AOWs can range from everyday objects that are actually firearms, such as an umbrella that can fire a round, to other weapons the Bureau of Alcohol, Tobacco, Firearms and Explosives ("ATF") decides to place in this category. The tax is $200 if you make or transfer an item other than the transfer of AOWs; the tax for transferring AOWs is $5. The NFA is also referred to as Title II of the federal firearms laws. *See* Chapter 18 for more information on how to navigate the NFA while remaining legal.

F. Protection of Lawful Commerce in Arms Act

In 2005, Congress passed the Protection of Lawful Commerce in Arms Act ("PLCAA") to protect firearm retailers and manufacturers from certain lawsuits seeking damages arising out of the criminal conduct of third parties. *See* 15 U.S.C. §§ 7901-7903. There are a few exceptions to this Act, namely the sale of a defective good or fraud. Interestingly, the Texas Supreme Court recently applied the PLCAA and held that a Texas retailer–Academy Sports and Outdoors, which sold a magazine prohibited under Colorado law to a resident of Colorado–was protected under the Act, effectively dropping the suit against the retailer. *In re Academy, Ltd.*, ___ S.W.3d ___ (Tex. June 25, 2021) (No. 19-0497).

IV. DO TEXANS HAVE A RIGHT TO KEEP AND BEAR ARMS IN THE TEXAS CONSTITUTION?

Yes. The Texas Constitution acknowledges the right to keep and bear arms in Article I, Section 23. This provision of the Texas Constitution has never been amended. Article I, Section 23 reads:

> Every citizen shall have the right to keep and bear arms in the lawful defense of himself or the State; but the Legislature shall have power, by law, to regulate the wearing of arms, with a view to prevent crime.

The more observant will notice that, as opposed to the Second Amendment of the United States Constitution, this description specifically allows for regulation. The courts in Texas have acknowledged that Section 23 allows the legislature to create laws to prohibit certain types of weapons, and have upheld "unlawful carrying" laws and license requirements. *See Collins v. State,* 501

S.W.2d 876 (Tex. Crim. App. 1973); *Roy v. State,* 552 S.W.2d 827 (Tex. Crim. App. 1977). Additionally, Texas recently reaffirmed its commitment to the right to keep and bear arms by declaring itself a Second Amendment sanctuary. Therefore, Texas will not use state resources to enforce federal gun control laws enacted after January 19, 2021.

A. Can Texas prohibit local municipalities from making certain gun laws?

Yes. The Texas Legislature can (and does) prohibit local municipalities from making certain gun laws by the legal doctrine known as "preemption." A preemption statute is a mechanism by which the Texas Legislature sets certain areas off-limits to local governments, which helps ensure the uniformity of law across the state—in this case, firearms law.

B. What local governments may not regulate

The Texas preemption statute can be found in Texas Local Government Code Section 229.001. It states what areas of law municipalities (cities) are not allowed to regulate. Local municipalities cannot regulate:

- Anything relating to the transfer, possession, wearing, carrying, ownership, storage, transportation, licensing, or registration of firearms, air guns, knives, ammunition, or firearm supplies or accessories (Section 229.001(a)(1));
- Commerce in firearms, air guns, knives, ammunition, or firearm or air gun supplies or accessories (Section 229.001(a)(2));
- The discharge of a firearm at a sport shooting range (Section 229.001(a)(3));
- The discharge of a shotgun, air rifle, air pistol, BB gun, or bow and arrow on a tract of land of 10 acres or more and more

than 150 feet from a residence or occupied building located on another property in a manner not reasonably expected to cause a projectile to cross the boundary line (Section 229.002(1)(A)); or
- The discharge of a center or rim fire rifle or pistol of any caliber on a tract of land of 50 acres or more, more than 300 feet from a residence or occupied building located on another property in a manner not reasonably expected to cause a projectile to cross the boundary line (Section 229.002(2)).

Further, in response to the City of San Antonio attempting to zone gun stores out of existence, the 2019 Texas Legislature made some large changes to statutory preemption laws located in Texas Local Government Code § 229.001. Effective September 1, 2019, a municipality may not adopt or enforce a zoning ordinance, land use regulation, fire code, or business ordinance designed or enforced to effectively restrict or prohibit the manufacture, sale, purchase, transfer, or display of firearms, firearms accessories, or ammunition that is otherwise lawful in the state.

This new law contains a powerful catchall which states that an ordinance, resolution, rule, or policy adopted or enforced by a municipality, or an official action, including in any legislative, police power, or proprietary capacity, taken by an employee or agent of a municipality in violation of Section 229.001 is void (invalid). Additionally, an action taken by a municipality could subject it to being sued by the Attorney General, who may recover all attorney's fees and litigation costs.

C. What local governments may regulate
Local municipalities under state law are empowered to and may regulate the following:

- The discharge of firearms within the limits of the municipality other than at a sport shooting range (Section 229.001(a)(3));
- The use of property under a generally applicable zoning ordinance, land use regulation, fire code, or business ordinance (Section 229.001(b)(3));
- The use of firearms in the case of an insurrection, riot, or natural disaster if it is found necessary to protect public health and safety (Section 229.001(b)(4));
- The storage and transportation of explosives to protect public safety:
  - The statute provides an exception, that local municipalities cannot regulate 25 pounds or less of black powder for each private residence, or 50 pounds or less for each retail dealer (Section 229.001(b)(5)); and
- The carrying of a firearm or air gun, other than a handgun carried by a non-prohibited person, at a public park, public meeting of a governmental body, non-firearms-related school, college, or professional athletic events:
  - This does not apply to a firearm carried to or from an area designated for lawful hunting, fishing, or other sporting events where firearms are commonly used in the activity (Section 229.001(b)(6)).

Preemption even applies to municipal housing authorities, their municipal housing codes, or mass transit authorities; for example, it would be unlawful for a public housing project to prohibit the possession of firearms within the public housing project, or evict anyone who violated such prohibition, as the preemption statute above prohibits such regulations. *See* Tex. Att'y Gen. Op No. DM-71 (1991).

> CHAPTER TWO ◄

KNOW YOUR RIGHTS: PART I
THE FOURTH AMENDMENT:
Understanding Police Power
Some Basic Legal Concepts

I. INTRODUCTION AND OVERVIEW

It's 3 a.m. and the police barge into your home with a search warrant. They're at the wrong address and your family is terrorized; what are your rights? An officer approaches you on the street and asks to pat you down for weapons; what are your rights? The government listens to your private telephone calls or looks through your private documents; what are your rights? An officer wants to search your vehicle during a traffic stop; what are your rights? The answers to all these questions are found in the jurisprudence of the Fourth Amendment to the U.S. Constitution. The court cases and legislation coming out of this area are some of the fastest changing and most hotly contested in the country right now. Everything from when the government can take your DNA, to what parts of your house the police can look in, the use of "no knock warrants," to searching a smartphone are disputed topics. Commonly known as the law of "search and seizure," this is the most crucial protection we have from the government prying into our private lives and property. Let's take a closer look at Fourth Amendment rights.

II. WHAT IS THE FOURTH AMENDMENT?

The constitutional restriction on governmental searches and seizures is one of the first attempts by any society to protect the people from the government itself. Simply put, the Fourth Amendment stops government agents (often the police, but applicable to any person acting under government authority) from interfering with, searching, or seizing a person without first establishing "probable cause" and securing a warrant. The actual text of the Fourth Amendment reads:

> The right of the people to be secure in their persons, houses, papers, and effects, against unreasonable searches and seizures, shall not be violated, and no Warrants shall issue, but upon probable cause, supported by Oath or affirmation, and particularly describing the place to be searched, and the persons or things to be seized.

A. Why was this protection included in the Bill of Rights?

The men who drafted the U.S. Constitution and its first 10 amendments, the Bill of Rights, wanted to keep the government from gaining overarching power to abuse its citizens. The Fourth Amendment, specifically, is a result of these founding fathers' disgust and concern with the British "writ of assistance." These writs were widely used by Great Britain in the American colonies, and functioned as general search and seizure warrants with no requirement they state what locations to search or what items to seize. To make matters even worse, they never expired and could be transferred from person to person. The result was a blanket authorization by the British government to interfere with the private affairs of the colonists, with no real restrictions, checks, or balances. The goal of the Fourth Amendment was to restrict the police and provide "security" to Americans against a snooping, abusive government.

B. How is the government limited today?
Today's driving force in Fourth Amendment law is called the "reasonable expectation of privacy." This concept recognizes that private affairs follow the person, and are not necessarily confined to a particular location (such as a home or car). When an individual is guaranteed a reasonable expectation of privacy, the government must obtain a warrant from a neutral magistrate (or satisfy an exception as discussed in Chapter 4) before conducting a lawful search or seizure. This reasonable expectation of privacy is what we think of as our "right to privacy." While it is not a right specifically guaranteed in the Bill of Rights, it is a principle that comes from courts interpreting the Fourth Amendment over the decades.

III. LEGAL LEVELS OF PROOF
Officers must meet certain standards of proof before engaging in many police encounters with citizens. In order to lawfully detain, search, or arrest, the police must obtain certain levels of proof to believe that a person is connected to some criminal activity. What are these levels of proof, and how are they defined in Texas?

A. Reasonable suspicion
Reasonable suspicion is the legal standard that a police officer must have in order to legally stop and detain a person or "pat down" a

person for weapons or contraband (a *Terry Stop,* discussed below). What does this murky concept mean? It is a very low standard of proof, and requires a minimal level of objective evidence. Reasonable suspicion occurs when a police officer has "specific articulable facts that, when combined with rational inferences from those facts, would lead him to reasonably suspect that a person has engaged or is (or soon to be) engaging in criminal activity." *York v. State,* 342 S.W.3d 528, 536 (Tex. Crim. App. 2011). Reasonable suspicion cannot be based on a mere hunch or guess. Unfortunately, the facts and reasons can be subject to interpretation, and the U.S. Supreme Court and the Texas Court of Criminal Appeals have found reasonable suspicion from conduct that is as consistent with innocent activity as it is with criminal activity. For example, reasonable suspicion can come from your car being too clean, being too dirty, driving under the speed limit, or driving the exact speed limit, depending on the situational factors.

TERRY v. OHIO, 392 U.S. 1 (1968)

THE FACTS

John Terry was stopped and frisked by a veteran police officer when the officer spotted Terry and another man repeatedly walking up and down a street and peering into store windows. During the search, the officer found a concealed handgun in Terry's possession, which was a violation of Ohio law. The officer testified that he conducted the frisk because he suspected the men were "casing" a store for a potential robbery.

THE LEGAL HOLDING

The Supreme Court held that an officer may stop a suspect and perform a brief search for weapons when he has a reasonable belief that the person may be engaging in criminal activity and is potentially armed. This ruling made history by providing the government an avenue to search on a standard less than probable cause.

As you can see, Mr. Terry did nothing more than lawfully walk up and down the street and look in some store windows—an activity that is done by millions on a daily basis.

B. Probable cause

Probable cause is the minimum legal standard of proof required by law before a police officer may lawfully arrest someone or search a vehicle without a warrant or for a judge or magistrate to issue a search warrant or arrest warrant. This relatively low level of proof is defined by the U.S. Supreme Court as available trustworthy facts that would lead a reasonable person to believe that the person under investigation had committed or is committing an offense. *See Beck v. Ohio,* 379 U.S. 89 (1964). Probable cause is evaluated on a case-by-case basis and has no precise formula. Sometimes, a person is eligible for certain defenses or exceptions to shield him from criminal responsibility. Unfortunately, an officer does not need to investigate and rule out all possible defenses and exceptions before developing probable cause that an offense is being committed.

C. Preponderance of the evidence/clear and convincing evidence

Preponderance of the evidence and clear and convincing evidence are standards of proof that predominantly apply to civil causes of action. *See* Chapter 16 for more information on these terms, and civil liability in general.

D. Beyond a reasonable doubt

This is the highest level of legal proof, and is the standard of proof that must be established in trial before a person can be convicted of a criminal act. How is it defined? In the past, the Texas courts placed a lengthy definition on this term to guide juries in criminal cases. However, the definition of this concept was extremely controversial, and the subject of much debate and many legal challenges. Consequently, in 2000 the definition was scrapped by the Texas Court of Criminal Appeals, and the decision was made that "beyond a reasonable doubt" should not have a standard definition. Instead, it is up to each individual juror to decide what this term means for himself or herself. *Paulson v. State*, 28 S.W.3d 570, 573 (Tex. Crim. App. 2000). In general, it has been described as the level of certainty that a reasonable person should have before unplugging the life support system for a loved one, or the certainty that a person would need in packing their parachute before jumping out of a perfectly good aircraft. The government must provide this level of evidence before a conviction may occur. In short, the government needs reasonable suspicion to detain a person, probable cause to arrest a person, and proof beyond a reasonable doubt to convict a person.

IV. WHAT IS A SEARCH?

What definition do courts give to the term "search" under the Fourth Amendment? A search is: 1) an intrusion into an individual's reasonable expectation of privacy; and 2) made by a government agent. If the examination or investigation of a person, place, or property does not violate someone's reasonable expectation of privacy, or was not done by a government agent, it is not subject to the restrictions of the Fourth Amendment. See *Katz v. United States*, 389 U.S. 347 (1967).

The most common searches are of the home, vehicle, and person. However, the Fourth Amendment is not limited to these areas. As stated above, a search can occur anywhere a person has a reasonable expectation of privacy. For example, searches often include private documents, bank records, electronic communications, DNA samples, and countless other intrusions into private affairs.

V. WHAT IS A SEIZURE?

If the government demonstrates the appropriate level of proof, its agents may make a seizure of either a person or property.

A. What is a seizure of a person?

Someone is "seized" when a reasonable person would understand from the conduct of a police officer and the circumstances surrounding the encounter that he or she was not free to terminate the encounter and leave the interaction. Two elements must be satisfied for an act to constitute a seizure of a person: 1) there is a show of authority by the officer; and 2) the citizen submits to that authority. *See California v. Hodari*, 499 U.S. 621 (1991). This kind of seizure occurs during investigatory stops, detentions, and arrests.

B. What is a seizure of property?

The government has "seized" property under the Fourth Amendment anytime a government agent creates a meaningful interference with a person's possessory right in the property. *See U.S. v. Jacobsen*, 466 U.S. 109, 113 (1984). To seize, the government must show probable cause that the property was: 1) illegal; 2) evidence of a crime; or 3) "fruit" or property acquired as a result of a crime.

VI. POLICE POWER

The power of police is bestowed through legislation, and it affects the rights of individuals when the balance of interests favors the health, safety, and maintenance of the general public over the individual's rights to act as he or she pleases free from government interruption, intrusion, or prohibition.

A. What is the role of police?

There are many different police organizations. Most often, we encounter police employed by the State of Texas, individual counties, municipalities, school districts, *etc.* There is no general federal police power. However, there are law enforcement bodies controlled by the U.S. government that enforce laws in arenas specifically under federal control. Federal law enforcement bodies (often referred to as "bureaus") include the Federal Bureau of Investigation; the Bureau of Alcohol, Tobacco, Firearms and Explosives; United States Immigration and Customs Enforcement; United States Park Police; and many others.

Though it's hard to generalize the day to day routines of these vastly different agencies, law enforcement functions performed by police can be broken down into three broad areas: 1) maintaining order through general patrols and surveillance, particularly with high visibility policing; 2) enforcing the laws against violators and apprehending and arresting those suspected of breaking the law; and 3) providing services unrelated to criminal activity, such as rendering first aid, helping distressed citizens, *etc.* For example, a patrol officer on a usual day can patrol streets, investigate a burglary, and help get a cat out of a tree—all before lunchtime.

It's the "law enforcement" function that we are most concerned about in this Chapter. This is where the police commit the most intrusion and are most likely to run up against (or through!) the rights of individuals.

B. Limits on police power

The Texas and U.S. Constitutions serve as the greatest restraint on police power. Specifically, the Fourth, Fifth, and Sixth Amendments to the U.S. Constitution, and the case law that has flowed from these amendments, function to keep the government in check with strict consequences for violations. *See* Section IX below for a detailed explanation of what happens when the police violate your rights.

VII. ENCOUNTERS WITH THE POLICE
A. When do my Fourth Amendment rights matter?
The Fourth Amendment is designed to protect citizens during encounters with the police and other government agents. These encounters take several different forms. The Fourth Amendment does not cover a private citizen interacting with other private citizens.

B. Voluntary encounter
A police officer can approach any person who is located in a "public place" and engage them in ordinary conversation, just as any other person could do. This can be very casual; "lovely weather," or "nice boots." A person who finds themselves in a voluntary encounter with a police officer is fully within their rights to not engage in conversation or to walk away. *See U.S. v. Drayton*, 536 U.S. 194 (2002).

Courts have decided that the act of walking away from a police officer during a voluntary encounter does not create a reasonable suspicion that they are involved in criminal activity. However, any statements given or observations made during a voluntary encounter may establish reasonable suspicion to detain or probable cause to search or arrest a person. Any evidence found during the voluntary encounter may be used in court based on the person's consent in talking with the police officer. *See* Chapter 4 for more issues on consent.

EXAMPLE:
Jim is walking to a bus stop when the police approach and ask where he is going. Jim ignores them just as the bus pulls up. Jim has a legal right to get on the bus without being detained by the police.

C. Temporary detention

A temporary detention occurs when a police officer stops and holds a person, restricting their right to walk away. A police officer is legally justified in conducting a temporary detention when the officer has "reasonable suspicion" based on specific articulable facts that a person has broken, is breaking, or will break the law. While lawfully detained, a police officer may check arrest warrants, frisk the outside of clothing, remove weapons, or handcuff and place a person in the back of a squad car.

There is no requirement for a police officer to read a person their Miranda Rights warning during a temporary detention. *See* discussion of *Miranda v. Arizona*, below. What a person says to the police and the surrounding circumstances of the detention may give rise to probable cause to arrest even if the detention was based on completely different suspicion. Any evidence obtained during the temporary detention may be used against that person in court.

> **EXAMPLE:**
> Police receive a call about a man wearing a red shirt who is causing a commotion at the park. Upon arrival, the police observe a man matching the description who appears intoxicated. The police have reasonable suspicion to detain this man for criminal investigation.

D. Arrest

Police may arrest a person if they have probable cause to believe a crime has been or is being committed. In Texas, a formal arrest occurs when someone is placed into custody in a manner such that a reasonable person would believe they have been deprived of their freedom. At the point of arrest, most of the person's legal rights and protections are triggered, including the right to remain silent, the right to counsel, *etc.* Remember: Don't waive your rights without talking to your lawyer!

EXAMPLE:
Police are called to the scene of a convenience store robbery. While the police are talking to the clerk, the clerk says, "There he is!" and points to Sam walking down the street. The police lawfully detain him, pat him down, and find a pistol and a wad of cash in his jacket. Sam can now be lawfully arrested based on probable cause.

E. "Community caretaking"

This encounter doesn't fit nicely into the categories of police interactions. An officer may approach a citizen if he "reasonably believes" the citizen is in need of assistance. It was expressly allowed in Texas by the Court of Criminal Appeals in the case of *Wright v. State,* 7 S.W.3d 148 (Tex. Crim. App. 1999), which relied on the U.S. Supreme Court case of *Cady v. Dombrowski,* 413 U.S. 433 (1973). Courts will determine whether the officer was reasonable by looking at the level and nature of distress exhibited, the location of the individual, the ability to receive assistance from others, and the extent to which the individual posed a danger to himself or others. A community caretaking encounter does not provide the right to search absent independent reasonable suspicion or probable cause, and generally only applies to public property. However, the incriminating information an officer gets from this encounter can give him reasonable suspicion for an investigation or probable cause for an additional detention or arrest. In a recent development, the United States Supreme Court's decision in *Caniglia v. Strom*, 593 U.S. ___ (2021), refused to extend *Cady's* "community caretaking" exception to the warrant requirement to searches of private homes. Justice Thomas wrote for the Court, "neither the holding nor the logic of *Cady* justified" the warrantless search and seizure inside the private home. *Id.*

> **EXAMPLE:**
> A police officer observes Dylan vomiting out of the passenger window of a moving vehicle. The officer can lawfully conduct a traffic stop of the automobile to determine whether he needs medical attention. While he is conducting the stop, he determines that both Dylan and the driver are intoxicated and arrests him for public intoxication and the driver for driving while intoxicated.

F. Traffic stops

The most common encounters with the police are traffic stops. The police have the ability to make a traffic stop for any violation that they witness. It is commonly said that a police officer could follow any car for 10 minutes and observe some traffic violation that would allow him to stop a car. In 2014, the U.S. Supreme Court in the case of *Navarette v. California,* 572 U.S. 393 (2014), held that the police can make a traffic stop or other temporary detention based upon information provided by an anonymous person. This ruling could profoundly impact Fourth Amendment law in the future.

VIII. THE FIFTH AMENDMENT
A. What are my rights against self-incrimination?

The Fifth Amendment to the U.S. Constitution protects an individual from being compelled to be a "witness against himself," among other rights. This means the state cannot force a person to make statements or testify in court, especially when they are against their own self-interest or are incriminating.

B. Do the police have to read the Miranda Rights warning after every arrest?

No! The Miranda Rights warning is not required simply because a person is placed into handcuffs and charged with a crime. This warning is only required when the police: 1) place a person in custody; and 2) wish to interrogate that person.

Whether or not someone is in "custody" for the purposes of Miranda Rights is determined by analyzing the facts and circumstances to determine if his or her freedom of action has been deprived in a significant way. Generally, an arrest will equate to "custody." However, there are some circumstances in which a person has not been arrested, but is in "custody" for the purposes of the Miranda Rights warning. If the police do not wish to interrogate the person in custody, there is no need for a Miranda Rights warning. However, if the police wish to ask questions of the individual in custody to further their own investigation or to obtain a confession, they must administer this warning.

MIRANDA v. ARIZONA, 384 U.S. 436 (1966)

THE FACTS

The decision of *Miranda v. Arizona* actually addressed four different cases. In each case, the criminal suspect was questioned by law enforcement for many hours, isolated in an interrogation room with no outside communication, and ultimately each suspect gave a confession to law enforcement. None of the four defendants were advised of their Fifth Amendment rights during the interrogation process.

THE LEGAL HOLDING

The Court held that "there can be no doubt that the Fifth Amendment privilege is available outside of criminal court proceedings and serves to protect persons in all settings in which their freedom of action is curtailed in any significant way from being compelled to incriminate themselves." The Court concluded that, "the prosecution may not use statements, whether exculpatory or inculpatory, stemming from custodial interrogation of the defendant unless it demonstrates the use of procedural safeguards effective to secure the privilege against self-incrimination. By custodial interrogation, we mean questioning initiated by law enforcement officers after a person has been taken into custody or otherwise deprived of his freedom of action in any significant way." The result of this holding is the "Miranda Warning" we are familiar with today. When a suspect is subjected to a custodial interrogation by law enforcement officers, the resulting statements are not admissible unless the suspect first knowingly waived his or her rights.

IX. WHAT HAPPENS IF THE POLICE VIOLATE MY RIGHTS?
A. Exclusionary rule

What can you do when the government has overstepped its limits and violated your Fourth or Fifth Amendment rights? If a person is found to be in possession of criminal evidence or contraband, and they are successful in persuading a judge that the police officer's search, seizure, or interrogation was unconstitutional, their recourse is found in a legal principle called the exclusionary rule. The exclusionary rule states that illegally obtained evidence is "fruit of the poisonous tree" and cannot be used as evidence in the criminal trial of the person, even if this results in a guilty person going free. The exclusionary rule exists at both the federal level and the state level.

B. The federal exclusionary rule

There are a few judicially recognized exceptions to the exclusionary rule where the "illegally obtained" evidence may still be admissible against the accused. This includes evidence found in "good faith" reliance on a search warrant later determined to be legally defective, or a statute later declared to be unconstitutional. Evidence may also be admitted if it has become sufficiently disassociated from the illegal police action, it was legally obtained from an independent source, or it would have been inevitably discovered through other legal means. The U.S. Supreme Court has also ruled that the government may use illegally obtained evidence if the police officer made a "reasonable" mistake of fact or of law. Further, any evidence excluded during the prosecution phase of a criminal trial can later be admissible if the defendant or defendant's attorney "opens the door" to the issue by referring to it in the testimony at trial.

In order to take advantage of the exclusionary rule, the person charged with the crime has to have "standing" to make the evidentiary challenge. What does this mean? Simply that the person making the challenge had an expectation of privacy, was wronged by the police action, and their personal Fourth or Fifth Amendment rights were violated.

C. The Texas exclusionary rule

Texas has its own statutory version of the exclusionary rule found in the Texas Code of Criminal Procedure Article 38.23. The Texas exclusionary rule is broader than the federal exclusionary rule because it excludes evidence obtained in violation of Texas statutes and the Texas Constitution. Also, it excludes evidence illegally obtained by both the police and private citizens, and does not provide for the admission of "inevitable discovery" evidence. Where appropriate, a good Texas defense lawyer always moves to exclude evidence under both Texas and federal law.

D. Section 1983 Claim

When a person's civil rights, including their rights against illegal searches are violated by a police officer, a person may file a civil lawsuit under Title 42, Section 1983, of the United States Code, which is commonly referred to as a "Section 1983 Claim." The United States Supreme Court has ruled that a police officer and his or her department may be liable for monetary damages if a person's civil rights are violated. *Monell v. New York City Dept. of Social Services*, 436 U.S. 658 (1978). However, there is a huge exception to this rule. If the court finds a reasonable police officer could have believed a search, seizure, or other action was lawful, a police officer will be cloaked with qualified immunity that legally excuses the officer from civil liability. This means a person whose rights have been violated will have to show that a police officer knew his or her conduct was objectively unreasonable under a clearly established rule of law. *Anderson v. Creighton*, 483 U.S. 635 (1987). This is a very high burden and will make a Section 1983 Claim an uphill battle for any aggrieved person. To bring a successful Section 1983 Claim, a person must show:

1) a person acting under the color of law (for example, a police officer acting within the scope of their employment as a police officer);
2) deprived the individual of their rights guaranteed by the U.S. Constitution or laws of the United States; and
3) is not protected by qualified immunity.

Now that we have laid a groundwork for the basic legal concepts underlying Fourth Amendment law, the following chapters will discuss the practical applications.

> CHAPTER THREE ◄

KNOW YOUR RIGHTS: PART II
THE FOURTH AMENDMENT:
Understanding The Warrant Requirement In Texas

I. INTRODUCTION AND OVERVIEW

The text of the Fourth Amendment requires that the government have a warrant based on probable cause when they want to invade our privacy or place us under arrest. Unfortunately, the words of the Fourth Amendment are not the end of the story. Over the years, the courts and the legislature have chipped away at the warrant requirement and created an incredible number of exceptions. So many, in fact, that today there are far more searches and seizures conducted without a warrant than with one. Despite this sad reality, warrants remain the general rule, and it is important to understand how they are obtained and executed.

II. WHAT IS THE WARRANT REQUIREMENT?

Let's start with the most basic question—what is a warrant? A warrant is a document issued by a government official, typically a magistrate judge, authorizing a police officer to arrest a person, or search and/or seize property. A search warrant gives the government authority to conduct a search of a specified place and seize evidence of criminal acts or to install monitoring equipment in or on certain property. A magistrate can also issue a warrant that authorizes the "seizure" of a human being. This is called an arrest warrant, and it directs a law enforcement officer to arrest and bring "the body of the person" accused of criminal wrongdoing in front of the court.

> **PRACTICAL LEGAL TIP**
>
> What is a magistrate? Nearly every type of judge is a magistrate. The most common magistrate is a justice of the peace or a municipal judge. Part of their duties include issuing warrants and advising those who have been arrested of their charges and initial legal rights. –Richard

A. How is a warrant issued?

First, police learn of activity leading them to believe a search or seizure of property will reveal evidence of a crime or that a person has committed a criminal act. Police might gather this information through their own investigation and first-hand knowledge or through information gathered by a confidential informant ("CI"). Next, the police officer drafts a sworn statement supporting the request to arrest or search. He will include all relevant facts he has gathered in his investigation or from his CI. He will often include photos, maps, or other visual evidence with his sworn statement. After the warrant is drafted, a neutral magistrate judge reviews the sworn statement and determines whether or not the officer has articulated probable cause for the arrest or search. *See* Chapter 2 for the definition of probable cause. If probable cause has been established, the magistrate judge signs the warrant, and police may then execute the warrant. This means the police now have full authority to search and/or seize property or persons described in the warrant.

EXAMPLE:

Justin is arrested for possession of crack cocaine. Justin tells police where he bought the crack. Police write an affidavit describing details given by Justin about the crack house on Maple Street. The requested search warrant and attached affidavit are given to a magistrate who signs both, thus authorizing police to raid the crack house.

THE WARRANT PROCESS:

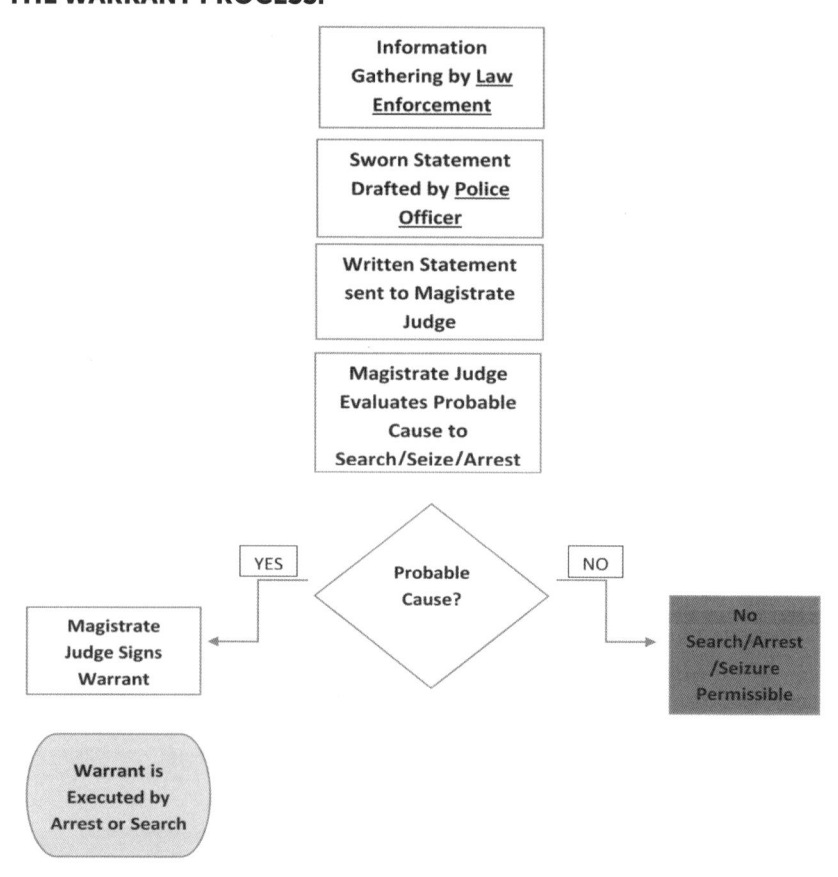

```
Information Gathering by Law Enforcement
         │
         ▼
Sworn Statement Drafted by Police Officer
         │
         ▼
Written Statement sent to Magistrate Judge
         │
         ▼
Magistrate Judge Evaluates Probable Cause to Search/Seize/Arrest
         │
         ▼
     Probable Cause?
    /              \
  YES              NO
   │                │
   ▼                ▼
Magistrate      No Search/Arrest
Judge Signs     /Seizure
Warrant         Permissible
   │
   ▼
Warrant is Executed by Arrest or Search
```

B. The "particularity requirement"

The text of the Fourth Amendment dictates that warrants must "particularly describe" the person or place at issue. How does this "particularity requirement" look in practical application? The warrant must specifically identify the person to be arrested, or describe the property to be searched and seized. It must be done in such a manner that the average person could find the location or identify the persons and places named in the warrant. In an arrest warrant, particularity is generally satisfied by including the name and date of birth of the person to be arrested, the crime alleged, and the name of the victim, if any. A search warrant's requirements are a little more complicated. To cover all bases, a search warrant generally includes three separate descriptions of the location—the street address, visual characteristics of the land or building, and descriptors from the county property records. More often than not, police officers will attach a photo of the location to the search warrant. The warrant must also describe the items the police want to seize and what they believe will be found in the location. Once probable cause is established and the warrant is signed, it may be executed by a police officer.

C. How is a warrant executed?
1. General rule—police must "knock and announce"
It is generally required that the government "knock and announce" their presence before entering a premises to execute a warrant. However, there is an exception to this requirement, and this exception swallows the rule. If the police can state reasonable suspicion to believe that if they knocked or announced before entering it would be "dangerous, futile, or would frustrate the search's purpose," then they may disregard the knock and announce requirement. The police can ask in advance that the warrant dispense with the knock and announce requirement, or they may claim the circumstances surrounding the actual search justified dispensing with the knock and announce requirement at the time the warrant was executed. In practice, the potential for destruction of evidence and issues of officer safety will almost always supersede the knock and announce requirement. What does this mean? The police may possibly break down your door without any warning to execute their warrant.

2. Is there a limit on destruction of your property?
It is a violation of the Fourth Amendment to cause unnecessary

and excessive destruction of property when executing a search warrant. However, as the U.S. Supreme Court clarified in *U.S. v. Ramirez,* 523 U.S. 65, 73 (1998), this violation does not mean that the evidence against you should be thrown out. *See* the previous chapter's discussion of the exclusionary rule. Practically speaking, the police can justify highly destructive acts in the course of their search. If it is "necessary" in the execution of the search warrant, the police may go as far as ripping up your carpets or tearing open your furniture to find what they are looking for.

3. How long do the police have to execute a warrant?

Article 18.06 of the Texas Code of Criminal Procedure states that a search warrant must be executed within three days, exclusive of the date the warrant was signed and the final date the warrant is valid. Though the code describes this as a "three-day" requirement, in practice it amounts to five days. For example, a warrant that is signed on Monday must be executed on or before Friday. Is Friday three days from Monday? No, but excluding Monday (the date it was signed) and Friday (the final date the warrant is valid) the three-day requirement is met.

4. What if you are in the wrong place at the wrong time?

You are at a friend's home when the police knock on the door with a search warrant for that address; what happens to you, the innocent bystander? In the event that the police do not have probable cause to arrest or search other individuals present at the scene, they may be temporarily detained during the course of the search for purposes of controlling the scene, officer safety, the preservation of evidence, or checks for outstanding arrest warrants. Additionally, an arrest outside a house, depending on the circumstances, can justify a protective sweep as much as an arrest inside. *Rios v. State*, No. 14-18-00886-CR (Tex. App. — Houston [14th Dist.] Aug. 27, 2020). If there exists no probable cause that a detained person who is not named in the warrant is involved in criminal activity, they must be released. However, you may find yourself detained for several hours before the police decide to release you.

D. Do the police always need a warrant to perform a search and seizure?

No! The following chapter describes the many ways in which the warrant requirement has been eroded.

E. In Texas, what can be searched and/or seized?

The Texas Code of Criminal Procedure lays out in detail what may be searched and/or seized. Under Article 18.02, a search warrant may be issued to search for and seize:

1) stolen property, or any property obtained by criminal means;
2) property designed to be used, or commonly used, in the commission of crimes;
3) arms and munitions kept or prepared for the purposes of insurrection or riot;
4) weapons prohibited by the Penal Code;
5) gambling devices or equipment, altered gambling equipment, or gambling paraphernalia;
6) obscene materials kept or prepared for commercial distribution or exhibition;
7) a drug, controlled substance, chemicals used as an immediate precursor to drugs, and drug paraphernalia;
8) any illegal property;
9) implements or instruments used in the commission of a crime;

10) property or items, except personal writings, that are evidence of a criminal offense;
11) persons;
12) contraband;
13) electronic customer data held in electronic storage; or
14) cellular telephone or other wireless communications device.

As you can see, almost anything is subject to a search and/or seizure with a warrant. What about when the police don't have a warrant? In the next chapter, we will discuss in detail the many, many exceptions to the warrant requirement.

> CHAPTER FOUR ◄

KNOW YOUR RIGHTS: PART III
THE FOURTH AMENDMENT:
Exceptions To The Warrant Requirement

I. INTRODUCTION AND OVERVIEW

You are driving late at night when you look into your rearview mirror and see flashing blue and red lights. When the officer approaches your window, he tells you he is going to search your car because he saw you making "furtive movements." What are your rights? You are walking around your neighborhood when an officer approaches and tells you that you match the description of a burglary suspect. He frisks you for weapons. Can he do this without a warrant? When does the law allow police to avoid the warrant process to make an arrest or conduct a search of your private property?

Courts have eroded the strong protection of the warrant requirement over the years—there are so many present day exceptions to obtaining a warrant that the exceptions now swallow the rule. This Chapter will discuss the many ways police can conduct warrantless arrests and warrantless searches of your body, vehicle, and home.

II. WHEN CAN THE POLICE SEARCH OR ARREST ME WITHOUT A WARRANT?

A. Stop and frisk

If a police officer has developed reasonable suspicion a person has committed a crime, he can detain and pat down that person to search for weapons. This "stop and frisk" is commonly referred to as a *Terry Stop*. Named after *Terry v. Ohio,* 392 U.S. 1 (1968), this type of search is confined to "…guns, knives, clubs, or other hidden instrumentalities for the assault of the police officer." Recall from Chapter 2 that reasonable suspicion is an extremely low standard. An officer has to have just a little more than a hunch that you might be involved in criminal activity. A *Terry Stop* is limited to an over-the-clothes search for weapons; however, if an officer can determine through touch alone that a person is in possession of contraband (the "plain feel" doctrine), he can confiscate the contraband and charge the person with a criminal violation. How far does plain feel go? While the officer cannot squeeze, move, or manipulate the things in your pockets to see if the items feel like contraband, it is not uncommon for police officers to claim they could tell by plain feel that someone was in possession of a crack rock or a marijuana joint. If he feels contraband in your pockets, he can arrest you, and the evidence he found on your body is admissible in court.

Just how easy is it for an officer to decide he has reasonable suspicion to search you? In Texas, a quick-thinking officer can justify a *Terry Stop* and frisk of virtually anyone he decides is suspicious. Texas currently has a law on the books that criminalizes the "obstruction of a public roadway." Not only does this include roads and highways, but it has also been extended to cover city sidewalks! If an officer sees you walking down the sidewalk and decides that he wants to search you, all he has to do is wait for you to stop and look at your phone, bend over to tie your shoe, or stop to look into a storefront. He now has reasonable suspicion that you are committing the crime of obstructing the public sidewalk! *Terry v. Ohio* gives him permission to detain and search you for weapons and other contraband.

In 2017, the United States Fourth Circuit Court of Appeals issued an opinion in the case *U.S. v. Robinson,* 846 F.3d 694 (4th Cir. 2017), which addressed a stop and frisk search situation that is relevant to all legal firearm owners. The Court reasoned that an anonymous tip about the presence of a firearm triggered a police officer's right to engage in a *Terry Stop,* even if the act of carrying a firearm is not illegal under state law. Under the reasoning of the Fourth Circuit's opinion, anyone exercising their Second Amendment rights effectively surrenders their Fourth Amendment rights against warrantless detentions and searches.

B. On-site arrest

In Texas, the police have been given broad powers of arrest any time an officer has probable cause to believe someone is violating almost any law, from serious felonies to minor municipal ordinances. There are only two exceptions:
1) a person must be given a summons and cannot be arrested for speeding less than 25 miles over the speed limit; or
2) having an open container of alcohol in their car.

Because the police in Texas may arrest when they have probable cause that almost any infraction has occurred or is occurring, there are literally thousands of criminal offenses for which a person may be arrested. Almost everyone who drives a car or walks around in public violates some minor law on a daily basis and is subject to arrest if a police officer so desires. For example, if you are driving an automobile, you can be arrested for having a burnt out light around your license plate, an expired registration sticker, crossing a solid line on the roadway, failing to signal a lane change, failing to signal 100 feet prior to turning, or hundreds of other infractions. This can be equally true if you are on a bicycle or even on foot, because the Texas Transportation Code regulates pedestrian and bicycle riders in public. Arrestable offenses include crossing a street in the wrong place, stepping out of a crosswalk, or crossing against a "Don't Walk" sign.

C. Warrantless apprehension of suspected dangerous persons with mental illness

In recent years, there has been a nationwide push for "extreme risk protective orders" or "red flag laws" specifically designed to remove firearms from individuals who are accused of engaging in conduct or making statements that others may deem "dangerous." As of 2021, the Texas Legislature has resisted the reactionary enactment of legislation that could be viewed as too broad, too vague, subject to abuses, and lacking due process. However, for the last several decades, Texas has had a process which allows law enforcement to seize a person without a warrant and remove their firearms based upon that person's mental illness.

Texas Health and Safety Code Chapter 573 provides that the police may take a person into custody without a warrant under certain circumstances based on the theory that there is no time to secure a warrant. If the officer "has reason to believe and does believe that the person is a person with a mental illness; and because of that mental illness there is a substantial risk of serious harm to the person or to others unless the person is immediately restrained," they may seize all firearms in that person's possession. *See* Tex. Health & Safety Code § 573.001. The apprehended individual will then be taken to a mental health facility to be examined by mental health professionals and provided a hearing before a judge or magistrate. If the individual is judicially determined to be mentally incompetent, they will lose their right to purchase and possess firearms.

III. WHEN CAN THE POLICE SEARCH MY HOME WITHOUT A WARRANT?

Your home is about as private as any place can get. The government should always be required to get a warrant to search this ultra-private space, right? Wrong! There are several scenarios where the police can legally search your home or its surrounding areas without a warrant. The following is a discussion of the most important exceptions.

A. Exigent circumstances

The police may enter and search a home in response to "exigent circumstances." Police officers typically claim exigency in order to protect life, protect property, prevent the destruction of evidence, or pursue a fleeing felon.

Once the crisis is contained, a further search of the home is not permitted. However, officers may seize any evidence or contraband that is in plain view inside the home. Further, what they see while in the home may be used to support probable cause for a search warrant.

> **EXAMPLE:**
>
> The police are chasing Curtis, a robbery suspect, through a neighborhood. Unfortunately, Curtis decides to evade the cops by running into Eric's home! Because the police are in hot pursuit of an alleged felon, they have every right to enter Eric's home without a warrant, and may search any place in his house that Curtis could possibly be hiding. To make matters worse, they see on Eric's kitchen counter what they believe is drug paraphernalia. They can now seize these items to investigate and use them to develop probable cause for a search warrant or to arrest Eric.

B. Open fields

The police don't need a warrant to march around and search the open fields outside your home. What is an open field? It's any area "out of doors in fields, except in the area immediately surrounding the home." *Oliver v. United States,* 466 U.S. 170, 178 (1984). The area immediately surrounding your home is the "curtilage," and the police have to get a warrant to search this area. Why are the open fields different from the spaces immediately adjacent to your home? Courts have said that people do not have a reasonable expectation of privacy in the open fields outside because open fields aren't private enough to invoke the protections of the Fourth Amendment.

C. Abandoned property

Courts have consistently held that persons cannot object to the seizure and evidentiary admission of abandoned property. An officer only has to have a reasonable belief that a person has abandoned the property. Because of that, any reasonable expectation of privacy in the property is lost. The most notable example of abandoned property is your garbage on the street awaiting collection.

What does it take to abandon an object? In the unpublished Texas case of *Bernard v. State,* the front seat occupant of a car stuffed his bag containing drug paraphernalia as far into the back of the car as he could manage, then told the officer the bag was not his. Unfortunately for him, the acts were visible on the officer's dash cam. The court ruled that the man could not challenge the admissibility of the contraband in his trial, because he had abandoned the bag!

D. Plain view

An officer may, without a warrant, seize contraband and evidence of criminal activity that is in plain view. The plain view doctrine, as courts have analyzed, has three requirements:

1) the officer must lawfully make an initial intrusion or be in a lawful position to see the items;

2) the officer must make the discovery inadvertently and may not use plain view as pretext; and

3) it must be immediately apparent that the items are contraband or evidence of a crime.

See *Horton v. California*, 496 U.S. 128 (1990).

What does it mean to be in a "lawful position" to see the items? An officer walks up to your front door, and through your living room window, he sees your elaborate methamphetamine operation. He may enter and seize the items because they are in plain view. By contrast, if an officer suspects you have a meth lab somewhere in your home and decides to jump your fence to look into your back window, anything he sees from that vantage does not fall under the "plain view" doctrine.

1. Can the police use sense-enhancing devices?

It depends. Law enforcement's use of binoculars to peer into your home or your property is lawful and can constitute plain view. Similarly, aerial views of your property by airplane or helicopter are plain view and do not require a warrant. Infrared imaging and dog sniffs of your home, however, require warrants based on probable cause and do not constitute plain view (or smell). In the 2013 legislative session, the Texas Legislature passed a bill which requires that police obtain a warrant for drone surveillance on misdemeanor cases, but police may conduct the same surveillance for felony offenses on reasonable suspicion alone! No probable cause or warrant required!

2. Can the police claim "plain view" if you have "no trespassing" signs?

Yes. A "no trespassing" sign does not stop law enforcement officials from seizing items in plain view on your property. A "no trespassing" sign might stop an officer from searching through your abandoned property or from physically setting foot on your property (unless one of the exceptions applies), but courts often allow officers to skirt this requirement by claiming they did not see any posted "no trespassing" sign before entering the property.

IV. WHEN CAN THE POLICE SEARCH MY VEHICLE WITHOUT A WARRANT?

Many Americans would be shocked to learn that the Fourth Amendment provides very little protection for their personal vehicles. The Supreme Court justified this lessened expectation of privacy in the 1925 case of *Carroll v. United States*, 267 U.S. 132 (1925). In *Carroll,* the Court reasoned that a car's mobility makes it more difficult for the police to secure a search warrant, and because automobiles are already subject to increased government regulation, people should not expect the same security against warrantless searches that they have in their homes. As a result, there are very few circumstances in which the police have to seek a warrant to search a vehicle.

A. The probable cause search

This is the farthest reaching exception to searching without a warrant. In order to legally search a vehicle, a police officer only has to articulate probable cause that a crime has been, will be, or is being committed. *See* detailed discussion of probable cause, Chapter 2. Once this occurs, an officer can search anywhere in the vehicle that could contain evidence of that crime without the requirement of obtaining a warrant.

It is a common misconception that a police officer cannot search containers, bags, or other self-contained personal items present in a vehicle. Unfortunately, this is most often not the case. A police officer may search any part of the vehicle, including the glove box or trunk, which could contain evidence of the crime for which they developed probable cause.

For example, if an officer smells the odor of marijuana in a vehicle, he may search anywhere in the vehicle that could contain marijuana. Since marijuana could be stored in a very small space, there will be virtually no restrictions on where the officer may look. By contrast, if the officer has probable cause to believe you are a felon in possession of an AR-15, he will not be able to look in your glove box, center console, or small locked briefcase, as an AR-15 could not reasonably be stored in any of these locations.

What about the wheel well and body panel of the vehicle? An

officer must have probable cause that contraband or evidence of a crime is specifically contained within these areas of your vehicle to justify a warrantless search. This makes some sense, because searching these areas is more intrusive and damaging to your personal property than searching the passenger compartment.

How does the law treat other modes of transportation? Boats and planes are treated like motor vehicles, and warrantless searches are lawful based on probable cause. RVs and houseboats, however, are a different story—if the RV or houseboat is stationary and being used as a home at the time law enforcement wishes to conduct a search, they must seek a warrant. If the RV or houseboat is traveling, it is likely subject to a warrantless search.

B. Plain view in a motor vehicle

Just like an officer may seize contraband and evidence of a crime in plain view from your home and/or person (described in detail above), they may seize these items if they are in plain view in your vehicle. So, if you leave your unholstered handgun lying out in plain view on your dashboard, an officer can seize it as evidence and arrest you for unlawfully carrying a firearm—no warrants required.

C. Search incident to arrest

Regardless of what the arrest was for, there is an exception to the warrant requirement that permits an officer to perform a warrantless search during or immediately after a lawful arrest. The exception is limited to the person arrested and the area immediately surrounding the person in which the person may gain possession of a weapon, in some way effect an escape, or destroy or hide evidence.

What about personal items at the time of arrest? A decision out of the Court of Appeals in Fort Worth may shed some light. Personal items that are "immediately associated" with an arrestee may be searched incident to arrest. What does "immediately associated" mean? Purses, wallets, bags, and even "a small tin can" are likely to meet this standard, while luggage, foot lockers, and other "untypical objects" generally do not. *See State v. Drury*, 560 S.W.3d 752, 754 (Tex. App.—Fort Worth 2018).

If a person is arrested in the very near vicinity of his vehicle, this power to search will often extend to the passenger compartment of the vehicle. In 2009, the U.S. Supreme Court addressed this authority to search in the case of *Arizona v. Gant,* 556 U.S. 332 (2009). In *Gant,* the Court held that a search of the passenger compartment of the vehicle was lawful only if it was reasonable to believe the arrestee might access the vehicle at the time of search, or that the vehicle contained evidence of the crime for which the person has been arrested. Assume that an officer slaps the cuffs on you right outside your open car door for the aforementioned crime of unlawful carry. Now, the police can search your entire passenger compartment incident to your arrest! However, if you are arrested several yards away from your parked car, *Gant* does not allow the search of your car as being "incident" to the arrest.

D. Inventory search

The inventory search is the all-encompassing catch-all that will allow a thorough search of your vehicle anytime it comes into police custody. Anytime you are arrested with your vehicle, the police are authorized to remove the car and impound it for safe keeping. The contents of the car must be "inventoried" to protect the property of the person arrested as well as to protect the police from any false allegations of stealing or losing the property. For the search to provide admissible evidence, courts require that the police department must have procedures in place for performing inventories of automobiles. *South Dakota v. Opperman*, 428 U.S. 364 (1976). In practice, virtually every police agency has a valid inventory search policy. Many times, the police will use this opportunity to perform a thorough search of the car, its trunk, and all of its contents. The courts have determined that this "inventory" can be done without a warrant and any contraband or other evidence of criminal activity that is lawfully obtained constitutes admissible evidence. Note: as an example of the continued evolution of Fourth Amendment jurisprudence, the Fourteenth Court of Appeals in Texas issued an opinion that vastly expands the government's right to conduct an inventory search. In *State v. Jackson,* 468 S.W.3d 189 (Tex. App.—Houston [14th Dist.] 2015, no pet.), the Court ruled that an officer could conduct an inventory search of a vehicle even though that vehicle was eventually released to a third party instead of impounded.

E. Consent

In practice, this is the most common way police officers gain access to your home or vehicle to conduct a search. Most people are conditioned to respect the authority of a police officer, and so many people have a hard time saying no when an officer demands permission to search. An officer can ask permission to search for any reason or no reason at all. There is no evidentiary standard required to ask a person for consent to conduct a search. The officer must simply obtain consent "voluntarily."

What is "voluntariness"? Texas courts have decided that "voluntariness" as it applies to consent to search means more than just the literal meaning of "a knowing choice." The state must prove that consent was voluntary by a clear and convincing evidence standard, and the court will look to the totality of the circumstances to make this determination. *Reasor v. State*, 12 S.W.3rd 813, 818 (Tex. Crim. App. 2000). If an officer demands to search your vehicle, or else he is going to beat you to a bloody pulp, your consent is not voluntary under Texas law.

Do people have the right to refuse consent? Yes! However, an officer does not need to inform you of your right to refuse consent. In fact, in Texas, an officer may gain consent to search your vehicle by saying something to the effect of "I'm going to search your vehicle now, okay?" If you agree, you have given voluntary consent! How far does consent go? A person may limit the scope of their consent, and anything found outside that scope will not be admissible evidence. For example, if you grant an officer consent to look in your glove compartment, he may not use that same consent to conduct a search of your trunk.

V. OTHER SEARCH ISSUES
A. Inventory once in custody
No warrant is required to search an individual once they are in custody and booked into jail. Personal possessions are accounted for and logged into police custody. Depending on the officers and the offense you are suspected of committing, this search can be very invasive. Unfortunately, once you are in custody, there is no more permission needed for an officer to bring out the rubber gloves.

B. GPS tracking
The U.S. Supreme Court decision of *U.S. v. Jones*, 565 U.S. 400 (2012), determined that the installation and tracking of a GPS

device on a vehicle is a Fourth Amendment search requiring a warrant. However, the Court has not yet issued any guidelines as to what conditions are required for the issuance of a warrant for GPS tracking.

C. Smartphones

In today's day and age, you might be hard-pressed to find someone who does not carry a smartphone on their person at all times. Most of these tiny, portable computers are overflowing with personal information such as texts, personal contacts, schedules, emails, and photos. What happens when police find a smartphone, say in an inventory search like the one above? How has Fourth Amendment jurisprudence kept up with this technological development? In 2014, the U.S. Supreme Court handed down *Riley v. California*, 573 U.S. 373 (2014), which directly addresses this issue. In *Riley*, the Court distinguished cell phones from other objects found on an individual by stating:

> Cell phones differ in both a quantitative and a qualitative sense from other objects that might be kept on an arrestee's person. The term "cell phone" is itself misleading shorthand; many of these devices are in fact minicomputers that also happen to have the capacity to be used as a telephone. They could just as easily be called cameras, video players, rolodexes, calendars, tape recorders, libraries, diaries, albums, televisions, maps, or newspapers. One of the most notable distinguishing features of modern cell phones is their immense storage capacity. Before cell phones, a search of a person was limited by physical realities and tended as a general matter to constitute only a narrow intrusion on privacy.

Due to these distinguishing features, the Court ultimately concluded that police must obtain a warrant based on probable cause to search the contents of a cell phone. However, the Court left open the question of whether or not a smartphone can be searched without a warrant if there are exigent circumstances or if the phone itself is the instrumentality of the crime.

D. Highly regulated businesses

Warrantless searches have been permitted by the courts if carried out by the state's administrative agents in any business or activity that is closely regulated by the government. For example, agents from the ATF may conduct an audit of a gun store, or the Texas Alcoholic Beverage Commission ("TABC") may send their agents to inspect liquor stores or bars.

E. Airports/international borders

Warrantless searches are permitted at borders and airports under the legal theory that individuals have implicitly consented to be searched while traversing an international border or getting on an airplane. Further, warrantless searches are justified by public interest and the great risk to public safety in these areas.

F. Probationers/parolees

Persons on probation and parole have a lessened expectation of privacy due to their highly monitored status. As a result, they may be searched on reasonable suspicion alone. This standard even applies to the person's cell phone! Persons subject to government supervision lose nearly all of their Fourth Amendment rights.

G. Dog sniffs

As it applies to vehicles, a dog sniff is not considered a search under the Fourth Amendment. An officer may detain you for a reasonable amount of time to await a canine to conduct a sniff. If the dog alerts on your vehicle, the officer then has probable cause to conduct a search of the vehicle for narcotics without a warrant. However, a dog sniff of the front porch of a home is a search under the Fourth Amendment, and cannot be done in the absence of a warrant. This is because the dog sniff takes place on the curtilage of the home, which is a place where the occupant of the home has an expectation of privacy.

What is a "reasonable" amount of time? Courts examine this under the totality of the circumstances on a case-by-case basis. For example, in a large city with many canine officers, it is probably unreasonable to detain someone for over an hour to await the dog. In a small county with only one canine officer, this long wait may not be unreasonable if the dog is out on another crime scene. Ultimately, the lengths to which an officer is allowed to go to detain and search a particular person will be fought after the fact in the courtroom on this kind of "totality of the circumstances" analysis.

The U.S. Supreme Court in *Rodriguez v. United States*, 575 U.S. 348 (2015), added some clarity to the legality of dog sniff detentions at the conclusion of a traffic stop. The Court ruled that once the officer has concluded his investigation into the traffic stop, he may not detain a citizen to wait for a drug dog without independent reasonable suspicion that the person is in possession of illegal narcotics. Expect to see many lengthy traffic stops in the future as police officers attempt to stay on the right side of this decision.

H. Drones

The use of drones has become more and more prevalent. This includes aerial surveillance by both private individuals and law enforcement. Wherever a member of the public is allowed to fly their drones, the police are allowed to fly theirs. However, as police expand the use of drones, the Fourth Amendment will certainly be implicated. It will be up to the courts to determine when the use of police drones without a warrant violates a person's expectation of privacy. Additionally, it will be important to see how a court addresses Fourth Amendment privacy concerns when a private citizen flies their drone over property and reports any suspicious activity to local law enforcement.

➢ CHAPTER FIVE ◄

LEGAL DEFINITIONS AND CLASSIFICATIONS OF FIREARMS:
WHAT IS LEGAL?

I. INTRODUCTION AND OVERVIEW

Before discussing the law of firearms and all its different facets, it is important first to understand what the law defines as a "firearm." Firearms laws are governed on both the federal and state levels; therefore, throughout this Chapter we will explore the interactions that federal and state law have on the purchase and possession of firearms.

A. What is a firearm?

FEDERAL DEFINITION

Under federal law, a firearm is defined as "any weapon (including a starter gun) which will or is designed to or may readily be converted to expel a projectile by the action of an explosive." 18 U.S.C. § 921(a)(3). The federal definition of a firearm also includes the frame or receiver of any such weapon, any firearm muffler or silencer, or any "destructive device." This is similar to the Texas definition, but not exactly the same.

TEXAS DEFINITION

In the State of Texas, for purposes of applying state and not federal law, a firearm is defined by the Texas Penal Code in Chapter 46. Section 46.01(3) defines a firearm as "any device designed, made, or adapted to expel a projectile through a barrel by using the energy generated by an explosion or burning substance or any device readily convertible to that use."

Why might it be important to know the different ways the term "firearm" is defined under federal and state law? It is because if a person finds themselves charged with a crime by federal authorities, the federal definition of a firearm will apply. Likewise, if the charge is under a violation of state law, then the Texas definition will apply. Thus, the primary difference in the definitions and their impact on a defendant charged with a crime involving a firearm lies with how a person may be in trouble with the law. As we will see in the next section, the definitions of what does and does not constitute a firearm, although similar in many aspects, contain an array of differences that make violating the law unwittingly easy.

B. Unfinished "80 percent" frames and receivers

During the firearm manufacturing process, raw materials such as metals and polymers eventually emerge from their unmanufactured form into something readily identifiable and usable as a firearm. This necessitates the question: at what point does a block of raw material become a firearm? The federal government (through the ATF) has drawn a distinction between unfinished firearm frame or receiver blanks, which are unregulated, and finished firearm frames or receivers, which are subject to federal regulation under the Gun Control Act. The unfinished frame or receiver blanks are commonly sold as 80 percent lowers. Therefore, generally it is only after a frame or receiver is machined or manufactured beyond 80 percent that it becomes a firearm and is subject to federal and state regulation. Keep in mind, the ATF does not use the term "80 percent" but simply classifies items as "finished" or "unfinished." Therefore, an unfinished frame or receiver can be sold and shipped through the mail without regulation. It is not considered a firearm in its unfinished format but merely a metal or plastic block, akin to a paperweight. Once the item is finished, it becomes classified as a firearm and governed by all applicable laws, including possession and transfer.

On May 20, 2021, the ATF submitted a proposed rule amending the definition of "firearm" in 27 CFR 478.11 by adding "[t]he term shall include a weapon parts kit that is designed to or may readily be assembled, completed, converted, or restored to expel a projectile by the action of an explosive." *Definition of "Frame or Receiver" and Identification of Firearms*, 86 Fed. Reg. 97, 27720 (May 20, 2021)(Proposed Rules). As of the writing of this material, this rule is not effective and is still in the rulemaking process.

C. Definitions for handguns, rifles, and shotguns

In addition to defining what constitutes a firearm, federal and Texas law further classify and define firearms into categories of handguns and long guns (rifles and shotguns). This section will provide an overview of how federal and state laws classify firearms as well as the physical requirements for a firearm to be legal.

1. What is a handgun?

Ultimately, whether looking at the federal or Texas definition, the term "handgun" is defined in the same manner; it simply refers to any firearm that is designed to be fired by using only one hand. While it is true that most individuals will use two hands when firing a handgun for safety and accuracy purposes, the emphasis in the legal definition of a handgun rests purely in its design to be held or fired with a single hand.

FEDERAL DEFINITION

The United States Code of Federal Regulations defines a handgun as "(a) any firearm which has a short stock and is designed to be held and fired by the use of a single hand; and (b) any combination of parts from which a firearm described in paragraph (a) can be assembled." 27 CFR § 478.11.

TEXAS DEFINITION

Under Texas law, handguns are defined by the Penal Code in Chapter 46. A handgun "means any firearm that is designed, made, or adapted to be fired with one hand." Tex. Penal Code § 46.01(5).

2. What is a rifle?

Federal law defines a rifle as "a weapon designed or redesigned, made or remade, and intended to be fired from the shoulder, and designed or redesigned and made or remade to use the energy of the explosive in a fixed metallic cartridge to fire only a single projectile through a rifled bore for each single pull of the trigger." See 27 CFR § 478.11. In addition, a legal rifle must have a barrel length of 16 inches or greater, and includes any weapon made from a rifle that is at least 26 inches overall in length. Texas law does not provide a definition for a rifle under the Penal Code, but it does classify illegal short-barreled firearms, including rifles, in the same manner as the federal definition. See Tex. Penal Code § 46.01(10).

Minimum lengths

In order for a rifle to not be subject to the National Firearms Act or classified as a short-barreled firearm under Texas law, it must have a barrel of at least 16 inches in length. The ATF procedure for measuring barrel length is accomplished by measuring from the closed bolt (or breech-face) to the furthermost end of the barrel or permanently attached muzzle device. Below is an example of a rifle that does not meet the minimum barrel length requirement after measurement.

The barrel is measured by inserting a dowel rod into the barrel until the rod stops against the bolt or breech-face. The rod is then marked at the furthermost end of the barrel or permanently attached muzzle device, withdrawn from the barrel, and then measured. Any measurement of less than 16 inches will classify the rifle as being short-barreled under Texas and federal law and subject the firearm to the NFA. *See* Chapter 18, which discusses the NFA for short-barreled rifles and other non-compliant firearms. Note: for overall length, rifles with collapsible/folding stocks are measured from the "extreme ends," unless the stock is "easily detachable," in which case it is measured without the stock.

3. What is a shotgun?

Federal law defines a shotgun as "a weapon designed or redesigned, made or remade, and intended to be fired from the shoulder, and designed or redesigned and made or remade to use the energy of the explosive in a fixed shotgun shell to fire through a smooth bore either a number of ball shot or a single projectile for each single pull of the trigger." *See* 27 CFR § 478.11. Like rifles, legal shotguns have requirements for minimum barrel and overall lengths. Shotgun barrels must be at least 18 inches long and must also comply with the same 26-inch overall length requirement. Under Texas law, shotguns are classified in the same manner as they are under federal law. *See* Tex. Penal Code § 46.01(10).

Minimum lengths

In order for a shotgun to not be subject to the National Firearms Act or classified as a short-barreled firearm under Texas law, it must have a barrel of at least 18 inches in length. The ATF procedure for measuring the barrel length of a shotgun is the same as it is for a rifle.

Above is an example of a shotgun that does not meet the minimum barrel length requirement after measurement. Any measurement of less than 18 inches will classify the shotgun as a short-barreled weapon and illegal under Texas and federal law unless the requirements of the NFA are satisfied. *See* Chapter 18 for short-barreled shotguns and other non-compliant firearms. Note: the collapsible/folding-stock rule that applies to rifles applies to shotguns as well.

Numerous questions have surrounded the Mossberg 590 Shockwave. The firearm has a pistol grip, shoots shotgun shell ammunition, has a barrel length of 14 inches, and an overall length of around 26½ inches. On March 2, 2017, the ATF issued a letter that states the Shockwave is not a firearm regulated by the NFA. Instead, it is a GCA firearm that is regulated as any other common firearm that is available to the public. Consequently, Mossberg has marketed the 590 Shockwave as a non-NFA weapon that does not require a tax stamp for possession. The ATF determination relies on the fact that it is made without a shoulder stock and instead has a "birdshead" grip. However, since the Texas definition of a short-barreled firearm does not include the element of "intended to be fired from the shoulder" the question remained: "is this legal, and can I have one in Texas?"

The ATF's determination that the 590 Shockwave was not an NFA weapon occurred during the 2017 session of the Texas Legislature. The 85th Texas Legislature responded by amending Texas Penal Code Section 46.05 to state that weapons that are not subject to NFA registration are not classified as prohibited weapons under Texas law. Therefore, the Mossberg Shockwave and any other firearm that the ATF determines to not be a short-barreled firearm is not illegal in Texas.

D. Antique firearms and replica firearms

When is a firearm not legally a "firearm"? It is when the law defines it as not being one, such as with "antique" firearms.

1. Federal definition of "antique firearm"
1898 or prior

The federal definition of firearm under Title 18, Section 921 of the United States Code excludes "antique firearms." Even though an antique firearm still functions ballistically similar to a "modern" firearm, under federal law, antique firearms are regulated differently. An antique firearm under federal law includes any firearm with a matchlock, flintlock, percussion cap, or similar type of ignition system manufactured in or before 1898 or any replica of a firearm just described so long as the replica "is not designed or redesigned for using rimfire or conventional centerfire fixed ammunition, or uses rimfire or centerfire ammunition that is no longer manufactured in the United States and is not readily available in ordinary channels of commerce." *See* 18 U.S.C. § 921(a)(16)(A) and (B). So, an "antique firearm" is not a "firearm" for purposes of federal regulation; it is an "antique firearm."

Muzzle loading

In addition, federal law does not consider "any muzzle loading rifle, muzzle loading shotgun, or muzzle loading pistol, which is designed to use black powder, or a black powder substitute, and which cannot use fixed ammunition" as a firearm. Be aware, however, that the term "antique firearm" does not include: any weapon which incorporates a firearm frame or receiver; any firearm which is converted into a muzzle loading weapon; or any muzzle loading weapon which can be readily converted to fire fixed ammunition by replacing the barrel, bolt, breechblock, or any combination of these parts. *See* 18 U.S.C. § 921(a)(16)(C).

2. Texas definition of "antique firearm"
Pre-1899

The Texas definition of firearm excludes "antique firearms" by not including any firearm that is an antique firearm manufactured before 1899, or a replica of an antique firearm manufactured before 1899, but only if the replica does not use rim fire or center fire ammunition. *See* Tex. Penal Code § 46.01(3). This is similar to the federal definition, simply stated differently.

3. Differences in federal and Texas law

The area where the federal and Texas definitions of what is not a firearm differ the most is in the use of black powder firearms. Although the language appears different, the years of manufacture for firearms that are classified as "antiques" are both the same under federal and Texas law; antique firearms are ones that were manufactured before 1899. However, the federal law takes things one step further by providing a separate section exempting muzzle loading firearms designed to use black powder or a black powder substitute so long as the firearm cannot be readily converted to fire fixed ammunition. Texas law has no such exception for black powder firearms; only firearms that were produced prior to 1899, or which are replicas of weapons that were actually produced prior to 1899, are excluded.

This demonstrates one of the few examples where federal law is less restrictive than state law. By these definitions, a person who could not otherwise legally possess a firearm under federal law, could legally possess a muzzle loading rifle or pistol designed to use black powder that is not a replica of any weapon that was actually previously manufactured before 1899, because federal law does not consider such a weapon to be a firearm due to its mere use of black powder. However, under Texas law, if a black powder gun is a modern black powder firearm and not a replica of an "old" pre-1899 firearm, it is considered a firearm under the Texas Penal Code, and it is not an "antique firearm." The possession or use of such a black powder firearm would be subject to all other Texas laws governing the use of firearms. Texas only excludes from its definition of firearms weapons designed to use black powder if they were actual weapons manufactured prior to 1899 or replicas of actual weapons manufactured prior to 1899.

E. Which firearms are illegal?

Under Texas Penal Code Section 46.05, certain firearms are prohibited or illegal under Texas law when they are not registered with the ATF pursuant to the National Firearms Act. *See* Chapter 18 for more information on the NFA. These firearms include:
- Explosive weapons;
- Machine guns; and
- Short-barreled firearms.

Note that due to this phrasing, possession of the NFA item itself is no longer inherently a crime; possessing the item without it being registered, however, is still a crime. This means a law enforcement official would need reasonable suspicion that you did not register the item to inquire about your registration status; as opposed to previously when you could theoretically be arrested and have to show up in court with your tax stamp proving registration. Functionally, however, it is always a good idea to carry around your proof of NFA compliance any time you are in possession of your weapon.

There are also zip guns (a term which includes any device which was not originally a firearm, but is adapted to become and act like one) which are illegal without exception. Zip guns are absolutely prohibited. *See* Tex. Penal Code § 46.05.

This section of the Penal Code also makes illegal other weapons such as chemical dispensing devices and armor-piercing ammunition.

Under federal law, the same firearms that are prohibited weapons under state law without registration are regulated by the National Firearms Act. These firearms include:
- Short-barreled shotguns;
- Short-barreled rifles;
- Machine guns;
- Firearm silencers or suppressors;
- Weapons or devices capable of being concealed on the person from which a shot can be fired;
- Pistols or revolvers having a smooth bore (as opposed to rifled bore) barrel designed to fire a fixed shotgun shell;
- Pistols or revolvers with a vertical handgrip;

- Destructive devices; and
- Weapons classified as "Any Other Weapon," or AOWs.

See 26 U.S.C. § 5845.

On the surface, the prohibited firearms list is similar between both federal and state law, with the primary difference existing merely in classification only (federal law classifies most of these items as firearms, whereas Texas classifies the items not as firearms but prohibited weapons). However, although these firearms and/or weapons are prohibited by statute, it does not mean a person absolutely cannot possess one. Many of these weapons may be legally possessed with proper compliance under the National Firearms Act. *See* Chapter 18 for more information on these prohibited weapons and the NFA.

F. How big of a gun can a person possess?

Federal law dictates that any firearm which has any barrel with a bore of more than one-half inch in diameter is a "destructive device" and is subject to the National Firearms Act. Possession of any such firearm without the proper paperwork associated with NFA firearms is illegal. Note, however, that some shotguns are regulated differently. *See* Chapter 18 for more information on destructive devices and the NFA.

II. AMMUNITION AND THE LAW

No discussion concerning firearm law would be complete without examining laws concerning the ammunition that goes into a firearm. Just like firearms, the law regulates the possession, sale, and even composition of "legal" ammunition. This section addresses the essential aspects of the law concerning ammunition and what gun owners need to know, both under federal and Texas law.

A. How does the law define ammunition?

Under federal law, the term "ammunition" is defined under 18 U.S.C. § 921(a)(17)(A) and means "ammunition or cartridge cases, primers, bullets, or propellant powder designed for use in any firearm." Thus, the federal definition of ammunition includes the finished product and all of the components in making a round of ammunition. However, the federal definition of ammunition does not include:
1) any shotgun shot or pellet not designed for use as the single, complete projectile load for one shotgun hull or casing; or
2) any unloaded, non-metallic shotgun hull or casing not having a primer.

See 27 CFR § 478.11.

In other words, individual ammunition components are legally defined as ammunition themselves, even if they are simply parts, except that shotgun ammunition components, if not completely assembled, are not ammunition.

Under Texas law, there is no statutory definition for mere "ammunition." Texas law only provides a definition for armor-piercing ammunition (which we will discuss later in this Chapter) and a definition for the way firearms are discharged: a "projectile [that is expelled] through a barrel by using the energy generated by an explosion or burning substance." Tex. Penal Code § 46.01(3).

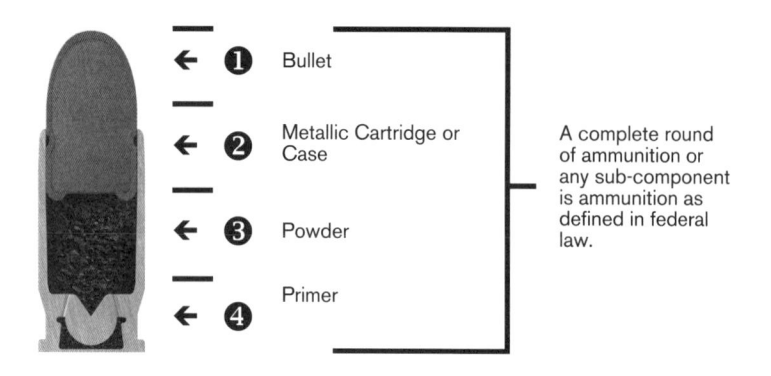

- ① Bullet
- ② Metallic Cartridge or Case
- ③ Powder
- ④ Primer

A complete round of ammunition or any sub-component is ammunition as defined in federal law.

B. Is there a difference in ammunition that is used in different types of firearms?

Yes. Ammunition can be divided into two classifications: ammunition for handguns and ammunition for long guns. Long gun ammunition can be further divided into ammunition for rifles and ammunition for shotguns.

Handgun ammunition means ammunition that is meant to be fired from a handgun, and it comes in many different calibers. Rifle ammunition is meant to be fired from a rifle and is similar to handgun ammunition in that it comes in many different calibers. Shotgun ammunition, on the other hand, comes in self-contained cartridges loaded with some form of shot or a shotgun slug which is designed to be fired from a shotgun.

C. What ammunition is illegal?

Armor-piercing handgun ammunition is the only ammunition that has explicit prohibitions under both federal and Texas law. The federal definition of armor-piercing ammunition is found in 18 U.S.C. § 921(a)(17)(B) and means "[1] a projectile or projectile core which may be used in a handgun and which is constructed entirely (excluding the presence of traces of other substances) from one or a combination of tungsten alloys, steel, iron, brass, bronze, beryllium copper, or depleted uranium; or [2] a full jacketed projectile larger than .22 caliber designed and intended for use in a handgun and whose jacket has a weight of more than 25 percent of the total weight of the projectile."

FEDERAL LAW
Under federal law, while there is no blanket prohibition on the mere possession of armor-piercing ammunition, it is prohibited under four conditions:

Prohibition one: it is illegal to make or import armor-piercing ammunition.
Under 18 U.S.C. § 922(a)(7) it is unlawful for any person to manufacture or import armor-piercing ammunition unless:
1) the manufacture of such ammunition is for the use of the United States, any department or agency of the United States, any state, or any department, agency, or political subdivision of a state;
2) the manufacture of such ammunition is for the purpose of exportation; or
3) the manufacture or importation of such ammunition is for the purpose of testing or experimentation and has been authorized by the United States Attorney General.

Prohibition two: it is illegal for manufacturers and importers to sell or deliver armor-piercing ammunition.
Federal law states that it is unlawful for any manufacturer or importer to sell or deliver armor-piercing ammunition unless such sale or delivery is:
1) for the use of the United States, any department or agency of the United States, any state, or any department, agency, or political subdivision of a state;

2) for the purpose of exportation; or

3) for the purpose of testing or experimentation and has been authorized by the United States Attorney General. *See* 18 U.S.C. § 922(a)(8).

Prohibition three: an FFL or other license-holder cannot sell or deliver armor-piercing ammunition without the proper documentation.
Under 18 U.S.C. § 922(b)(5), it is unlawful for any licensed importer, licensed manufacturer, licensed dealer, or licensed collector to sell or deliver armor-piercing ammunition to any person unless the licensee notes in his records, as required under 18 U.S.C. § 923, the name, age, and place of residence of such person if the person is an individual, or the identity and principal and local places of business of such person if the person is a corporation or other business entity.

Prohibition four: it is illegal to possess armor-piercing ammunition if a person is involved in a crime of violence or drug trafficking.
Pursuant to 18 U.S.C. § 924(c)(5), it is unlawful for "any person who, during and in relation to any crime of violence or drug trafficking crime (including a crime of violence or drug trafficking crime that provides for an enhanced punishment if committed by the use of a deadly or dangerous weapon or device) for which the person may be prosecuted in a court of the United States, uses or carries armor piercing ammunition." Individuals who use or carry armor-piercing ammunition in the commission of a crime of violence or during a drug-trafficking crime are subject to heightened sentencing standards should they be found guilty.

As you can see, while possession of armor-piercing ammunition itself is not illegal, obtaining armor-piercing ammunition without violating one of the foregoing prohibitions is almost impossible.

TEXAS LAW

Texas Penal Code Section 46.01(12) defines armor-piercing ammunition as "handgun ammunition that is designed primarily for the purpose of penetrating metal or body armor and to be used principally in pistols and revolvers." Texas Penal Code Section 46.05(a)(3) makes the intentional or knowing possession, manufacture, transport, repair, or sale of armor-piercing ammunition a third degree felony.

A couple of notable exceptions to this law are available. One is in the form of a defense to prosecution, and the other is an affirmative defense. First, under Texas Penal Code Section 46.05(b), it is a defense to prosecution that a person's intentional or knowing possession, manufacture, transport, repair, or sale was "incidental to the performance of official duty by the Armed Forces or National Guard, a governmental law enforcement agency, or a correctional facility." Persons employed in any of these agencies should not be prosecuted so long as their use of armor-piercing ammunition was a part of their official duties. Second, it is an affirmative defense that a person's intentional or knowing possession, manufacture, transport, repair, or sale of armor-piercing ammunition was incidental to dealing with armor-piercing ammunition solely for the purpose of making the ammunition available to the Armed Forces or National Guard, a governmental law enforcement agency, or a correctional facility. *See* Tex. Penal Code § 46.05(d)(2).

PS90

By definition, it should be noted that not all ammunition that can pierce armor is actually armor-piercing. Both the federal and Texas definitions contain specific requirements for a particular round of ammunition's composition in order to qualify as armor-piercing. Federal law requires that the ammunition be composed of certain alloys, while Texas law requires that the ammunition be designed primarily for the purpose of penetrating armor. For instance, 5.7 millimeter ammunition for an FN Five-seveN handgun or a PS90 rifle, while capable of piercing armor based on its size and velocity, is not ammunition that is armor-piercing as defined under the law because such ammunition, sold commercially, is primarily for sporting purposes according to the ATF.

D. Does modifying traditional ammunition make it illegal?

No. Outside of armor-piercing ammunition, there is no handgun or long gun ammunition that is prohibited under federal or Texas law. In fact, there are many examples of hollow-point rounds which are modified in a way to become more lethal, such as the R.I.P. ammunition, Critical Duty, *etc.*, which star outward upon impact in order to do more internal damage. Such ammunition, though it looks different from traditional ammunition, is perfectly legal.

Factory and Expanded Hollow-Point Rounds

E. Is it legal to use ammunition that works in both handguns and rifles?

Yes, except for armor-piercing ammunition that is used principally in handguns. This is because the federal and Texas definitions of armor-piercing ammunition contemplate handguns only. Armor-piercing ammunition for a rifle is perfectly legal, though it may complicate matters at trial in trying to demonstrate to the jury any differentiation. Beyond armor-piercing ammunition, it is legal to use ammunition that is available in common calibers and that functions in both handguns and rifles.

With a solid understanding of what is and is not a firearm and ammunition, as well as what firearms and ammunition a person may legally possess without the necessity of obtaining additional documentation, we are now ready to move to the next chapter discussing the purchase and possession of firearms.

> **PRACTICAL LEGAL TIP**
>
> Even with firearms, having the right tool for the job is important. Practically speaking, you should choose the firearm and ammunition you feel most comfortable in using. At the end of the day, why you started shooting in self-defense is always more important than which firearm you chose to shoot. —Emily

> CHAPTER SIX ◄

PURCHASING, TRANSFERRING, AND POSSESSING FIREARMS

I. LAWS OF PURCHASING AND POSSESSING: THE BASICS

The laws of purchasing, selling, gifting, or otherwise transferring a firearm are distinct and different from the laws of possessing a firearm. It may be legal for someone to possess a firearm, and it still be illegal for them to "purchase" the firearm. Further, the laws for "purchasing" or "possessing" have a federal and a state component, both of which must be satisfied in order to stay on the right side of the law.

On the federal level, the ATF is charged with regulating firearms, including sales, purchases, and transfers through Federal Firearms Licensees ("FFLs" or "dealers"); however, a multitude of federal agencies can be involved in any given firearms law investigation or police function, and most fall under a branch of the U.S. Department of Justice. Texas has no direct state-level counterpart to the ATF.

A. What is an FFL?

An FFL or Federal Firearms License is a license required by federal law for those persons or entities that are engaged in the business of buying and selling firearms. When an individual purchases, sells, or transfers a firearm through a dealer, the FFL and the individual must both comply with specific federal law requirements, paperwork, and procedures concerning the buying, selling, or transferring of those firearms. These requirements will be addressed throughout this Chapter.

B. Who must obtain an FFL?

Federal law requires an FFL if a person is engaged in business as a firearms dealer, manufacturer, or importer. For the purposes of our discussion in this Chapter, a person is engaged in the business when the person "devotes time, attention, and labor to dealing in firearms as a regular course of trade or business with the principal objective of livelihood and profit through the repetitive purchase and resale of firearms, but such term shall not include a person who makes occasional sales, exchanges, or purchases of firearms for the enhancement of a personal collection or for a hobby, or who sells all or part of his personal collection of firearms." *See* 18 U.S.C. § 921(a)(21)(C).

C. What is a private sale?

A private sale is just what it sounds like: a sale, purchase, or transfer of a firearm by parties that are not licensed dealers. A private sale is perfectly legal for both handguns and long guns in Texas, as long as all other legal requirements are met. We will discuss the ins-and-outs of private sales in greater detail in this Chapter under Section IV.

D. What is the legal age to purchase and possess a firearm?

Federal law controls all FFL firearms transactions and requires that a person be 21 years of age or older before they may purchase a handgun or 18 for the purchase of a long gun. However, under Texas law, a handgun or long gun may be purchased in a private sale by a person who is 18 or older. Texas Penal Code Section 46.06(a)(2) makes it a crime if a person "intentionally or knowingly sells, rents, leases, or gives or offers to sell, rent, lease, or give to any child younger than 18 years of age any firearm, club, or location-restricted knife." Note the exceptions to follow.

MINIMUM AGE TO PURCHASE FIREARMS	FEDERAL LAW: FROM DEALER	TEXAS LAW: PRIVATE SALE
Handgun	21	18
Long gun	18	18

Under federal law, a person must be at least 18 years of age to legally possess a handgun or ammunition for a handgun. *See* 18 U.S.C. § 922(x)(2). Unlike the law on purchasing a long gun, there is no federal age requirement for the possession of a rifle or shotgun. There is no Texas law directly specifying that persons under a certain age are prohibited from possessing a firearm; however,

Texas law does specify that persons under 17 must be supervised or that certain other conditions must be met in order for a juvenile to possess a firearm.

E. Can I buy a firearm if I have a note from my parents?

If a person finds themselves charged with selling a firearm to a minor, Texas law does provide an affirmative defense to prosecution under state law if the sale or transfer of the firearm was made "to a minor whose parent or the person having legal custody of the minor had given written permission for the sale or, if the transfer was other than a sale, the parent or person having legal custody had given effective consent." *See* Tex. Penal Code § 46.06(c). This is the law whether the sale is for a handgun or a long gun. For the federal law regarding juveniles and handguns *see* 18 U.S.C. § 922(x). Note, however, that this state-law exception does not apply to FFL transactions, and an individual must be 21 years old to purchase a handgun from an FFL.

F. Criminal liability for allowing a minor access to firearms

In Texas, under Texas Penal Code Section 46.13, a person may be guilty of a crime if a child (younger than 17) gains access to a readily dischargeable firearm and the person with "criminal negligence: (1) failed to secure the firearm; or (2) left the firearm in a place to which the person knew or should have known the child would gain access."

If the child discharges the firearm and causes death or serious bodily injury to himself or another person, it is a Class A misdemeanor. Otherwise, it is a Class C misdemeanor.

The law defines "readily dischargeable firearm" as a "firearm that is loaded with ammunition, whether or not a round is in the chamber." The statute also defines "secure" as meaning to "take steps that a reasonable person would take to prevent the access to a readily dischargeable firearm by a child, including but not limited to placing a firearm in a locked container or temporarily rendering the firearm inoperable by a trigger lock or other means." *See* Tex. Penal Code § 46.13(a)(3).

However, if a minor commits a crime to gain access to a firearm, the firearm's owner is not guilty of a crime. It is an affirmative defense to prosecution when a child gains access to a firearm "by entering property in violation of this code." *See* Tex. Penal Code § 46.13(c)(3). This means that if a child illegally breaks into a person's home or vehicle and then takes possession of a weapon illegally, the gun owner has not committed a crime.

G. When may children legally possess firearms?

Texas law allows for the legal possession of firearms under specific exceptions included in the law. These exceptions or "affirmative defenses" include the following:

1. Exception for hunting or sporting purposes

The first affirmative defense is that the child's access to the firearm "was supervised by a person older than 18 years of age and was for hunting, sporting, or other lawful purposes." *See* Tex. Penal Code § 46.13(c)(1). An adult is legally permitted to take a child hunting or to the shooting range and permit the child to have access to a firearm, so long as that adult supervises the child.

2. Self-defense

Second, if the child's access to the firearm "consisted of lawful defense by the child of people or property." *See* Tex. Penal Code

§ 46.13(c)(2). For obvious reasons, if a child uses a firearm in self-defense, or in defense of another person or property, there is a general public policy interest in not prosecuting those persons.

> **EXAMPLE:**
> One night, armed intruders break into Nicole's home and hold Nicole's parents at gunpoint while burglarizing the home. Nicole, who is 12, covertly sees what is transpiring from the top of the stairs and, knowing that her father keeps a loaded handgun in his nightstand, retrieves the weapon. Nicole then shoots the burglar threatening her parents.

Two questions arise in this scenario: first, is Nicole legally justified in shooting the armed burglar? As we will see later in Chapters 7, 8, and 10, yes, she is. Nicole is justified in defending a third person and property with deadly force under these circumstances. Second, is Nicole's father in trouble legally for leaving his firearm accessible to Nicole? No, he is not in trouble. Nicole's access to the firearm was the result of her necessity in defending her parents who were staring down the barrel of a home invader's gun! This accessibility to a firearm is contemplated under the Texas Penal Code in the form of the affirmative defense—"lawful defense by the child."

3. Exception for ranching or farming

There is an affirmative defense if the child has a firearm during a time when the child was "engaged in an agricultural enterprise." *See* Tex. Penal Code § 46.13(c)(4). This affirmative defense covers situations where a child may need a firearm for protection or other necessary situations that arise while farming, ranching, or other activities associated with agriculture.

H. Special duty of firearms dealers involving minors

Texas law requires that a dealer of firearms post in a conspicuous place on the premises where the dealer conducts his business a sign that contains the following warning written in block letters, not less than one inch in height:

"IT IS UNLAWFUL TO STORE, TRANSPORT, OR ABANDON AN UNSECURED FIREARM IN A PLACE WHERE CHILDREN ARE LIKELY TO BE AND CAN OBTAIN ACCESS TO THE FIREARM."
Tex. Penal Code § 46.13(g)

Federal law requires that FFLs who deliver handguns to non-licensees display at their licensed premises (including temporary business locations at gun shows) signs that customers can readily see. These signs are provided by the ATF and contain the following language:

1) the misuse of handguns is a leading contributor to juvenile violence and fatalities.
2) safely storing and securing firearms away from children will help prevent the unlawful possession of handguns by juveniles, stop accidents, and save lives.
3) federal law prohibits, except in certain limited circumstances, anyone under 18 years of age from knowingly possessing a handgun, or any person from transferring a handgun to a person under 18.
4) a knowing violation of the prohibition against selling, delivering, or otherwise transferring a handgun to a person under the age of 18 is, under certain circumstances, punishable by up to 10 years in prison.

See 27 CFR § 478.103(b).

In addition to the displayed sign, federal law requires FFLs to provide non-licensee customers with a written notification containing the same four points as listed above as well as Sections 922(x) and 924(a)(6) of Title 18, Chapter 44 of the United States Code. This written notification is available as a pamphlet published by the ATF entitled "Youth Handgun Safety Act Notice" and is sometimes referred to as ATF Information 5300.2. Alternatively, this written notification may be delivered to customers on another type of written notification, such as a manufacturer's brochure accompanying the handgun or a sales receipt or invoice applied to the handgun package. Any written notification delivered to a customer other than the one provided by the ATF must include the language described here, and must be "legible, clear, and conspicuous, and the required language shall appear in type size no smaller than 10-point type." See 27 CFR § 478.103(c).

II. FEDERAL LAW DISQUALIFICATIONS FOR PURCHASING AND POSSESSING FIREARMS

Federal law lists categories of persons disqualified from legally purchasing and possessing a firearm. This list comprises disqualifications that come from several different pieces of federal legislation, including the Gun Control Act of 1968, the Brady Handgun Violence Prevention Act, and the Violence Against Women Act. If a person buys or attempts to buy a firearm from an FFL, they must not be disqualified under any of the laws. Before an FFL may sell or otherwise transfer a firearm, the purchaser must fill out an ATF Form 4473. This form has questions concerning each of the criteria that disqualify a person to purchase a firearm under federal law. These disqualifications include:

1) if the person is not the actual purchaser of the firearm—also known as a "straw man purchaser";

2) if the person is under indictment or information in any court for a felony or any other crime for which the judge could imprison the person for more than one year;
3) if the person has ever been convicted in any court for a felony or other crime for which the judge could imprison the person for more than one year;
4) if the person is a fugitive from justice;
5) if the person is an unlawful user of, or addicted to, marijuana, or any depressant, stimulant, narcotic drug, or controlled substance;
6) if the person has ever been adjudicated as a mental defective or has been committed to a mental institution;
7) if the person has been dishonorably discharged from the Armed Forces;
8) if the person is subject to an active protective order restraining the person from harassing, stalking, or threatening the person's child, or an intimate partner or child of such partner;
9) if the person has been convicted in any court for a misdemeanor crime of domestic violence;
10) if the person has ever renounced their United States citizenship;
11) if the person is an alien illegally in the United States; and
12) if the person is admitted under a non-immigrant visa and does not qualify for an exception.

The purchaser must legally affirm that they are not subject to any of the criteria listed above before they may purchase a firearm. If a prospective purchaser answers any question on the form in a manner that indicates they are legally disqualified, it is illegal for the FFL to sell that person the firearm, and it is illegal for the purchaser to complete the transaction or possess the firearm.

A. Understanding who is disqualified

1. Can I buy a firearm for another person?

No. This would be a "straw man" purchase. In order to legally purchase a firearm from a dealer, you must be the "actual purchaser or transferee." If you are not the actual purchaser or transferee, it is illegal for you to complete the transfer or sale under federal law. Purchases for third persons are often called "straw man" purchases and are illegal. If you are not the actual purchaser, beware!

In fact, the ATF has a campaign called "Don't Lie for the Other Guy" that is targeted at (as they term it on their website) detection and deterrence of "straw man" purchases. The ATF website lists numerous examples of prosecutions for "straw man" purchases and a United States Supreme Court case examined and upheld federal law on this matter. *See Abramski v. United States,* 134 S.Ct. 2259 (2014).

So who is the "actual" buyer or transferee so as not to be a "straw man"? The ATF states that you are the actual "transferee/buyer if you are purchasing the firearm for yourself or otherwise acquiring the firearm for yourself (*e.g.*, redeeming the firearm from pawn/retrieving it from consignment, or a firearm raffle winner)." The ATF goes on to state "you are also the actual transferee/buyer if you are legitimately purchasing the firearm as a gift for a third party."

> **EXAMPLE:**
>
> Jim asks his sister Crystal to purchase a firearm for him because he will be out of town during the gun sale. Jim gives Crystal the money for the firearm. Crystal then buys the firearm with Jim's money and gives him the firearm.

Crystal is not the "actual buyer" (she is legally a "straw man") of the firearm and if she indicates that she is the "actual buyer" of the firearm on ATF Form 4473, she has committed a federal crime. However, it should be noted that the Supreme Court ruling in *Abramski* reaffirmed that "gifts" of firearms are not illegal straw man purchases. The important element in this crime is who provided the money for the purchase.

When completing ATF Form 4473, if a person checks "yes" to the box asking if the person is the "actual purchaser," then that person cannot have engaged in a separate transaction to sell or transfer the firearm privately. Please note: the Supreme Court's ruling held that a person cannot legally purchase a firearm on behalf of another even if the person receiving the firearm would not otherwise be prohibited from making the purchase themselves. So don't buy a firearm for another person no matter how good a friend, relative, or person they are—it is a crime!

> **FREQUENTLY ASKED QUESTIONS FROM THE ATF WEBSITE**
>
> **Q: TO WHOM MAY AN UNLICENSED PERSON TRANSFER FIREARMS UNDER THE GCA?**
>
> A: A person may sell a firearm to an unlicensed resident of his State, if he does not know or have reasonable cause to believe the person is prohibited from receiving or possessing firearms under federal law. [...] A person may loan or rent a firearm to a resident of any State for temporary use for lawful sporting purposes, if he does not know or have reasonable cause to believe the person is prohibited from receiving or possessing firearms under federal law. [...] A person may sell or transfer a firearm to a licensee in any State. However, a firearm other than a curio or relic may not be transferred interstate to a licensed collector. [18 U.S.C. 922(a)(3) and (5), 922(d), 27 CFR 478.29 and 478.30]
>
> **Q: MAY A PARENT OR GUARDIAN PURCHASE FIREARMS OR AMMUNITION AS A GIFT FOR A JUVENILE (LESS THAN 18 YEARS OF AGE)?**
>
> A: Yes. However, possession of handguns by juveniles (less than 18 years of age) is generally unlawful. Juveniles generally may only receive and possess handguns with the written permission of a parent or guardian for limited purposes, *e.g.*, employment, ranching, farming, target practice or hunting.
> [18 U.S.C. 922(x)]

Bureau of Alcohol, Tobacco, Firearms and Explosives. (2021). Firearms - Frequently Asked Questions - Unlicensed Persons [online] Available at: https://www.atf.gov/firearms/firearms-frequently-asked-questions-unlicensed-persons [Accessed 12 August 2021].

Instead of the previous example where Jim gave Crystal money to purchase a firearm for him, if Crystal decides to buy a firearm with her own money and then give the firearm to Jim as a present, Crystal is the actual buyer/transferee of the firearm. Since Crystal is the actual buyer, there exists no sham or "straw man," and the purchase is legal.

2. A person cannot purchase a firearm if they have been convicted or are under "indictment or information" for a felony or certain misdemeanors

If a person has been convicted of a felony or other crime for which a judge may sentence, or could have sentenced, the person to more than one year imprisonment, that person may not legally purchase a firearm (unless the crime was a state misdemeanor punishable by imprisonment of two years or less). *See* 18 U.S.C. § 921(a)(20)(B).

Likewise, if a person is under "indictment" or "information" for a felony, or any other crime for which a judge may sentence the person to more than one year imprisonment, that person is disqualified from purchasing a firearm. An "indictment" or "information" is a formal accusation of a crime punishable by imprisonment for a term exceeding one year. It is important to point out that the actual sentence received is not the determining factor for disqualification; rather, it is the possible maximum sentence. A person may have only been sentenced to 30 days imprisonment, but if the crime for which they were charged allowed a maximum penalty of five years, then that person is disqualified. *See Schrader v. Holder*, 704 F.3d 980 (D.C. Cir. 2013).

3. What does it mean to be a "fugitive from justice" so as to be disqualified from purchasing a firearm?

A "fugitive from justice" is a person who, after having committed a crime, flees from the jurisdiction of the court where the crime was committed. A fugitive from justice may also be a person who goes into hiding to avoid facing charges for the crime of which he or she is accused. Such individuals are not eligible to purchase or possess firearms.

4. Unlawful users of or persons addicted to drugs are disqualified from purchasing firearms

Federal law is very broad in that it disqualifies persons from the purchase of firearms if they are either users of or addicted to marijuana or any depressant, stimulant, narcotic drug, or any controlled substance. Under federal law, an "addict" is defined as a person that "habitually uses any narcotic so as to endanger the public morals, health, safety, or welfare, or who is so far addicted to the use of narcotic drugs as to have lost the power of self-control with reference to his addiction." *See* 21 U.S.C. § 802(1). However, in using the terms "users of," no such frequency or dependence seems contemplated in the words, nor did Congress give further guidance. Illegal users and addicts are prohibited from purchasing firearms from any person under federal law, and are likewise prohibited from possessing firearms. *See* 18 U.S.C. § 922(d) and (g). In late 2016, the ATF felt compelled to revise its Form 4473 to include the following statement in bold lettering:

> **WARNING: THE USE OR POSSESSION OF MARIJUANA REMAINS UNLAWFUL UNDER FEDERAL LAW REGARDLESS OF WHETHER IT HAS BEEN LEGALIZED OR DECRIMINALIZED FOR MEDICAL OR RECREATIONAL PURPOSES IN THE STATE WHERE YOU RESIDE.**

This has caused a great amount of concern as to whether or not a person who holds a prescription or license to buy marijuana is automatically prohibited from purchasing or possessing firearms.

As more and more states decriminalize marijuana, this is an issue that must ultimately be resolved.

5. A person can't legally buy or possess firearms if they are a "mental defective"

What does "mental defective" mean? A person is considered to have been adjudicated as a "mental defective" if there has been a "determination by a court, board, commission, or other lawful authority that a person, as a result of marked subnormal intelligence, or mental illness, incompetency, condition, or disease: is a danger to himself or others, or lacks the mental capacity to contract or manage his own affairs." The term mentally defective includes a finding of insanity by a court in a criminal case, and those persons found incompetent to stand trial or found not guilty by reason of lack of mental responsibility. *See* 27 CFR § 478.11.

Mentally defective also includes a person who has been committed to a mental institution by a court, board, commission, or other lawful authority, or a commitment to a mental institution involuntarily. The term includes commitment for mental defectiveness or mental illness, and also includes commitment for other reasons, such as drug use. However, it does not include a person in a mental institution for observation or a voluntary admission to a mental institution. Individuals who have been adjudicated as a mental defective are also prohibited from possessing firearms under federal law. *See* 18 U.S.C. § 922(g)(4).

6. A person subject to a restraining order may not purchase or possess a firearm

Under 18 U.S.C. § 922(g)(8), firearms may not be sold to or received by a person subject to a court order that: (a) was issued after a hearing which the person received actual notice of and had an opportunity to participate in; (b) restrains the person from harassing, stalking, or threatening an intimate partner or child of such intimate partner or person, or engaging in other conduct that would place an intimate partner in reasonable fear of bodily injury to the partner or child; and (c) includes a finding that such person represents a credible threat to the physical safety of such intimate partner or child; or by its terms explicitly prohibits the use, attempted use, or threatened use of physical force against such intimate partner or child that a person would reasonably be expected to cause bodily injury. An "intimate partner" of a person is the spouse or former spouse of the person, the parent of a child of the person, or an individual who cohabitates with the person. *See* 18 U.S.C. § 921(a)(32).

7. Domestic violence issues and disqualifications
A person who has ever been convicted of the crime of domestic violence may not purchase or possess firearms under federal law. The two primary factors considered are the use of force (or threatened force) and who the force or threatened force was against. This is an often misunderstood law, and, in fact, the ATF has numerous "Frequently Asked Questions" concerning this disqualification on its website: www.atf.gov. The ATF does a good job of explaining the scope of this subject in its FAQs. Due to the complexity of this issue, the ATF examples are included here:

FREQUENTLY ASKED QUESTIONS FROM THE ATF WEBSITE

Q: WHAT IS A "MISDEMEANOR CRIME OF DOMESTIC VIOLENCE"?

A "misdemeanor crime of domestic violence" is an offense that:
  (1) Is a misdemeanor under federal, state, or tribal law;
  (2) Has, as an element, the use or attempted use of physical force, or the threatened use of a deadly weapon; and
  (3) Was committed by a current or former spouse, parent, or guardian of the victim, by a person with whom the victim shares a child in common, by a person who is cohabiting with or has cohabited with the victim as a spouse, parent, or guardian, or by a person similarly situated to a spouse, parent, or guardian of the victim.

However, a person is not considered to have been convicted of a misdemeanor crime of domestic violence unless:
  (1) The person was represented by counsel in the case, or knowingly and intelligently waived the right of counsel in the case; and
  (2) In the case of a prosecution for which a person was entitled to a jury trial was tried, either –
    (a) the case was tried by a jury, or
    (b) the person knowingly and intelligently waived the right to have the case tried by a jury, by guilty plea or otherwise.

In addition, a conviction would not be disabling if it has been expunged or set aside, or is an offense for which the person has been pardoned or has had civil rights restored (if the law of the jurisdiction in which the proceedings were held provides for the loss of civil rights upon conviction for such an offense) unless the pardon, expunction, or restoration of civil rights expressly provides that the person may not ship, transport, possess, or receive firearms, and the person is not otherwise prohibited by

the law of the jurisdiction in which the proceedings were held from receiving or possessing firearms.
[18 U.S.C. 921(a)(33); 27 CFR 478.11]

Editor's note: A significant number of people make the mistake of overlooking or forgetting about a court issue or family law judicial proceeding. However, if you meet the above criteria, you are federally disqualified from possessing a firearm. The fact that it may have happened a long time ago, or that you did not understand the ramifications, is legally irrelevant.

Q: MUST A MISDEMEANOR CRIME OF DOMESTIC VIOLENCE (MCDV) BE DESIGNATED AS A "DOMESTIC VIOLENCE" OFFENSE?

A: No. A qualifying offense does not need to be designated as a domestic violence offense. For example, a conviction for assault may qualify as a misdemeanor crime of domestic violence even if the offense is not designated as a domestic violence assault. [18 U.S.C. 921(a)(33) and 922(g)(9); 27 CFR 478.11 and 478.32(a)(9)]

Q: DOES THE PROHIBITION ON RECEIPT OR POSSESSION OF FIREARMS AND AMMUNITION APPLY IF THE PERSON WAS CONVICTED OF AN MCDV PRIOR TO THE ENACTMENT OF 18 U.S.C. 922(g)(9) ON SEPTEMBER 30, 1996?

A: Yes.

Editor's note: For those wondering why this is not an unconstitutional *ex-post facto* law, multiple federal appeals courts have ruled against that argument and the Supreme Court has consistently declined to review any of those cases, effectively accepting the ruling of the courts of appeals and upholding this interpretation of the law.

Q: IS AN INDIVIDUAL WHO HAS BEEN PARDONED, OR WHOSE CONVICTION WAS EXPUNGED OR SET ASIDE, OR WHOSE CIVIL RIGHTS HAVE BEEN RESTORED, CONSIDERED CONVICTED OF A MISDEMEANOR CRIME OF DOMESTIC VIOLENCE?

A: No, as long as the pardon, expungement, or restoration does not expressly provide that the person may not ship, transport, possess, or receive firearms. A restoration of civil rights, however, is only effective to remove the federal firearms disability if the law of the jurisdiction provides for the loss of civil rights for a conviction of such a misdemeanor. [18 U.S.C. 921(a)(33); 27 CFR 478.11]

Q: IS THE RELATIONSHIP BETWEEN THE PARTIES AN ELEMENT OF A MCDV?

A: No. The "as an element" language in the definition of "misdemeanor crime of domestic violence" only applies to the use of force provision of the statute and not the relationship provision. However, to be disabling, the offense must have been committed by someone whose relationship to the victim meets the definition in the Gun Control Act (GCA). [18 U.S.C. 921(a)(33); 27 CFR 478.11]

Editor's note: This basically means that if illegal force was used against another person, regardless of the language in the underlying statute, if the illegal force was used against a protected person under the statute, federal law will deem this as satisfying the requirements and disqualify the individual from purchasing and possessing firearms.

Q: IN DETERMINING WHETHER A CONVICTION IN A STATE COURT IS A "CONVICTION" OF A MISDEMEANOR CRIME OF DOMESTIC VIOLENCE, DOES FEDERAL, STATE OR TRIBAL LAW APPLY?

A: The law of the jurisdiction determines whether a conviction has occurred. Therefore, if the law of the jurisdiction does not consider the person to be convicted, the person would not have the federal disability. [18 U.S.C. 921(a)(33); 27 CFR 478.11]

Q: DOES THE MCDV DISABILITY APPLY TO LAW ENFORCEMENT OFFICERS?

A: Yes. The Gun Control Act was amended so that employees of government agencies convicted of misdemeanor crimes of domestic violence would not be exempt from disabilities with respect to their receipt or possession of firearms or ammunition. Thus, law enforcement officers and other government officials who have been convicted of a disqualifying misdemeanor may not lawfully possess or receive firearms or ammunition for any purpose, including performance of their official duties. The disability applies to firearms and ammunition issued by government agencies, purchased by government employees for use in performing their official duties, and personal firearms and ammunition possessed by such employees. [18 U.S.C. 922(g)(9) and 925(a)(1); 27 CFR 478.32(a)(9) and 478.141]

Q: ARE LOCAL CRIMINAL ORDINANCES "MISDEMEANORS UNDER STATE LAW" FOR PURPOSES OF 18 U.S.C. 922(d)(9) AND (g)(9)?

A: Yes, assuming a violation of the ordinance meets the definition of "misdemeanor crime of domestic violence" in all other respects.

> **Q: WHAT STATE AND LOCAL OFFENSES ARE "MISDEMEANORS" FOR PURPOSES OF 18 U.S.C. 922(d)(9) AND (g)(9)?**
>
> A: The definition of misdemeanor crime of domestic violence in the Gun Control Act (GCA) includes any offense classified as a "misdemeanor" under federal, state or tribal law. In States that do not classify offenses as misdemeanors, the definition includes any State or local offense punishable by imprisonment for a term of 1 year or less or punishable by a fine. [18 U.S.C. 921(a)(33); 27 CFR 478.11]

> **Q: WHAT SHOULD AN INDIVIDUAL DO IF HE OR SHE HAS BEEN CONVICTED OF A MISDEMEANOR CRIME OF DOMESTIC VIOLENCE?**
>
> A: Individuals subject to this disability should immediately dispose of their firearms and ammunition, such as by abandonment to a law enforcement agency. [18 U.S.C. 922(g)(9); 27 CFR 478.32]

Bureau of Alcohol, Tobacco, Firearms and Explosives. (2021). Misdemeanor Crime of Domestic Violence. [online] Available at: https://www.atf.gov/qa-category/misdemeanor-crime-domestic-violence [Accessed 19 July 2021].

PRACTICAL LEGAL TIP

If you or a loved one are going through court proceedings involving family issues and a restraining or protective order is entered in your case, it can suspend your ability to purchase or possess firearms. Language in the court order prohibiting any acts of family violence, whether or not family violence actually occurred, make it so the person whom the order impacts is legally barred from the purchase or possession of any firearm. Believe it or not, the family courts have the ability to suspend your Second Amendment rights. —Emily

8. Illegal aliens or aliens admitted under a non-immigrant visa

Persons who are illegally in the United States may not legally purchase, possess, or transport firearms. Generally, non-immigrant aliens are also prohibited from legally purchasing, possessing, or transporting firearms. *See* 18 U.S.C. § 922(g)(5).

Exceptions for non-immigrant aliens

However, a non-immigrant alien who has been admitted under a non-immigrant visa is not prohibited from purchasing, receiving, or possessing a firearm if the person falls within one of the following exceptions:
1) if the person was admitted to the United States for lawful hunting or sporting purposes or is in possession of a hunting license or permit lawfully issued in the United States;

2) if the person is an official representative of a foreign government who is accredited to the United States Government or the Government's mission to an international organization having its headquarters in the United States;
3) if the person is an official representative of a foreign government who is *en route* to or from another country to which that alien is accredited;
4) if the person is an official of a foreign government or a distinguished foreign visitor who has been so designated by the Department of State;
5) if the person is a foreign law enforcement officer of a friendly foreign government entering the United States on official law enforcement business; or
6) if the person has received a waiver from the prohibition from the Attorney General of the United States.

See 18 U.S.C. § 922(y).

III. TEXAS LAW DISQUALIFICATIONS: WHO CANNOT BUY A FIREARM UNDER TEXAS LAW?

As mentioned earlier, Texas has restrictions on the sale, transfer, and possession of firearms that are separate and distinct from the federal restrictions. If a person runs afoul of the law, they could potentially face prosecution in both state and federal court.

A. Texas law disqualifications for selling a firearm

The disqualifications for selling firearms under Texas law are contained in Section 46.06 of the Texas Penal Code and apply to all transactions in Texas. This section of the Penal Code makes it a crime—a Class A misdemeanor or, under certain circumstances, state jail felony—for a person to:

1) sell, rent, lease, loan, or give a handgun to a person that the seller knows intends to commit an unlawful act;
2) intentionally or knowingly sell, rent, lease, or give (or even offer to do so) a firearm to any child;
3) intentionally, knowingly, or recklessly sell a firearm or ammunition to an intoxicated person;
4) knowingly sell a firearm or ammunition to any person convicted of a felony before the lapsing of five years from release from confinement or supervision; or
5) sell, rent, lease, loan, or give a handgun to a person knowing that the person is subject to an active protective order.

If a person falls under any of the categories (*see* full explanations below) listed in the foregoing sections, Texas law makes it illegal to sell that person a firearm.

B. Texas law disqualifications for purchasing a firearm

Unlike the disqualifications for selling, which place criminal penalties on the seller, the disqualifications for purchasing a firearm are located in Texas Penal Code Sections 46.06(a)(6) and (a)(7). These Sections criminalize certain conduct for purchases. Specifically, it is unlawful for a person to knowingly purchase, rent, lease, or receive a handgun as a loan or gift from another while the recipient is subject to an active protective order. It is also unlawful for a person, while prohibited from possessing a firearm under state or federal law, to knowingly make a material false statement on a federal firearm transaction form.

C. Texas law disqualifications for possessing firearms

Similar to the disqualifications for selling and purchasing firearms under Texas law, Chapter 46 of the Penal Code also includes prohibitions on the possession of firearms. These prohibitions on possession are specifically found in Section 46.04 of the Penal Code and include:

1) persons convicted of a felony until after the fifth anniversary of the person's release from confinement, supervision under community supervision, parole, or mandatory supervision—whichever date is later; and after the time expires, it cannot be possessed in any other place than the person's home;
2) persons convicted of domestic or family violence punishable as a Class A misdemeanor before the fifth anniversary of the later of the date of the person's release from confinement, or the date of release from community supervision following the conviction of the misdemeanor;
3) persons (other than law enforcement officers) who are subject to a domestic protective order, have received notice of the order, and before the expiration of the order; or
4) persons who are members of a criminal street gang, as defined by Texas Penal Code Section 71.01, and intentionally, knowingly, or recklessly carry on or about their person a handgun in a motor vehicle or watercraft.

Note: even though a person may not be disqualified from possession of a firearm under state law, that person may nevertheless still be disqualified to possess a firearm under federal law.

EXAMPLE:
Richard was convicted of a state crime Class A misdemeanor involving family violence in 1992. He has a Smith & Wesson .357 Magnum in his nightstand for self-defense.

Under Texas law, Richard may be in legal possession of his firearm because more than five years have elapsed following either his conviction or his release from community supervision. However, if push comes to shove and the Feds ever care, Richard is in unlawful possession of a firearm under 18 U.S.C. § 922(g)(9) and 27 CFR § 478.32(a)(9), regardless of Texas law.

D. Understanding who is disqualified under Texas law
1. How does a seller know a person intends to commit an unlawful act?
Under Texas Penal Code § 46.06(a)(1), a person is prohibited from selling a firearm to another person when the seller knows that the buyer intends to commit some unlawful act. Let's take a look at a couple of examples to highlight the difficulties a seller can face.

The issue of knowledge as it relates to the law can be a minefield to navigate. Under the law, whenever a statute prohibits a person from doing something because they know a condition exists, the government must prove actual knowledge. *See City of San Benito v. Cantu,* 831 S.W.2d 416, 421 (Tex. App.—Corpus Christi 1992). In fact, Texas Penal Code § 6.03(b) states that a "person acts knowingly, or with knowledge, with respect to the nature of his conduct or to circumstances surrounding his conduct when he is aware of the nature of his conduct or that the circumstances exist. A person acts knowingly, or with knowledge, with respect to a result of his conduct when he is aware that his conduct is reasonably certain to cause the result." That is, a person must actually know that something is prohibited, as opposed to being "pretty sure," "probable," or even "likely." Knowing is also a much higher standard than "should have had reason to know." A person's knowledge can only be established by the facts of each incident.

EXAMPLE:

Tony arranges to sell a handgun to Paul. When Paul arrives at the pre-arranged meeting location to conduct the transaction, he inspects the handgun and, without humor, tells Tony, "This will be perfect to rob the First State Bank down the street this afternoon. I've been looking for a gun just like this one! Now I don't have to wait any longer!"

Can Tony legally sell his handgun to Paul? No. Paul has clearly communicated his plan to commit a serious crime with Tony's handgun.

EXAMPLE:

Allen arranges to sell a hunting rifle to Jerry, a man he met briefly at a gun show a couple of weeks prior. When Jerry comes over to buy the rifle, he remarks while examining the firearm, "Boy, it'd sure be great to get on my neighbor's land sometime and shoot some deer."

In this example, does Allen have actual knowledge that Jerry is going to commit an unlawful act, like trespassing or hunting without a license? No, he only has an idea of what Jerry would like to do sometime. He does not know if the hunting is with or without the land owner's permission, whether it would even be legal to shoot deer, or if a neighbor or deer even exists at all. With only this information in hand, it would not be illegal for Allen to sell the rifle to Jerry. Ultimately, what a seller did or did not know can only be established by looking at the totality of the circumstances and may ultimately be decided by a jury in court.

2. What does Texas law define as a child for the purpose of selling a firearm?

A child refers to any person who is under 18 years of age. *See* Section I(D) of this Chapter for a discussion of age restrictions.

3. A person may not sell a firearm or ammunition to an intoxicated person

A person may not intentionally, knowingly, or recklessly sell a firearm to an intoxicated person. *See* Tex. Penal Code § 46.06(a)(3).

What is intoxicated?

Texas Penal Code § 46.06(b)(1) provides the most relevant definition for "intoxicated" with respect to the purchase of a firearm. Under that section of the Penal Code, intoxicated means "substantial impairment of mental or physical capacity resulting from introduction of any substance into the body." Note that under this definition, intoxication is not limited to alcohol, and there is not a specific legal limit on the amount of impairing-substance found in the body. Under Texas law, no person who is intoxicated can be sold a firearm. Again, when a person knew another may be intoxicated or knew whether a person was actually intoxicated may ultimately be decided by a jury.

Mental state

The law has three different mental states under which a person may be guilty of a crime for selling a firearm to an intoxicated person: intentionally, knowingly, or recklessly. Intentionally and knowingly are the higher standards and reckless the lesser.

When does a person recklessly sell a firearm to an intoxicated person? Texas Penal Code Section 6.03(c) states that "a person acts recklessly, or is reckless, with respect to circumstances surrounding his conduct or the result of his conduct when he is aware of but consciously disregards a substantial and unjustifiable risk that the circumstances exist or the result will occur. The risk must be of such a nature and degree that its disregard constitutes a gross deviation from the standard of care that an ordinary person would exercise under all the circumstances as viewed from the actor's standpoint." Likewise, if a person's mental state when selling a firearm or ammunition to an intoxicated person rises above reckless to knowingly or intentionally, that is also illegal.

4. Illegal to sell to certain felons

If a person knows that another person was convicted of a felony, they may not legally sell that other person a firearm under Texas law unless the person has been out of imprisonment or released from community supervision for five years—whichever is later. Note, however, that a person may still be guilty of unlawfully transferring a firearm to a felon under federal law.

5. Differences in federal and Texas law concerning convicted felons possessing firearms

Under federal law, a person convicted of a felony is prohibited from possessing firearms. Texas law, however, relaxes such restrictions. Under Texas law, a convicted felon is permitted to possess firearms in the person's home after five years from the date of the person's release from confinement, supervision under community supervision, parole, or mandatory supervision—whichever date is later. *See* Tex. Penal Code § 46.04(a).

6. Will my juvenile record prevent me from purchasing and possessing a firearm?

Generally, if any person, including a juvenile, has been convicted of a crime that carries a punishment of imprisonment for more than one year, then that person will not be permitted to purchase a firearm under federal law unless their firearm rights are restored. In Texas, juvenile adjudications of delinquent conduct are not convictions and therefore are not disqualifying under federal law. *See* 18 U.S.C. § 922(g); and *United States v. Walters,* 359 F.3d 340 (4th Cir. 2004).

IV. UNDERSTANDING "PRIVATE SALES" LAWS
A. What are the legal restrictions on "private sales" of firearms?

Private individuals may legally buy, sell, gift, or otherwise transfer firearms to another private individual in Texas. However, when doing so, careful attention needs to be paid to not violate the laws regulating these transactions. So, what are the legal restrictions? First, the ATF website has an informative pamphlet entitled "Best Practices: Transfers of Firearms by Private Sellers" located on its website. https://www.atf.gov/file/58681/download. This pamphlet should be a must-read before entering into a "private sale" transaction involving a firearm. So, what are the rules in Texas regarding private sales?

1. Residency requirements

In order for the private sale of a firearm to be legal in Texas, both parties must reside in the same state. This means, for our purposes, that both the buyer and seller of the firearm must be Texas residents. Similarly, under federal law, an unlicensed (non-dealer) may only "transfer" a firearm to another unlicensed person in the same state. This means that if a person is a resident of Texas, federal law prohibits the person from directly (not through a dealer) selling or transferring the firearm to a resident of another state. Federal law makes these transactions illegal from both the buyer/transferee and seller/transferor perspective. It is illegal for a private individual to transport into or receive within his own state a firearm that was purchased in another state from a private seller. *See* 18 U.S.C. § 922(a)(3). Likewise, it is illegal for a private seller to sell or deliver a firearm to an individual whom the private seller knows or has reason to believe is not a resident of the seller's state. *See* 18 U.S.C. § 922(a)(5).

EXAMPLE:

Bernie, a Texas resident, is visiting his brother-in-law Justin in Louisiana. While visiting, Bernie and Justin decide to go hunting in the swamps around Lafayette, and Bernie borrows one of Justin's handguns to shoot snakes. Bernie is impressed with Justin's handgun. Bernie asks Justin if he could buy it from him. Since they've been in-laws for so many years, Justin agrees and gives him a good price. Bernie happily pays Justin and brings his new handgun back home to San Antonio.

Has Justin committed a crime in selling the handgun to Bernie? Has Bernie committed a crime in purchasing the handgun from Justin? The answer to both questions is yes! Under federal law, Bernie is not allowed to privately purchase a handgun in another state and transport it back to his home state. Likewise, Justin is not allowed to sell a firearm legally to a person he knows lives in another state. In this example, both Bernie and Justin know that Bernie is not a Louisiana resident—the place where Justin has sold his handgun. Bernie has committed the crime of willfully receiving a firearm from an out-of-state unlicensed person while Justin has committed the federal crime of willful sale of a firearm to an out-of-state person. *See* 18 U.S.C. § 924(a)(1)(D). The penalties for these crimes include jail time up to 5 years and/or a fine of $250,000!

What if the situation is less obvious? Let's take a look at an example where "reasonable cause to believe" comes into play.

> **EXAMPLE:**
>
> Felicia, a Texas resident, recently posted her Kimber 1911 for sale on an internet message board. Felicia receives an email from a person named Thomas who would like to buy the handgun. Felicia and Thomas agree, via email, on a purchase price and arrange to meet at a place in Texas one week later to complete the transfer. When Thomas pulls up in his 1999 Ford F-150, Felicia notices the truck's Oklahoma license plates. Nevertheless, Felicia shrugs and sells Thomas the gun anyway without going through any of the formalities of making a bill of sale, or asking for Thomas's identification. Two weeks later, Felicia finds herself at an ATF field office in Houston answering questions about a shooting that took place in Tulsa with her (former) Kimber 1911.

Is Felicia in trouble? It is highly likely. Although Felicia is not the center of the shooting investigation, she is probably under investigation for illegally selling the firearm to an out-of-state resident under federal law. If Felicia admits to noticing the Oklahoma license plate, the ATF will assert that she had reasonable cause to believe that she was engaging in a prohibited firearm transfer.

2. Private sales: don't knowingly sell to the "wrong" people

A private individual may sell a firearm to a private buyer in the same state so long as the seller does not know or have reasonable cause to believe that the person purchasing the firearm is prohibited from possessing or receiving a firearm under federal or state law. *See* 18 U.S.C. § 922(d). *See also* Sections II and III of this Chapter for our discussion on disqualifications.

> **EXAMPLE:**
> Gene and Jezebel are friends, and Jezebel tells Gene that she has just attempted to buy a gun from a local FFL dealer and that she was denied because she was disqualified for some reason under federal law (something about a conviction or restraining order or drug use or psychiatric problems—Jezebel was too mad to remember!). Gene says, "no problem, I'll just sell you one of mine," and he does.

Gene has just committed a crime, because he knew (or at least had reasonable cause to believe) that Jezebel was prohibited from purchasing a firearm under the law.

B. How does the law determine a person's residence when buying or selling a firearm?

1. Individuals with one residence

For the purpose of firearms purchases, the person's state of residence is the state in which the person is present and where the individual has an intention of making a home. *See* 27 CFR § 478.11.

2. What if a person maintains a home in two states?

If a person maintains a home in two (or more) states and resides in those states for periods of the year, he or she may, during the period of time the person actually resides in a particular state, purchase a firearm in that state. However, simply owning property in another state does not qualify a person as a resident for the purpose of purchasing a firearm in that state. To meet the residency requirements, a person must actually maintain a home in a state which includes an intention to make a particular state a residence. *See* 27 CFR § 478.11. This issue may ultimately be a fact question with evidence of residency being things like a driver's license, insurance records, recurring expenses in the state, as well as other things related to making a particular state a person's residence.

3. Members of the Armed Forces

A member of the Armed Forces on active duty is a resident of the state in which his or her permanent duty station is located. If a member of the Armed Forces maintains a home in one state and the member's permanent duty station is in a nearby state to which he or she commutes each day, then the member has two states of residence and may purchase a firearm in either the state where the duty station is located or the state where the home is maintained. *See* 18 U.S.C. § 921(b). *See also* ATF FAQs on residency at www.atf.gov.

4. Immigrant aliens

Persons who are legally present in the United States are residents of the state in which they reside and where they intend to make a home. Such persons, provided they meet all other requirements and are not otherwise prohibited from purchasing a firearm, are lawfully permitted to purchase a firearm.

C. Best practices to document a private firearms sale

Protect yourself! This is practical advice that should not be ignored. If you engage in the private sale of a firearm in the State of Texas, here are some practical tips:
- Ask for identification whether you are the buyer/transferee or seller/transferor to establish residency;

- Get and/or give a bill of sale for the transfer and keep a copy—identify the firearm including make, model, and serial number, as well as the date and place of transfer;
- Put the residency information on the bill of sale including names, addresses, and phone numbers; and
- Do not sell or transfer a firearm or ammunition if you think the person may not be permitted or is prohibited from receiving the firearm.

Why do this? Not only will it help establish residency, but if you unfortunately happen to buy or sell a firearm that was previously used in a crime, or if you sell or transfer a gun that is later used in a crime, you want to be able to establish when you did and did not own or possess the firearm.

Further, as a matter of good course, if you are a seller or transferor in a private sale, you might ask whether there is any reason the buyer/transferee cannot own a firearm. Why? So that if there is an issue later, you can at a minimum say that you had no reason to know the buyer could not legally possess firearms. However, do not overlook behavior that may indicate the buyer is not telling you the truth, because law enforcement will not overlook facts that show you knew or had reasonable cause to believe that the buyer/transferee could not own a firearm at the time of the transfer if a legal issue arises later. Protect yourself!

V. BUYING, SELLING, AND TRANSFERRING THROUGH AN FFL
A. Basic procedures

Persons purchasing firearms through dealers must comply with all legal requirements imposed by federal law. These include both paperwork and appropriate background checks or screenings to ensure that the purchaser is not prohibited from the purchase or possession of a firearm under federal law.

When purchasing through a dealer, the first thing a prospective buyer will do is select a firearm. Once a selection has been made, the prospective purchaser is required to show proper identification and complete ATF Form 4473. This form requires the applicant, under penalty of law, to provide accurate identifying information, as well as answer certain questions in order to establish whether a person may legally purchase a firearm. The information provided on Form 4473 is then provided to the National Instant Criminal Background Check System ("NICS") for processing and approval in order to proceed with the transfer (however, no NICS background check may be required if the transferee is legally exempt for reasons such as possessing a state-issued firearms license like a Texas LTC). An FFL dealer can submit the check to NICS either by telephone or through the online website, and only after the FFL completes all of these steps successfully is a purchaser/transferee allowed to take possession of the firearm.

B. What is Form 4473?

ATF Form 4473 is known as the Firearms Transaction Record, which must be completed when a person purchases a firearm from an FFL dealer. *See* 27 CFR § 478.124. Form 4473 requires the applicant provide their name, address, birth date, state of residence, and other information including a government-issued photo identification. The form also contains information blanks to be completed, including the NICS background check transaction number, the make, model, and serial number of the firearm to be purchased, and a series of questions that a person must answer. *See* 27 CFR § 478.124(c). This series of questions and the corresponding answers help determine a firearm purchaser's eligibility under federal law. Once the form is completed, the prospective purchaser will sign the form and attest that the information provided is truthful and accurate under penalty of federal law. This means that if you lie or make false statements on this form, the Feds can and will prosecute you!

Likewise, the dealer must also sign the Form 4473 and retain it for at least 20 years. The ATF is permitted to inspect as well as receive a copy of the Form 4473 from the dealer both during audits and during the course of a criminal investigation. The 4473 records must be surrendered to the ATF in the event the FFL dealer retires or ceases business.

Texas law also prohibits lying on a federal firearm transaction form. Texas Penal Code Section 46.06(a)(7) makes it a state jail felony to knowingly make a material false statement on this form while being prohibited from possessing a firearm under state or federal law. If you "lie and try" to purchase a firearm, you are committing a crime under both Texas and federal law!

C. How are background checks administered when purchasing a firearm?

1. NICS: National Instant Criminal Background Check System

Background checks by dealers when transferring firearms are completed through the National Instant Criminal Background Check System or ("NICS"), if required, prior to the transfer of a firearm from an FFL dealer to a non-dealer. When the prospective purchaser/transferee's information is given to NICS, the system will check the applicant against at least three different databases containing various types of records. Applicants are checked against the records maintained by the Interstate Identification Index ("III"), which contains criminal history records, the National Crime Information Center ("NCIC"), which contains records including warrants and protective orders, as well as the NICS Index, which contains records of individuals who are prohibited from purchasing or possessing firearms under either federal or state law. In addition, if the applicant is not a United States citizen, the application is processed for an Immigration Alien Query ("IAQ") through the Department of Homeland Security's Immigration and Customs Enforcement Division.

2. Responses from NICS
NICS responses to background checks come in three basic forms: proceed, delay, or deny. The "proceed" response allows for the transfer to be completed. The "delay" response means that the transfer may not legally proceed. If the dealer receives a response of "delay," NICS has three business days to research the applicant further. See 27 CFR 478.102. If the dealer has not received a notice that the transfer is denied after the three business days, then the transfer may proceed. "Deny" means the transfer should not take place; a transferee's options after a "deny" are discussed below.

3. What transactions require background checks?
A background check is required before each and every sale or other transfer of a firearm from an FFL to a non-licensee unless an exception is provided under the law. For every transaction that requires a background check, the purchaser/transferee must also complete ATF Form 4473. This includes:
• The sale or trade of a firearm;
• The return of a consigned firearm;
• The redemption of a pawned firearm;

- The loan or rental of a firearm for use off of an FFL's licensed premises; and
- Any other non-exempt transfer of a firearm.

> **PRACTICAL LEGAL TIP**
>
> Thinking about pawning a firearm for a little emergency cash? Be sure you are eligible to purchase a firearm when you redeem your pawn ticket. Since most pawn shops are FFL dealers, you will need to complete an ATF Form 4473 and pass a NICS background check simply to get your own firearm out of pawn. −Edwin

4. What transactions do not require a background check?

A background check is not required under the following circumstances:

- The sale or transfer of a firearm where the transferee presents a valid state permit/license that allows the transferee to possess, acquire, or carry a firearm (for example, a Texas LTC) from the state where the FFL is located and the state permit/license is recognized by the ATF as a qualifying alternative to the background check requirement;
- The transfer of a firearm from one FFL to another FFL;
- The return of a repaired firearm to the person from whom it was received;
- The sale of a firearm to a law enforcement agency or a law enforcement officer for official duties if the transaction meets the specific requirements of 27 CFR § 478.134, including providing a signed certification from a person in authority on

agency letterhead stating that the officer will use the firearm in official duties and where a records check reveals the officer does not have any convictions for a misdemeanor crime of domestic violence;
- The transfer of a replacement firearm of the same kind and type to the person from whom a firearm was received; or
- The transfer of a firearm that is subject to the National Firearms Act if the transfer was pre-approved by the ATF.

Note: a Texas License To Carry a Handgun ("LTC") currently qualifies as an alternative to the NICS background check requirement as long as the license was issued within five years of the date of the transfer. A complete permit chart for all states is available on the ATF's website at www.atf.gov.

5. If a person buys multiple handguns, a dealer must report that person to the ATF

Under federal law, FFLs are required to report to the ATF any sale or transfer of two or more pistols, revolvers, or any combination of pistols and revolvers totaling two or more to an unlicensed (non-FFL) individual that takes place at one time or during any five consecutive business days. *See* 18 U.S.C. § 923(g)(3). This report is made to the ATF on Form 3310.4 and is completed in triplicate with the original copy sent to the ATF, one sent to the designated state police or local law enforcement agency in the jurisdiction where the sale took place, and one retained by the dealer and held for no less than five years.

6. FFLs must report persons who purchase more than one rifle in southwest border states

In Texas, Arizona, New Mexico, and California, FFL dealers are required by the ATF to report the sale or other transfer of more than one semi-automatic rifle capable of accepting a detachable magazine and with a caliber greater than .22 (including .223 caliber/5.56 millimeter) to an unlicensed person at one time or during any five consecutive business days. This report is made via ATF Form 3310.12 and must be reported no later than the close of business on the day the multiple sale or other disposition took place. This requirement includes (but is not limited to) purchases of popular semi-automatic rifles such as AR-15s, AK-47s, Ruger Mini-14s, and Tavor bullpup rifles.

VI. WHAT IF I'M DENIED THE RIGHT TO PURCHASE A FIREARM?
A. If I am denied the right to purchase, how do I appeal?

Persons who believe they have been erroneously denied or delayed a firearm transfer based on a match to a record returned by NICS may request an appeal of their "deny" or "delay" decision. All appeal inquiries must be submitted to the NICS Section's Appeal Service Team ("AST") in writing, either via mail or online on the FBI's website at www.fbi.gov. An appellant must provide their complete name, complete mailing address, and NICS transaction number. For persons appealing a delayed transaction, a fingerprint card is required and must be submitted with the appeal, while the fingerprint card is merely recommended on appeals for denied applications. This may seem counter-intuitive, but it is required per the FBI's website.

B. What if I keep getting erroneously delayed or denied when I am attempting to buy a firearm?

Apply for a Unique Personal Identification Number ("UPIN") that is designed to solve this issue. Some individuals may have a name which is common enough (or happens to be flagged for other reasons) that it causes undue delays or denials in the background check verification process through NICS. For that reason, NICS maintains the Voluntary Appeal File database ("VAF"), which allows any applicant to apply by submitting an appeal request and then obtain a UPIN. A person who has been cleared through the VAF and received a UPIN is able to use their UPIN when completing Form 4473 in order to help avoid further erroneous denials or extended delays. A person can obtain a UPIN by following the procedures outlined on the FBI's website at www.fbi.gov.

Traditionally, there has been a long delay in processing a UPIN application; there may be an alternative. Another option available to a prospective purchaser that may yield a quicker resolution is a firearm-related challenge (appeal). You may only challenge a denied (not a delay) firearm transaction in this manner. This process will provide the reason a background check was denied and allow the challenging of a denial. Unlike with the VAF application, the applicant will not receive a UPIN. Rather, if a firearm-related challenge is successful, the FBI will clear the denial for a singular purchase. If you are repeatedly delayed or denied a firearm purchase, the VAF is recommended to expedite future purchases as well. A person can obtain a UPIN or request a firearm-related challenge by following the procedures outlined on the FBI's website at www.fbi.gov.

VII. ADDITIONAL CONSIDERATIONS IN FIREARMS PURCHASING AND POSSESSION LAWS

A. How can I legally purchase a firearm from someone in another state?

Any individual who wishes to purchase a firearm from a person that lives in another state than the purchaser must complete the transaction through an FFL. Sellers or transferors are legally authorized to facilitate a private transaction or transfer by shipping the firearm to the purchaser's FFL in the recipient/buyer's state, where the FFL will complete the transfer process. *See* ATF Procedure 2020-2. It is a federal crime to sell or transfer a firearm between persons who are residents of different states, or where a transfer takes place in a state other than the transferee/transferor's singular state of residence.

B. Can I purchase firearms on the internet?

Yes. However, all legal requirements for a transfer must be followed. If the buyer and seller are both residents of Texas, then the two may lawfully conduct a private sale so long as all other legal issues are satisfied (*see* our earlier discussion on disqualifications to purchasing and possessing firearms in this Chapter). However, if buyer and seller are not residents of the same state, the transaction can only be legally facilitated through an FFL.

C. Shipping firearms

1. Can I ship my firearm through the United States Postal Service ("USPS")?

Long guns: yes. Handguns: no. However, under federal law, a non-licensed individual may not transfer (and this would include shipping to someone) a firearm to a non-licensed resident (non-FFL) of another state. However, a non-licensed individual may mail a long gun to a resident of his or her own state, and they may also mail a long gun to an FFL of another state. To that end, the USPS recommends that long guns be mailed via registered mail and that the packaging used to mail the long gun be ambiguous so as to not identify the contents. Handguns are not allowed to be mailed via USPS. *See* 18 U.S.C. §§ 1715, 922(a)(3), 922(a)(5), and 922(a)(2)(A). Rather, handguns must be shipped using a common or contract carrier (*e.g.*, UPS, FedEx, *etc.*).

2. Shipping handguns and other firearms through a common or contract carrier

Under federal law, a non-licensed individual may ship a firearm (including a handgun) by a common or contract carrier (*e.g.*, UPS, FedEx, *etc.*) to a resident of his or her own state, or to an FFL in another state. However, it is illegal to ship any firearm to a non-FFL in another state. It is a requirement that the carrier be notified that the shipment contains a firearm; however, carriers are prohibited from requiring any identifying marks on the package which may be used to identify the contents as containing a firearm. *See* 18 U.S.C. §§ 922(a)(2)(A), 922(a)(3), 922(a)(5), 922(e), 27 CFR 478.31 and 478.30.

D. Can I ship my firearm to myself for use in another state?

Yes. In accordance with the law as described in the preceding section, a person may ship a firearm to himself or herself, in care of another person in another state where he or she intends to hunt or engage in other lawful activity. The package should be addressed to the owner, and persons other than the owner should not open the package and take possession of the firearm.

E. If I am moving out of Texas, may I have movers move my firearms?

Yes. A person who lawfully possesses firearms may transport or ship the firearms interstate when changing the person's state of residence, so long as the person complies with the requirements for shipping and transporting firearms as outlined earlier. *See* 18 U.S.C. § 922(e) and 27 CFR § 478.31. However, certain NFA items such as destructive devices, machine guns, short-barreled shotguns or rifles, and so forth require approval from the ATF before they can be moved interstate. *See* 18 U.S.C. § 922(a)(4) and 27 CFR §

478.28. It is important that the person seeking to move the firearms also check state and local laws where the firearms will be relocated to ensure that the movement of the firearms into the new state does not violate any state law or local ordinance.

F. May I loan my firearm to another person?

Yes. There is no prohibition on loaning a firearm to another person, so long as the person receiving the firearm may lawfully possess one. However, under Texas Penal Code § 46.06(a)(2), it is unlawful for a person to intentionally or knowingly sell, rent, lease, give or offer to sell, rent, lease, or give a firearm to any child younger than 18 years of age. The law does provide an affirmative defense for persons charged with a crime of unlawful transfer of weapons in the event that the loan of the firearm to a minor was done with the effective consent of the parent with legal custody of the child. Although this statute does not specifically use the word "loan," the term "give" is not defined. Thus, Texas firearms owners should be aware of this statute anytime the loan of a firearm to a minor takes place.

G. What happens if a firearm is stolen?

A stolen firearm can be a headache no gun owner wants to deal with. However, if the proper steps are taken, the risks associated with a firearm loss can be minimized. The first and most crucial part of a lost or stolen gun incident is preparing before such an event with proper documentation. The information you should track is each firearm's make, model, and serial number. Additionally, you should keep a copy of the purchase record, such as a sales receipt or bill of sale. This information should be kept separately from the location where you store your firearms, such as a safety deposit box.

Texas law does not require a lost or stolen gun be reported to law enforcement, but in most instances it is the prudent course of action. With that said, if a firearm goes missing, it is important to speak with an attorney before reporting the loss to law enforcement. This may avoid inadvertently creating criminal liability (*e.g.*, disclosing the loss leads police to discover another crime).

Reporting the gun lost or stolen breaks what is commonly referred to as the "chain of custody." It clearly delineates when you had the gun and when it left your possession. If you decide to report your firearm as lost or stolen, law enforcement will enter the gun's information into the National Crime Information Center database maintained by the Federal Bureau of Investigation.

H. What happens to my firearms when I die?

Depending on the manner in which a person leaves his or her estate behind, firearms may be bequeathed in a customary manner like other personal property because federal law provides an exception to the interstate transfer restrictions for firearms acquired by bequest or intestate succession. *See* 27 CFR 478.30. Does this mean you can leave your firearms to your nephew who is a convicted felon? Or that you can leave firearms with "high-capacity magazines" to your daughter in California? No. Careful consideration needs to be given in estate planning with consideration for firearms law of both the jurisdiction in which the estate is located as well as consideration of who is to receive the firearms.

VIII. AMMUNITION: THE LAW OF PURCHASING AND POSSESSION
A. Who is legally prohibited from purchasing ammunition under federal law?

Under federal law, there are six primary situations where a person is prohibited from buying, selling, or possessing ammunition (beyond armor-piercing ammunition, which was discussed in Chapter 5).

(1) Under 18 U.S.C. § 922(b)(1), it is unlawful for a person to sell long gun ammunition to a person under the age of 18;

(2) Under 18 U.S.C. § 922(b)(1), it is unlawful for a person to sell handgun ammunition to a person under the age of 21;

(3) Under 18 U.S.C. § 922(x)(2)(B), it is unlawful for a juvenile to possess handgun ammunition;

(4) Under 18 U.S.C. § 922(d), it is unlawful to sell ammunition to a person who is prohibited from purchasing firearms;

(5) Under 18 U.S.C. § 922(g), it is unlawful for a person who is disqualified from purchasing or possessing firearms to possess firearm ammunition if such ammunition has moved in interstate commerce (which is nearly all ammunition); and

(6) Under 18 U.S.C. § 922(h), it is unlawful for a person who is employed by a person who is disqualified from purchasing or possessing ammunition to possess or transport ammunition for the disqualified individual.

For the statutes that involve juveniles, there are a couple of notable exceptions to the law. First, the law against selling handgun ammunition to a juvenile and possession of handgun ammunition by a juvenile does not apply to a temporary transfer of ammunition to a juvenile or to the possession or use of ammunition by a juvenile if the handgun and ammunition are possessed and used in the course of employment, in the course of ranching or farming-related activities at the residence of the juvenile (or on property used for ranching or farming at which the juvenile, with the permission of the property owner or lessee, is performing activities related to the operation of the farm or ranch), target practice, hunting, or a course of instruction in the safe and lawful use of a handgun. The law also does not apply to the temporary transfer to or use of ammunition by a juvenile with prior written consent from his or her parent or guardian who is not prohibited by federal, state, or local law from possessing firearms. *See* 18 U.S.C. § 922(x)(3).

Second, the law against selling ammunition to juveniles does not apply to juveniles who:
1) are members of the Armed Forces of the United States or the National Guard who possess or are armed with a handgun in the line of duty;
2) receive ammunition by inheritance; or
3) possess ammunition in the course of self-defense or defense of others in the residence of the juvenile or a residence in which the juvenile is an invited guest.

B. When is a person prohibited from purchasing or possessing ammunition under Texas law?

The Texas Penal Code provides two occasions where the sale of ammunition is prohibited:
1) to intoxicated persons; and
2) to felons prior to the fifth anniversary of their release from confinement, community supervision, parole, or mandatory supervision.

However, there is no crime for the purchase or possession of ammunition by those or any other individuals, with the exception of armor-piercing handgun ammunition. *See* Chapter 5.

Under Texas Penal Code Section 46.06(a)(3), it is a Class A misdemeanor if a person "intentionally, knowingly, or recklessly sells a firearm or ammunition for a firearm to any person who is intoxicated."

> **EXAMPLE:**
>
> Max comes into Larry's pawn shop to browse around. Larry notices that Max has red watery eyes, slurred speech, strong odor of an alcoholic beverage on his breath, and he is staggering around. Additionally, Max is carrying a half-empty Jim Beam bottle. Max says that he wants to buy a .38 Special and some ammo. Larry happily obliges him, and Max stumbles out the door with his new purchase. Max then gets arrested for public intoxication a few blocks from the shop, and the police find the gun, ammo, and a receipt from Larry's pawn shop showing the time and date of purchase. The police then show up at the pawn shop to arrest Larry for violating Texas Penal Code Section 46.06(a)(3).

Larry will claim that he did not know that Max was intoxicated, but the prosecutor will argue that Larry consciously disregarded all of the signs of Max's intoxication and he therefore "recklessly" sold him the gun and ammunition.

Likewise, under Section 46.06(a)(4), it is a Class A misdemeanor if a person "knowingly sells a firearm or ammunition for a firearm to any person who has been convicted of a felony before the fifth anniversary of the later of the following dates: (A) the person's release from confinement following conviction of the felony; or (B) the person's release from supervision under community supervision, parole, or mandatory supervision following conviction of the felony." Texas law only criminalizes selling of ammunition to these individuals; it does not criminalize the possession or purchase of it.

C. Is a person disqualified from purchasing ammunition if they are disqualified from purchasing firearms?

Yes. Under federal law 18 U.S.C. Section 922(g), it is unlawful for a person who is disqualified from purchasing or possessing firearms to purchase ammunition if the ammunition has moved in interstate commerce. Since nearly all ammunition or ammunition components move through interstate commerce in one form or another, this disqualification includes essentially all ammunition. Under Texas law, there is no such disqualification.

D. Can a person purchase ammunition that is labeled "law enforcement use only"?

Yes. Although some handgun ammunition is sold with the label "law enforcement use," such a label has no legal meaning and is only reflective of a company policy or a marketing strategy.

CHAPTER SEVEN

WHEN CAN I LEGALLY USE MY GUN: PART I
UNDERSTANDING THE LAW OF JUSTIFICATION
Some Basic Legal Concepts

I. IGNORANCE OF THE LAW IS NO EXCUSE!

Now we can start our discussion: when is it legal to use a gun as a weapon? The purpose of this Chapter is to look at the essential, basic legal concepts of when and under what circumstances a person is legally justified in using force or deadly force against other persons or animals. Know when you may legally shoot, because ignorance of the law holds no weight in a courtroom! That is why it is critical you know the law so that you are in the best possible situation to preserve your legal rights if you ever need them.

II. GUN OWNERS NEED TO KNOW CHAPTER 9 OF THE TEXAS PENAL CODE

In Texas, legal justifications appear in numerous places and areas of the law. Of particular importance to gun owners are the defenses found in Chapter 9 of the Texas Penal Code entitled "Justification Excluding Criminal Responsibility," which we cover in detail throughout this book.

III. TO LEGALLY USE FORCE OR DEADLY FORCE, YOU MUST BE "JUSTIFIED." WHAT IS LEGAL JUSTIFICATION?

A. Basic definition of justification: an acceptable excuse

So, when is it legal to use force or deadly force against another person? When is it legal to even threaten to use force or deadly force against another? The answer is when there is a legal justification or defense. A legal justification is an acceptable reason or excuse under the law for committing an act that would otherwise be a crime.

> **EXAMPLE:**
>
> Richard sees Ben standing on the guardrail at the top of the Galveston Causeway, and Ben is threatening to end it all. Richard runs up behind Ben and grabs him and throws him to the ground. Ben breaks his arm and claims that Richard has assaulted him, causing bodily injury.

Richard intentionally made physical contact with Ben that caused bodily injury, which is ordinarily the crime of assault. Why will Richard likely be not guilty of the crime of assault causing bodily injury? The reason is that he was legally justified under Texas Penal Code Section 9.34 because he prevented Ben's suicide. That is, the law will likely say the excuse for assaulting Ben—preventing him from jumping off the bridge—makes Richard's action of pulling Ben to the ground reasonable and, therefore, legally justified.

> **PRACTICAL LEGAL TIP**
>
> A defense to prosecution is not the same as a bar to prosecution. A bar to prosecution is where a person can't be prosecuted for engaging in certain conduct, whereas a defense to prosecution allows prosecution for the conduct, but offers defendants a justification that must be demonstrated with evidence in court. —Kirk

B. Basic requirement: confession and avoidance

If a person wants the potential protection of legal justification in Texas, in order to raise the defense the law requires them to admit (or at a minimum, not deny) the charged conduct. *See Bowen v. State,* 162 S.W.3d 398 (Tex. Crim. App. 2005). Then, the person must present "some evidence" of justification before a jury will be given an instruction that "a person is legally justified to use force if…" In plain English, a person will not be allowed to say, "I didn't do it, but if I did do it, I was justified!" You must admit the underlying conduct of the charge. *See Young v. State*, 991 S.W.2d 835 (Tex. Crim. App. 1999).

> **EXAMPLE:**
>
> Melissa is out with her boyfriend, Thomas, in the parking lot of a restaurant. Thomas is attacked from behind by a masked perpetrator. Melissa retrieves her pocket knife and stabs the masked man in the back. Melissa is charged with aggravated assault with a deadly weapon.

Because justification is a legal defense in Texas, if Melissa's case goes all the way to trial, in order to offer a legal justification for committing aggravated assault, she must admit in court that she pulled her knife and stabbed Thomas's attacker. Then, in order for the jury to consider a legal justification defense (*i.e.*, receive a jury instruction from the judge), she must offer some evidence of why she is legally justified under the law for having stabbed a man (in this example, Melissa believed she was defending Thomas). The result is that Melissa is entitled to have the judge instruct the jury that they may find her "Not Guilty" because she was justified in her action. The jury will then decide if they believe Melissa and whether she is guilty or not guilty of the crime of aggravated assault. On the other hand, if Melissa does not admit to the conduct of the offense she is charged with, she will not be allowed to offer a legal justification defense under Chapter 9 of the Texas Penal Code. Legal justification is, therefore, literally the law of "Yes, I did it, BUT...!"

> **PRACTICAL LEGAL TIP**
>
> A jury instruction is a statement made by the judge to the jury informing them of the law applicable to the case in general, or some aspect of it. —Edwin

IV. CATEGORIES OF FORCE FOR JUSTIFICATION UNDER CHAPTER 9

Anytime a person takes a physical action against another person, they have used force. Chapter 9 of the Texas Penal Code divides or categorizes uses of force into different levels. Whether or not a use of force was justified under the law often depends on how that force is categorized. These categories, which we will address throughout this book, are: 1) force, 2) deadly force, and 3) the threat of force.

A. What if a person uses greater force than the law allows?

The use of a legally appropriate level of force is important because if a person uses more force than is "reasonably believed to be immediately necessary," that person may not be legally justified in using that level of force. It is important to understand the differences in the levels of force and the circumstances under which the law allows the use of each. *See* Section V.

For example, if a person uses deadly force, and the law allows only for the use of force, that person will not be legally justified. Likewise, if a person uses force when no force is legally allowed, that use of force will not be legally justified.

EXAMPLE:

Dwayne looks out his window and sees a person walking through his backyard toward his tool shed. Dwayne yells at the fellow to get off his land. The fellow in the backyard does not respond and keeps walking toward the tool shed. Dwayne rushes out to confront him and demands that he leave the backyard.

This man is clearly a trespasser! What degree of force may Dwayne use to remove the trespasser? The law, as discussed later, will show that Dwayne is only allowed to use force in response to a mere trespasser. If Dwayne uses deadly force against the trespasser, he will not be legally justified and would be guilty of unlawfully using more force than is reasonably necessary against the trespasser. Ultimately, using the correct degree of force is critical in determining whether a person has committed a crime or a legally justified action.

B. What is the legal definition of "force"?

Surprisingly, force is not defined in the Texas Penal Code. However, deadly force is defined. Under Chapter 9 of the Penal Code, a prerequisite for being able to legally use deadly force is that a person must be able to use force in the same situation. Therefore, one may conclude that mere force must be something less than deadly force. Texas courts have helped define force by holding that in the absence of a statutory definition, the commonly understood meaning is used. *See Olvede v. State* 650 S.W.2d 408 (Tex. Crim. App. 1983). Force is usually defined as violence, compulsion, or constraint exerted against another person or thing. Therefore, force occurs anytime a person engages in conduct that inflicts harm on another person or puts another person in fear of harm.

> **EXAMPLE:**
> Mikey is being harassed and insulted by Clay, a bully at school. One day, Clay stops Mikey on the playground and suddenly clenches his fist and takes a swing at him, but misses. Mikey reacts to the swing by kicking Clay in the shin.

Clay's action was a use of force. Even though Clay missed Mikey, he placed Mikey in fear of imminent harm. Mikey's reaction of kicking Clay was likewise a use of force, and as will be discussed later, a legally justified use of self-defense.

C. What is deadly force?

> **DEFINITION OF DEADLY FORCE**
> **TEX. PENAL CODE § 9.01(3)**
>
> "Deadly force" means force that is intended or known by the actor to cause, or in the manner of its use or intended use is capable of causing, death or serious bodily injury.

1. Deadly force does not have to cause death
On the surface, the legal definition of deadly force seems simple. However, the meaning of what is and is not deadly force can be legally tricky. A particular action does not necessarily have to result in death to be legally defined as deadly force—it just needs to be capable of causing death or serious bodily injury. Note: serious bodily injury is defined as bodily injury that creates a substantial risk of death or that causes death, serious permanent disfigurement, protracted loss, or protracted loss or impairment of the function of any bodily member or organ. *See* Tex. Penal Code § 1.07(a)(46).

> **EXAMPLE:**
> Jerry is being robbed and beaten by a group of individuals when he manages to draw his handgun and fire it at one of the most aggressive assailants. His shot misses his intended target but breaks the group up, causing the would-be robbers to flee.

In this example, even though the bullet did not kill or even strike any of his assailants, Jerry legally used deadly force because his conduct fit the legal definition of "capable of causing death or serious bodily injury." Thus, death is not a prerequisite for the existence of deadly force! Likewise, almost any object can be used as a weapon in a particular circumstance. Therefore, in this section of the law, the focus is on the object's intended use and not just on the object itself.

2. "Intended or known" as a component of deadly force
Deadly force, by its legal definition, occurs when a person takes an action that is intended or known by the actor to cause death or serious bodily injury. This knowledge or intention to cause serious bodily harm or death is called a person's mental state. A prosecutor

must prove beyond a reasonable doubt that a person possessed a particular mental state applicable to a crime in order to meet the state's burden of proof and convict someone of that crime.

Often a person's intent is easily ascertainable by the circumstances. For example, if a person is the would-be victim of robbery, and the person resists by pulling his or her gun and firing at the robber, the law will likely find the victim used justifiable deadly force, because the victim used force intended to cause death or serious bodily injury.

However, the weapon used is not always dispositive evidence of someone's intent to use deadly force. Hammers, toasters, knives, baseball bats, and almost any other object can be "capable of causing" serious bodily injury or death under a particular circumstance. The case legally turns, then, on how the person is using the force.

> **THREATS AS JUSTIFIABLE FORCE**
> **TEX. PENAL CODE § 9.04**
>
> The threat of force is justified when the use of force is justified by this chapter. For purposes of this section, a threat to cause death or serious bodily injury by the production of a weapon or otherwise, as long as the actor's purpose is limited to creating an apprehension that he will use deadly force if necessary, does not constitute the use of deadly force.

D. What are threats of force? "Stop or I will…"
Texas law provides that if you are legally justified to use force in any particular situation, then you may also legally threaten to use

force in the same situation. Likewise, if you are justified in using deadly force in a particular situation, you may legally threaten the use of deadly force in the same situation.

Section 9.04 of the Texas Penal Code states that if a person threatens deadly force by the production of a weapon, it is not a use of deadly force so long as the person's only purpose is to create an apprehension that they will use deadly force, if necessary.

EXAMPLE:
Barry is walking to his car after work when he sees his nemesis, Carl, keying his car. Barry confronts Carl in the middle of his act of criminal mischief. Barry draws his gun and clearly demands that Carl stop destroying his car's paint. Carl stops his criminal act and flees from the scene.

Has Barry used deadly force by showing his gun? Probably not under the plain language of Section 9.04. Barry's threat was to create apprehension that he would use deadly force if necessary if Carl attacked him. Thus, the legal argument would say Barry's production of a weapon was a use of force and not the use of deadly force.

By defining the action of the production of a weapon to create apprehension as not "the use of deadly force," the legislature (by its express language and the legislative history) wanted to make the action only a use of force. Therefore, a person could be legally justified to produce a weapon to create apprehension when the use of force was legally justified—not just when the use of deadly force was justified! This is what the text of the law says.

A warning about warnings

Section 9.04 clearly shows the legislature intended the "production" of a weapon (as opposed to the "use" of a weapon) in defense to be a use of force—not deadly force. Absent justification, the use of force ordinarily constitutes a misdemeanor, whereas the use of deadly force constitutes a felony. Contrary to the plain language of Section 9.04, historically some Texas courts indicated that a person may only legally produce a weapon as a threat in response to deadly force (and prosecutors and trial courts followed)—although the plain language of Section 9.04 appears to give a legal justification for a person to threaten force by producing a weapon in response to an unlawful use of force or deadly force.

The Texas Court of Criminal Appeals has held that it was judicial error of a trial court when it failed to give a jury instruction on Section 9.04 in cases where a defendant has claimed self-defense and stated that they displayed a weapon but did not use it. *See Gamino v. State,* 537 S.W.3d 507 (Tex. Crim. App. 2017); *State v. Sciacca,* 518 S.W.3d 480 (Tex. App.—Hou.[1st Dist.] 2016). The Texas Court of Criminal Appeals determined that Section 9.04 is incorporated into the self-defense justification of Section 9.31. It adopted the Fort Worth Court of Appeals language that states:

> [i]f Section 9.04 applies, then the use of a gun does not constitute 'deadly force,' and, therefore, [S]ection 9.32 would become inapplicable. If [S]ection 9.04 applies, then the use of the gun would, by default, be the use of 'force' in self defense, and section 9.31 would be the applicable provision. *Gamino,* 537 S.W.3d 507, 510-511, citing *Gamino v. State,* 480 S.W.3d 80, 87 (Tex. App.—Fort Worth 2015).

Unfortunately, police and prosecutors frequently misapply Section 9.04 and treat exhibiting (producing) a weapon the same as using a weapon. Thus, it is not uncommon for a person who merely pointed a firearm as a warning to be charged with the same crime as if they shot and seriously injured that person. While that is an unfortunate position to be in, thankfully, the *Gamino* case has offered significant clarity on this issue.

E. Warning shots

Warning shots get a lot of good folks in legal trouble! Warning shots are commonly portrayed in movies and television as a good idea—and people like to mimic what they see in movies and on TV! Leaving completely aside all practical issues of whether under a particular set of circumstances a warning shot is a good idea (and experience has taught us that very rarely are they a good idea), what does Texas law say about warning shots?

1. Are warning shots a use of deadly force?

The term "warning shot" does not appear in the Texas Penal Code. Without clear guidance from statutory law, courts are left to determine if the action of firing a warning shot is to be considered under either the use of force standard or the use of deadly force standard.

Although the firing of a warning shot is not *per se* legally forbidden, you should be aware that if you fire a warning shot, it is highly likely that your conduct will be judged under the legal standard that you have used deadly force and not just mere force. This means that a person may only be allowed the legal argument of justification if a warning shot is fired in situations in which deadly force is justified under the law. There is little appellate court case law demonstrating how Texas courts have addressed the issue of warning shots. Every gun owner should be aware that one likely argument a prosecutor may put forth against a defendant at trial is that the simple discharge of a firearm is an action that is capable of causing death or serious bodily injury. Such an argument, if successful, will shift the analysis of warning shots into the use of deadly force arena, whether a person intended that action or not.

Why is it important whether the law classifies a warning shot as a use of force or a use of deadly force, even if no one is injured? Let's take a look at an example.

> **EXAMPLE:**
> Wanda hears some laughter coming from the back of her property during broad daylight and sees two trespassers on her property. Not knowing what the trespassers are doing, Wanda grabs her shotgun to investigate. Wanda confronts the trespassers, who are picking berries in her woods, and demand that they leave the property, but the trespassers ignore Wanda. Both scared and agitated, Wanda fires a warning shot to get their attention and compliance.

Does Wanda's firing of her shotgun fit the definition of the use of deadly force? Likely, yes. Wanda may be guilty of a crime and not have a justification available as a defense because she used a higher degree of force than the law allows against both trespassing and theft during the daytime.

2. Warning shots: "But, I never meant to hurt anyone!"

Going back to the above example, assume Wanda will say she fired the warning shot, but that she never aimed at or even meant to hit anyone. In fact, assume Wanda will say she only shot into the air to get the trespassers to leave. How will the law view Wanda's warning shot?

Wanda was confronted with trespassers who may have also been thieves. Under Texas law, a person may legally use force, but not deadly force, to remove a trespasser or thief during the daytime. Therefore, if the warning shot fired by Wanda is legally classified as deadly force, she will not be legally justified, and instead, a jury may decide she is guilty of a crime such as aggravated assault. So, the classification is the difference between guilt and innocence.

Now, let us change the example a bit to see how things may get even more complicated.

EXAMPLE:

Wanda confronts the same trespassers, Adam and Jane, as before and fires a warning shot. This time, however, the shot startled Adam and Jane out of their zoned state of blissful courtship. They were so completely consumed with one another they didn't realize that they had accidentally wandered onto Wanda's property. In fact, Adam and Jane were so deep in enjoying each other's company and the Texas air that they didn't even hear Wanda's verbal demands, but the sound of Wanda's 12 gauge got their full attention! As a result, Adam does exactly what his Army training has taught him—he draws and fires at Wanda, believing that she had meant to kill him and Jane.

Wanda has very likely used unlawful deadly force against mere trespassers. After Wanda's shot, does this turn our absent-minded, wandering Adam and Jane into victims who reasonably believe that their lives are threatened? Does this fact then allow Adam some legal justification to return fire?

Continuing the issue, if our wandering Adam then returns fire at Wanda, is Wanda then legally justified in using deadly force to defend herself? Or, because Adam and Jane are accidental trespassers, is Adam required to retreat first before he takes any action? Keep in mind that Wanda knows nothing about Adam and Jane's courtship stroll. She is just confronted with two trespassers who did not respond to her verbal requests, and now have responded to her warning shot with muzzle flashes from a pistol. Ultimately, you can see how messy this type of scenario can become, and it started with a well-intentioned warning shot.

After the dust clears (assuming perfect knowledge), Wanda likely used a higher degree of force than the law allows. But who decides if a warning shot is just a warning and not a shot at someone that simply missed? Who decides if a response to a situation is reasonable? In the vast majority of cases in Texas, a jury ultimately decides. There are no bright lines on warning shots, so be advised that a warning shot can potentially be viewed as a use of deadly force, whether you subjectively intended it to be or not. Therefore, it should never be used without careful consideration.

V. WHAT DOES IT MEAN TO "REASONABLY BELIEVE FORCE IS IMMEDIATELY NECESSARY"?

Under Texas law, the legal standard for a justified use of force is generally expressed as: a person must "reasonably believe" that the use of force is "immediately necessary" to protect against the unlawful use of force. *See* Tex. Penal Code § 9.31.

But what does "reasonably believe" mean? Further, when is something immediately necessary—and who decides whether it is or not? The answers to these questions are how the legal process decides guilt or justification. For all gun owners, these concepts are critical.

A. How does the law determine what is "reasonable"?

In determining what is reasonable, Texas law uses a standard known as the "reasonable person" standard to evaluate a person's conduct. Texas Penal Code Section 1.07(42) states, "Reasonable belief means a belief that would be held by an ordinary and prudent man in the same circumstances as the actor." So, who is this ordinary and prudent person, and how does he or she act? Ultimately, a reasonable person is whatever a jury says it is.

> **PRACTICAL LEGAL TIP**
>
> Throughout this book, we refer to juries making the ultimate determination of fact. There are, however, some limited occasions where a judge makes the determinations. For example, if all parties waive their right to a jury, the court may conduct what is called a bench trial.
> –Kirk

The legal analysis behind the reasonable person standard goes like this: if a person used force or even deadly force, they must act like a reasonable person would have acted under the same or similar circumstances in order to be legally justified! However, if a person fails to act like a reasonable person, their conduct will fall below the acceptable legal standard and will not be justified. The reasonable person standard is the law's attempt to make the concept of reasonableness an objective and measurable test.

Under this standard, the law does not focus on whether you subjectively (or personally) believed force was reasonable, but whether a reasonable person would have considered it reasonable, an objective standard. If the legal system (again, this could ultimately be a jury) determines that a reasonable person would have believed that force was immediately necessary in response to another person unlawfully using force against you, then you will be found legally justified in using force.

Keep in mind, however, that judges, juries, and prosecutors are simply human beings, and people can have vastly different ideas of how a reasonable person should act under any given circumstances. This is particularly true if asked to decide whether force or deadly force was immediately necessary or not.

B. What does "immediately necessary" mean under the law?

When does someone have a reasonable belief that force is immediately necessary? In Texas, it ultimately may be a jury that is tasked with determining whether someone had a reasonable belief that an action was immediately necessary or not. With that said, courts have held that "immediately necessary" means when a person took his action, he had to take that action right then, right there, and without delay, otherwise he may have suffered harm or injury. *See McGarity v. State*, 5 S.W.3d 223 (Tex. App.— San Antonio, 1999, no pet.). Clearly, "immediately necessary" attempts to convey a sense of urgency for the use of force, but again, it usually falls back to the jury to decide if this standard was met in a particular case.

C. Legal presumptions: stop legal second-guessing

Under certain circumstances, a person's belief in the immediate necessity of force or deadly force will be presumed reasonable under Texas law. This legal presumption can be a very powerful legal tool to stop legal second-guessing or "Monday morning quarterbacking" of the timing or the degree of force used. A jury will be told that if a given set of circumstances exists (*e.g.*, a person is the victim of a sexual assault), the law will presume reasonable a person's belief in the immediate necessity of using force or deadly force, and that use of force or deadly force would, therefore, be legally justified. *See* Tex. Penal Code §§ 9.31, 9.32.

EXAMPLE:

Sam is asleep in his house when he hears a noise in his kitchen. Sam enters his kitchen with his 1911 drawn and confronts an armed burglar. Sam fires his weapon; the intruder has invaded his last home!

In this situation, was Sam's use of deadly force in firing his gun immediately necessary, or more precisely, was Sam's belief that deadly force was immediately necessary reasonable? Did Sam legally have to take additional actions before firing in order to have acted reasonably? In Sam's current situation, the law will give him a powerful legal presumption that his belief that the use of deadly force was immediately necessary was reasonable. In this example, Section 9.32 of the Texas Penal Code will provide Sam with this presumption of reasonableness (as a victim of a home invasion in his occupied habitation). In Texas statutes, these legal presumptions read: "the actor's belief that deadly force was immediately necessary is presumed to be reasonable if... "(fill in the appropriate circumstances: *e.g.*, it was used to prevent murder, sexual assault, *etc.*). This presumption will prevent any second-guessing by prosecutors that deadly force was not immediately necessary. This has a practical effect of preventing arguments such as a person should have used no force, less force, or retreated before using force. The legal presumption of reasonableness is a powerful tool for anyone facing a criminal charge and claiming legal justification.

> **PRACTICAL LEGAL TIP:** A legal presumption is not an absolute ticket to victory. A prosecutor may attempt to overcome the presumption with other evidence that shows you did not act in self-defense. —Edwin

D. No presumption of reasonableness: prosecutors are allowed to second-guess

As we discussed above, under certain circumstances, the law will presume the reasonableness of a person's belief that force or deadly force is immediately necessary. However, if a person uses force or deadly force under circumstances that do not qualify for this presumption, the issue of whether a belief of the immediate necessity to use force or deadly force was reasonable is left to the jury, and prosecutors are allowed to second-guess the reasonableness of the timing and/or degree of force used by a defendant. Accordingly, when a defendant does not qualify for a legal presumption, a prosecutor has the opportunity to argue that a person's use of force or deadly force was not immediately necessary. This allows for arguments in court like "should have retreated," "should have used lesser force," and so forth. In many circumstances (such as situations involving defense of property), no legal presumption of reasonable belief is afforded for uses of force or deadly force at all!

In those cases, a jury will decide the reasonableness of a person's belief and, ultimately, whether or not a person is guilty of a crime.

VI. THE BURDEN OF PROOF IN CRIMINAL CASES

In criminal cases, the state attorneys or prosecutors have the burden of proof. This means that it is the state's responsibility to present enough evidence to prove the defendant committed a crime. The burden of proof the prosecutor bears is a standard called "beyond a reasonable doubt." It is the highest level of proof used in the American justice system. The state's job at trial in attempting to prove the defendant's guilt includes eliminating any reasonable doubt that the defendant's conduct was justified.

We are now ready to look at the circumstances under which Texas law allows a person to use deadly force to protect themselves and others in the next chapter.

PRACTICAL LEGAL TIP

A word about juries: juries are not "picked" in Texas. Rather, they are the first 12 people who are not "struck" from the pool of folks called a jury pool. Most of the time, in my opinion, juries get it "right," but after years of practice, some juries' decisions leave you scratching your head... That's why a legal presumption can be critical.
—Edwin

> CHAPTER EIGHT ◂

WHEN CAN I LEGALLY USE MY GUN: PART II
SELF-DEFENSE AND DEFENSE OF OTHERS
Understanding When Force And Deadly Force Can Be Legally Used Against Another Person

I. INTRODUCTION AND OVERVIEW

The question of "when can a person legally use deadly force against another person" is of critical importance if you are a legal Texas firearms owner. Although a firearm is nothing more than a tool, it is a tool that by its very nature has the ability to deliver deadly force. Thus, all responsible firearms owners should understand when they are justified in using force and deadly force under the law. Failure to understand the law gets lots of good folks in serious trouble!

The primary Texas statutes dealing with self-defense and defense of other people are contained in three Texas Penal Code Sections:
9.31: Self-Defense
9.32: Deadly Force In Defense of Person
9.33: Defense of Third Persons

The law of justified self-defense is split between justification for the use of *force* in Section 9.31 and justification for the use of *deadly force* in Section 9.32. Each of these sections also contain legal presumptions of reasonableness that are available under certain circumstances and are extremely powerful when deciding if a use of force or deadly force was legally justified. Likewise, the language of both sections contains Texas's version of the "Castle Doctrine" and "Stand Your Ground" laws, even though those specific terms are not mentioned in the statutes. Section 9.33 combines force and deadly force in providing justification for "Defense of Third Persons."

In the previous Chapter, several legal concepts such as reasonableness, immediate necessity, and the categorization of force and deadly force were discussed. Those concepts have practical applications in this Chapter. Here, we will expand upon those topics to include when a person may be justified in using force or deadly force in self-defense, as well as those circumstances when the law specifically prohibits the use of force or deadly force.

II. DEFENDING PEOPLE WITH FORCE OR DEADLY FORCE
A. General self-defense justification: no presumption of reasonableness

The primary self-defense statutes in Texas are Sections 9.31 and 9.32 of the Texas Penal Code. Section 9.31(a) lays out the legal requirements for the justified use of force, but not deadly force, for self-defense. This section establishes that a person is legally justified in using force against another "when and to the degree the actor reasonably believes the force is immediately necessary to protect the actor against the other's use or attempted use of unlawful force."

Likewise, Section 9.32(a) establishes the general standard for the justified use of deadly force. The first requirement is that force must be justified under Section 9.31; a person must legally be able to use force before the law will ever allow deadly force to be justified. Thereafter, a person is legally justified in using deadly force for self-defense "when and to the degree the actor reasonably believes the deadly force is immediately necessary" to protect himself or herself against another's use or attempted use of unlawful deadly force. As discussed previously, what a person believes is immediately necessary and whether that belief is reasonable is the difference between justification (not guilty) and conviction (guilty).

Who decides whether an actor's belief that force or deadly force is immediately necessary is reasonable? Who decides if the degree of force used by someone was reasonable under a particular set of circumstances? The answer to both of these questions is typically the jury.

Therefore, if a person finds himself or herself facing a criminal charge and is claiming self-defense under the general self-defense provisions of Sections 9.31 and 9.32, the jury will decide if that person's belief was or was not reasonable regarding the immediate necessity of the use of force or deadly force. As can be imagined, this leaves a lot of room for juries to interpret what actions are reasonable or not. It also leaves the door open for legal second-guessing by prosecutors as to when and how much force was used, including arguments that there was no imminent threat and as such, the force or deadly force was not really "immediately necessary." If the prosecutor convinces a jury that a person used force or deadly force when or to a degree that was not "reasonably" believed to be immediately necessary, a person's use of force or deadly force will not be legally justified, and that person will be guilty of using unlawful force or deadly force. However, under certain circumstances, Sections 9.31 and 9.32 give persons a powerful additional protection in the form of a legal presumption of reasonableness in their belief that the use of force or deadly force was immediately necessary.

B. Presumption under Sections 9.31 and 9.32

Sections 9.31 and 9.32 of the Texas Penal Code contain several circumstances when the law gives far more protection than is available under the general self-defense standard. Under certain circumstances, a person's belief that it was immediately necessary to use force or deadly force will be legally presumed reasonable. This legal presumption, if available, is a potentially powerful legal argument and limits prosecutors in court from second-guessing either when, or the amount of force used by the accused, in defending himself or herself (*e.g.*, should have used non-deadly force, dispute resolution methods, or should have retreated, and so forth). If a defendant meets the conditions enabling him or her to be afforded the protection of this presumption, the law will deem "reasonable" a belief that the force used was immediately necessary, limiting any argument that the force used was unreasonable.

> **PRACTICAL LEGAL TIP**
>
> In law school, they taught us that "reasonable minds can differ." Yet, reasonableness is a standard that we are held to whenever we face a legal issue. Thankfully, Texas provides us with presumptions of reasonableness so that even when reasonable minds do differ, you know where you stand with the law. –Emily

C. Legal presumptions for victims of certain violent crimes

If a person is a victim or would-be victim of unlawful force or deadly force, Texas law allows for the justified use of force or deadly force when and to the degree that the person reasonably believes it is immediately necessary to protect himself or herself. However, if a person is forced to defend himself or herself against someone who is committing or is about to commit one of the six crimes listed in Sections 9.31 and 9.32 and satisfies the other requirements of the statutes, the law will provide a legal presumption that a victim's belief in the immediate necessity of force or deadly force was reasonable. These six crimes are: aggravated kidnapping, murder, sexual assault, aggravated sexual assault, robbery, and aggravated robbery.

1. Victims of aggravated kidnapping

If a person is a victim or a would-be victim of an aggravated kidnapping, a first degree felony, then the law will presume reasonable his or her belief that the use of force (Section 9.31) or deadly force (Section 9.32) was immediately necessary to defend against an attacker, and therefore, force or deadly force will be legally justified.

What is aggravated kidnapping? Generally, aggravated kidnapping occurs anytime a person abducts another person and "uses or exhibits a deadly weapon during the commission of the offense." *See* Tex. Penal Code § 20.04(b).

However, under Texas law, the crime of aggravated kidnapping can actually occur in several different circumstances. Texas Penal Code Section 20.04(a) defines aggravated kidnapping as anytime a person: intentionally or knowingly abducts another person with the intent to:
- Hold him for ransom or reward;
- Use him as a shield or hostage;
- Facilitate the commission of a felony or the flight after the attempt or commission of a felony;
- Inflict bodily injury on him or violate or abuse him sexually;
- Terrorize him or a third person; or
- Interfere with the performance of any governmental or political function.

EXAMPLE 1:

Leslie is out jogging one evening, when a white van pulls up next to her and a masked man with a gun jumps out, trying to grab her and drag her into his van. Leslie pulls out her pepper spray, sprays the man in the face, and runs away to call police.

EXAMPLE 2:

Leslie is out jogging one evening, when a white van pulls up next to her and a masked man with a gun jumps out, trying to grab her and drag her into his van. Leslie pulls out her Glock 42 and fires two shots, killing her attacker.

In the first example, was Leslie legally justified in her use of force against the man? What about her use of deadly force in example two? The answer to both is yes. Leslie's belief that the use of force (pepper spray) was immediately necessary will be presumed reasonable under Section 9.31, because the man in the white van was attempting to commit aggravated kidnapping! Likewise, in the second example, under Section 9.32, Leslie's belief that deadly force was immediately necessary will also be presumed reasonable for the same reason, and also results in the conclusion that Leslie's use of deadly force was justified.

In these hypotheticals, the masked man with the gun was trying to abduct Leslie. Whatever his ultimate purpose for trying to grab her, if Leslie reasonably believed she was about to be a victim of an aggravated kidnapping, she will be entitled to a legal presumption that her belief was "reasonable." Thus, with this presumption, prosecutors will be limited in their ability to second-guess whether Leslie should have used less force than she did, or whether she should have retreated first. The law will deem her belief in the immediate necessity of her use of force or deadly force reasonable. These are clear examples. We will discuss later how the law is applied in more ambiguous cases.

2. Victims of attempted murder

It is basic self-preservation set forth in the law that if someone is trying to end your days, you may defend yourself with force or deadly force. Thus, it is no surprise that Sections 9.31 and 9.32 of the Texas Penal Code combine to allow for the use of force or deadly force to prevent someone from murdering you. As with the other listed violent crimes, a person who defends himself or herself against murder is justified in using force or deadly force in self-defense against the attacker. The victim is also given a legal presumption of "reasonableness" to any belief that force or deadly force was immediately necessary to defend his or her life.

MURDER

So, what is murder? Texas Penal Code Section 19.02 defines murder as any time a person:
- Intentionally or knowingly causes the death of an individual;
- Intends to cause serious bodily injury and commits an act clearly dangerous to human life that causes the death of an individual; or
- Commits or attempts to commit a felony, other than manslaughter, and in the course of and in furtherance of the commission or attempt, or in immediate flight from the commission or attempt, commits or attempts to commit an act clearly dangerous to human life that causes the death of an individual.

How should the law under Sections 9.31 and 9.32 be applied after a self-defense shooting?

EXAMPLE:
> David is working quietly in his office at his computer repair shop when he hears an angry voice yell out, "Y'all ripped me off and I'm gonna kill everyone in here!" David looks out of his office and sees a deranged-looking man wielding an axe. The disgruntled customer turns toward David with an evil look. David draws a gun from his desk drawer. As the man rushes toward David holding the axe over his head, David fires two shots at the attacker, killing him.

In this situation, the law allows David to use force or deadly force when and to the degree he reasonably believes it is immediately necessary to defend himself. Here, David skipped mere force and immediately used deadly force. Was this reasonable? Should David have first used non-deadly force? Should he have used a method of dispute resolution? If he could have retreated out of a back door, was his use of deadly force really immediately necessary? If there were no legal presumptions under Sections 9.31 and 9.32, these are the types of questions and issues that would be presented for the jury to determine.

However, in this example, because David is about to be a victim of murder at his business, the law will deem "reasonable" his belief that deadly force was immediately necessary! This is a powerful legal presumption and limits prosecutorial arguments regarding the reasonableness of when the force was used or the degree of force used, because it is legally deemed reasonable. How do we know David acted in self-defense? In this example, the attacker makes it easy, because he cleared up any ambiguity of his intentions when he declared, "I am gonna kill everyone in here!" while wielding an axe. Thus, under Texas law, David, as a would-be victim of murder, is entitled to a legal presumption that he had a reasonable belief that it was immediately necessary to use force or deadly force against the attacker to prevent his own murder. Therefore, David is legally justified in using deadly force.

If, for some reason, David was ever charged with a crime for killing the would-be murderer, and David puts forth "some evidence" in trial that he was about to be the victim of murder, the jury would then get to decide whether David acted in self-defense under Sections 9.31 and 9.32. For a discussion of the legal concept of "some evidence," *see* Section D. The jury will be told that if David reasonably believed he was about to be murdered, the law will presume reasonable that deadly force was immediately necessary. The prosecution would then have the burden of establishing beyond a reasonable doubt that David did not act in self-defense (*i.e.*, David did not know or have reason to believe he was about to be murdered). If the jury finds that the prosecution did not meet this burden of proof, it will decide his use of deadly force was legally justified.

But how does the self-defense statute work when the example is not so clear?

EXAMPLE:

Police respond to a two-car collision in a parking lot. When the police arrive, they discover that the collision has sparked a shooting. At the scene, one man is dead on the ground with a tire iron beside him. The other driver, Matt, a 45-year-old man with no previous criminal record, fired two shots and is now the police's prime suspect in a murder investigation. Matt claims that the other driver became irate while exchanging information, threatened him, and aggressively came toward him swinging the tire iron. However, the position of the physical evidence made it unclear as to who was the true victim in this incident. In fact, one of the officers thinks Matt is lying. Unfortunately for Matt, there are no other witnesses.

If Matt ultimately faces criminal charges for murder and claims self-defense at his trial, how does the court determine whether or not the jury will be told of the legal presumption and, ultimately, legal justifications under Sections 9.31 and 9.32?

In order to receive the protection of a presumption of "reasonableness" for victims of crimes under Sections 9.31 and 9.32, Matt has the initial burden of producing some evidence in court to support that he "knew or had reason to believe" that he was about to be the victim of murder (*e.g.*, the man screamed threats at him and was about to strike him with the tire iron, and Matt was in fear of his life, so he shot the man). If Matt puts forth some evidence that the dead man was about to murder him, the law requires the prosecution to then prove beyond a reasonable doubt that the accused (in this case, Matt) did not act in self-defense. See *Saxton v. State,* 804 S.W.2d 910 (Tex. Crim. App. 1991), and *Jenkins v. State,* 740 S.W.2d 435 (Tex. Crim. App. 1987). The prosecution will have an opportunity to put forth evidence that Matt was not about to be the victim of murder based on the physical evidence found at the scene as well as the investigating officer's testimony. This presumption of reasonableness puts Matt's legal defense in a much better legal position than it would be without it.

If the jury believes Matt acted in self-defense to prevent an attempted murder or, more precisely, that the prosecution did not prove beyond a reasonable doubt that Matt did not act in self-defense, Sections 9.31 and 9.32 act to give him a legal presumption of "reasonableness" to his belief that the use of force or deadly force was immediately necessary. This is a very powerful legal tool in court. Having the presumptions of Sections 9.31 and 9.32 could just be the difference between a verdict of guilty or not guilty!

3. Victims of sexual assault and aggravated sexual assault

Like murder, if a person is the victim of a sexual assault or an aggravated sexual assault, Texas law allows for the legally justified use of force (Section 9.31) or deadly force (Section 9.32) to stop the assault. These two self-defense statutes will also provide any victim of these crimes who resists with force or deadly force a powerful legal presumption of "reasonableness" to his or her belief in the immediate necessity of force or deadly force against the attacker. How does the law define sexual assault and aggravated sexual assault?

SEXUAL ASSAULT

Section 22.011 of the Texas Penal Code classifies sexual assault as a second degree felony, or under certain circumstances, a first degree felony. A person commits sexual assault in the State of Texas any time that person intentionally or knowingly:

- Causes the penetration of the anus or sexual organ of another person by any means, without that person's consent;
- Causes the penetration of the mouth of another person by the sexual organ of the actor, without that person's consent;
- Causes the sexual organ of another person, without that person's consent, to contact or penetrate the mouth, anus, or sexual organ of another person, including the actor;
- Causes the penetration of the anus or sexual organ of a child by any means;
- Causes the penetration of the mouth of a child by the sexual organ of the actor;
- Causes the sexual organ of a child to contact or penetrate the mouth, anus, or sexual organ of another person, including the actor;
- Causes the anus of a child to contact the mouth, anus, or sexual organ of another person, including the actor; or
- Causes the mouth of a child to contact the anus or sexual organ of another person, including the actor.

AGGRAVATED SEXUAL ASSAULT

The crime of aggravated sexual assault under Texas law is found in Section 22.021 and is a first degree felony. Aggravated sexual assault occurs when a person commits an intentional or knowing action of sexual assault under Section 22.011, and the person:

- Causes serious bodily injury or attempts to cause the death of the victim or another person in the course of the same criminal episode;
- By acts or words places the victim in fear that any person will become the victim of [human trafficking] or that death, serious bodily injury, or kidnapping will be imminently inflicted on any person;
- By acts or words occurring in the presence of the victim threatens to cause any person to become the victim of [human trafficking] or to cause the death, serious bodily injury, or kidnapping of any person;
- Uses or exhibits a deadly weapon in the course of the same criminal episode;
- Acts in concert with another who engages in conduct described by [the sexual assault statute in Section 22.011] directed toward the same victim and occurring during the course of the same criminal episode;
- Administers or provides to the victim of the offense any substance capable of impairing the victim's ability to appraise the nature of the act or to resist the act;
- Commits the offense against a victim younger than 14 years of age; or
- Commits the offense against an elderly individual or a disabled individual.

4. Victims of robbery and aggravated robbery

Like the other violent crimes listed in Sections 9.31 and 9.32 of the Texas Penal Code, if a person is a victim or would-be victim of a robbery or aggravated robbery, Texas law allows the victim to protect himself or herself against the robber with legally justified force or deadly force. Further, like the other crimes listed in these two sections, the presumptions of reasonableness of force or deadly force being immediately necessary without a duty to retreat are available if all statutory requirements are met. How does Texas law define robbery and aggravated robbery?

ROBBERY

Under Section 29.02 of the Texas Penal Code, robbery, a second degree felony, occurs when a person, in the course of committing theft and with the intent to obtain or maintain control of the property:
- Intentionally, knowingly, or recklessly causes bodily injury to another; or
- Intentionally or knowingly threatens or places another in fear of imminent bodily injury or death.

For a robbery to occur, a robber does not actually have to acquire the property.

AGGRAVATED ROBBERY

Aggravated robbery is a first degree felony and is defined in Texas Penal Code Section 29.03 as when, during the commission of robbery, the robber:
- Causes serious bodily injury to another;
- Uses or exhibits a deadly weapon; or
- Causes bodily injury to another person or threatens or places another person in fear of imminent bodily injury or death, if that person is 65 years of age or older, or a disabled person.

> **EXAMPLE:**
>
> Tanya is on her way home from work. She stops by a local convenience store for some bread and milk. As she enters the store, a masked man suddenly approaches her with a knife, grabs her by the arm, and demands her money. Tanya, scared and shaken, remembers her training, opens her purse, pulls a .357 revolver, and fires, killing the masked robber.

In this example, because an aggravated robbery was happening, Sections 9.31 and 9.32 allow for the justified, legal use of force or deadly force when and to the degree Tanya reasonably believes it is immediately necessary to stop the aggravated robbery. In addition, the law will provide Tanya with a powerful legal presumption of "reasonableness" to her belief in the immediate necessity of deadly force to stop the aggravated robbery, and she has no legal duty to retreat. Thus, her use of deadly force is legally justified.

What if the example is less clear?

> **EXAMPLE:**
>
> Homer, a 66-year-old disabled man, works downtown. He has to park four blocks from his company's office building and walk through some rough parts of town in order to get to his car. A man suddenly appears in front of him and says, "Hey man—give me some money!" Homer, feeling very frightened and intimidated, walks on with the now more loud and aggressive panhandler demanding, "Hey! Man! I said give me some money!" Homer now becomes extremely concerned for his safety. About that time, Homer makes a wrong turn into an alley where he is cornered. He again hears, "HEY! MAN! I SAID GIVE ME SOME MONEY!" When Homer turns around, he sees the same man, now very aggressive, with something in his hand.

Is the panhandler just being annoying, or is Homer about to be the victim of a robbery or aggravated robbery? This is the ultimate issue Homer may face if he decides to use force or even deadly force against the alleged aggressor. How will the law evaluate a use of deadly force under Sections 9.31 and 9.32?

This is an example with a lot of gray areas. The man never verbally threatened Homer, nor did he ever physically touch him. All the man said was "give me some money"; he didn't even demand all of Homer's money—just some. Do robbers ever demand just some money? If Homer is in genuine fear of an aggravated robbery, does he have a duty to retreat? What about the fact that Homer was cornered in an alley? If Homer takes out his legally carried handgun and fires it to defend himself, what happens? Was Homer really about to be robbed, or is he a paranoid trigger-happy fellow as the prosecutor may try to portray him? Beyond that, who decides what the facts really were? This goes to show that there are lots of questions and gray areas.

If Homer finds himself charged with unlawfully using force or deadly force against his alleged attacker, he can assert a legal justification based on self-defense under Sections 9.31 and 9.32 of the Texas Penal Code. Again, the law will allow Homer to use force or deadly force for self-defense when and to the degree he reasonably believes it is immediately necessary to stop unlawful force against him. In this example, before a jury will be allowed to decide if Homer acted in self-defense, he must present some evidence at trial that he reasonably believed he was about to be robbed.

Homer may attempt to satisfy the "some evidence" requirement by testifying that he was in fear for his safety and had seen the panhandler acting violently on the same street many times in the past. Homer may also say the man raised a weapon in his hand and was moving aggressively toward him, and that the assailant outweighed Homer by 75 pounds and was about a foot taller. Homer will absolutely testify he felt he was being robbed. If he puts forth some evidence in court that he was the victim of an attempted aggravated robbery, the jury will get to decide if Homer is credible and if his belief was reasonable, and the law then requires the prosecution to prove beyond a reasonable doubt that he did not act in self-defense. *See Saxton v. State,* 804 S.W.2d 910 (Tex. Crim. App. 1991). However, if Homer fails to put forth some evidence that he acted in self-defense, he will not be entitled to a self-defense jury instruction concerning Sections 9.31 and 9.32, and the jury will not get to decide the issue.

D. What is "some evidence"?

So, how much evidence does a person have to offer in a trial to constitute "some evidence" in order to be entitled to a jury charge regarding self-defense? Multiple Texas appeals courts have stated that "if [any] evidence raises the issue of self-defense, the defendant is entitled to have it submitted to the jury, whether that evidence is weak or strong, unimpeached or contradicted, and regardless of what the trial court may or may not think about the credibility of the defense." *Guilbeau v. State,* 193 S.W.3d 156, 159 (Tex. App.—Houston [1st Dist.] 2006, pet. ref'd). Interestingly enough, the Court of Criminal Appeals recently held that "[I]n the case of conflicting evidence and competing inferences, the [defensive] instruction should be given." *Rodriguez v. State,* ___ S.W.3d ___ (Tex. Crim. App. 2021) (No. PD-1130-19). The *Rodriguez* Court found that the admission to otherwise criminal conduct (in this case) "kill[ing] the victim in response to the victim's aggression," should create an inference necessitating a defensive instruction. This applies even when the actor expressly denies their intent to kill but nonetheless, their defensive conduct resulted in the death of another. For example, if an actor shot a defensive "warning shot" in response to a threat that resulted in the death of the aggressor, even if the actor claims it was an accident, they would be entitled to a self-defense instruction to any criminal charge. This means that in court, a defendant could literally offer anything as evidence that raises the issue of self-defense, and he is entitled to receive a jury instruction regarding self-defense under Sections 9.31 and 9.32. The only requirement is that the evidence offered must be related to the incident of self-defense at issue.

The "some evidence" requirement may be satisfied where the evidence offered is as simple as the defendant's own testimony, which "alone may be sufficient to raise the defensive theory requiring a charge." *Guilbeau,* 193 S.W.3d at 159; *see also Hayes v. State,* 728 S.W.2d 804 (Tex. Crim. App. 1987). In other words, a defendant testifying in court at his own trial that he was attacked first and feared for his life as a result of the attack, would have submitted sufficient evidence to be entitled to a jury instruction on self-defense. The defensive instruction may also expand if the defendant is attacked by multiple attackers. *Jordan v. State,* 593 S.W.3d 340 (Tex. Crim. App. 2020). It is important to note that "in determining whether the testimony of a defendant raises an issue of self-defense, the truth or credibility of the defendant's testimony is not at issue." *Guilbeau,* 193 S.W.3d at 159. Rather, determining the truth or credibility of the defendant's testimony is the role the jury undertakes in its deliberations.

Of course, relying on a defendant's testimony to be the sole source of evidence in order to obtain a jury instruction on self-defense can be fraught with peril as well. All defendants have the right to not testify at their trial—which can be a sound trial tactic in that it prevents the government from examining the defendant under oath and on the witness stand. Once a defendant takes the witness stand, however, that defendant will be subject to examination by not only his attorney, but also by the state, an examination which may ultimately contain evidence that sways a jury away from seriously considering acquittal on self-defense grounds.

> **PRACTICAL LEGAL TIP**
>
> My experience in over 25 years as a trial lawyer is that many people serving on juries tend to ignore the principle of "innocent until proven guilty." Even though every person has a Constitutional right to not testify against themselves, not doing so can cloud a juror's mind so as to make the notion of "innocent until proven guilty" be viewed with skepticism. –Edwin

E. The "Castle Doctrine" and "Stand Your Ground" laws
1. The "Castle Doctrine"

The term "Castle Doctrine" does not appear in Texas statutory law. However, the legal concept comes from the philosophy that every person is a king or queen of his or her "castle." As such, no king or queen is required to retreat before using force or deadly force against an intruder in their castle. In Texas, the "Castle Doctrine" type laws are implemented under Sections 9.31 and 9.32 of the Texas Penal Code and take the form of powerful presumptions of reasonableness similar to those provided for the six violent crimes in these two sections. Texas "Castle Doctrine" laws extend to a person's occupied habitation, occupied vehicle, or occupied place of business or employment.

As we discussed earlier, the general rule is that a person is legally justified in using force or deadly force:

> When and to the degree a person reasonably believes the force or deadly force is immediately necessary to protect against the unlawful use of force or deadly force.

If you are a victim of unlawful force or deadly force when you are in your occupied habitation, occupied vehicle, or occupied place of business or employment, the law will provide you protection beyond the general rule. In these "Castle Doctrine" circumstances, the law will presume "reasonable" a person's belief that force or deadly force was immediately necessary to defend against unlawful force. This presumption applies to you when:
(A) a person has unlawfully and with force entered, or was attempting to enter your: occupied habitation, vehicle, or place of business or employment; or
(B) a person has unlawfully and with force removed, or is attempting to remove you from your occupied habitation, vehicle, or place of business or employment.

As can be seen, section (A) covers conditions when someone is entering or attempting to enter your "castle" and section (B) covers situations when you are being unlawfully removed from your "castle." Like the presumptions available for victims of violent crimes, a "Castle Doctrine" presumption of "reasonableness" is a powerful legal tool for any person who is accused of a crime and claiming justification. The presumption will be further enhanced by having no duty to retreat. This will prevent prosecutors in court from second-guessing when or the amount of force that was used. These presumptions are available only for occupied habitations, vehicles, or places of business or employment.

2. What is a habitation under the "Castle Doctrine"?

Texas law, in defining "Castle Doctrine" rights, does not use the term home, house, or property; it uses the term "habitation." The presumptions under Sections 9.31 and 9.32 are specific, limited, and do not cover an entire piece of real property—just a habitation. The term "habitation" is defined by Texas Penal Code Section 30.01 as:

> A structure or vehicle adapted for the overnight accommodation of persons; and includes each separately secured or occupied portion of the structure or vehicle; and each structure appurtenant to or connected with the structure or vehicle.

This means that structures that are detached from the building where you sleep at night are not considered to be your habitation.

EXAMPLE:

Jethro sees a stranger going into his tractor shed, which sits 50 yards from his house. Jethro grabs his rifle and shoots at the stranger from the comfort of his back porch. When the police show up, Jethro claims that his actions are presumed reasonable under the "Castle Doctrine."

Unfortunately, Jethro is wrong. Texas law does not consider your detached garage, shed, or barn part of your habitation. Therefore, any use of force or deadly force would not qualify for presumptions of reasonableness under this particular part of the law. However, if your garage or front or back porch is connected to the structure containing your sleeping quarters (as exists in many suburban communities), it is considered part of your habitation as defined by the Texas Penal Code.

3. What is a vehicle under the "Castle Doctrine"?

Texas "Castle Doctrine" legal presumptions and protections are applicable to occupied vehicles. If a person is attempting to "car-jack" you, which is to unlawfully and with force enter your vehicle while you are in it, or unlawfully and with force remove you from your vehicle, your actions will fall under the "Castle Doctrine." What does Texas define as a vehicle? Under Texas Penal Code Section 30.01, a vehicle is defined as:

> Any device, in, on, or by which any person or property is or may be propelled, moved, or drawn in the normal course of commerce or transportation.

This is a very broad definition and appears to include anything that carries people or property from one place to another, including cars, trucks, boats, airplanes, golf carts, and so forth.

4. In Texas, "Stand Your Ground" means no duty to retreat

"Stand Your Ground" is a common term for laws that provide that a person has no legal duty to retreat before using force or deadly force against a person that is a threat. The words "Stand Your Ground" are not used in the Texas Penal Code but do appear in Texas case law. Prior to the amendments passed by the Texas Legislature in 2007, Texas Penal Code Section 9.32 imposed a requirement that deadly force could only be used when "a reasonable person in the actor's situation would not have retreated." The 2007 amendments to the self-defense statutes added provisions that allow a person under certain listed circumstances to "Stand Their Ground" while defending himself or herself, and eliminated any legal duty to retreat. However, for circumstances that are not covered by the provisions of Sections 9.31 and 9.32, "the failure to retreat may be considered in determining whether a defendant reasonably believed that his conduct was immediately necessary…" *Morales v. State,* 357 S.W.3d 1, 5 (Tex. Crim. App. 2011). Thus, the existence of no duty to retreat is also a powerful legal tool for any defendant.

The provisions establishing no duty to retreat are located in the self-defense statutes of Sections 9.31(e) and (f), and Section 9.32(c) and (d). These provisions will act to limit a prosecutor from arguing in court that a person's use of force or deadly force was not really immediately necessary because the person could have or should have first retreated.

In order to receive the "No Duty to Retreat" protection under these statutes, first, a person must satisfy all the conditions in the Penal Code:
1) he or she has a legal right to be at the location where force or deadly force was used;
2) he or she did not provoke the person against whom force or deadly force was used; and
3) he or she is not engaged in criminal activity at the time force or deadly force was used.

All three of these conditions must be satisfied in order for the "No Duty to Retreat" provisions to apply. Further, if a person does not qualify for "No Duty to Retreat" provisions, it does not mean that the person's use of force or deadly force was not legally justified. It simply means that a jury will evaluate whether the person's failure to retreat when they used force or deadly force was reasonable. If a person cannot satisfy all three requirements, the prosecutor will be free to argue that because the accused could have but did not retreat, the accused's belief that the use of force or deadly force was immediately necessary was not reasonable.

EXAMPLE:

One day, looking for a shortcut through the neighborhood, Simon hops a fence (a trespass) and is walking across open property to reach the street on the other side of the property. Simon is confronted by the property owner and tries to explain that he meant no harm and was just taking a shortcut. However, the property owner becomes irate and cocks his gun, aims it at Simon, and says "I'm going to kill you!"

Under this example, Simon is a trespasser, and since this is considered being "engaged in criminal activity" under the statute, Simon is disqualified from any legal presumptions under Sections 9.31 and 9.32. *See* discussion later in this Chapter regarding not being engaged in criminal activity. As such, any presumption of reasonableness to a belief in the immediate necessity of force or deadly force will not be given to Simon, even though the property owner made his intention to kill Simon very clear. Further, because he is a trespasser and has no legal right to be at his location, Simon will not be entitled to the "No Duty to Retreat" protections of the law. The highest Texas criminal court has held that "the failure to retreat may be considered in determining whether a defendant reasonably believed his conduct was immediately necessary to defend himself or a third person" *Morales,* 357 S.W.3d at 5. Thus, a prosecutor could argue that before the use of force or deadly force by Simon was immediately necessary, Simon should have retreated. It does not mean Simon may not be ultimately legally justified in defending himself; it just makes it more difficult to convince a jury of his justification. Now, let us look a little further.

EXAMPLE:

Simon is scared out of his mind as he looks down the barrel of the property owner's shotgun. The two are about 20 feet apart. Simon, hearing the property owner's threat to kill him, draws his own firearm and fires two shots, killing the property owner.

In this example, because Simon is not eligible for the presumptions under Section 9.32, a prosecutor would be allowed to question and second-guess the use of deadly force. The prosecutor may argue that Simon did not really need to use deadly force immediately because a reasonable person would have retreated under the circumstances. Simon does not lose his legal right to self-defense under this example; he only loses the presumption of reasonableness, and the protection that the "No Duty to Retreat" provisions offer.

PRACTICAL LEGAL TIP

Numerous jurisdictions like Texas have "No Duty to Retreat" laws that do not require fleeing before the legal use of deadly force. However, several states impose a duty on a person to retreat if reasonably available as a prerequisite to using deadly force. So when traveling, make sure you know the law of the state you are visiting.
–Emily

F. A person who provokes an attack is not entitled to a presumption of reasonableness

Sections 9.31 and 9.32 of the Texas Penal Code contain a requirement that in order for a person to take advantage of legal presumptions of reasonableness, the person must not have provoked the attack that led to the use of force or deadly force in the first place. *See also* Section H discussing "Provocation" later in this Chapter.

G. Is a person legally entitled to a presumption of reasonableness if they were involved in criminal activity?

Sections 9.31(a)(3) and 9.32(b)(3) of the Texas Penal Code also contain a requirement that you cannot be engaged in a crime (other than a Class C misdemeanor regulating traffic) at the time force or deadly force is used in order to obtain a presumption that you have a reasonable belief in the immediate necessity of the use of force or deadly force. Interestingly, the "Stand Your Ground" or no duty to retreat language in Sections 9.31(e) and 9.32(c) use the even broader words "not engaged in criminal activity" and do not exempt Class C misdemeanors regulating traffic.

> **EXAMPLE:**
> Paul, a Texas LTC holder, carries his handgun past effective 30.06 and 30.07 signs into his favorite movie theater. During the movie, Paul hears a series of loud bangs and sees a gunman in dark clothes making his way down the aisle. Paul draws his handgun and unloads it into the perpetrator.

Can Paul legally stand his ground since he has his handgun in violation of the theater's criminal trespass warning? No, the police and prosecutors can consider his failure to retreat when deciding if they believe he acted reasonably. A classic example of this principle is a drug deal gone bad: the drug dealer may not lose his legal right to self-defense, but the law will not allow the dealer a legal presumption of reasonableness. The general idea is that individuals involved in criminal activity should not receive the power of presumed legal justification in protecting themselves when they were doing things they were not legally entitled to be doing in the first place!

H. When is the use of force or deadly force explicitly not legally justified under Texas Penal Code Sections 9.31 and 9.32?

Texas Penal Code Section 9.31(b) outlines five specific situations where a person is not justified in using force. Being justified in the use of force is an absolute prerequisite to the use of deadly force; therefore, any time a person is not justified to use force under Section 9.31, that person is also automatically disqualified from being justified to use deadly force under Section 9.32.

1. Force never legally justified in response to verbal provocation alone

> **NO JUSTIFICATION FOR WORDS ALONE**
> **TEX. PENAL CODE § 9.31(b)(1)**
>
> The use of force against another is not justified in response to verbal provocation alone.

If you think back to your childhood, you probably remember the saying: "sticks and stones will break my bones, but words will never hurt me!" Believe it or not, the law agrees wholeheartedly with this concept. Under Texas law, a person is not justified in using force when words are the only provocation to a situation.

> **EXAMPLE:**
>
> Samantha is walking to her local polling place to cast her vote for mayor. A woman who supports the other candidate starts screaming at her, "You're an idiot if you vote for that guy!" Samantha runs over to the woman and punches the woman in the face.

In this instance, Samantha is not legally justified in her use of force because the only thing happening was the other woman screaming at her—a mere verbal provocation.

2. Force not legally justified to resist arrest or search

> **RESISTING ARREST OR SEARCH NOT JUSTIFIED**
> **TEX. PENAL CODE § 9.31(b)(2)**
>
> The use of force against another is not justified to resist an arrest or search that the actor knows is being made by a peace officer, or by a person acting in a peace officer's presence and at his direction, even if the arrest or search is unlawful.

> **EXAMPLE:**
>
> Jeremy has been pulled over for speeding and is removed from his vehicle by a uniformed police officer. While sitting on the curb, the officer begins to search Jeremy's vehicle without his consent and without probable cause. Jeremy says, "Hey, what are you doing?" and the officer responds, "Shut up, I do what I want!" Feeling violated, Jeremy gets up and pulls the officer out of his car and throws the officer to the ground.

Even though the officer's behavior is unusual for a mere speeding violation, and even though it appears Jeremy is being subjected to an illegal search and seizure, his legally justifiable recourse is to pursue the matter through the court system—not to use force against the officer!

Unfortunately, there really are instances where police officers exceed their authority and use more force than they are allowed under the law. Sometimes there are many factors leading to that excessive use of force, but officers have to follow the law, too! For that reason, the legislature crafted a very limited and specific exception to this rule in Texas Penal Code Section 9.31(c).

> **JUSTIFICATION FOR USE OF FORCE AGAINST PEACE OFFICER**
> **TEX. PENAL CODE § 9.31(c)**
>
> The use of force to resist an arrest or search is justified if, before the actor offers any resistance, the peace officer (or person acting at his direction) uses or attempts to use greater force than necessary to make the arrest or search; and when and to the degree the actor reasonably believes the force is immediately necessary to protect himself against the peace officer's (or other person's) use or attempted use of greater force than necessary.

This exception in the self-defense statute is crafted to protect a person in those scenarios where an officer is using greater force than necessary to make an arrest or search. Having said that, pay very close attention to how narrow and specific this statute is in its application. A person must meet some very specific requirements before he or she is afforded any legal protection:

1) a person must *not be resisting* when the officer uses *greater force than necessary;* and

2) that person must *reasonably believe* that resistance is *immediately necessary* to protect himself or herself from the officer's use of greater force than necessary to make the arrest or search.

The point of this section is to give fair warning: any time a person uses force against a law enforcement officer, he or she should be aware that the cards are stacked against him or her from the beginning! Ultimately, the lack of available evidence may make it so exceptionally difficult to claim this statute's protections legitimately that it loses its value except in rare instances.

> **PRACTICAL LEGAL TIP**
>
> The right to remain silent is a fundamental Constitutional right, which is why it is so disturbing that in 2010, the U.S. Supreme Court held that you have to say the magic words of "I invoke my right to remain silent and to counsel" in order to trigger it. Seemingly, by the Court's standard, if you don't say the magic words, police could interrogate you until the end of time. –Edwin

3. Cannot claim self-defense and consent at the same time

NO JUSTIFICATION WHEN YOU CONSENT TO FORCE
TEX. PENAL CODE § 9.31(b)(3)

The use of force against another is not justified if the actor consented to the exact force used or attempted by the other.

This statute serves the purpose of preventing individuals who arrange to fight each other from avoiding criminal responsibility for their actions by claiming self-defense. The statute here is clear: if a person agrees to the force used against him or her by another person, that person cannot later claim that he or she fought back in self-defense! *See Gustin v. State*, 02-17-00376-CR, 2019 (Tex. App.—Fort Worth, May 9, 2019 no pet.); *see also Padilla v. State*, No. 03-07-00513-CR 2008, WL 5423139 (Tex. App.—Austin, Dec. 31, 2008 no pet.). However, there may be situations where a defendant who is not able to claim self-defense because of the issue of consent may have relief because Texas Penal Code Section 22.06 provides the defense of consent to specific situations.

CONSENT AS DEFENSE TO ASSAULTIVE CONDUCT
TEX. PENAL CODE § 22.06

(a) The victim's effective consent or the actor's reasonable belief that the victim consented to the actor's conduct is a defense to prosecution under Section 22.01 (Assault), 22.02 (Aggravated Assault), or 22.05 (Deadly Conduct) if:
  (1) the conduct did not threaten or inflict serious bodily injury; or
  (2) the victim knew the conduct was a risk of:
    (A) his occupation;
    (B) recognized medical treatment; or
    (C) a scientific experiment conducted by recognized methods.

(b) The defense to prosecution provided by Subsection (a) is not available to a defendant who commits an offense described by Subsection (a) as a condition of the defendant's or the victim's initiation or continued membership in a criminal street gang, as defined by Section 71.01.

This section allows the defendant to argue that their use of force, or even deadly force in the three recognized circumstances, is not subject to criminal liability because of the victim's consent. This includes situations where the parties are engaged in mutual combat (except street gang initiations) that does not threaten or result in serious bodily injury. Additionally, the defense of consent is what keeps professional football players from being charged with aggravated assault when they inflict career-ending injuries on each other and doctors from being charged every time they cut someone open with a scalpel. It is important to remember that this defense is only available for the crimes of assault, aggravated assault, or deadly conduct.

EXAMPLE:
Richard and Curtis are having an argument about whose favorite football team will win the championship. In the heat of the argument, Richard calls Curtis a bad name and Curtis asks if Richard wants to take it outside. Richard agrees, and they both begin fighting in the parking lot. Shortly after they begin fighting, the police show up and arrest them for assault.

Neither Curtis nor Richard will be permitted to claim the self-defense justifications of Texas Penal Code Section 9.31 because they consented to the exact force used. However, they may have a defense available under Section 22.06.

4. Provocation/abandoning an encounter
Under Texas Penal Code Section 9.31(b)(4), if a person has provoked an attack, self-defense is not available as a defense to a resulting criminal charge.

> **NO JUSTIFICATION FOR PROVOKING ANOTHER PERSON**
> **TEX. PENAL CODE § 9.31(b)(4)**
>
> The use of force against another is not justified if the actor provoked the other's use or attempted use of unlawful force.

What does it mean to provoke an attack so as to lose your right to self-defense presumptions? At the time of writing, there are no appellate cases directly interpreting this issue under Texas Penal Code Sections 9.31 and 9.32. However, Texas's highest criminal court, the Court of Criminal Appeals, generally defined what it means to provoke an attack. The Court held that a person who provokes an attack loses the legal right of self-defense (so certainly any legal presumption would be lost as well) when three requirements are met:

1) a person must do some act or use some words which provoke the attack;
2) the act or words from a person must be reasonably calculated to provoke the attack; and
3) a person's action or the words used must have been used for the purpose and with the intent that the defendant would have a pretext for inflicting harm on the other.

See Smith v. State, 965 S.W.2d 509 (Tex. Crim. App. 1998).

What the *Smith* Court is saying is that a person cannot effectively "bait" another person into a violent confrontation and then hide behind the law by claiming that their (the provocateur's) conduct should be presumed reasonable because the other fellow took the first swing! While the Court is considering protection in a different context, courts in the future will likely use this opinion with changes in statutory law to decide when a person has "provoked" another person under Sections 9.31 and 9.32. The legal doctrine of provocation is best summed up in a 1914 case:

> A man may not take advantage of his own wrong to gain favorable interpretation of the law. He seeks the law in vain who offends against it... One cannot willingly and knowingly bring upon himself the very necessity which he sets up for his own defense. *Sorrell v. State,* 169 S.W. 299 (Tex. Crim. App. 1914).

What if a person who started a fight soon realizes they bit off more than they can chew? Under the law, that person can abandon or clearly communicate his or her desire to abandon the encounter. If, after a person abandons or attempts to abandon the encounter, the person who was provoked pursues and uses unlawful force against the provocateur, the provocateur may then be legally justified to fight back.

ABANDONMENT OF PROVOCATION MAY ALLOW JUSTIFICATION
TEX. PENAL CODE § 9.31(b)(4)(A) AND (B)

The use of force against another is not justified if the actor provoked the other's use or attempted use of unlawful force, unless the actor abandons the encounter, or clearly communicates to the other his intent to do so reasonably believing he cannot safely abandon the encounter, and the other nevertheless continues or attempts to use unlawful force against the actor.

> **EXAMPLE:**
>
> Dylan is at a restaurant when he notices another man checking out his girlfriend. Dylan tells the other man, "take a hike or you'll regret it" and slightly shoves the admirer. The other man responds by punching Dylan in the face. Dylan, who didn't really want a confrontation, holds both his hands up in surrender and says, "I don't want any more trouble!" However, the other man pulls out a knife and lunges at Dylan. In response, Dylan draws his concealed handgun and puts one right between his eyes.

In this scenario, Dylan is legally justified to fight back with deadly force; he attempted to abandon the incident and made his intention known to the other person. When the other man continued to attack, Dylan is now legally justified to defend himself, even though he made the initial provocation.

5. Settling differences

Use of force is not justified when the actor "sought an explanation from or discussion with the other person concerning the actor's differences with the other person" while unlawfully carrying a weapon or possessing a prohibited weapon. *See* Tex. Penal Code § 9.31(b)(5). The purpose of the statute is to discourage people from seeking a confrontation to settle a dispute when in possession of a weapon illegally. Situations invoking things like road rage, cheating spouses, and "where is my money?" are confrontations that are completely different from facing an armed burglar in your home at night. Therefore, if you violate the statute, you lose your legal justification for self-defense.

III. DO I HAVE A LEGAL RESPONSIBILITY TO DEFEND ANOTHER PERSON?

Under Texas law, the average person has no duty to come to the defense of another, so long as that actor was not the cause of the situation or occurrence. This is true even if a crime is in progress. Note: this lack of a legal duty does not include police officers and other professionals that may have affirmative legal duties to assist. If you see a third person that is the victim of what you believe to be the unlawful use of force or deadly force, you have no legal duty to aid that person—it is your decision. This is equally true if you are legally carrying a gun pursuant to an LTC or Texas Constitutional Carry. But what if you decide to help the third person?

A. When does Texas law allow for the justifiable use of force or deadly force to protect someone else?

In the last sections, we addressed the law of legal justification for the use of force or deadly force for self-defense. We now turn to when the law allows the justified use of force or deadly force to protect another person or persons.

> **DEFENSE OF THIRD PERSON**
> **TEX. PENAL CODE § 9.33**
>
> A person is justified in using force or deadly force against another to protect a third person if: (1) under the circumstances as the actor reasonably believes them to be, the actor would be justified under Section 9.31 or 9.32 in using force or deadly force to protect himself against the unlawful force or unlawful deadly force he reasonably believes to be threatening the third person he seeks to protect; and (2) the actor reasonably believes that the intervention is immediately necessary to protect the third person.

In general, if you place yourself in the "shoes" of the third person, and the law would allow the third person to use force or deadly force to protect themselves, then you are legally justified to use the same level of force to protect the third person. Texas Penal Code Section 9.33 allows a person to protect a third person from the unlawful use of force or deadly force by another in the same circumstances in which a person could justifiably use force under Section 9.31 or deadly force under Section 9.32 to protect themselves, so long as the person reasonably believes that the intervention is immediately necessary. By referencing back to the self-defense statutes in Sections 9.31 and 9.32, the law makes the legal analysis for defending third persons the same as for self-defense.

Therefore, the same legal justifications and presumptions of reasonableness for self-defense are also available for the defense of third persons. If a person decides to aid a third person, the law of justifiable use of force will allow a person to defend a third person to the extent they may defend themselves. As long as the person defending another reasonably believes that the third person would be justified in using force or deadly force to protect him or herself, the person defending may step in and use force or deadly force on that person's behalf. *See Hughes v. State,* 719 S.W.2d 560 (Tex. Crim. App. 1986). However, please note that the law still imposes a requirement that a person's belief in the immediate necessity of the use of force or deadly force be reasonable. If a person decides to defend a third person, prudence dictates that the person defending must be sure they know what is truly happening in a situation before using force or deadly force. If a belief in the immediate necessity of the use of force or deadly force turns out to be unreasonable, the use of force or deadly force will not be legally justified, no matter how well-intentioned a person may be.

B. What if the situation is not as I thought it appeared to be?

A third person and a "Good Samaritan" might not see things as they really are. When a person elects to use force or deadly force to defend a third person, it can all go terribly wrong.

> **EXAMPLE:**
> Peter, carrying a handgun under Texas Constitutional Carry, visits his local big box store. He parks and exits his vehicle, whereupon he witnesses a man struggling to get a handbag away from an elderly woman. Peter, believing the elderly woman is a victim of robbery, drops to one knee while drawing his handgun. Still seeing the man pulling the handbag away from the woman, Peter decides to protect the would-be victim of robbery and fires his gun, striking the robber.

If there was in fact a robbery taking place, Peter's use of deadly force is likely legally justified, because if we put Peter in the shoes of the third person (the elderly woman in the example), Peter would be legally justified in using deadly force to stop the robbery. Thus, the law will deem Peter's belief that the use of deadly force was immediately necessary as reasonable. But what if there was no robbery?

In fact, what would happen if in the instant after Peter fires his gun, the woman Peter sought to protect immediately turns to help the wounded, suspected robber yelling "murderer!" at Peter while screaming in fear and grief, "why did you shoot my son?" It turns out that there was no robbery, just a son attempting to retrieve his mother's car keys because she has Alzheimer's disease, and after a frantic search he had found her wandering in the store's parking lot. How does the law deal with this scenario?

In such a situation, Peter's perspective and knowledge of the situation are very different from the person he sought to defend. In this situation, if Peter's belief that a robbery was in progress was reasonable, then Peter will be legally justified. However, if a jury finds that his belief was unreasonable, Peter will not be legally justified, and he will likely be guilty of aggravated assault or murder.

C. Do I have a duty to report a crime?

Yes, under certain circumstances. Texas Penal Code Section 38.171 makes it a Class A misdemeanor for a person who "observes the commission of a felony under circumstances in which a reasonable person would believe that an offense had been committed in which serious bodily injury or death may have resulted" and the person fails to report the crime where he or she reasonably believes the crime has not been reported and where doing so would not have placed the person "in danger of suffering serious bodily injury or death."

IV. THE USE OF FORCE IN PREVENTING SUICIDE

Texas law provides that a person may be justified in using force to prevent another from committing suicide or inflicting serious bodily injury on him or herself. If a person has a reasonable belief that it is immediately necessary to use force in order to prevent another from committing suicide or inflicting serious bodily injury, then the use of force is justified. Of course, the use of deadly force is not justified in that scenario; the purpose of this statute is to preserve life, not end it!

> **JUSTIFIED USE OF FORCE TO PROTECT LIFE OR HEALTH**
> **TEX. PENAL CODE § 9.34**
>
> (a) A person is justified in using force, but not deadly force, against another when and to the degree he reasonably believes the force is immediately necessary to prevent the other from committing suicide or inflicting serious bodily injury to himself.
>
> (b) A person is justified in using both force and deadly force against another when and to the degree he reasonably believes the force or deadly force is immediately necessary to preserve the other's life in an emergency.

Section (b) of this statute refers to the rare instances where it may be necessary to use what would be considered deadly force to perform some type of emergency procedure in order to save a life, such as an amputation or tracheotomy. Although the language seems somewhat misleading, it is not suggesting that a person be justified in killing another in order to save their life!

> CHAPTER NINE ◄

WHEN CAN I LEGALLY USE MY GUN: PART III
UNDERSTANDING WHEN DEADLY FORCE
Can Be Used Against Animals

I. CAN I LEGALLY USE DEADLY FORCE AGAINST ANIMALS?

When it comes to the law of use of force and deadly force to defend yourself, others, or property from animal attacks, Texas law is a hodgepodge of different laws that are not contained in one section of statutes.

A. No general defense against animals statute

Texas has no general self-defense or defense of others statute that deals with all animals. There are statutes that justify conduct against certain specific "dangerous wild animals" and ones for protection of domestic animals, crops, and livestock, but not a justification statute for protecting people against animal attacks. For example, if a dog is attacking you, and you have to shoot the dog, there exists no provision of the Texas Penal Code that specifically justifies the use of deadly force. In this situation, persons will be forced to rely on a general defense called "necessity." *See* Tex. Penal Code § 9.22. The typical laws you would expect to find such as self-defense against an animal attacking a human being don't exist under Texas law at all! What this means is that one may not find specific legal justification for using force or deadly force against an animal that is attacking if the animal is not a certain type of animal. Under this condition, a person may be forced to argue the general law of necessity. This Chapter will examine the laws that do exist relating to the use of deadly force against an animal and how your right to self-preservation can best be accomplished.

B. The doctrine of necessity

Because there is no specific Texas law that allows a person to use deadly force against an animal in self-defense, often the best claim for legal justification a person can make in a court is one of justification by necessity. Texas law recognizes a very broad justification to potential criminal liability called "necessity," which is defined in Texas Penal Code Section 9.22.

> **NECESSITY**
> **TEX. PENAL CODE § 9.22**
>
> Conduct is justified if:
>
> 1. the actor reasonably believes the conduct is immediately necessary to avoid imminent harm;
>
> 2. the desirability and urgency of avoiding the harm clearly outweigh, according to ordinary standards of reasonableness, the harm sought to be prevented by the law proscribing the conduct; and
>
> 3. a legislative purpose to exclude the justification claimed for the conduct does not otherwise plainly appear.

As this law applies to animal attacks, a person may be legally justified in using force or deadly force (such as firing their gun) against an attacking animal if that person has a reasonable belief that force or deadly force is immediately necessary to avoid imminent harm. However, the imminent harm a person is trying to avoid (by otherwise breaking the law) must be evaluated by a desirability and urgency test under the statute using a reasonable person standard. Further, there exist no legal presumptions of reasonableness such as ones that exist for human-on-human attacks. So, how does this all work in practice?

> **EXAMPLE:**
>
> Jose is walking in his neighborhood when out of nowhere, three large pit bulls spot him and immediately begin running toward him, barking with sharp fangs showing. Jose barely has time to draw and fire his .40 caliber Glock at the lead dog, just before it lunges at him. Having dispatched one dog, the other two flee.

If, for some reason, Jose finds himself charged with any form of crime for his shooting of the dog (this could be anything from cruelty to animals to discharge of a firearm in city limits, *etc.*) Jose will not be able to rely on a specific statute for self-defense because there are none. Rather, Jose will have to rely on the general legal doctrine of necessity as described above. This means that a jury would ultimately decide whether Jose's conduct met the requirements of Section 9.22. First, did Jose "reasonably" believe his conduct (in this case, drawing and firing his gun) was immediately necessary to avoid imminent harm (being bitten, mauled, *etc.*)? Without legal presumptions available under either of the Texas versions of "Castle Doctrine" or "Stand Your Ground" types of laws, a prosecutor will fully be able to argue that Jose should have retreated, that he used too much force, or that the threat really was not imminent.

Second, if a defendant satisfies the first part, he or she must still pass a desirability and urgency test according to the standards of reasonableness. In the case of Jose, he would argue that the desirability of a human (in this case, himself) not being bitten by a dog when walking in his neighborhood outweighs the law against either discharging a firearm in the city limits or a charge of cruelty to animals, *etc.* However, a prosecutor would be free to question all aspects of his conduct and second-guess him in court. In this case, it will be for the jury to decide if Jose, or any person in a similar situation, acted reasonably.

> **PRACTICAL LEGAL TIP**
>
> Beware! Using deadly force against a dog or cat that is only digging into your flowerbed, trespassing, or getting into your garbage is not justified, even under the doctrine of necessity.
> –Edwin

C. Lions and tigers in Texas: "dangerous wild animals"

Frankly, it's amazing that there's a law specifically protecting you from prosecution in the event you need to kill a caracal—which is a wild cat found primarily in Africa, Asia, and India—but not one which would protect you from an attacking dog in your neighborhood. Nevertheless, Texas Penal Code Section 42.092(d)(1) makes that the case.

> **DEFENSE FOR CRUELTY TO ANIMALS; DANGEROUS WILD ANIMAL**
> **TEX. PENAL CODE § 42.092(d)(1)**
>
> It is a defense to prosecution under this section that the actor had a reasonable fear of bodily injury to the actor or to another person by a dangerous wild animal as defined by Section 822.101, Health and Safety Code.

The dangerous wild animals referenced in this section only include: a lion, tiger, ocelot, cougar, leopard, cheetah, jaguar, bobcat, lynx, serval, caracal, hyena, bear, coyote, jackal, baboon, chimpanzee, orangutan, gorilla, or any hybrid of one of the animals listed here. If the animal is not on the list, it is not covered.

This list is very important because these are the only animals for which a specific justification of self-defense of a person is statutorily authorized. Further, the legislature also addresses using a firearm for self-defense against these specific animals in the disorderly conduct statute. Texas Penal Code Section 42.01(e) makes it a defense to the crime of disorderly conduct by discharging a firearm in a public place or across a public road if the person who discharged the firearm had a reasonable fear of bodily injury to the person or to another by one of these dangerous wild animals.

You may be asking yourself, "why cougars, bears, and gorillas?" The answer lies in the purpose of Chapter 822 of the Health and Safety Code, which governs the owning of wild animals for entertainment, exhibition, or profit. This list is comprised of animals that are not traditionally domesticated animals but are in some cases allowed to be kept in captivity. So, if you are out and about and are confronted by one of the animals listed in Section 822.101 which has escaped from confinement, and you have a reasonable fear of bodily injury, you may shoot without fear of prosecution for disorderly conduct or cruelty to animals. This list is conspicuously short and does not cover every non-native wild animal which may be held in a zoo, circus, or safari park. Many animals not included on the list can kill or maim at will, such as the hippopotamus, elephant, or ferocious cape buffalo. What if our favorite peanut-eating pachyderm charges in a rage? You are left with the defense of necessity as the elephant is not a "dangerous wild animal."

D. Protecting livestock and crops

> **DEFENSE FOR CRUELTY TO ANIMALS; PROTECTING LIVESTOCK**
> **TEX. PENAL CODE § 42.092(e)(1)**
>
> It is a defense to prosecution under Subsection (b)(2) [killing, administering poison, or causing serious bodily injury to an animal] or (b)(6) [causing bodily injury to an animal] that the animal was discovered on the person's property in the act of or after injuring or killing the person's livestock animals or damaging the person's crops and that the person killed or injured the animal at the time of this discovery.

With regard to cruelty to a non-livestock animal, Texas Penal Code § 42.092(e)(1) provides a specific statutory defense for killing or injuring an animal if a person discovers the animal on his property and it is in the act of or has just killed or injured that person's livestock or crops. Subsections (b)(2) and (b)(6) of Section 42.092 deal with the moments when you are forced to "intentionally, knowingly, or recklessly" kill, poison, or cause serious bodily injury to another person's animal.

> **EXAMPLE:**
> Ted is weeding his garden when he hears a commotion by the chicken coop and sees his neighbor's dog attacking his chickens. Bloody feathers fill the air of the coop. Ted runs over and uses his garden hoe to kill the dog.

Although there is no question that Ted intended to kill the dog, Texas law *exempts him* from any criminal liability for cruelty to animals because he was protecting his livestock. If you catch an animal killing or destroying your livestock or crops, you will be justified in using force or deadly force against it.

E. Dogs and coyotes attacking livestock or domestic animals

> **AUTHORIZATION TO KILL ATTACKING DOGS/COYOTES**
> **TEX. HEALTH AND SAFETY CODE § 822.013**
>
> A dog or coyote that is attacking, is about to attack, or has recently attacked livestock, domestic animals, or fowls may be killed by: any person witnessing the attack; or the attacked animal's owner or a person acting on behalf of the owner if the owner or person has knowledge of the attack.

Texas Health & Safety Code § 822.013 specifically allows a person to kill a dog or coyote that is attacking livestock, domestic animals, or fowls. This statute came into application in 2010 when then-Texas Governor Rick Perry was out jogging and a coyote attacked his dog. Governor Perry dispatched the coyote with his .380 Ruger. The Governor was fully within the scope of Section 822.013. The Texas Court of Criminal Appeals approved this authorization statute as a defense to the crime of animal cruelty in the case of *Chase v. State*, 448 S.W.3d 6 (Tex. Crim. App. 2014).

It is notable that this section is specifically limited to dog and coyote attacks on animals, not people. This statute does not address the issue of defending people against animal attacks; you must look elsewhere for your legal justification. If Governor Perry had not had his dog with him that day and the coyote had instead attacked him, he would have had to employ the general legal defense of necessity under Texas Penal Code Section 9.22.

F. Fur-bearing animals

> **DEFENSE FOR ILLEGAL COLLECTION OF FUR-BEARING ANIMAL**
> **TEX. PARKS AND WILDLIFE CODE § 71.004**
>
> This chapter does not prohibit a landowner or his agent from taking a fur-bearing animal causing depredation on that person's land.

It is not uncommon to be troubled by fur-bearing pests on your property, such as wild beavers, otters, minks, ring-tailed cats, badgers, skunks, raccoons, muskrats, opossums, foxes, or nutria. Many of these animals destroy property, crops, and so forth in their attempt to build their own habitats. It is for that reason this section of the Parks and Wildlife Code exists: to provide you with some recourse in the event you and your property are troubled by one of these animals. Unlike the Health and Safety Code section for dogs and coyotes, this appears to be a defense, much like other sections, rather than an affirmative authorization to use deadly force against a fur-bearing animal. Chapter 71 of the Parks and Wildlife Code also defines a "taking" of a fur-bearing animal to include killing that animal. Interestingly, if you kill a fur-bearing animal that is destroying your crops, the law does not allow you to use or keep its fur. Therefore, you cannot make a coon-skin cap out of that nuisance raccoon.

G. Federal law defenses

The federal law, in a comprehensive fashion, has actually had the foresight to specifically provide that a person may kill an animal protected by federal law in self-defense, such as the regulations concerning the Mexican wolf in 50 CFR § 17.84(k)(7)(i), or the grizzly bear in 50 CFR § 17.40(b)(i)(B). Unlike the Texas statutes, this makes the federal law clear and comprehensible. Therefore, if you are carrying a firearm in a national park (*see* Chapters 12 and 13) and you find yourself face to face with a grizzly bear, you will have a legal defense for protecting yourself.

› CHAPTER TEN ‹

WHEN CAN I LEGALLY USE MY GUN: PART IV
UNDERSTANDING WHEN DEADLY FORCE
Can Be Used To Protect Property

I. OVERVIEW AND LOCATION OF THE LAW TO PROTECT PROPERTY

Texas law allows a person to protect, with force, their property from another's unlawful interference or trespass on their property or the property of another. Further, Texas law, under certain circumstances, will also allow a person to use legally justified deadly force to protect property. The sections of the Texas Penal Code dealing with legally justified force or deadly force to defend property are as follows:

9.41: Protection of One's Own Property;
9.42: Deadly Force to Protect Property; and
9.43: Protection of a Third Person's Property.

Protection of property will be analyzed under the same "reasonable person" standard discussed in Chapters 7 and 8 and will have the same requirements for a person reasonably believing that the force or deadly force used was "immediately necessary." In addition to the above sections, Texas Penal Code Section 9.44 addresses the law of devices to protect property.

II. WHEN IS SOMEONE LEGALLY JUSTIFIED TO USE FORCE BUT NOT DEADLY FORCE TO PROTECT THEIR OWN PROPERTY?

A. Prevent or terminate interference with property

The law answers this question based upon the statutory law of the justified use of force to protect property contained in Section 9.41 of the Penal Code. This section divides the justified use of force (but not deadly force) into two categories: the first category, under Subsection 9.41(a), is when a person is justified in using force to prevent or terminate another person's unlawful trespass or interference with their property, *e.g.*, stealing property, vandalizing property, *etc.*

If you catch someone in the act

In plain terms, if someone is unlawfully taking your personal property, you are justified in using force to stop them. Of course, just like instances of self-defense, you must also meet the standard of reasonable belief in the immediate necessity of the use of force.

> **EXAMPLE:**
> Shaun looks out his peephole and sees a man taking a package that the delivery driver had just left on Shaun's front porch. Shaun opens his door, chases the man down the sidewalk, and wrestles the package away from him.

Shaun is legally justified because he used only enough force necessary to protect his property from theft during the daytime.

> **JUSTIFIED USE OF FORCE TO PROTECT YOUR PROPERTY**
> **TEX. PENAL CODE § 9.41(a)**
>
> A person in lawful possession of land or tangible, movable property is justified in using force against another when and to the degree the actor reasonably believes the force is immediately necessary to prevent or terminate the other's trespass on the land or unlawful interference with the property.

B. Recovery of property

The second category, under Texas Penal Code Section 9.41(b), is the justified use of force in recovering property that has been unlawfully taken from the person or to reenter land that has been unlawfully taken from them.

> **JUSTIFIED USE OF FORCE TO RECOVER YOUR PROPERTY**
> **TEX. PENAL CODE § 9.41(b)**
>
> A person unlawfully dispossessed of land or tangible, movable property by another is justified in using force against the other when and to the degree the actor reasonably believes the force is immediately necessary to reenter the land or recover the property if the actor uses the force immediately or in fresh pursuit after the dispossession and: (1) the actor reasonably believes the other had no claim of right when he dispossessed the actor; or (2) the other accomplished the dispossession by using force, threat, or fraud against the actor.

Fresh pursuit after property is taken

In the event a person's property has already been stolen, a person is only legally justified to use force to recover it immediately after it was stolen or in "fresh pursuit." A person is not allowed to use force that is not immediate, or in fresh pursuit, to go and recover the property days, weeks, or months later. What does it mean to recover property immediately after or in fresh pursuit? Let's consider our example from the previous section.

> **EXAMPLE:**
>
> Shaun is not able to catch the thief immediately after the theft because the man jumped into a waiting car. However, Shaun sees the thief at the grocery store the next day. Shaun grabs the guy and throws him to the ground while shouting, "Give me back my box!"

Shaun is no longer justified in his use of force because he is no longer in fresh pursuit. Shaun should have called the police for help. While it appears that the appellate courts in Texas have been reluctant to provide a bright-line definition of what it means to be in fresh pursuit, they have provided some guidance on what is not considered to be fresh pursuit. For instance, one court stated that the use of force was not immediately after or in fresh pursuit after the dispossession of the defendant's property when the defendant walked down to his van, retrieved a shotgun, returned upstairs, and then shot the complainant who had refused to return the defendant's revolver. *See Salley v. State,* No. 14-97-0656-CR, 2000 WL 552193 (Tex. App.—Houston [14th Dist.] 2000, pet. ref'd). In another case, a court held that a defendant who used force in an attempt to recover a wrecker approximately one hour after it was taken did not act immediately or in fresh pursuit. *See Hall v. State,* No. 01-88-00511-CR, 1989 WL 21835 (Tex. App.—Houston [1st

Dist.] 1989, no pet.). Finally, a case in Houston cited the Black's Law Dictionary by stating that fresh pursuit is sometimes referred to as "hot pursuit." *See Ordonez v. State,* No. 14-10-00132-CR, 2010 WL 5395808 (Tex. App.—Houston [14th Dist.] 2010, no pet.) (citing Black's Law Dictionary, 667 (6th ed. 1990)). Ultimately, it appears that courts view fresh pursuit to mean "immediate without delay," as even taking a few minutes to arm oneself is sufficient to lose legal justification in using force to recover property.

In addition to attempting recovery immediately after or in fresh pursuit after dispossession of property, a person must have a reasonable belief that the other person wasn't entitled to take it in the first place. In other words, if an ordinary, reasonable person would take the item back believing the thief had no right to it, then a person may be justified in doing the same thing. Keep in mind, though, this section only justifies the use of force, not deadly force.

C. No legal presumption of reasonableness when defending property

Texas law provides no legal presumptions of reasonableness for uses of force to protect property, whether it is preventing or terminating a trespass or interference with or the recovery of property. Thus, the jury will be the ultimate arbiter of the reasonableness of conduct.

The analysis so far leads us to the question: if force may legally be used to prevent or terminate trespass or interference with property, what constitutes a trespass or interference with property?

D. What is trespassing?

The commonly understood meaning of trespass is "an unlawful interference with one's person, property, or rights." This definition has been expanded to refer typically to "any unauthorized intrusion or invasion of private premises or land of another." *See* Black's Law Dictionary, 6th ed. This commonly understood definition of trespass is different and more expansive than the offense of criminal trespass found in Section 30.05 of the Texas Penal Code. The Penal Code defines a criminal trespass as when:

> A person...enters or remains on or in property of another, including residential land, agricultural land, a recreational vehicle park, a building, ... or an aircraft or other vehicle, without effective consent and the person:
> (1) had notice that the entry was forbidden; or
> (2) received notice to depart but failed to do so.

In other words, unlike the common definition of trespass where a person becomes a trespasser whether they realized it or not (unwittingly walking across the King's hunting grounds, for instance), under the Texas Penal Code, prior to committing a criminal offense, a person must have knowledge they are in a place they do not belong or are not welcome. In addition, the crime of criminal trespass is strictly limited to when a person is found in or on a piece of property without permission; the offense does not cover situations involving personal property.

E. Trespass, for legal justification, is not just "criminal trespass"

How is "trespasser" defined in Texas Penal Code Section 9.41 for purposes of defending property? Because the plain language of Section 9.41(a) refers only to terminating "the other's trespass" and does not reference a "criminal trespass," it is clear that the statute intends to follow a broader definition of trespass than just the offense of criminal trespass found in Texas Penal Code § 30.05. In other words, a person may be potentially legally justified in using force against a person found trespassing on their land—even if that person has not committed the crime of criminal trespass—but only so long as the use of force is accompanied with a reasonable belief that it is immediately necessary to terminate the trespass.

However, in the event an unwitting trespasser has no intention of remaining on or damaging the property, at least one Texas court has held that the use of force is not immediately necessary. *See Hudson v. State,* 145 S.W.3d 323 (Tex. App.—Fort Worth 2004, pet. ref'd). Further, without a specific definition of what "trespass" means as found in Section 9.41, in the vast majority of cases, a jury will make the ultimate decision as to whether or not a person had a reasonable belief that it was immediately necessary to terminate another person's trespass on the land.

> **EXAMPLE:**
> Elijah wanders past a fence post that has a large purple stripe. Unbeknownst to him, he is trespassing on Jacob's land. Instead of confronting Elijah, Jacob calls the sheriff, who responds and detains Elijah for questioning.

Should Elijah be prosecuted for criminal trespass if he says that he did not know that a post with a purple stripe on it has the same legal effect as a fence or "No Trespassing" sign? Would Jacob have been justified if he would have tackled him rather than calling the sheriff? In this instance, a jury would evaluate the justification.

F. What is unlawful interference with property?

You have a legal right to prevent or terminate "interference with property," but what does this mean? It can be a theft, destruction, vandalism, or anything else that diminishes a person's right to their property. Whether particular conduct rises to interference with property is an issue that a jury decides.

G. Is there a statutory minimum value of property before force may be legally used to protect it?
No. There exists no statutory minimum value for property before force may be used to protect it. Texas Penal Code Sections 9.41 and 9.42 do not specify that property a person seeks to protect must be of a certain, minimum dollar value in order for a person to legally protect it. Having said that, what the Texas Penal Code does specify is that a person must have a reasonable belief that the use of force or deadly force is immediately necessary to protect that property before a person would be justified in using force or deadly force.

Realistically, even though a person may be in the process of taking tangible, movable property (as specified in Section 9.41), some property may be of so little value that the use of force or deadly force to protect or recover it would not be deemed reasonable by a jury.

EXAMPLE:
One day at work, Fred walks into Ricky's office and takes a red stapler off of Ricky's desk and walks away. Ricky, upset at having his favorite stapler pilfered from his desk, jumps up, chases Fred down, shoves him to the ground, and starts beating on Fred to recover his property. On his way to chase Fred, Ricky also passes the office supply closet where black staplers are available for anyone to take and use.

Was Ricky's use of force against Fred legally justified? Maybe, but probably not. It will be a very hard sell to a jury that a person was beaten up over a red stapler. However, some members of a jury may value a red stapler much differently than a black stapler. What if a thief is stealing irreplaceable family photos? There's no monetary value to be placed there—only personal sentiment. Again, the law is silent on the subject of any monetary value of property to be defended.

> **PRACTICAL LEGAL TIP**
>
> There are plenty of clever signs and bumper stickers out there advocating the use of a firearm. "Keep honking, I'm reloading," and even "Trespassers Will Be Shot" are seen often on the bumpers of Texas cars and the fence posts of Texas homeowners. But these signs, despite the chuckle they may elicit from a passerby, are not a good idea. Even if meant only to prompt a laugh, if you are forced to use your firearm to defend yourself and end up in court, you can bet that the prosecutor will bring these signs up to the jury for consideration. Remember, a prosecutor will use every avenue to paint you in the worst light possible. Keep the laughs to yourself and take the signs down! —Emily

The point to be made here is that some items simply may not have enough value (financial, sentimental, or otherwise) to provide a person with a reasonable belief that the use of force or deadly force is necessary to protect or recover the item. In this example, not only does the stapler have little monetary value, but there are others readily available for replacement from the supply closet. It would be hard to imagine a jury finding a person to be justified in even using force, let alone deadly force, for such a petty larceny! To that end, in a case of deadly force in 1893, the Texas Court of Criminal Appeals held that the taking of a nickel (which is worth about $1.52 today), did not justify the owner of the nickel in killing the thief who was fleeing with the money. *Bowman v. State,* 21 S.W. 48 (Tex. Crim. App. 1893). Remember, your conduct will always be evaluated under a reasonable person standard, and there are no legal presumptions available for defending property under Texas Penal Code Sections 9.41 and 9.42.

III. WHEN IS SOMEONE LEGALLY JUSTIFIED IN USING DEADLY FORCE TO PROTECT OR RECOVER THEIR OWN PROPERTY?

When a person may legally use deadly force (force that is intended to cause or causes serious bodily injury or death) to defend his or her property is addressed in Section 9.42 of the Texas Penal Code.

> **JUSTIFIED USE OF DEADLY FORCE TO PROTECT YOUR PROPERTY**
> **TEX. PENAL CODE § 9.42**
>
> A person is justified in using deadly force against another to protect land or tangible, movable property:
> (1) if he would be justified in using force against the other under Section 9.41; and
> (2) when and to the degree he reasonably believes the deadly force is immediately necessary:
>   (A) to prevent the other's imminent commission of arson, burglary, robbery, aggravated robbery, theft during nighttime, or criminal mischief during the nighttime; or
>   (B) to prevent the other who is fleeing immediately after committing burglary, robbery, aggravated robbery, or theft during the nighttime from escaping with the property; and
> (3) he reasonably believes that:
>   (A) the land or property cannot be protected or recovered by any other means; or
>   (B) the use of force other than deadly force to protect or recover the land or property would expose the actor or another to a substantial risk of death or serious bodily injury.

A. Three requirements for legal justification under Section 9.42

Legal justification for deadly force to protect property under Texas Penal Code Section 9.42 is not accompanied with any legal presumptions of reasonableness; the jury will be the ultimate arbiter in deciding whether a person acted reasonably in a given incident. Because Section 9.42 requires three separate elements of reasonable belief, this means a jury will have their work cut out for them in determining whether a person is justified or not.

1. Step one: justified under Section 9.41 to use force
First, the jury will be responsible for determining whether the person (now a defendant) involved in the use of deadly force was justified in using mere force under Texas Penal Code Section 9.41. Because justification under Section 9.41 requires a reasonable belief in the immediate necessity of the use of force, the jury's first task is to establish whether the use of force would have even been justified. That is, was there an interference with property or a trespass in the first place? If not, a person will not be legally justified in using deadly force; the analysis stops and no legal justification exists under Section 9.42.

2. Step two: prevent crimes or stop those fleeing with property
Second, the jury must decide whether a defendant had a reasonable belief that deadly force was immediately necessary to prevent the imminent commission of arson, burglary, robbery, aggravated robbery, theft during the nighttime, or criminal mischief during the nighttime, or if deadly force was used to prevent a person who was fleeing immediately after the commission of burglary, robbery, aggravated robbery, or theft during the nighttime from escaping with property. The jury must decide whether the person had a reasonable belief that deadly force was immediately necessary to prevent the other from escaping with property.

> **PRACTICAL LEGAL TIP**
>
> Notice the difference between Texas Penal Code Sections 9.42(a) and (b) is that a person is not provided with a justification to use force or deadly force against a person who has completed arson or criminal mischief and shows no intent on committing another one! —Kirk

3. Step three: no other means of recovery available

The third step to legal justification under Texas Penal Code Section 9.42 is the person who used deadly force to protect property must have reasonably believed that the property could not have been protected or recovered by other means or using something less than deadly force would expose the person to a substantial risk of death or serious bodily injury to themselves or another.

If the jury finds that a person acted reasonably under all three of these steps, only then will the person be legally justified in using deadly force. Again, there are no legal presumptions available for justified uses of force or deadly force to protect property.

EXAMPLE:

After a long day at work, Gary finally pulls into his driveway just in time to see two masked men running out of his front door with his favorite television and his grandfather's expensive watch on one of the men's wrists. Gary gets out of his car and demands that the men stop where they are, but they ignore him and run away. Gary pulls his Glock 17 and fires at the fleeing men, killing one and injuring the other.

Was Gary justified under Section 9.42 to use deadly force? To answer this question, start the three-step analysis under Section 9.42. First, is Gary justified under Section 9.41 to use force? Gary has to show a jury he had a reasonable belief that it was immediately necessary to use force to stop the interference with his property or a trespass. It seems pretty clear that with his TV and watch being stolen, there is both interference with property and a trespass. So if Gary reasonably believes (as decided by a jury) that force is necessary to stop the threat, he may use force under Section 9.41. Gary likely passes step one.

Next, under Section 9.42, the jury will decide if Gary had a reasonable belief that his use of deadly force was immediately necessary to prevent burglary, theft during nighttime, or to prevent the person he shot from fleeing immediately after the person committed a burglary or theft during the nighttime from escaping with his TV and watch. This second requirement seems fairly straightforward, and Gary likely passes step two, as well.

Finally, a jury must find Gary's belief reasonable that his TV and watch could not have been protected or recovered by other means, or that using less than deadly force would have endangered him or another under the language of Section 9.42. In this case, the jury is again the ultimate arbiter, and persons may reasonably disagree. Because there are no legal presumptions of reasonableness available to Gary in protecting property, we do not know how the jury will decide this case, but the facts definitely seem to be in Gary's favor.

IV. CAN I PROTECT ANOTHER PERSON'S PROPERTY?

> **JUSTIFIED USE OF DEADLY FORCE TO PROTECT ANOTHER'S PROPERTY**
> **TEX. PENAL CODE § 9.43**
>
> A person is justified in using force or deadly force against another to protect land or tangible, movable property of a third person if, under the circumstances as he reasonably believes them to be, the actor would be justified under Section 9.41 or 9.42 in using force or deadly force to protect his own land or property and:
>
> (1) the actor reasonably believes the unlawful interference constitutes attempted or consummated theft of or criminal mischief to the tangible, movable property; or
>
> (2) the actor reasonably believes that:
>
>   (A) the third person has requested his protection of the land or property;
>
>   (B) he has a legal duty to protect the third person's land or property; or
>
>   (C) the third person whose land or property he uses force or deadly force to protect is the actor's spouse, parent, or child, resides with the actor, or is under the actor's care.

Section 9.43 of the Texas Penal Code establishes a two-prong test in determining if force or deadly force may be legally used to defend another person's property. First, before force or deadly force may be used to protect another's property, a person must have been justified under Texas Penal Code Sections 9.41 or 9.42, respectively, as if the land or property were his or her own. The inverse is also true: you can't legally protect another person's property if you wouldn't be justified in protecting your own.

If a person satisfies the first prong of the test, they must also satisfy the second. The second prong of Section 9.43 may be satisfied in one of the following ways:
1) the person using the force must reasonably believe that the interference with property they are preventing or stopping is a theft or criminal mischief to tangible, movable property;
2) the owner of the property has requested the property's protection;
3) the person seeking to protect the property has a legal duty to protect the property (*e.g.*, security officer); or
4) the property belongs to a spouse, parent, child, another person who is residing with the person, or is another person who is under the person's care seeking to protect the property.

If a person satisfies one of these requirements, then both prongs of the test are met and the person may be justified. Let's return to our earlier example with Gary and see how things would play out if another person's property was involved.

> **EXAMPLE:**
> After a long day at work, Gary pulls into his own driveway one night and witnesses two men climbing out of his neighbor's window, which appears to be broken, and with what looks to be his neighbor's television. Gary exits his vehicle, gun drawn, and demands the two men stop. When the men ignore his command, Gary shoots and wounds both men.

Is Gary legally justified in using deadly force under this scenario? Possibly yes. We evaluate legal justification by determining first, would Gary have been justified in using deadly force if the property he was protecting was his own? The answer seems clear that he would have been (*e.g.*, burglary or theft during the nighttime, *etc.*). The second requirement of Section 9.43 must also be satisfied for there to be legal justification. In this scenario, even if Gary's neighbor had not specially asked Gary to protect his property (although such a request would have satisfied the second prong of the test), because Gary's belief was likely reasonable that the persons he shot were attempting or consummating a theft to tangible, movable property, he likely will be legally justified. Keep in mind, because there are no legal presumptions for the defense of property, a jury could determine that shooting someone over his neighbor's television is not reasonable.

V. HOW ARE THE CRIMES ASSOCIATED WITH DEFENDING PROPERTY DEFINED UNDER TEXAS LAW?

In the previous sections, we discussed circumstances where if certain crimes are being or have been committed, a person may have a legal justification in using force or deadly force to defend their property. How does Texas law define those crimes?

A. Arson

When a person starts a fire, regardless of whether the fire continues after ignition, or causes an explosion with the intent to destroy or damage any vegetation, fence, or structure on open-space land, or any building, habitation, or vehicle under certain circumstances. *See* Tex. Penal Code § 28.02.

B. Burglary

Anytime a person, without the consent of the owner, enters a habitation or building (or any portion of a building) not then open to the public, or remains concealed in a habitation or building with the intent to commit a felony, theft, or assault, or enters a habitation or building and actually commits or attempts to commit a felony, theft, or assault. *See* Tex. Penal Code § 30.02.

C. Burglary of a Motor Vehicle
When a person breaks into or enters a vehicle or any part of a vehicle without the effective consent of the owner and with the intent to commit any felony or theft. *See* Tex. Penal Code § 30.04.

D. Burglary of a Coin-Operated Machine
When a person breaks or enters into any coin-operated machine, coin collection machine, or other coin-operated or coin collection receptacle, contrivance, apparatus, or equipment used for the purpose of providing lawful amusement, sales of goods, services, or other valuable things, or telecommunications with the intent to obtain property or services without the effective consent of the owner. *See* Tex. Penal Code § 30.03.

A note about "burglary"
Texas Penal Code § 9.42 uses the word burglary in the most general sense of the word. The statute gives no qualifiers or limitations on what type of burglary a person would be justified in using deadly force to thwart. This is important because there are four types of burglary that are criminalized in Chapter 30 of the Texas Penal Code. It is generally accepted that deadly force is justified to prevent a burglary of a habitation and burglary of a building that is not a habitation; since these are both felonies, they are contained in a penal code section simply titled "Burglary," and they are crimes of a more personal nature where the perpetrator intends on committing other felonies or a theft. However, there is an unresolved potential legal issue of whether the crimes of "burglary of a motor vehicle"

as defined in Texas Penal Code Section 30.04 or "burglary of a coin-operated machine" as defined in Texas Penal Code Section 30.03 are included in the scope of the term "burglary" under Texas Penal Code Section 9.42. There exist legal arguments both for the inclusion and exclusion of these two crimes; however, until a court of appeals addresses the issue, they remain mere arguments.

E. Robbery

When, in the process of committing theft, a person intentionally, knowingly, or recklessly causes bodily injury to another; or intentionally or knowingly threatens or places another person in fear of imminent bodily injury or death while intending to obtain or maintain control of the stolen property. *See* Tex. Penal Code § 29.02.

F. Theft

When a person unlawfully appropriates property with the intent to deprive the owner of the property. *See* Tex. Penal Code § 31.03.

G. Criminal Mischief

When a person, without the effective consent of the owner: intentionally or knowingly damages or destroys the tangible property of another; tampers with the tangible property of another and causes pecuniary loss or substantial inconvenience to the owner or a third person; or makes markings, including inscriptions, slogans, drawings, or paintings, on the tangible property of another. *See* Tex. Penal Code § 28.03.

H. Nighttime

The period of time beginning thirty minutes after sunset and ending thirty minutes before sunrise. *See* Tex. Transp. Code § 541.401.

VI. HOW CAN I ASSIST LAW ENFORCEMENT?
A. Acting under a police officer's direction

Almost without fail, as attorneys we are regularly asked about whether you can make a citizen's arrest, and how you can best assist law enforcement in dicey situations. Since every legal situation is unique, here we'll just provide a brief summary of the general law, as well as reference some of the statutes governing the use of citizen's arrests and how to assist authorities.

First, Texas Penal Code Section 9.51(a) states that you may detain an individual who is committing a crime if you are authorized and directed by a police officer to do so, and if you are in that officer's presence. This would appear to eliminate the very idea of a "citizen's arrest" in the traditional sense and looks much more like a field-commission to deputy! In addition, be aware that this section of the Texas Penal Code only authorizes you to use force; you are not authorized to use deadly force. Finally, any person assisting law enforcement must identify themselves as a person acting at an officer's direction, unless such identification is either impossible or already known to the person being arrested.

Section 9.51(a) operates as the statute under which law enforcement is able to use force against a suspect. In order to enable officers to use all available resources at their disposal (such as an ordinary citizen), the statute is expanded to include individuals acting at an officer's direction.

B. Not acting under a police officer's direction

More in the area of authorizing a citizen's arrest is the language found in Texas Penal Code Section 9.51(b), the text of which is found in the following box, and which removes the obstacle of being in an officer's presence.

> **JUSTIFIED USE OF FORCE ASSISTING LAW ENFORCEMENT**
> **TEX. PENAL CODE § 9.51(b)**
>
> A person other than a peace officer (or one acting at his direction) is justified in using force against another when and to the degree the actor reasonably believes the force is immediately necessary to make or assist in making a lawful arrest, or to prevent or assist in preventing escape after lawful arrest if, before using force, the actor manifests his purpose to and the reason for the arrest or reasonably believes his purpose and the reason are already known by or cannot reasonably be made known to the person to be arrested.

This statute allows an ordinary person to use force when making or assisting in making an arrest, since it does not require the person to be in a peace officer's presence! Once again, you must meet the same "reasonable belief" and "immediate necessity" standards we've outlined throughout this Chapter before you may use force. Where possible, you also need to identify yourself and the reason you're making the arrest, unless you believe such is already known or can't be made known. Take notice, however, this statute does not authorize the use of deadly force.

In addition, the Texas Code of Criminal Procedure authorizes the warrantless citizen's arrest of an individual in the event the offense is "committed in his presence or within his view, if the offense is one classed as a felony or as an offense against the public peace."

Tex. Code Crim. Proc. Art. 14.01(a). This statute also closely follows the authorization granted by the Texas Court of Criminal Appeals in *Miles v. State* authorizing the warrantless arrest of a person committing a "misdemeanor within the citizen's presence or view or if the evidence shows that the person's conduct poses a threat of continuing violence or harm to himself or the public." *See Miles v. State,* 241 S.W.3d 28, 42 (Tex. Crim. App. 2007).

C. When can a person use deadly force in assisting law enforcement?

In order to be legally justified in using deadly force to help law enforcement, a person must comply with the requirements of Texas Penal Code Section 9.51(d).

> **JUSTIFIED USE OF DEADLY FORCE ASSISTING LAW ENFORCEMENT**
> **TEX. PENAL CODE § 9.51(d)**
>
> A person other than a peace officer acting in a peace officer's presence and at his direction is justified in using deadly force against another when and to the degree the person reasonably believes the deadly force is immediately necessary to make or assist in making a lawful arrest, or to prevent escape after lawful arrest if, the use of force would have been justified under Subsection (b) and:
>
> 1. the actor reasonably believes the felony or offense against the public peace for which the arrest is authorized included the use or attempted use of deadly force; or
> 2. the actor reasonably believes there is a substantial risk that the person to be arrested will cause death or serious bodily injury to another if the arrest is delayed.

Like nearly every law authorizing the use of deadly force, this statute also only justifies using deadly force if you would first be justified in using mere force. However, deadly force may only legally be used to assist the police if a police officer is present and directing you to do so.

In other words, there is not a circumstance under Section 9.51 where you, as an ordinary citizen, are legally justified in using deadly force to execute an arrest if no police officer is present and has so directed. That doesn't mean you won't have any justification under other sections of the law, such as self-defense, just not under Section 9.51.

D. Detaining potential thieves: "retailer's privilege"

The Texas Civil Practice and Remedies Code grants a person authority to detain a person in order to investigate potential theft.

> **AUTHORIZATION TO DETAIN POTENTIAL THIEF**
> **TEX. CIVIL PRACTICE AND REMEDIES CODE § 124.001**
>
> A person who reasonably believes that another has stolen or is attempting to steal property is privileged to detain that person in a reasonable manner and for a reasonable time to investigate ownership of the property.

The most common application of this particular statute is in a retail setting. Thus, it is often called "retailer's" or "shop-keeper's" privilege" or right. Common scenarios include when a loss prevention officer for the store will take a person into some type of custody while they investigate whether an item was stolen from their business.

PRACTICAL LEGAL TIP

If you use your firearm for defensive purposes, the first number you should call is 911. But keep your call brief: you only need to tell the operator that you have been the victim of a crime, where you are located, and some identifying information. After that, hang up! You are not required to remain on the line, and doing so could cause you problems later. Remember, all 911 calls are recorded, and operators are trained to gather as much information as possible. No matter how justified you are in your use of a firearm, something you say on a 911 call may become a real headache later at trial. –Edwin

➤ CHAPTER ELEVEN ◂

WHAT CRIMES CAN I BE CHARGED WITH WHEN MY USE OF DEADLY FORCE IS NOT JUSTIFIED?

I. INTRODUCTION AND OVERVIEW

Now it's time to give a brief summary of where you'll find yourself in legal trouble if you don't meet the elements of justification as we've discussed throughout this book. This Chapter describes some of the crimes involving the use of deadly force or a firearm, and where relevant provisions may be found in Texas law.

II. CRIMES AGAINST PERSONS

When a person uses force or deadly force in a defensive incident, it is specifically directed at a particular individual or individuals, the criminal aggressors. In the event that the investigators do not believe this force or deadly force is justified, it can lead to criminal charges for crimes against persons.

A. Murder

The most severe crime a person can be charged with when they use deadly force is murder. Murder under Texas Penal Code Section 19.02 is intentionally or knowingly causing the death of another person, or intending to cause serious bodily injury and committing an act clearly dangerous to human life that causes the death of another person.

B. Manslaughter

Manslaughter under Texas Penal Code Section 19.04 is recklessly causing the death of another person. This charge is used in situations where the prosecution believes the defendant killed the victim, however, may not have enough credible evidence to prove that the killing was intentional. Manslaughter is often included as a lesser offense in the jury instruction in a trial for murder.

C. Assault and Aggravated Assault

In the event a person used deadly force that did not result in the death of another person, they can be charged with aggravated assault. This offense starts with an assault on another person. An assault can occur when a person intentionally, knowingly, or recklessly causes bodily injury to another; intentionally or knowingly threatens another with imminent bodily injury; or intentionally or knowingly causes offensive or provocative contact with another that does not cause bodily injury. As you can see, almost all hostile confrontations can fit under any of these three scenarios. An assault becomes "aggravated" under Texas Penal Code § 22.02 when it results in serious bodily injury or a deadly weapon is used or exhibited. It is usually the presence of a firearm, as a deadly weapon, that causes an incident which would otherwise be a Class C misdemeanor assault to suddenly get elevated to a second degree felony of aggravated assault.

D. Terroristic Threat

Many prosecutors have chosen to use the terroristic threat statute to prosecute people who have expressed a threat to use force against another. This statute is found in Texas Penal Code Section 22.07(a)(2), wherein it is a Class B misdemeanor to threaten to commit any offense involving violence to any person with the intent to place any person in fear of imminent serious bodily injury. This is the easiest of the assaultive offenses to charge and prove because it is not necessary for the prosecutor to show that a person actually suffered an injury or had a fear of harm, but only that the defendant wanted to put the victim in fear.

CRIMES INVOLVING DEADLY FORCE

1. **Murder:** *See* Tex. Penal Code § 19.02
2. **Manslaughter:** *See* Tex. Penal Code § 19.04
3. **Aggravated Assault:** *See* Tex. Penal Code § 22.02
    - Includes pointing a gun at another, shooting at another without provable intent to kill, and firing warning shots.
4. **Terroristic Threat:** *See* Tex. Penal Code § 22.07

III. CRIMES AGAINST SOCIETY

Many crimes do not have a direct victim (also known as a complainant). A person who displays a firearm or discharges a firearm when it is not a direct threat to a specific individual falls into this category of crime.

A. Disorderly conduct

People commonly call the display of a handgun "brandishing," although this word is not used in the Texas Penal Code. Texas law criminalizes the general display of a firearm as either disorderly conduct or deadly conduct. If a person intentionally or knowingly displays a firearm or other deadly weapon in a public place in a manner calculated to alarm, this is an act of disorderly conduct. It is important to remember that this crime includes the display of any deadly weapon, such as knives and clubs. It also includes black powder weapons, even though these guns are excluded from the definition of "firearm" in Texas Penal Code Section 46.01(3). It is an undisputed historical fact that a lead ball shot from a black powder gun can kill a human. The complicated language of the disorderly conduct statute (Texas Penal Code Section 42.01(a)(8)) had gone uninterpreted by the appellate courts for decades. In May 2019, the Texas Court of Criminal Appeals finally clarified the proper standard to apply to the conduct of a person who displays a deadly weapon, including a firearm, in public. "[T]o be guilty of disorderly conduct under Penal Code Section 42.01(a)(8), a person must intentionally and knowingly display a firearm in a public place in a manner that he knows is likely, under an objective standard of reasonableness, to frighten the average, ordinary person." *See State v. Ross*, 573 S.W.3d 817, 825 (Tex. Crim. App. 2019).

The discharge of a firearm can be an act of disorderly conduct in two different ways. If a firearm is discharged on or across a public road, it is a Class C misdemeanor. It is a separate act of disorderly conduct to discharge a firearm in a public place that is not a shooting range, which is a Class B misdemeanor. You may think to yourself that shooting across a road is inherently more dangerous than shooting in a different public place, so why is the punishment lower? Sometimes the answer is simply, "because that's the way the Texas Legislature wrote it."

B. Deadly conduct

Somewhat similar to disorderly conduct, the crime of deadly conduct can be committed in two separate fashions, displaying and discharging a firearm. *See* Tex. Penal Code § 22.05. The display of a firearm is an act of deadly conduct if a person recklessly points a firearm at or in the direction of another person, putting that person in imminent danger of serious bodily injury. It is immaterial if the firearm is loaded or unloaded. The discharge of a firearm can constitute the crime of deadly conduct if it is done at or in the direction of an individual or a habitation, building, or vehicle when the shooter is reckless about whether or not the habitation, building, or vehicle is occupied.

C. Discharging a firearm within the city limits

Virtually every city, town, or village has adopted an ordinance against discharging a firearm within its incorporated limits. Violations of municipal ordinances are generally Class C misdemeanors punishable by a fine of up to $500. These city ordinances can run the gamut of being narrowly drawn with several defenses, *i.e.* discharge in self-defense or discharge by a police officer, to very broad with no defenses.

However, the State of Texas has determined that if the discharge of a firearm is done recklessly and it occurs in a city of 100,000 or more people, then that act is severe enough to constitute a Class A misdemeanor. *See* Tex. Penal Code § 42.12. The legislature has concluded that there is a greater risk of harm to persons and property because of the larger population.

CRIMES AGAINST THE PUBLIC INVOLVING A FIREARM

1. **Display of Firearms:**
   a. It is disorderly conduct to intentionally or knowingly display a firearm or other deadly weapon in a public place in a manner calculated to alarm. See Tex. Penal Code § 42.01(a)(8);
   b. It is deadly conduct to recklessly engage in conduct with a firearm that places another person in imminent danger of serious bodily injury. See Tex. Penal Code § 22.05(a);
   c. It is the unlawful carrying of a handgun if a person carries a handgun and intentionally displays the handgun in plain view of another person in a public place when not carried in a holster. See Tex. Penal Code § 46.02(a-5).
2. **Discharge of Firearms:**
   a. It is disorderly conduct to intentionally or knowingly discharge a firearm in a public place (other than a public road or shooting range). See Tex. Penal Code § 42.01(a)(7);
   b. It is disorderly conduct to intentionally or knowingly discharge a firearm across a public road. See Tex. Penal Code § 42.01(a)(9);
   c. It is prohibited to recklessly discharge a firearm in a city of 100,000 persons or more. See Tex. Penal Code § 42.12(a);

> **CRIMES AGAINST THE PUBLIC INVOLVING A FIREARM (CONT'D)**
>
> d. It is deadly conduct to knowingly discharge a firearm at or in the direction of one or more people, or if you discharge a firearm at or in the direction of a habitation, building, or vehicle and you do so with reckless disregard as to whether that habitation, building, or vehicle is occupied. *See* Tex. Penal Code § 22.05(b);
>
> e. It may also be a crime under a specific city ordinance (check your local statutes).

EXAMPLE:

Jim is entering the freeway. He inadvertently cuts off Marvin, who takes great exception to having to hit his brakes while cruising at 70 mph. Jim exits the freeway a mile later, and Marvin follows him onto the feeder road. As they both approach the next red light, Marvin stops next to Jim and begins screaming obscenities at him. Jim is startled by this act of aggression and wants to do something to make Marvin leave him alone. Jim then grabs his handgun from his console, rolls down his window, and shows it to Marvin. Jim achieves his objective and Marvin backs off, but Marvin calls 911, gives the operator his location, and says that Jim pointed a gun at him. The police respond and pull Jim over a few miles down the road; Marvin pulls over, also. The police talk to Marvin first since he was the one who called 911. They then speak to Jim, who tells them where to find the handgun in his console. Jim explains that Marvin randomly pulled up beside him and began yelling at him and that he showed Marvin his gun for the purposes of warning him so that he would be left alone, but Jim emphatically states that he did not point the gun at Marvin.

After calling the district attorney's office, the police arrest Jim. What crimes can Jim be charged with? You may have noticed that many of the crimes discussed in this Chapter have very similar elements. Technically, Jim's action of displaying his handgun in an effort to scare Marvin into leaving him alone could result in Jim being charged with aggravated assault because he exhibited a deadly weapon in a way that threatened Marvin with imminent bodily injury; deadly conduct because he recklessly displayed a firearm that put another person in imminent danger of bodily injury; terroristic threat because he intended to cause fear in Marvin; or disorderly conduct because he displayed his firearm in a public place in a manner calculated to alarm. During Jim's prosecution for any of these crimes, he may argue self-defense if he can articulate any facts that show that Marvin's provocation of him was more than verbal. Ultimately, the jury would have the job of determining whether or not Jim had a reasonable belief (a belief that would be held by an ordinary and prudent person in the same circumstances) that at the time he displayed his handgun, Marvin's actions presented an imminent threat of unlawful force or deadly force.

IV. THE AFTERMATH

When a person has found themselves in a position where they have used force or deadly force, what should they do to help increase the chances the police investigation will exonerate them and implicate the aggressive law-breaker?

WHAT DO I DO IMMEDIATELY AFTER I USE MY FIREARM?

1. Make sure that the threat is contained or neutralized;
2. Return your firearm to safekeeping;
3. Call 911 and tell them you (or another person) have been the victim of a crime. Give the operator your location and description. Avoid giving any unnecessary information, and avoid telling them you shot someone. It may be wise to suggest an ambulance is needed. Then hang up with 911.
4. Call the U.S. LawShield Emergency Hotline and follow the instructions your program attorney gives you;
5. Wait for the police, and do not touch any evidence;
6. If directed by your attorney, provide the police only simple details of the crime against you;
7. Be careful of police questions, and always be ready to invoke your right to silence and your right to counsel at any time.

› CHAPTER TWELVE ‹

LAW OF HANDGUN CARRY: PART I
QUALIFICATIONS
To Carry A Handgun

In 1995, the Texas Legislature passed a law allowing for the issuance of Concealed Handgun Licenses ("CHL"). It was a great change in the law as it existed prior to 1995, but carrying a visible handgun continued to be strictly prohibited. On June 13, 2015, Governor Greg Abbott signed a bill which forever altered over 140 years of Texas firearms law. It took a great deal of political wrangling, but Texas became the 46th state in the Union to recognize some form of legalizing the open carry of handguns in public places. Therefore, on January 1, 2016, a CHL in Texas officially became simply a License to Carry a Handgun.

It was not necessary for people who held a Texas CHL to apply for a new license, undergo any additional training, or otherwise alter or supplement their valid CHL. Once a CHL holder renewed their license, they would receive a Texas LTC.

In Texas, qualified individuals may still obtain an LTC, which allows the carrying of a concealed or visibly carried holstered handgun on or about their person for any lawful purpose. To obtain an LTC, a person must meet certain requirements and submit an application to the Texas Department of Public Safety ("DPS"). An LTC only allows for the lawful carry of handguns; the license does not cover long guns or any other type of weapon.

The latest major change occurred on June 16, 2021, with the signing of House Bill 1927 (The Firearm Carry Act of 2021), which allowed for "Texas Constitutional Carry." Although people can still acquire, renew, and retain an LTC, HB 1927 primarily allowed an additional subset of qualifying individuals to carry a firearm in non-prohibited places without first obtaining a recognized license or permit to carry a handgun.

I. THE EVOLUTION OF THE TEXAS HANDGUN CARRY LAW

Despite its reputation as being a "gun-friendly state," various concealed carry laws were proposed but ultimately defeated in every Texas legislative session from 1983 to 1991. In 1993, the legislature passed a law calling for a statewide referendum on CHLs, but Governor Ann Richards vetoed the bill. It wasn't until 1995 that the legislature finally passed "shall-issue" concealed carry, which then Governor George W. Bush signed into law. The law went into effect on January 1, 1996, and the Texas Department of Public Safety was able to train 2,000 instructors in time to meet the more than 200,000 initial applicants that followed. As of December 31, 2020, there were 1,626,242 LTC holders in the State of Texas.

Texas Government Code Chapter 411, Subchapter H, entitled "License to Carry a Handgun," contains the law on how handgun licenses are administered in Texas. Throughout this Chapter, we will discuss the qualifications, requirements, application process, and benefits of having an LTC in the State of Texas.

Additionally, this Chapter will discuss the Texas Constitutional Carry alternative, volunteer emergency services personnel, and first responders.

II. QUALIFICATIONS FOR AND STEPS TO GET AN LTC
A. Persons who are legally qualified to obtain an LTC

In this section, we will discuss the requirements to apply for a Texas LTC, as well as potential disqualifications. In addition to the requirements listed below, applicants must also complete state-mandated education with an LTC instructor certified by the Texas Department of Public Safety and demonstrate proficiency with a handgun, which can be of any caliber.

Section 411.172 of the Texas Government Code states that to be eligible for an LTC in Texas, a person must:
1) be a legal resident of the state for the six-months prior to an application (this requirement is inapplicable for non-resident LTC applications);
2) be at least 21 years of age, or age 18 if the person is an active or honorably discharged member of the armed forces or a protected person under certain family violence protective orders;
3) not have been convicted of a felony;

4) not have been charged with a Class A or B misdemeanor or convicted of one within the five years preceding an application;
5) not be charged with the crime of Disorderly Conduct as outlined in Section 42.01 of the Texas Penal Code, or be convicted of Disorderly Conduct within the five years preceding an application;
6) not be a fugitive from justice for any felony, Class A misdemeanor, Class B misdemeanor, or any equivalent offense;
7) not be a chemically dependent person;
8) not be incapable of exercising sound judgment with respect to the proper use and storage of a handgun;
9) be fully qualified under federal and state law to purchase a handgun;
10) not have been finally determined by a court to be delinquent in making child support payments;
11) not have been finally determined by a court to be delinquent in the payment of state taxes;
12) not be currently restricted under a court protective order or subject to a restraining order affecting the spousal relationship, other than a restraining order solely affecting property interests;
13) not have been adjudicated as a juvenile delinquent for a felony-level offense within the 10 years preceding an application; and
14) not make any material misrepresentation, and a person must not fail to disclose any material fact in the application.

Most of the qualifications are straightforward; however, some require further explanation.

B. What does it mean to be a "chemically dependent person" so as to be disqualified from receiving an LTC?

A person is legally disqualified from receiving an LTC if that person is "chemically dependent." Texas Government Code Section 411.172(c) states that a person is a chemically dependent person if he or she has been convicted at least twice within the 10-year period prior to an application for an LTC of any Class B misdemeanor or greater offense involving alcohol or controlled substances, or if he or she is found by a court to be a chemically dependent person in any other proceeding. In addition, Texas Government Code Section 411.171 specifically defines "chemically dependent person" to include a "person who frequently or repeatedly becomes intoxicated by excessive indulgence in alcohol or uses controlled substances or dangerous drugs so as to acquire a fixed habit and an involuntary tendency to become intoxicated or use substances as often as the opportunity is presented." Individuals who possess any of the characteristics listed in this section will not legally qualify for an LTC under Texas law.

> **PRACTICAL LEGAL TIP**
>
> Texas Government Code Section 411.173 allows non-residents, who are otherwise qualified, to obtain a Texas License To Carry a Handgun. –Kirk

C. What does it mean to be "incapable of exercising sound judgment" so as to be disqualified from receiving an LTC?

Texas Government Code Section 411.172(d) states the different ways in which a person may be deemed incapable of exercising sound judgment. First, it may mean that a person "has been diagnosed by a licensed physician as suffering from a psychiatric disorder or condition that causes or is likely to cause substantial impairment in judgment, mood, perception, impulse control, or intellectual ability." The statute goes on to state that if the condition is in remission but is reasonably likely to redevelop at a future time, or if the person "requires continuous medical care" to avoid redeveloping the condition, the person is incapable of exercising sound judgment and may be disqualified from obtaining an LTC.

Second, it may mean that a person "has been diagnosed by a licensed physician, determined by a review board or similar authority, or declared by a court to be incompetent to manage the person's own affairs."

Finally, it may mean that a person "has entered a plea of not guilty by reason of insanity" in any criminal proceeding. If any of these apply to an applicant, then that person will be deemed incapable of exercising sound judgment and will not meet one of the basic requirements to qualify for an LTC in Texas. *See* Tex. Gov't Code § 411.172(d).

Persons who are currently receiving psychiatric treatment may be disqualified from holding a Texas LTC while undergoing treatment. The State of Texas considers the following to constitute evidence that a person has a psychiatric disorder or condition described in Texas Government Code Section 411.172(e):

1) involuntary psychiatric hospitalization;
2) psychiatric hospitalization;
3) inpatient or residential substance abuse treatment in the preceding five-year period;
4) diagnosis in the preceding five-year period by a licensed physician that the person is dependent on alcohol, a controlled substance, or a similar substance; or
5) diagnosis at any time by a licensed physician that the person suffers or has suffered from a psychiatric disorder or condition consisting of or relating to:

(A) schizophrenia or delusional disorder;
(B) bipolar disorder;
(C) chronic dementia, whether caused by illness, brain defect, or brain injury;
(D) dissociative identity disorder;
(E) intermittent explosive disorder; or
(F) antisocial personality disorder.

Although most individuals who fall into one of the above categories may be prohibited from holding an LTC, if an applicant can provide a certificate from a licensed physician practicing psychiatry stating that the person's disorder or condition is in remission and is not likely to develop at a future time, then the applicant may still qualify for an LTC, because the applicant will not be judged to be incapable of exercising sound judgment.

D. If you don't disclose, you can expect your application to be delayed or denied!

The factor that delays the majority of applications revolves around when a person fails to make a full disclosure of material fact in their application. To qualify for a Texas LTC, a person must not make any material misrepresentation or fail to disclose any material fact in his or her LTC application. *See* Tex. Gov't Code § 411.172(a)(14). Most often, this is due to a person failing to disclose a criminal conviction of one nature or another.

Many applicants forget about things that may have happened many years ago, but which require disclosure in the application. The best practice is: when in doubt, disclose! Otherwise, a person may face unwanted delays or even a denial of their application. Note: be very careful in the wording of your disclosures. We have seen many applicants encounter difficulties from not using precise descriptions of their legal history, medical condition, *etc.* Be careful with your words!

E. What if I received deferred adjudication? Can I get an LTC?

If a person received deferred adjudication, probation without a conviction, as a result of a criminal charge, that person may still be eligible for an LTC under specific conditions. Section 411.1711 of the Texas Government Code states that orders of deferred adjudication against a person for certain crimes—including felonies—will not prevent a person from obtaining an LTC.

If a person has been charged with a crime which resulted in an order of deferred adjudication more than 10 years prior to his or her application for an LTC and the person received deferred adjudication for any crime except the following felony offenses, then the person may be eligible to apply for an LTC. Persons who received deferred adjudication for any of the following felony offenses are permanently barred from holding an LTC:
1) Title 5 of the Texas Penal Code: violent crimes against people;
2) Chapter 29 of the Texas Penal Code: robbery;
3) Sections 25.07 or 25.072 of the Texas Penal Code: violating a court-issued protective order; or
4) Section 30.02(c)(2) or (d): burglary of a habitation.
See Tex. Gov't Code § 411.1711.

What this means is that persons who have received deferred adjudication for criminal offenses not listed above may be eligible to apply for and obtain a Texas LTC after 10 years from the date of their deferred adjudication order.

F. What is "deferred adjudication"?

Under Article 42A.101 of the Texas Code of Criminal Procedure, "if in the judge's opinion the best interest of society and the defendant will be served, the judge may, after receiving a plea of guilty or plea of *nolo contendere*, hearing the evidence, and finding that it substantiates the defendant's guilt, defer further proceedings without entering an adjudication of guilt, and place the defendant on community supervision."

Deferred adjudication is, therefore, the legal act of either accepting culpability for a crime or refusing to contest the culpability of a crime, without being actually convicted of the crime. Deferred adjudication is effectively a form of probation: a defendant is released back into society under the condition that the defendant will stay out of legal trouble for a period of time imposed by a judge. At the conclusion of the probationary period, the defendant will not be considered convicted for most purposes.

G. Suspension and revocation of an LTC

1. What is the difference between suspension and revocation?

To begin, it is important to know that there is a difference between a suspension and a revocation of a person's LTC. A suspension is only temporary, and a person's license may be reinstated without the necessity of submitting a new application for an LTC. This means that a person will not have to go through the rigors of the application process or the classroom requirements again in order to regain their LTC. On the other hand, a revocation means that the Texas DPS has decided that a person's LTC shall be terminated and in order for the person to ultimately regain the LTC, they must reapply from step one by attending an LTC class and submitting the application with the applicable fees. *See* Tex. Gov't Code §§ 411.186, 441.187.

2. Under what circumstances can the Texas DPS revoke an LTC?

Texas Government Code Section 411.186 governs LTC revocation and states that a person's LTC may be revoked for any of the following reasons:

If the person was not entitled to an LTC at the time it was issued

If an LTC is revoked because a person was not entitled to be issued an LTC, the person may apply as a new applicant two years after the date of revocation so long as the reason for revocation no longer applies when the new application is made. If the reason for revocation exists on the two-year anniversary, the person may apply for a new LTC two years after the cause no longer exists. *See* Tex. Gov't Code § 411.186(a).

Misrepresentations and failure to disclose

If the person made a material misrepresentation or failed to disclose a material fact on their original application or on their renewal application, DPS may revoke their LTC. If an LTC is revoked for this reason, the person may apply as a new applicant two years after the date of revocation so long as the reason for revocation no longer applies when the new application is made. If the reason for revocation does apply on the two-year anniversary, the person may apply for a new LTC two years after the cause no longer exists. *See* Tex. Gov't Code § 411.186(a).

No longer meets the requirements

If, after receiving their LTC, the person no longer meets one of the eligibility requirements for possessing an LTC, the license may be revoked. If an LTC is revoked for this reason, the person may apply as a new applicant two years after the date of revocation so long as the reason for revocation no longer applies when the new application is made. If the reason for revocation does apply on the two-year anniversary, the person may apply for a new LTC two years after the cause no longer exists. *See* Tex. Gov't Code § 411.186(a).

Three strikes

If the Texas DPS determines that the person's license has already been suspended twice before for the same reason, the license is revoked on the third occurrence of the same suspendable conduct. If an LTC is revoked for this reason, the person may apply as a new applicant two years after the date of revocation so long as the reason for revocation no longer applies when the new application is made. If the reason for revocation does apply on the two-year anniversary, the person may apply for a new LTC two years after the cause no longer exists. *See* Tex. Gov't Code § 411.186(a).

Failure to pay fee

If the person submits an application fee that is dishonored or reversed, DPS may revoke the LTC. *See* Tex. Gov't Code § 411.186(a).

The requirement of Texas Government Code Section 411.186 that a person whose LTC was revoked be free of the ineligibility for two years leads to the apparent result that a person whose LTC is revoked for a Class A or B misdemeanor or crime of disorderly conduct would have to wait for two additional years after the five-year ineligibility period. An LTC holder whose license was revoked because they were placed on deferred adjudication for a felony that is exempt from permanent disqualification has to wait two additional years after the 10-year ineligibility period.

3. Under what circumstances can the Texas DPS suspend an LTC?

Texas Government Code Section 411.187 governs suspensions of Texas LTCs and states that a person's LTC may be suspended for any of the following reasons:

Charged with a crime

The person is charged with a Class A or B misdemeanor, a crime of disorderly conduct, or a felony by information or indictment. In such cases, the LTC is suspended for as long as the charges are pending, and depending on the outcome of the case, when the matter is resolved, the person's LTC will either be reinstated in the event of dismissal or acquittal, or revoked upon the person's conviction. *See* Tex. Gov't Code § 411.187.

Failure to update information

The person fails to notify DPS of a change of name, address, or special status as an LTC instructor, a judge, a spouse of a judge, or a prosecutor. A suspension under these circumstances lasts for 30 days. *See* Tex. Gov't Code § 411.187.

Family violence protective order

If the person commits an act of family violence and is the subject of an active protective order under the Texas Family Code, then that person's LTC is suspended for as long as the protective order is active. *See* Tex. Gov't Code § 411.187.

Emergency protective order

If the person was arrested for an offense of family violence or stalking, and is the subject of a magistrate's emergency protective order issued under the Code of Criminal Procedure, then that person's LTC is suspended for as long as the order for emergency protection is active. *See* Tex. Gov't Code § 411.187.

4. What happens if my LTC expires while it is suspended?

If you are unfortunate enough to have your Texas LTC expire during your period of suspension, you may or may not be able to renew your license. A Texas LTC must be renewed within one year after the expiration to avoid retaking the class, paying fees, and submitting a new application. If more than a year has elapsed since expiration or during the period of suspension, you will have to reapply from step one. *See* 37 Tex. Admin. Code § 6.16.

5. Procedure for revocation or suspension of an LTC

LTCs are not automatically suspended or revoked even if one of the elements of revocation or suspension as discussed above apply—the revocation or suspension requires law enforcement action before it actually occurs. Texas law allows a law enforcement officer to seize the physical LTC card of a person who the officer suspects will be subject to revocation or suspension. Once dispossessed of their physical LTC card, a person effectively no longer possesses an LTC because they must have physical possession of their LTC to carry under the authority of an LTC. However, regardless of whether the officer does seize the physical LTC card, the officer will complete an affidavit stating the reasons why revocation or suspension is recommended and forward the affidavit to DPS. DPS will then make a decision on whether to revoke or suspend the license. If DPS decides to proceed with the revocation or suspension, then DPS will send the LTC holder a letter stating the reason for revocation or suspension and require the LTC holder to surrender their license to DPS within 10 days of receipt of the letter unless the person requests a hearing and the request is received by DPS within 30 days of receipt of the letter. *See* Tex. Gov't Code § 411.185.

In addition, there are two scenarios where a person's LTC can be suspended before DPS takes action. If a person is the subject of an emergency protective order pursuant to the Code of Criminal Procedure, a magistrate shall suspend the LTC of the person who is the subject of the order, pursuant to Texas Code of Criminal Procedure Article 17.292(l). Once DPS becomes aware of the matter, DPS will also follow its procedures as outlined in Texas Government Code Section 411.187 as stated above. Likewise, for individuals who are subject to a protective order issued under the Texas Family Code, the court that issues a protective order shall suspend the LTC of the person who was found to have committed family violence, pursuant to Texas Family Code Section 85.022(d). DPS will then also follow its procedures for revocation or suspension as outlined in Texas Government Code Section 411.187.

6. If my LTC is denied, revoked, or suspended, can I appeal?
Any LTC denial, revocation, or suspension may be appealed within 30 days of receiving official notice in the form of the notice letter discussed above from Texas DPS that the LTC has been denied, revoked, or suspended. A person must request a hearing in writing, and the written request for a hearing must be received by DPS within 30 days of the date the letter was received by the LTC holder. *See* Tex. Gov't Code § 411.180(e). A person can request a hearing online or by mail, *see* the Texas DPS website for additional information.

If no hearing is requested, then the denial, revocation, or suspension will be final and unappealable after the 30th day from receipt of written notice from DPS that the license was denied, revoked, or suspended, pursuant to Texas Government Code Section 411.180(g).

III. THE LTC APPLICATION AND PROCESS
A. The LTC application

A Texas LTC application packet containing all required information is necessary to obtain a license. The packet must be completed and submitted to the Texas Department of Public Safety. The packet can be downloaded and printed out or completed electronically at the Texas DPS website. Either method of submission is acceptable as applicants can begin the application process online, or they can print the application forms and mail them back to the DPS. The application requires personal identifying information including a valid driver's license or identification card; current demographic, address, and contact information; residential and employment information for the last five years; a valid email address; as well as personal background information, including information regarding any psychiatric, drug, alcohol, or criminal history from the applicant as described in Section 411.174 of the Texas Government Code. Back in 2017, the Texas Legislature added an incentive for Texans to get their Texas LTC by lowering the application fee from $140 to the true cost of processing the application, $40. This is one of the lowest fees for a handgun license in the United States. *See* Tex. Gov't Code § 411.174(6).

The process of completing the application requires a person to answer every question on the application—whether completed online or by hand. In addition, after the application has been submitted electronically, or DPS is in receipt of a paper application, applicants are required to submit fingerprints to DPS as part of a background check. LTC applicants must submit fingerprints electronically, unless the applicant resides in a county having a population of less than 46,000 and the applicant does not reside within a 25-mile radius of a facility with the capability to process digital or electronic fingerprints. Instructions on how to properly submit fingerprints to the DPS and the applicable fees for doing so are available on the DPS website. *See* Tex. Gov't Code § 411.175.

B. LTC class and shooting test

In order to obtain a Texas LTC, applicants must complete a state-mandated education course taught by a Texas DPS certified LTC instructor. These classes generally consist of a classroom portion of four to six hours of instruction, followed by a shooting test in which the applicant must demonstrate proficiency with their handgun. Any caliber of handgun may be used to demonstrate proficiency. This means that if a person does not have the physical capabilities to operate a large caliber handgun, they may use a .22 or a .25 to qualify for an LTC. Applicants for an LTC must take the class and pass both a written and shooting test in order to be qualified for an LTC. Without successfully passing both of these portions, a person's application will be denied. If a person fails either exam, the test results are required by law to be submitted to the Texas Department of Public Safety, where they will be kept on record. Applicants can take the classroom portion of the LTC qualification online. Of course, the shooting range portion must be done in person along with an additional one to two hours of range safety instruction for online course takers.

In order to obtain a passing score, applicants must complete the course with a minimum score of 70%. Once an applicant successfully completes both the written and shooting proficiency examinations, the LTC instructor may certify that he or she has established proficiency, and the applicant will be ready to submit his or her application to the DPS for approval and licensing. *See* 37 Tex. Admin. Code § 6.14.

C. LTC renewal

The expiration date of a license holder's LTC can be found on the front of their license. An original LTC may be valid up to the first birthday of the license holder after the fourth anniversary of the date of issuance. However, a renewed LTC is valid up to five years after the date of the expiration of the previous license. In either scenario, the LTC will expire on the license holder's birthday. *See* Tex. Gov't. Code § 411.183.

Typically, the DPS will contact the license holder by mail 60 days before the expiration of their LTC. However, even if a person has not received notice from the DPS, their license will still expire and they must still request a renewal (if they wish to do so). So long as a renewal applicant is eligible, the DPS must issue the renewed LTC within 45 days. For that reason, it is prudent to submit renewal materials no less than 45 days before the expiration. *See* Tex. Gov't. Code § 411.185.

A renewed LTC is valid for five years. An LTC may be renewed by mail by completing a Form LTC-77 and paying the applicable fee by money order, personal check, or cashier's check (note: the standard fee is $40); or online by visiting: https://txapps.texas.gov/txapp/txdps/ltc/. *See* Tex. Gov't. Code § 411.185.

IV. BENEFITS OF HAVING AN LTC

Generally, an LTC holder has more rights and privileges than a person carrying a handgun under Texas Constitutional Carry. Perhaps most appreciated benefit of having an LTC is that an LTC holder is allowed to carry at more locations than a Texas Constitutional Carrier, which will be discussed in depth later in this book. However, there are also other advantages to having an

LTC that often depend on one's lifestyle. These advantages come in many forms, but some of the biggest perks for an LTC holder include reciprocity with other states, ease in facilitating firearm transactions, and a heightened signage requirement for exclusion at an otherwise lawful location under Texas law.

A. Reciprocity with other states

Every state has the authority to determine whether or not their state will recognize a license or permit to carry a handgun issued by another state. Reciprocity is when states enter into an agreement with each other to recognize each other's carry licenses. However, states are not required to have reciprocity with one another, nor are they required to recognize another state's carry license. There are many states that issue their own licenses and refuse to recognize a carry license from another state. Conversely, there are states that choose to recognize some or all other states' carry licenses. Texas gives the governor authority to negotiate (with the assistance of the attorney general) reciprocity agreements with other states or to issue proclamations which will unilaterally recognize other states' carry licenses. Since each state is allowed to choose what other states' carry license will be recognized, there are several states that have carry licenses that Texas recognizes, but those states do not recognize a license to carry from Texas. There are also states that recognize a Texas LTC, but Texas does not recognize their license. In short, out-of-state recognition of a license or permit is of the utmost importance to many people. And, unless a state has permitless carry open to non-residents, generally, a person can only legally carry a handgun for self-defense through reciprocity while traveling in a different state.

States where you must have a Texas LTC

Many states honor a Texas LTC, and several states have permitless carry. *See* the end of Section V. However, as of the date of this writing, if you want to lawfully carry your concealed handgun in the following states, you will need to have an LTC:

Alabama	Colorado*	Delaware
Florida*	Georgia	Indiana
Louisiana	Michigan*	Nebraska
Nevada	New Mexico	North Carolina
North Dakota*	Ohio	Pennsylvania*
South Carolina*	Virginia	Wisconsin
Wyoming		

* Indicates that the state only recognizes a Texas LTC issued to a Texas resident.

Licenses or permits recognized by Texas

Alabama	Alaska	Arizona
Arkansas	California	Colorado
Connecticut	Delaware	Florida
Georgia	Hawaii	Idaho
Illinois	Indiana	Iowa
Kansas	Kentucky	Louisiana
Maryland	Massachusetts	Michigan
Mississippi	Missouri	Montana
Nebraska	Nevada	New Jersey
New Mexico	New York	North Carolina
North Dakota	Ohio	Oklahoma
Pennsylvania	Rhode Island	South Carolina
South Dakota	Tennessee	Utah
Virginia	Washington	West Virginia
Wyoming		

An out-of-state handgun carry license or permit holder must follow Texas law while in Texas, just like a Texas LTC holder must follow the law of the state they are visiting. Additionally, with the exceptions of firearms transactions and carrying in federal gun-free school zones, license or permit holders from other recognized states enjoy the same benefits as Texas LTC holders.

B. Facilitating firearm transactions

Generally, every person who purchases a firearm from a Federal Firearms Licensed dealer ("FFL") is subject to a background check through the National Instant Criminal Check System ("NICS"). Going through this system can sometimes lead to delays and erroneous denials due to mistaken identity. However, no NICS background check may be required if the transferee is legally exempt for reasons such as possessing a state-issued firearms license like a Texas LTC. *See* 18 U.S.C. § 922(t)(3).

Additionally, as many saw during the COVID-19 pandemic, firearms may be in such demand, and the availability so sparse, a license or permit to carry might get you that last firearm while the other guy is still waiting on his background check. For many who had LTCs, they were able to purchase a firearm without having to wait on NICS. For those who did not have an LTC and therefore needed a background check completed before they were allowed to purchase the firearm from the FFL dealer, they may have lost out on the ability to purchase. In times like these, although they may be rare, an LTC can be helpful for the law-abiding gun owner.

C. Signage requirement for LTC holders

Generally speaking, there is a heightened notice requirement when trying to exclude an LTC holder (compared to a Texas Constitutional Carrier) from carrying in an otherwise lawful place. *See* Tex. Penal Code §§ 30.06, 30.07.

Although this topic will be discussed more in Chapter 13, under the new law stemming from House Bill 1927, an unlicensed person may be excluded from property by several different forms; the only legal requirement is that the sign or notice is reasonably likely to come to the attention of the person entering the building. *See* Tex. Penal Code § 30.05. So, even signs such as these could be effective against a person carrying under Texas Constitutional Carry, and yet these signs are not considered effective notice to license holders:

As discussed more in Chapter 13, the courts in Texas will need to determine the legal effectiveness of any sign attempting to prohibit Texas Constitutional Carry that does not track language "substantially similar" to the new Texas Penal Code Section 30.05(c) signage requirement.

In short, because there is a specific statutory requirement on what is considered effective notice for an LTC holder, but there is a broad range of possibility of what notice is effective to exclude a Texas Constitutional Carrier, it is much easier to exclude a Texas Constitutional Carrier from an otherwise non-prohibited place.

D. Other perks

Lastly, some additional benefits of having an LTC include: additional protection in federal gun-free school zones and airports; added protection for school district employees; and heightened notice requirements to prohibit a license holder from carrying in a bar.

Added protection in federal Gun-Free School Zones

Generally, the federal Gun-Free School Zones Act prohibits carrying a firearm within 1,000 feet of a public, parochial, or private elementary, middle, or high school. This means that there is technically a law on the books that prohibits a person from carrying a firearm within 1,000 feet of school grounds. However, there are several exceptions to this law. Primarily among them is that this prohibition does not criminalize the carrying of a firearm by a person who holds a handgun permit or license from the state where the school is located. In other words, a person who has a Texas LTC can carry within 1,000 feet of Texas school grounds without committing a crime. So, a person will not be charged for violating the federal gun-free school zones law by merely carrying an accessible handgun in their vehicle while picking up or dropping off their child with a Texas LTC. However, people who do not have a resident LTC, and who do not fall under another exception, technically violate this federal law. *See* 18 U.S.C. § 922(q).

Added protection at airports
LTC holders are allowed "oopsies" at airports. When traveling by air, a license holder retains their ability to avoid arrest in the event they inadvertently leave their handgun in their carry-on baggage, as long as they promptly depart the secured area when notified they are in possession of a handgun and are allowed to depart. The unlicensed individual who leaves a handgun in their carry-on bag is given no such courtesies and may find themselves arrested and charged with a felony. *See* Tex. Penal Code § 46.03.

School district employees with an LTC
School district employees who have an LTC are protected if that person is an employee of a school district and has been issued a Texas LTC. Texas law protects that person's right to keep a firearm and ammunition concealed in his or her locked motor vehicle while it is parked in a school parking lot. In fact, Texas law prevents the school district from imposing any duties, restrictions, or reporting requirements on where or how firearms and ammunition are stored. However, these employment protections are not given to employees who do not possess a valid handgun license. *See* Tex. Edu. Code § 37.0815.

Surrounding the prohibition of carrying in a bar
Lastly, the statutory prohibition against carrying a handgun into a bar does not apply to a license holder unless the bar has posted its 51% sign in accordance with the law. So, in order to have notice that

a location is a bar, and thus a prohibited place, an LTC holder will need to be placed on notice by a 51% sign. For a Texas Constitutional Carrier, the individual will be liable for taking a handgun into a 51% establishment, even in the absence of a 51% sign. Whereas a license holder does not need to magically divine whether a place derives 51% or more of its income from the sale of alcohol for consumption on premises, that burden is on a Texas Constitutional Carrier. *See* Tex. Penal Code § 46.15(p).

V. QUALIFICATIONS FOR TEXAS CONSTITUTIONAL CARRY

In order to carry under the authority of Texas Constitutional Carry, in addition to meeting the qualifications to possess firearms and ammunition under federal law, a person:

1) must be 21 years of age or older;
2) must not be prohibited from possessing a firearm in a public place under Texas law; and
3) must not have been convicted in the previous five years of a misdemeanor crime of:
   (1) Assault Causes Bodily Injury;
   (2) Deadly Conduct;
   (3) Terroristic Threat;
   (4) Disorderly Conduct - Discharging a Firearm; or
   (5) Disorderly Conduct - Displaying a Firearm.

In other words, there are three main requirements in qualifying to carry a handgun under the authority of Texas Constitutional Carry:

Requirement 1: Must be 21 years of age or older.

Requirement 2: Must not be prohibited from possessing a firearm in a public place under Texas law.

Who is prohibited from possessing a firearm in a public place under Texas law?
1) felons: A person who has been convicted of a felony. *See* Tex. Penal Code § 46.04(a).
2) people convicted of Assault Family Violence: A person who has been convicted of a Class A misdemeanor assault involving a family or household member before the fifth anniversary or release from confinement or community supervision (whichever is later). *See* Tex. Penal Code § 46.04(b).
3) people under Certain Protective Orders: A person, other than a peace officer, subject to a protective order, who received notice of the order and before the expiration of the order. *See* Tex. Penal Code § 46.04(c).

Requirement 3: Within the past five years, the person must not have been convicted (a final judgment of guilt) of certain offenses:
1) Assault Causes Bodily Injury. *See* Tex. Penal Code § 22.01.
2) Deadly Conduct. *See* Tex. Penal Code § 22.05.
3) Terroristic Threat. *See* Tex. Penal Code § 22.07.
4) Disorderly Conduct - Discharging a Firearm. *See* Tex. Penal Code § 42.01(a)(7).
5) Disorderly Conduct - Displaying a Firearm. *See* Tex. Penal Code § 42.01(a)(8).

Note: Although carrying a handgun in a motor vehicle or watercraft is not generally referred to as "constitutional carry," a person who is a member of a criminal street gang and does not have an LTC is generally prohibited from carrying a handgun in a motor vehicle or watercraft. The law has moved from Texas Penal Code Section 46.02(a-1)(2)(C) to Texas Penal Code Section 46.04(a-1). Interestingly enough, this prohibition does not extend to a person who is a criminal street gang member but otherwise qualified to carry a handgun under the authority of Texas Constitutional Carry, carrying a handgun *outside* of their motor vehicle or watercraft (*e.g.*, on a public sidewalk). Chalk it up to another quirk of Texas gun law.

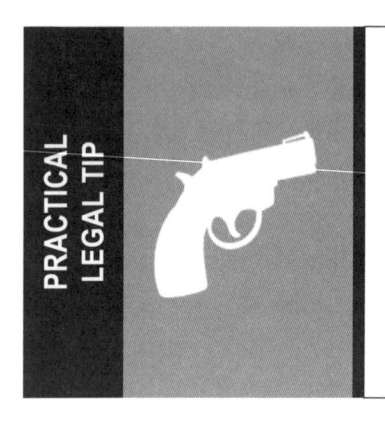

> **PRACTICAL LEGAL TIP**
>
> There is no requirement that a person carrying under the Firearm Carry Act of 2021 be a Texas resident. Meaning, an out-of-state person who otherwise meets the requirements above will qualify for Texas Constitutional Carry.
> –Emily

States that do not require a license or permit to carry a handgun
With the passage of the Firearm Carry Act of 2021, Texas joined an ever-growing list of states that do not require a license or permit to generally carry a handgun in public.

Alaska	Arizona	Arkansas
Iowa	Idaho	Kansas
Kentucky	Maine	Mississippi
Missouri	Montana	New Hampshire
North Dakota*	Oklahoma	South Dakota
Tennessee	Texas	Utah
Vermont	West Virginia	Wyoming*
Note: Current as of October, 2021.		

* Indicates you must be a resident of the state to qualify for permitless carry

› CHAPTER THIRTEEN ‹

LAW OF HANDGUN CARRY: PART II
METHODS AND NOTICE
For Legally Carrying in Texas

With the creation of Texas Constitutional Carry, the 87th Texas Legislature reorganized and changed several provisions of Texas law. Although the law surrounding LTC holders did not change as drastically, this Act, which added an additional subset of people who could otherwise legally carry in Texas without an LTC, changed Texas carry law as we know it.

For those unfamiliar with the law, "constitutional carry" is a broad term that applies to states that do not require a license or permit to carry a handgun. The name "constitutional carry" has caught on in recent years as a reference to the Second Amendment of the United States Constitution, with supporters pointing to the text of the Second Amendment as their "permit" or "license" to carry a handgun in public. It is important to note that every state that enacts constitutional carry has a unique version, and not every "constitutional carry" is the same.

Texas legislators have introduced constitutional carry legislation every session since 2013. But, in 2021, constitutional carry for handguns finally became a reality in Texas after the 87th Legislature passed, and Governor Abbott signed, House Bill 1927 (The Firearm Carry Act of 2021), introduced by State Representative Matt Schaefer.

The general idea of Texas Constitutional Carry is that every person who is not prohibited by law from legally owning a handgun should be free to carry it openly or concealed in public and not fear prosecution for simply exercising their right.

However, the law surrounding Texas Constitutional Carry is not simply common sense. We wish we could say it was easy—if you can legally buy a firearm, you can carry a handgun in public without a license—but that is not the case. As discussed in the previous chapter, age limitations, who may lawfully carry, how a person must carry, where carrying is allowed, and other restrictions apply.

Although where a person may carry will be discussed in depth in the next chapter, we first need to start with some basics: how to carry a handgun and what signs apply to what category of handgun carrier.

I. HOW TO CARRY A HANDGUN
A. Holster requirement simplified

Both license holders and constitutional carriers can carry openly or concealed. To conceal carry a firearm, it is critical that no part of the handgun be visible based on ordinary observation. Easy ways to conceal carry include keeping the firearm in a pocket, bag, holster, case, or jacket when no part of the handgun is visible in plain view. This law is still the same as before the passage of Texas Constitutional Carry.

However, the 87th Legislature's passing of HB 1927, SB 550, and HB 2112 did change the law of open carry in Texas. These bills struck all "belt or shoulder" references from Texas law, allowing an individual to carry a partially or wholly visible handgun in a belt holster, shoulder holster, ankle holster, appendix holster, pilot holster, chest holster, or backpack holster, to name a few. Whereas before September 1, 2021, a person would be limited to only carrying a visible handgun in a belt or shoulder holster, the types of holster now legal under Texas law are endless. Additionally, this change in law allows a person to use a mounted vehicle holster (such as a magnetic dashboard holster) when carrying in his or her vehicle.

B. Intentional display of a handgun when it is not in a holster remains a crime

When a handgun is purposely displayed and is not in a holster, it is the crime of "intentional display of a handgun" in public. Therefore, our discussion will focus on what is legal under this standard. *See* Tex. Penal Code § 46.02.

The law simply states that a person commits a crime "if the person carries a handgun and intentionally displays the handgun in plain view of another person in a public place." An unintentional, accidental, or inadvertent display is not a crime under Texas Penal Code Section 46.02. Likewise, to be a crime under this subsection, any intentional display of a handgun must take place in a public place; if you are on your own property, you are not in a public place. Additionally, there is a major exception to this crime: if the handgun was partially or wholly visible but was carried in a holster, the person has not violated Section 46.02. It is important to note that this prohibition extends to LTC holders. LTC holders are not exempt from Texas Penal Code Section 46.02 unless their handgun is carried concealed or in a holster. Since this offense involves intentionally displaying a handgun outside of a holster, the protection offered by Texas Penal Code Section 46.15(b)(6) does not apply.

Must have "intentionally" displayed to be a crime

The statute's use of the word "intentional" refers to a person's culpable mental state. In other words, a person must have "intended" to display the handgun outside of a holster. "Intentionally" is defined in Texas Penal Code Section 6.03(a): "[a] person acts intentionally, or with intent, with respect to the nature of his conduct or to a result of his conduct when it is his conscious objective or desire to engage in the conduct or cause the result." "Intentionally" is the highest degree of culpable mental state in the Texas Penal Code, meaning that it will be more difficult for a prosecutor to prove that you were intentional in your conduct than it would be to prove the lower-degree mental states of "knowingly" (being aware of the nature of your conduct or that a certain result will happen as a result of your actions) or "recklessly" (being aware of but consciously disregarding a substantial and unjustifiable risk that the circumstances exist or the result will occur).

Obvious examples of intentionally displaying your handgun would be pulling your shirt up to reveal to another person a portion or all of your handgun that is tucked into your waistband without a holster, while consciously desiring that they would see it. Another example would be simply pulling your handgun out of its holster and waving it in the air in front of somebody in order to frighten them. If you consciously desire that another person see your handgun or a portion of it, and you cause the other person to see it, then you have intentionally displayed your handgun. It is not enough that you were aware that it was possible for your handgun to become exposed, and it later does. You must have the conscious objective or desire to display or expose your handgun in a public place.

EXAMPLE:

Tony is in the grocery store to pick up a box of Frosted Flakes. When he reaches for the last box, Mildred snatches it away before he can grab it. Tony reacts by pulling up his shirt and showing Mildred that he has a Glock in his waistband. Mildred is startled and tells the store manager, who alerts the off-duty deputy sheriff who is working security.

Tony is very likely in trouble, because he engaged in an action to make sure that Mildred saw that he was carrying a handgun. The prosecutors will assert that it was his intention to display his gun in an effort to scare Mildred away from the last box of Frosted Flakes.

C. Unintentional displays of a handgun are not a crime

What do you do if a gust of wind picks up your shirt and shows off your 1911 handgun while it is not in a holster? What about when your pants accidentally split revealing your Spiderman underwear and your previously concealed Sig Sauer? How about the time your purse accidentally comes open, flashing your Glock? The good news is that none of these incidents are crimes under Texas law.

If a person's concealed handgun becomes unconcealed inadvertently and it is not being carried in a holster, such as by "flashing" or "printing," the person is not breaking the law. Texas law provides that a person must intentionally display his or her handgun in a public place to another person in order to be guilty of this crime under Section 46.02 of the Texas Penal Code.

> **EXAMPLE:**
> Tony is in the grocery store and reaches up to get a box of Frosted Flakes from the top shelf. While doing this, his shirt is pulled up and exposes the Glock he keeps tucked into his waistband so that he doesn't have to carry it in a holster. Mildred is standing next to him and sees that he has a gun. Mildred tells the store manager, who alerts the off-duty sheriff who then detains Tony.

Is Tony in trouble for displaying his handgun when it is not being carried in a holster? Probably not, because the crime requires a person to intentionally display their handgun to another individual. There is no evidence that Tony's handgun was displayed intentionally or that he knew Mildred was looking at him at the time his shirt came up.

> **PRACTICAL LEGAL TIP**
>
> A Texas LTC holder may present their license in place of his or her driver's license, except while driving, and it must be recognized as valid proof of personal identification by state and local governments and businesses. —Kirk

D. What is "printing," and is it a crime?

If you have chosen to carry your handgun concealed in your shirt or pants pocket instead of in a holster and it is "printing," are you committing a crime? First, printing is not a legal term, and printing is not a crime. Second, the word "printing" does not appear in the Texas Penal Code. "Printing" is a common street term. It generally refers to when the outline or characteristics of a handgun become visible under the clothing of a person. Imagine a person in a skin-tight spandex outfit who is carrying a full-size Glock 9mm pistol under the outfit. The outline of the gun would be clearly visible; however, since the gun is concealed by a layer of spandex, the gun is still concealed. It may be boorish behavior, bad taste, or even unwise, but under the plain language of the statute, it does not appear to be a crime, and no Texas appellate courts have construed printing to be a crime.

II. WHAT SIGNS APPLY TO ME?

A. Legally effective signage for license holders and for persons legally carrying under the Firearm Carry Act of 2021

Just as verbal notice (that firearms are not allowed in an otherwise lawful place) is enough to put anyone—license holder or constitutional carrier—on notice, there are also signs that apply to both license holders and constitutional carriers universally. Primary among them—51% signs and 46.03 signs.

51% sign
If an establishment sells alcohol for on-premises consumption and receives 51% or more of its income from alcohol sales, it must display a 51% sign to legally give notice to all persons that the place is prohibited. However, only license holders are provided relief from criminal liability under Texas Penal Code Section 46.15(p) if the establishment does not provide effective notice by posting signage in compliance with Texas Government Code Section 411.204. To make matters worse, unlawfully carrying into a 51% establishment is a felony of the third degree.

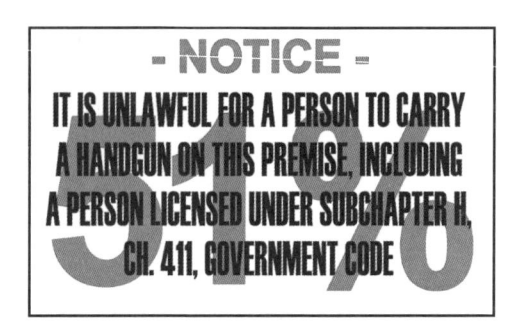

- NOTICE -
IT IS UNLAWFUL FOR A PERSON TO CARRY A HANDGUN ON THIS PREMISE, INCLUDING A PERSON LICENSED UNDER SUBCHAPTER H, CH. 411, GOVERNMENT CODE

As mentioned in the previous chapter, constitutional carriers **beware!** Although LTC holders require the presence of a 51% sign to receive notice that a place is a 51% establishment, constitutional carriers do not need to see a 51% sign to be in violation of carrying in a prohibited place. Meaning, constitutional carriers can be held responsible if they do not magically divine whether a place receives 51% or more of its income from the sale of alcohol for consumption on premises. *See* Tex. Penal Code § 46.15(p).

46.03 sign

A list of prohibited places is conveniently located in Texas Penal Code Section 46.03. Most notably, these prohibited locations include schools, courts, polling places, professional sporting events, and correctional facilities—places firearms are never allowed. In addition to firearms, location-restricted knives, clubs, and prohibited weapons are prohibited in Section 46.03 locations. For the most part, locations listed in Section 46.03 are off limits to both license holders and constitutional carriers, and signage or notice of prohibition is not required to exclude firearms, location-restricted knives, and clubs. However, these locations have the option to post a sign that alerts people to the prohibited nature of the premises.

This notice can be provided by a sign that is posted prominently at each entrance to the premises or property. If effective notice is provided by a 46.03 sign under Texas Penal Code Section 46.15(o), any person who carries a firearm (even accidentally) into that location will not have the benefit of the defense to prosecution intended to guard against mistakes. *See* Chapter 14 for a detailed discussion of 46.03 notice requirements and defenses to carrying into restricted locations.

- NOTICE -

WEAPONS PROHIBITED
PURSUANT TO SECTION 46.03, PENAL CODE (PLACES WEAPONS PROHIBITED), A PERSON MAY NOT CARRY A FIREARM OR OTHER WEAPON ON THIS PROPERTY.

ARMAS PROHIBIDAS
CONFORME A LA SECCIÓN 46.03 (LUGARES ARMAS PROHIBIDAS), PERSONAS NO PUEDE PORTAR UN ARMA DE FUEGO U OTRA ARMA EN ESTA PROPIEDAD.

> **TAKEAWAY:**
> - A location does not have to post a 46.03 sign to still be a prohibited place.
> - If a place does post a 46.03 sign, the presence of that sign removes any ability for a person who carried a firearm into that location to say, "I simply didn't know that this area was a prohibited location."
>
> –Emily

Regardless, if the location has or has not posted a 46.03 sign, it is still prohibited.

B. Legally effective signage for license holders

In order to legally prohibit an LTC holder from carrying a handgun on an owner's property, the owner must give the LTC holder notice, usually orally, in writing, or by signage. However, for written notice and signage, this notice must be specific, and there are legal requirements for the protection of LTC holders.

So, if someone wants to exclude LTC holders from carrying a handgun on his or her property, he or she must give effective legal notice that LTC holders are prohibited from carrying pursuant to either Texas Penal Code Section 30.06 (for concealed carry), Texas Penal Code Section 30.07 (for open carry), or both. These Sections pertain to criminal trespass, and as such, prohibitions can apply broadly to all property owned by the prohibiting party, depending upon the location of signage and/or the scope of notice given. For example, a grocery store might choose to post effective signage on its front door, which would serve as criminal trespass notice for the building. Or, it could post signage at the entrance to the parking lot, effectively prohibiting an LTC holder from walking through the lot *and* the building while armed.

What words must be in a 30.06 notice?

There is no specific wording required for oral notice, therefore a simple "We don't allow guns in here" would be sufficient. The statute allows effective notice to be given orally or by written communication. "Written communication" is: (1) a card or other document on which is written language identical to the following: "Pursuant to Section 30.06, Penal Code (trespass by license holder with a concealed handgun), a person licensed under Subchapter H, Chapter 411, Government Code (handgun licensing law), may not enter this property with a concealed handgun"; or (2) a sign posted on the property that includes the language described in the preceding sentence in both English and Spanish, appears in contrasting colors with block letters at least one inch in height, and is displayed in a conspicuous manner clearly visible to the public.

Under these specifications, a proper 30.06 sign will often look similar to the one pictured below:

HANDGUNS PROHIBITED

PURSUANT TO SECTION 30.06, PENAL CODE (TRESPASS BY LICENSE HOLDER WITH A CONCEALED HANDGUN), A PERSON LICENSED UNDER SUBCHAPTER H, CHAPTER 411, GOVERNMENT CODE (HANDGUN LICENSING LAW), MAY NOT ENTER THIS PROPERTY WITH A CONCEALED HANDGUN.

CONFORME A LA SECCIÓN 30.06 DEL CÓDIGO PENAL (TRASPASAR PORTANDO ARMAS DE FUEGO) PERSONAS CON LICENCIA BAJO DEL SUB-CAPITULO H, CAPITULO 411, CODIGO DE GOBIERNO (LEY DE PORTAR ARMAS), NO DEBEN ENTRAR A ESTA PROPIEDAD PORTANDO UN ARMA DE FUEGO.

Remember, the 30.06 sign is simply one way to give legal notice that a person carrying a concealed handgun pursuant to an LTC is trespassing.

Any place where 30.07 notice is given

Section 30.07 is virtually identical in its legal requirements for notice, violations, and penalties to 30.06, including that a valid warning can be given orally, in writing, or by signage. However, since a 30.07 sign pertains to the open carrying of a handgun, the language of 30.07 differs from 30.06 and states: "Pursuant to Section 30.07, Penal Code (trespass by license holder with an openly carried handgun), a person licensed under Subchapter H, Chapter 411, Government Code (handgun licensing law), may not enter this property with a handgun that is carried openly."

HANDGUNS PROHIBITED

PURSUANT TO SECTION 30.07, PENAL CODE (TRESPASS BY LICENSE HOLDER WITH AN OPENLY CARRIED HANDGUN), A PERSON LICENSED UNDER SUBCHAPTER H, CHAPTER 411, GOVERNMENT CODE (HANDGUN LICENSING LAW), MAY NOT ENTER THIS PROPERTY WITH A HANDGUN THAT IS CARRIED OPENLY.

CONFORME A LA SECCIÓN 30.07 DEL CÓDIGO PENAL (TRASPASAR PORTANDO ARMAS DE FUEGO) PERSONAS CON LICENCIA BAJO DEL SUB-CAPITULO H, CAPITULO 411, CODIGO DE GOBIERNO (LEY DE PORTAR ARMAS), NO DEBEN ENTRAR A ESTA PROPIEDAD PORTANDO UN ARMA DE FUEGO.

The requirements for a 30.07 sign are that it must contain this exact language in both English and Spanish, written in one-inch-high block letters in contrasting colors, and placed in a conspicuous place at each entrance to the property.

So, given that a 30.06 sign prohibits concealed carry by a license holder, and a 30.07 sign prohibits open carry by a license holder, a private property owner who wants to prohibit both concealed and open carry of handguns by *license holders* will need to post both a 30.06 sign and a 30.07 sign.

What if I did not see the 30.06 or 30.07 sign?

A very common question about 30.06 and 30.07 signs for LTC holders is, "what if I did not see the 30.06 or 30.07 sign—am I breaking the law if I have my handgun?" In short, an LTC holder who possesses a handgun and does not see a posted 30.06 or 30.07 sign at a place where they are caught carrying may still be charged with the crime of criminal trespass. However, the LTC holder will also have the opportunity to present an argument establishing that he or she did not see the sign, and, therefore, did not receive effective legal notice that the possession of a handgun was prohibited.

The critical element of Texas Penal Code Sections 30.06 and 30.07 is that the signs provide effective "notice" to an LTC holder that the carrying of a concealed or unconcealed handgun is prohibited as applicable. A person who does not see the sign because it was not visible, because the sign was placed in a location where a person would not ordinarily see it, or for any other reason, will have an opportunity to convince a jury that he or she did not receive the notice required under the law. It is important to keep in mind, however, that the purpose of the law is to provide notice, and such notice can be received in three different ways, as discussed earlier. Because an oral admonition is sufficient to provide notice (without any of the required language for written notice), it is possible that failing to see a posted sign may not be enough of an argument to prevail. *See* Tex. Penal Code §§ 30.06 and 30.07.

What if the 30.06 or 30.07 sign is defective or does not comply with the law?

Texas law requires under Texas Penal Code Sections 30.06 and 30.07 that a sign must be posted conspicuously and clearly visible to the public. (Interestingly, the Texas Legislature added a requirement to 30.07, but not to 30.06, that a sign be placed at each entrance to the property.) Signs must also be presented with contrasting colors between the lettering and background, and the letters must be in block letters at least one inch high. What happens, however, when an LTC holder encounters a sign which he or she believes does not comply with these requirements?

> **EXAMPLE:**
> Sherry, an LTC holder who always carries her handgun, walks to a new clothing store and notices a sign on the door that she believes does not meet the requirements of Texas Penal Code Section 30.06, in that the letters are white, only ½ inch tall, are in lower case, and on a piece of clear glass. She enters the store and chooses a pair of pants to try on. When she is in the changing room her concealed, holstered handgun falls to the floor, making a clattering noise that gets the sales representative's attention.

If the police are called, Sherry can attempt to explain to them why she was not given proper criminal trespass notice. As discussed in the preceding section, the purpose of Sections 30.06 and 30.07 is to provide notice. If an LTC holder encounters a nonconforming sign, and the person chooses to disregard the sign's admonition against carrying a handgun but later finds themselves charged with criminal trespass, then that person will have some strong legal arguments as to why the sign they saw failed to give them adequate statutory notice, meaning they are not guilty of criminal trespass. However, they only have a legal argument. This is an issue that has not been decided by the courts, yet.

The lack of case law on this subject makes scenarios such as a sign posted using white letters on a clear glass window difficult to judge beforehand. Is clear glass a sufficient contrasting background from the white letters as required by law? An argument could easily be made either way—which is exactly what will happen should such a case go to trial.

Beware, therefore! If you decide, as an LTC holder, to disregard a posted 30.06 or 30.07 sign because of a technical deficiency, you may be the first "test case" to help establish the bright lines of the law. Also, always remember that if a property owner ever gives you oral notice that LTC holders are not welcome to carry on their property, you have been given effective legal notice and must leave the property; otherwise, you are criminally trespassing.

What happens if I violate Sections 30.06 or 30.07?
Generally, a violation of Texas Penal Code Sections 30.06 or 30.07 is a Class C misdemeanor. But, if an LTC holder carrying a concealed handgun was personally given the notice by oral communication and subsequently failed to depart, it is a Class A misdemeanor. *See* Tex. Penal Code §§ 30.06 and 30.07. However, if you are given verbal notice to leave the premises and you promptly depart the property, then you will have a defense to prosecution.

A conviction or order of deferred adjudication for a Class A misdemeanor means the suspension of a person's LTC for seven years. *See* Tex. Gov't Code § 411.186(c). In addition, an LTC holder convicted of a Class A misdemeanor criminal trespass may face up to one year in county jail and/or up to a $4,000 fine or the person may receive a maximum of two years of probation with a minimum of 80 hours of community service. However, a conviction for a Class C misdemeanor criminal trespass by a license holder is punishable by a fine up to $200 and no jail time. Further, a conviction or order of deferred adjudication for a Class C misdemeanor criminal trespass by a license holder will not have any consequences on the LTC holder's license.

It is important to point out, however, that a violation of Sections 30.06 or 30.07 requires that a property owner who provided valid notice actually press charges to prosecute the crime of criminal trespass by a license holder. One question that is often asked is, "what if I am forced to use my handgun to stop a crime from happening in a place where a 30.06 or 30.07 sign was posted?" One can only speculate what would happen, but if an LTC holder saves the life of another person while violating Sections 30.06 or 30.07, a business owner may be hard-pressed to go forward with charges against a hero.

Other defenses to prosecution under Sections 30.06 and 30.07

It is a defense to prosecution that the license holder is a first responder who holds an unexpired certificate of completion under Section 411.184 of the Texas Government Code and, at the time of engaging in the applicable conduct, was engaged in the actual discharge of the first responder's duties while carrying the handgun and was employed or supervised by a municipality or county to which Chapter 179, Local Government Code, applies. *See* Tex. Penal Code §§ 30.06 and 30.07.

There is also a defense specific to violating Sections 30.06 and 30.07 at a hotel. It is a defense to prosecution if the license holder is a guest of the hotel and the license holder: carries or stores a handgun in the license holder's hotel room; carries a handgun directly en route to or from the hotel or the license holder's hotel room; carries a handgun directly en route to or from the license holder's vehicle located on the hotel property, including a vehicle in a parking area provided for hotel guests; or carries or stores a handgun in the license holder's vehicle located on the hotel property, including a vehicle in a parking area provided for hotel guests. *See* Tex. Penal Code §§ 30.06 and 30.07.

Are there property owners who cannot lawfully post a 30.06 or 30.07 sign?

Yes. According to Texas Penal Code Sections 30.06(e) and 30.07(e), buildings and other properties owned or leased by a governmental entity may not lawfully post a 30.06 or 30.07 sign, unless firearm possession on the property is otherwise prohibited by law. A handgun license holder may legally carry their handgun on property owned or leased by a governmental entity even if the government has attempted to post a 30.06 or 30.07 sign that is otherwise compliant with the law. An LTC holder should always be aware if the property is a place where a license holder is prohibited from carrying a handgun under Texas Penal Code Section 46.03. The Texas Legislature originally enacted subsection (e) to Texas Penal Code Section 30.06 in response to many cities, counties, and other governmental entities that were using the 30.06 law to prohibit LTC holders from carrying on government property where the Legislature passively allowed it by not specifically preventing it, such as public libraries, civic centers, and city halls. This prohibition on governments posting signs was later included in Texas Penal Code Section 30.07 as well.

Prior to 2015, the Texas Legislature did not provide a penalty for a local government that posts an unauthorized 30.06 sign. This oversight allowed anti-firearm local governments to confuse and intimidate lawful concealed handgun carriers by posting 30.06 signs even though it is prohibited by the statute. This oversight was remedied in 2015, when the civil penalty provided by Section 411.209 of Subchapter H, Chapter 411 of the Government Code went into effect for state agencies or political subdivisions of the state that post signs improperly. This law applies not only to proper 30.06 signs, but also to any sign referring to Section 30.06 of the Texas Penal Code, or to any sign referring to a concealed handgun licensee being prohibited from carrying, which would appear to include signs prohibiting openly carried handguns under Texas Penal Code Section 30.07.

This remedy was further clarified in 2019 to encompass all communications, not just signs, that state or imply that a license holder carrying a handgun on government property would be trespassing. In essence, unless it is a location prohibited by Section 46.03, a state agency or political subdivision that gives an express or implied communication barring handguns could incur a civil penalty.

However, this is the government we're talking about; that means there are some bureaucratic hoops a person will have to jump through. First, any citizen of Texas, or a Texas LTC holder, must inform the state agency or political subdivision, in writing, that the sign is invalid and note the specific location of the sign. If the improper sign is not taken down within three days, then a person may file a complaint with the attorney general. This complaint must contain evidence of the violation (*i.e.*, a picture of the sign) and a copy of the written notice (which is dated to show that the state agency or political subdivision has not complied). Next, the attorney general must investigate the complaint to determine whether legal action is warranted. If it is warranted, the attorney general must give the chief administrative officer of the agency or political subdivision a written notice that describes the violation, states the proposed penalty, and gives them 15 days from the date the agency or subdivision receives the notice to take down the sign to avoid the penalty. For repeat offenders that have already been found liable by a court for their sign, this notice is not required. That means it takes three days for the agency to ignore a written notice, the attorney general's "investigation" period, and possibly 15 days after the attorney general's notice is received until the improper sign gets taken down. *See* Tex. Gov't Code § 411.209.

How much liability does this statute create for the agency or political subdivision? For the first violation, the penalty is not less than $1,000 and not more than $1,500. What happens if it's the second violation? The penalty jumps all the way up to not less than $10,000 and not more than $10,500! Additionally, each day the sign is posted is considered a separate violation. Unfortunately, this fine isn't awarded as a prize to the citizen who catches the sign; it is deposited in the victims of crime fund instead. *See* Tex. Gov't Code § 411.209.

Can the government sue you for reporting a sign?

Some governmental entities want to stop people from exercising their Second Amendment rights so badly that they will happily trample First Amendment rights to do it. When Texas Government Code Section 411.209 was created to allow private citizens to put state and local governments and agencies on notice that they were unlawfully excluding LTC holders carrying handguns from government property, most of these entities bristled upon being called to account for their behavior. The county government of Waller County, Texas, took their defiance to a whole new level by suing the individual who sent them a Section 411.209 notice letter for its practice of excluding license holders from its multi-function courthouse. Fortunately, the Texas Court of Appeals found that the right to complain to the government is a protected First Amendment activity, and that Waller County's lawsuit violated the Texas Citizen's Participation Act. *Holcomb v. Waller County*, 546 S.W.3d 833 (Tex. App. [1st Dist.] 2018, pet. ref'd.).

Most governments have responded to Section 411.209 by taking down their 30.06 signs without any penalties being assessed. However, several governmental entities have steadfastly maintained that they are legally allowed to continue excluding and threatening LTC holders who are carrying handguns with criminal prosecution. The recalcitrance of these governmental entities has resulted in some ridiculous assertions, such as county-owned libraries and zoos claiming to be educational institutions, and city halls claiming to be courts. In short, non-prohibited places are trying to recategorize themselves as prohibited places and argue that they belong within the prohibited places listed in Texas Penal Code Section 46.03. Along these lines, counties have been the most adamant about claiming that their courthouses are entirely prohibited. However, this flies in the face of the actual text of Texas Penal Code Section 46.03(a)(3) which states that only "courts and offices utilized by the court" are prohibited, as well as Texas Attorney General Opinions KP-47 and KP-49. These opinions state that if a court and its offices occupy only a portion of a courthouse, and non-covered areas (*i.e.*, tax offices, auditor's offices, commissioner's offices, *etc.*) are also present in the courthouse, then LTC holders who are carrying handguns are only excluded from the courts and their offices. There are several lawsuits that have been filed, and the Texas Courts of Appeal and perhaps ultimately the Texas Supreme Court will have to settle this issue.

C. Legally effective signage for persons carrying under the Firearm Carry Act of 2021

Unlike the requirement for license holders, legally effective signage (appearing at an otherwise non-prohibited location) for a constitutional carrier is much broader.

Texas Penal Code Section 30.05(c) establishes a new option for a property owner to provide notice to exclude non-license holders carrying a firearm (including a handgun) in places governed by the general trespass statute. The text now reads, "[a] person may provide notice that firearms are prohibited on the property by posting a sign at each entrance to the property that: (1) includes language that is identical to or substantially similar to the following" sign:

- NOTICE -
UNLICENSED CARRYING OF FIREARMS PROHIBITED
PURSUANT TO SECTION 30.05, PENAL CODE (CRIMINAL TRESPASS), A PERSON MAY NOT ENTER THIS PROPERTY WITH A FIREARM.

PROHÍBEN PORTE SIN LICENCIADE DE ARMAS DE FUEGO
CONFORME A LA SECCIÓN 30.05 (TRASPASAR CRIMEN), PERSONAS NO PUEDE ENTRARA PROPIEDAD CON UN ARMA DE FUEGO.

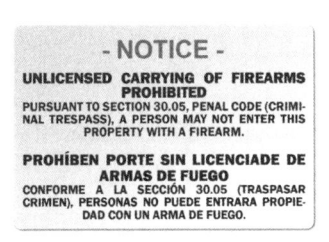

However, the "may" language of Section 30.05 leaves broad room for property owners. By including the word "may" rather than "shall,"

the code technically allows for any sign that would communicate this notice. So, the sign could come in many different forms; the only legal requirement is that it is reasonably likely to come to the attention of the person entering the building. As a result, even signs such as these could be effective against a person carrying under the authority of the Firearm Carry Act:

Still, it is important to remember that these signs would only apply to a person who is not carrying under the authority of a recognized license. For license holders, only the effective notice discussed earlier in this Chapter would apply.

Generally, for an unlicensed person to disregard these signs and violate Section 30.05, the offense is a Class C misdemeanor with a maximum fine of $200. However, a person will face a Class A misdemeanor if the person personally received notice from the owner or other person with apparent authority that the entry with a firearm or other weapon was forbidden and subsequently failed to depart. *See* Tex. Penal Code § 30.05.

D. Do private property owners have liability for not posting signs?

A big concern for private property owners is whether or not they should post 30.06 or 30.07 signs. Before 2019, state law did not provide adequate civil liability protections to business establishments that elected not to post 30.06 or 30.07 signs, leaving those establishments vulnerable to frivolous lawsuits. In effect, this provided incentives for businesses to adopt restrictive policies against the carrying of handguns by law-abiding citizens. In 2019, the legislature passed a law that states that evidence of a property owner's failure to forbid handguns carried by LTC holders on certain property will be inadmissible in certain civil lawsuits. *See* Tex. Civ. Prac. & Rem. Code § 95A.001.

E. TABC "blue signs" repealed

As of September 1, 2021, all "blue signs" are repealed and no longer have legal meaning. Constitutional carriers may carry into grocery stores, liquor stores, gas stations, and restaurants that sell alcohol so long as other trespass notice is not sufficiently provided. In short, even if you see these "blue signs" after September 1, 2021, you may disregard.

> **NOTICE**
> The unlicensed possession of a weapon on these premises is a felony with a maximum penalty of 10 years imprisonment and a fine not to exceed $10,000.
>
> Texas Alcoholic Beverage Commission
> P.O. Box 13127 - Austin, Texas 78711-3127
> TOLL FREE 1 - 888 - THE - TABC

➢ CHAPTER FOURTEEN ◄

LAW OF HANDGUN CARRY: PART III
WHERE A NON-PROHIBITED Person Can Legally Carry

The general law concerning the carrying of a handgun was greatly revised and reorganized with the Firearm Carry Act of 2021, also known as "Texas Constitutional Carry." Before Texas Constitutional Carry came into existence, a person without a recognized license or permit to carry was significantly limited in where that person could carry a handgun. Although non-prohibited and otherwise qualifying individuals can carry in non-prohibited public places as long as they are not given notice, the list of places that non-licensed individuals may carry increased substantially. Still, the basics of who can carry a firearm and where that person can carry a firearm apply. As mentioned in

Chapter 13, in order to carry a handgun in a public place, a person must either carry under the authority of a recognized license or permit or must meet the qualifications for Texas Constitutional Carry. Additionally, a handgun must be carried either openly in a holster or concealed. But what about all the other weapons a person may legally carry?

I. INTRODUCTION

There are a number of places in Texas where all firearms, including long guns and handguns, as well as other prohibited weapons such as knives with blades longer than 5½ inches, clubs, and the weapons listed in Section 46.05(a) of the Texas Penal Code, are prohibited. In some areas, all weapons are prohibited. *See* Tex. Penal Code § 46.03. Conversely, there are some places that only allow handguns to be carried by a license holder, or places where only a license holder may carry a handgun into that location. Then, there are places that are generally open to both LTC holders and constitutional carriers, subject to notice of prohibition. So, when trying to legally carry a weapon in Texas—especially a firearm—it is important that the person is educated on the legality of where a weapon is allowed. This Chapter discusses federal property, preemption law, prohibited places, and generally non-prohibited places, which locations allow weapons, and which do not.

II. FEDERAL PROPERTY

One place where a person generally may not carry is in federal buildings. Because an LTC is issued by the State of Texas and not the federal government, even an LTC holder may not legally carry their concealed or open handgun on federal property unless specifically authorized by federal law.

As a general reminder, an LTC is a product of state law and conveys no additional rights pertaining to carrying to the LTC holder that have been recognized under federal law. However, in certain instances, the federal government recognizes these state rights on certain federal property.

A. Federal buildings: firearms are prohibited

> **FIREARMS PROHIBITED IN FEDERAL FACILITIES**
> **18 U.S.C. § 930(a)**
>
> Whoever knowingly possesses or causes to be present a firearm or other dangerous weapon in a Federal facility (other than a Federal court facility), or attempts to do so, shall be fined under this title or imprisoned not more than 1 year, or both.

Under this statute, a "federal facility" refers to any building or part of a building that is owned or leased by the federal government and is a place where federal employees are regularly present for the purpose of performing their official duties. *See* 18 U.S.C. § 930(g)(1). However, this statute does not apply to "the lawful performance of official duties by an officer, agent, or employee of the United States, a State, or a political subdivision thereof, who is authorized by law to engage in or supervise the prevention, detection, investigation, or prosecution of any violation of law," nor does it apply to federal officials or members of the Armed Forces who are permitted to possess such a firearm by law, or the lawful carrying of a firearm incident to hunting or "other lawful purposes." *See* 18 U.S.C. § 930(d). This statute does not govern the possession of a firearm in a federal court facility. Still, "whoever knowingly possesses or causes to be present a firearm or other dangerous weapon in a Federal court facility, or attempts to do so, shall be fined under this title, imprisoned not more than 2 years, or both." *See* 18 U.S.C. § 930(e). It is important to note that there is a defense to prosecution built into 18 U.S.C. § 930. Subsection (h) states, "Notice ... shall be posted conspicuously at each public entrance to each Federal facility..." In short, federal facilities are required to post signage to put people on notice that entering the building with a firearm or other dangerous weapon is prohibited. What does that mean for folks who want to carry a firearm for self-defense? In the absence of signage or actual notice (*e.g.*, personal oral or written notice, *etc.*), there is a powerful defense to prosecution if charged with the crime of carrying a firearm into a federal facility. *See* 18 U.S.C. § 930(h).

B. National parks

> **FIREARMS IN NATIONAL PARKS**
> **16 U.S.C. § 1a-7b; 54 U.S.C. § 104906**
>
> Federal law allows possession of firearms in national parks and wildlife refuges so long as the person is not otherwise prohibited by law from possessing the firearm, and the possession of the firearm is in compliance with the law of the state in which the national park or wildlife refuge is located.

LTC holders and those carrying under the authority of the Firearm Carry Act of 2021 are permitted to carry in national parks in Texas but not buildings within the park, such as ranger stations, because these buildings usually qualify as a federal facility. As a reminder, the prohibition on carrying in federal facilities applies if a person has been provided actual notice or there is conspicuous notice at the facility's entrance that firearms or other dangerous weapons are prohibited. *See* 18 U.S.C. § 930(h).

Under federal law, for firearms purposes, all federal parks are subject to the state law of the state in which the park is located. *See* 16 U.S.C. § 1a-7b; 36 CFR § 2.4. In 1998, the executive director of the Texas Parks and Wildlife Department issued an executive order stating that the carrying of a concealed handgun in state parks by a license holder is governed by the laws concerning concealed handguns and that "nothing in the Public Hunting Lands Proclamation or State Parks Proclamation prohibits a person from possessing a concealed handgun." *See* Exec. Order No. 98-001 (July 8, 1998). In light of this order and expansion of firearm rights in Texas, the lawful carrying of a concealed handgun or openly carried handgun in a holster under state law is permissible by both license holders and constitutional carriers in national parks, federal wildlife preserves, and national forests in Texas.

C. VA Hospitals: firearms prohibited

> **FIREARMS PROHIBITED AT VETERANS AFFAIRS HOSPITALS**
> **38 CFR § 1.218(a)(13)**
>
> No person while on property shall carry firearms, other dangerous or deadly weapons, or explosives, either openly or concealed, except for official purposes.

One place where many law-abiding LTC holders fall victim is at the VA Hospital. Unlike the Texas laws on hospitals which allow an LTC holder to carry a handgun unless proper 30.06 or 30.07 signs are posted (or notice given), the VA Hospital system is governed by federal law, which prohibits the carrying of any firearm while on VA property. This includes the parking lot, sidewalks, and any other area which is the property of the VA.

Under federal law, the "official purposes" language refers specifically to the VA Hospital police. *See* 38 CFR § 1.218(a)(13). The area where this specific law gets good people in trouble is that the Department of Veterans Affairs has its own set of laws and guidelines and is not controlled strictly by the Gun Control Act and the general provisions regarding the prohibition of firearms on federal property. The VA law is much more restrictive, and many veterans have found themselves in trouble when they valet-park their vehicle and the valet discovers a handgun in the console, in the door storage area, or lying on the seat in a holster. How rigidly this law is enforced is determined by the individual hospital administrators as described in Title 38 of the Code of Federal Regulations, Section 1.218(a); however, regardless of how strictly the law is enforced, firearms are still prohibited, and the VA police are very aggressive in enforcing them.

D. United States Post Offices: firearms prohibited

> **FIREARMS PROHIBITED AT POST OFFICES**
> **39 CFR § 232.1(l)**
>
> Notwithstanding the provisions of any other law, rule or regulation, no person while on postal property may carry firearms, other dangerous or deadly weapons, or explosives, either openly or concealed, or store the same on postal property, except for official purposes.

Under this regulation, firearms or other deadly weapons are prohibited on postal property, which includes not only the building, but all property surrounding the building where a post office is located. This includes the parking lot (*e.g.*, a person's vehicle where a firearm may be stored), as well as the sidewalks and walkways (even though parking lots, sidewalks, walkways, and other related areas are generally not included when discussing the premises of a location where the carrying of a weapon is prohibited by law). Like the VA Hospital, United States Post Offices are another exception to the rule. In 2013, there was a decision by a United States District Court addressing this issue in Colorado which allowed a license holder to bring his firearm into the parking lot of the Avon, Colorado Post Office. However, in 2015, that case was reversed on appeal by the United States Tenth Circuit Court of Appeals. Then in 2016, the United States Supreme Court let the Tenth Circuit Court's ruling stand by refusing to review the decision. Still, it should be noted that the United States Tenth Circuit does not include Texas, and therefore the district court's initial ruling striking down the U.S. Post Office's rule has no legal bearing on the prohibition against possessing firearms on United States Post Office property in Texas.

E. Army Corps of Engineers Property: firearms prohibited

> **FIREARMS PROHIBITED AT PARKS, FORESTS, AND PUBLIC PROPERTY OF THE CORPS OF ENGINEERS**
> **36 CFR § 327.13(a)**
>
> The possession of loaded firearms, ammunition, loaded projectile firing devices, bows and arrows, crossbows, or other weapons is prohibited.

Under this regulation, loaded firearms, ammunition, and other projectile firing devices are generally prohibited on U.S. Army Corps of Engineers ("USACE") property. This applies to property owned and managed by the USACE, including bodies of water, but does not include easements or other rights of way that USACE may have near a project site (*e.g.*, private or state-owned shoreline near a USACE lake). Simply put, if the USACE does not own the property in whole, then the prohibition on the possession and carrying of firearms will not apply under this regulation. Unfortunately, these boundaries and ownership are oftentimes unclear. To be safe, be on the lookout for signs prohibiting the possession of these items and contact the office of the USACE project site for clarification. *See* 36 CFR § 327.30(d).

The exception to this general prohibition falls into the hands of USACE "District Commanders." The prohibition against the possession of loaded firearms, ammunition, loaded projectile firing devices, bows and arrows, crossbows, or other weapons does not apply if "written permission has been received from the District Commander." Additionally, the following evidence suggests that this exception may be used more often than you would think. *See* 36 CFR § 327.13(a)(4).

In 2018, the Chief of Operations and Regulatory Division Directorate of Civil Works promulgated a memorandum providing guidance on firearm possession requests. The memorandum explained that the primary consideration in determining whether a request is granted should be based on whether possession would interfere, impede, or disrupt the use of a project, or otherwise impair safety; however, District Commanders have complete discretion. As part of the memorandum, an example permission letter was provided with instructions on requirements the District Commander must impose if granting such a request.

If such permission to possess a loaded firearm is granted, district commanders are required to impose the following conditions:

1) possession must be in full compliance with Federal, state and local laws and will be revoked upon any violation of law that renders possession of a firearm illegal;
2) the individual must have a state-issued weapons permit, valid (including by reciprocal agreement) in the state where the project is located;
3) the authorization to carry a firearm may only be for carrying it concealed;
4) the authorization must require the individual to carry a copy of the Corps permission letter and the state-issued firearm carry permit at all times while on Corps property and the individual must be required to present a copy of the documents when requested by a law enforcement or Corps official;
5) the authorization must clearly specify at which Corps projects the authorization applies. The authorization must also specify where on the project the firearm can be carried; and
6) the authorization must specify a definite period of time for which it is valid.

F. Military bases and installations: firearms generally prohibited

Military bases and installations are treated much like the VA Hospital and United States Post Offices in that they have, and are governed by, a separate set of rules and regulations with respect to firearms on the premises of an installation or base and are generally prohibited. Military installations are governed by the federal law under Title 32 of the Code of Federal Regulations. Moreover, the sections covering the laws governing and relating to military bases and installations are exceedingly numerous. There are, in fact, sections which are dedicated to only certain bases, such as Title 32 of the Code of Federal Regulations, Section 552.98, which only governs the possessing, carrying, concealing, and transporting of firearms on Fort Stewart/Hunter Army Airfield.

III. GENERAL PREEMPTION LAWS FOR TEXAS

Generally, Texas preempts municipalities from enacting stricter regulations relating to the transfer, possession, wearing, carrying, ownership, storage, transportation, licensing, or registration of firearms, air guns, knives, ammunition, or firearm or air gun supplies or accessories; the commerce in firearms, air guns, knives, ammunition, or firearm or air gun supplies or accessories; or the discharge of a firearm or air gun at a sport shooting range.

As a result, generally, a municipality cannot restrict firearm rights or enact firearm laws or regulations regarding the carrying of a concealed or visibly holstered handgun that is more restrictive than state law. *See* Tex. Loc. Gov't Code § 229.001(a).

However, there are certain exceptions. Namely, state preemption described in subsection (a) of the above statute does not affect the authority of a municipality to regulate the carrying of an air gun or a firearm, other than a handgun carried by a person not otherwise prohibited by law from carrying a handgun, at a: public park; public meeting of a municipality, county, or other governmental body; a political rally, parade, or official political meeting, or non-firearms-related school, college, or professional athletic event. *See* Tex. Loc. Gov't Code § 229.001(b). In other words, municipalities cannot regulate the carrying of a handgun by a non-prohibited person in public parks, public meetings of government entities, political rallies, parades, or official political meetings, or non-firearms-related school, college, or professional athletic events. However, a handgun carrier must remember that other sections of the law, such as Texas Penal Code Section 46.03 (which lists prohibited places), intersect with this law. Just because this section may prohibit regulation on local levels does not mean that there are not other laws that apply.

A. General preemption laws not specific to LTC holders

In addition, Texas Local Government Code Section 229.001(a) prohibits municipalities from enacting regulations relating to the "transfer, possession, wearing, carrying, ownership, storage, transportation, licensing, or registration of firearms, air guns, knives, ammunition, or firearm or air gun supplies or accessories" for any person—not just LTC holders.

B. How big of a handgun can an LTC holder or constitutional carrier legally carry?

As we mentioned in Chapter 5, federal law dictates that any firearm which has any barrel with a bore of more than one-half inch in diameter (.50 caliber) is a "destructive device" and is subject to the National Firearms Act (except for certain shotguns). Possession of any such firearm without the proper paperwork associated with NFA firearms is illegal, whether a person is an LTC holder or not. *See* Chapter 17 for more information on destructive devices and the NFA.

Otherwise, there is generally no limit on how big a firearm a person can carry—a person may carry a long gun (in accordance with the law and in non-prohibited places) and a handgun as long as it is either concealed or in a holster while open carrying. The main issue with "scarier-looking" firearms is the carrier does not want to be seen as carrying in a manner calculated to alarm. *See* Tex. Penal Code § 42.01. Otherwise, as long as the item is legal, the carrier is legal, and the manner and place in which the firearm is carried is legal, the person is generally good to go.

IV. TEXAS PENAL CODE SECTION 46.03: PLACES PEOPLE SHOULD NOT CARRY

As a reminder, the Texas Firearm Carry Act of 2021 made many changes to firearm laws in the State of Texas. Included in these changes was a major reorganization of prohibited places within the Texas Penal Code.

In this Chapter, we will discuss the certain places where all firearms, including long guns and handguns, as well as other prohibited weapons such as knives with blades longer than 5½ inches, clubs, and the weapons listed in Section 46.05(a) of the Texas Penal Code, are forbidden. The most notable places a person may generally never carry are listed in Section 46.03 of the Texas Penal Code. In these places, a person is prohibited from possessing firearms or prohibited weapons on their premises, regardless of whether a person has an LTC or is legally allowed to possess firearms or other weapons. Remember, "premises" is defined in Texas Penal Code Section 46.03 as "a building or a portion of a building. The term does not include any public or private driveway, street, sidewalk or walkway, parking lot, parking garage, or other parking area." Tex. Penal Code § 46.03.

These prohibited places generally include schools, polling places, courts, racetracks, airports, within 1,000 feet of a place of execution, 51% locations, scholastic and professional sporting events, correctional facilities, civil commitment facilities, hospitals, amusement parks, and a room of an open government meeting.

PRACTICAL LEGAL TIP

Although there are limited exceptions provided in the Texas Penal Code for airports, open meetings of governmental entities, hospitals, nursing facilities, and amusement parks, it is generally not a defense to prosecution that the actor possessed a handgun and was licensed to carry. In other words, merely having an LTC will not necessarily save you if you violate Section 46.03, which usually results in a third degree felony offense! –Emily

A. Schools

> **WEAPONS PROHIBITED AT SCHOOLS**
> **TEX. PENAL CODE § 46.03(a)(1)**
>
> (a) A person commits an offense if the person intentionally, knowingly, or recklessly possesses or goes with a firearm, location-restricted knife, club, or prohibited weapon listed in Section 46.05(a):
>
> > (1) on the physical premises of a school or educational institution, any grounds or building on which an activity sponsored by a school or educational institution is being conducted, or a passenger transportation vehicle of a school or educational institution, whether the school or educational institution is public or private, unless:
> >
> > > (A) pursuant to written regulations or written authorization of the institution; or
> > >
> > > (B) the person possesses or goes with a concealed handgun that the person is licensed to carry under Subchapter H, Chapter 411, Government Code, and no other weapon to which this section applies, on the premises of an institution of higher education or private or independent institution of higher education, on any grounds or building on which an activity sponsored by the institution is being conducted, or in a passenger transportation vehicle of the institution.

Generally, it is prohibited for any person to possess or go with a firearm, location-restricted knife, club, or other prohibited weapon onto the premises of a school or educational institution. This prohibition applies to the physical premises of a school or educational institution, as well as any grounds or building where a school-sponsored activity is taking place. This means that if the marching band is practicing in the parking lot of a school—a place where a firearm is otherwise permitted—then while the band is participating in its activity, firearms and other weapons are prohibited.

It is important to note that the prohibition on firearms possession can be waived by the institution by giving written permission or creating written regulations.

B. Polling places

> **WEAPONS PROHIBITED AT POLLING PLACES**
> **TEX. PENAL CODE § 46.03(a)(2)**
>
> (a) A person commits an offense if the person intentionally, knowingly, or recklessly possesses or goes with a firearm, location-restricted knife, club, or prohibited weapon listed in Section 46.05(a):
>
> (2) on the premises of a polling place on the day of an election or while early voting is in progress; ...

The possession of firearms (both handguns and long guns) and other weapons is prohibited at any place where polling for an election is taking place, including places where early voting is in progress. Many polling locations are often at places where firearms are not ordinarily prohibited, such as churches, governmental buildings, and libraries. However, while voting is taking place, those locations become off-limits for firearms and other weapons.

C. Courts

> **WEAPONS PROHIBITED AT COURTS**
> **TEX. PENAL CODE § 46.03(a)(3)**
>
> (a) A person commits an offense if the person intentionally, knowingly, or recklessly possesses or goes with a firearm, location-restricted knife, club, or prohibited weapon listed in Section 46.05(a):
>
> (3) on the premises of any government court or offices utilized by the court, unless pursuant to written regulations; ...

Under Texas law, individuals are not permitted to possess firearms or other weapons in a court, or in any offices utilized by a court, including the judge's chambers and any court clerk or coordinator office, unless given explicit written authorization to do so. The Texas Attorney General has stated that this prohibition does not apply to the entire courthouse if the building contains non-prohibited rooms and offices. *See* Op. Tex. Att'y Gen. Nos. KP-47 and KP-49.

D. Racetracks

> **WEAPONS PROHIBITED AT RACETRACKS**
> **TEX. PENAL CODE § 46.03(a)(4)**
>
> (a) A person commits an offense if the person intentionally, knowingly, or recklessly possesses or goes with a firearm, location-restricted knife, club, or prohibited weapon listed in Section 46.05(a):
>
> (4) on the premises of a racetrack; ...

Texas law forbids the possession of all firearms and other weapons on the premises of a racetrack. How does the law define "racetrack"?

Texas Penal Code Section 46.01 defers to Texas Occupations Code Section 2021.003(41), which defines "racctrack" as "a facility that is licensed under this subtitle for the conduct of pari-mutuel wagering on horse racing or greyhound racing."

However, for security officers, it is a defense to prosecution that the actor possessed a firearm or club while traveling to or from the actor's place of assignment or in the actual discharge of duties as a security officer commissioned by the Texas Board of Private Investigators and Private Security Agencies, if: the actor is wearing a distinctive uniform; and the firearm or club is in plain view. *See* Tex. Penal Code § 46.03(h).

E. Airports

> **WEAPONS PROHIBITED AT AIRPORTS**
> **TEX. PENAL CODE § 46.03(a)(5)**
>
> (a) A person commits an offense if the person intentionally, knowingly, or recklessly possesses or goes with a firearm, location-restricted knife, club, or prohibited weapon listed in Section 46.05(a):
> (5) in or into a secured area of an airport; ...

No weapons are permitted in the secured area of an airport under Texas law. The "secured area of an airport" refers to all areas in the airport past security and metal detectors.

However, there are specific defenses pertaining to taking a handgun into the secured portion of an airport and one notable ability for a Texas LTC holder to avoid an arrest.

1. Defense for possessing a firearm or club in the secured areas of an airport

Subsection (d) says it is a defense to prosecution that the actor possessed a firearm or club while traveling to or from the actor's place of assignment or in the actual discharge of duties as: a member of the armed forces or national guard; a guard or employee of a penal institution; a security officer commissioned by the Texas Private Security Board if the actor is wearing a distinctive uniform and the firearm or club is in plain view; or a security officer who holds a personal protection authorization under Chapter 1702 of the Occupations Code, provided that the officer is either: wearing the uniform of a security officer or not wearing the uniform of a security officer and carrying the officer's firearm in a concealed manner. *See* Tex. Penal Code § 46.03(d).

In other words, members of the armed forces or national guard, guards employed by penal institutions, commissioned security officers wearing an official uniform with their firearm in plain view, private security officers authorized under Texas law wearing an official uniform with their firearm in plain view or while wearing plain clothes with their firearm concealed, all of whom must be either traveling to or from a place of assignment or are in the actual discharge of their official duties, are provided a defense to prosecution for possessing a firearm or club under Texas Penal Code Section 46.03(d) in the secured area of the airport.

If the person checked the firearm

Subsection (e) says it is a defense to prosecution that the actor checked all firearms as baggage in accordance with federal or state law or regulations before entering a secured area. *See* Tex. Penal Code § 46.03(e).

If the person is an LTC holder

Subsection (e-1) of Texas Penal Code Section 46.03 says it is a defense to prosecution that the actor: possessed, at the screening checkpoint for the secured area, a handgun that the actor was licensed to carry under Subchapter H, Chapter 411, Government Code; and exited the screening checkpoint for the secured area immediately upon completion of the required screening process and notification that the actor possessed the handgun.

In short, if a Texas LTC holder immediately exits the secured area screening checkpoint with their handgun upon completion of the screening process and notification that the Texas LTC holder possessed a handgun, that is a defense to prosecution.

Additionally, a Texas LTC holder receives even more protection under Texas Penal Code Section 46.03(e-2). Subsection (e-2) explains that a peace officer investigating conduct that could be seen as a breach of Texas Penal Code 46.03(a)(5) (taking a weapon into a secured area of an airport) that consists only of the actor's possession of a handgun as a Texas LTC holder, the officer may not arrest the actor for the offense unless: the officer advises the actor of the defense available under Subsection (e-1) and gives the actor an opportunity to exit the screening checkpoint for the secured area, and the actor does not immediately exit the checkpoint upon completion of the required screening process.

Meaning, if a Texas LTC holder takes a handgun into the secured area of an airport and it is found by security, before the officer can arrest the Texas LTC holder, the officer must tell the Texas LTC holder that the holder has the ability to exit the screening checkpoint after the required screening process. Then, the officer must allow the Texas LTC holder to depart. Only if the Texas LTC holder does not immediately depart may the officer arrest the actor for a violation under this section.

Still, it is important to remember that this defense is only applicable to the crime of violating Texas Penal Code Section 46.03(a)(5) and does not affect any penalties that the TSA may choose to impose on the person for violating its rules.

F. Places of execution

WEAPONS PROHIBITED AT PLACES OF EXECUTION
TEX. PENAL CODE § 46.03(a)(6)

(a) A person commits an offense if the person intentionally, knowingly, or recklessly possesses or goes with a firearm, location-restricted knife, club, or prohibited weapon listed in Section 46.05(a):

(6) within 1,000 feet of premises the location of which is designated by the Texas Department of Criminal Justice as a place of execution under Article 43.19, Code of Criminal Procedure, on a day that a sentence of death is set to be imposed on the designated premises and the person received notice that:

(A) going within 1,000 feet of the premises with a weapon listed under this subsection was prohibited; or

(B) possessing a weapon listed under this subsection within 1,000 feet of the premises was prohibited; ...

It is prohibited to take a weapon within 1,000 feet of the premises where an execution is scheduled to be carried out as long as the person possessing the weapon was provided with notice that possessing a weapon is prohibited. Note, however, that there is no specific statutory language required to provide notice that possessing a weapon within 1,000 feet of the premises is prohibited. *See* Tex. Penal Code § 46.03(a)(6).

However, persons who possess a firearm or club while driving a vehicle on a public road within 1,000 feet of a place of execution, as well as persons who possess a firearm or club in their own residence or place of employment that happens to be within 1,000 feet of a place of execution, are not subject to the statute prohibiting the possession of firearms and clubs within 1,000 feet of the premises of a place of execution as defined under Texas Penal Code Section 46.03(i).

G. 51% location

WEAPONS PROHIBITED AT 51% LOCATIONS
TEX. PENAL CODE § 46.03(a)(7)

(a) A person commits an offense if the person intentionally, knowingly, or recklessly possesses or goes with a firearm, location-restricted knife, club, or prohibited weapon listed in Section 46.05(a):

(7) on the premises of a business that has a permit or license issued under Chapter 25, 28, 32, 69, or 74, Alcoholic Beverage Code, if the business derives 51 percent or more of its income from the sale or service of alcoholic beverages for on-premises consumption, as determined by the Texas Alcoholic Beverage Commission under Section 104.06, Alcoholic Beverage Code; ...

Texas Penal Code Section 46.03(a)(7) makes it a crime for a person to carry a handgun, whether open or concealed, on the premises of an establishment that derives 51 percent or more of its income from the sale or service of alcoholic beverages for on-premises consumption. How does a person know if an establishment is a "51%" establishment? There is, by law, required to be a red 51% sign issued by the Texas Alcoholic Beverage Commission posted in the establishment.

Note: just because an establishment has a bar and sells alcoholic beverages does not necessarily mean that the establishment derives the majority of its income from the sale of the same. A proper 51% sign will give effective notice to a license holder where they may not carry their open or concealed handgun.

A proper 51% sign will look like this:

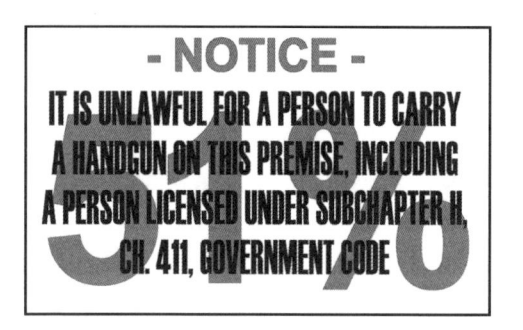

- NOTICE -
IT IS UNLAWFUL FOR A PERSON TO CARRY A HANDGUN ON THIS PREMISE, INCLUDING A PERSON LICENSED UNDER SUBCHAPTER H, CH. 411, GOVERNMENT CODE

However, there are some exceptions to 51% locations as prohibited places. Section 46.15(p) of the Texas Penal Code says the prohibition in Section 46.03 pertaining to 51% locations does not apply if the actor: (1) carries a handgun on the premises or other property, as applicable; (2) holds a Texas LTC; and (3) was not given effective notice under Section 411.204 of the Government Code.

Additionally, Texas Penal Code Section 46.15 explains that 46.03(a)(7) does not apply to an individual who carries a handgun as a participant in a historical reenactment performed in accordance with the rules of the Texas Alcoholic Beverage Commission.

Otherwise, if the business has not posted a 51% sign but derives the majority of its income from the sale and service of alcoholic beverages, an LTC holder has a defense if carrying in that location. However, as we mentioned previously, a person carrying under Texas Constitutional Carry does not have that defense and must magically divine whether or not the business is a 51% location. So, although LTC holders have an extra possible defense, constitutional carriers do not.

H. High school, collegiate, or professional sporting events

WEAPONS PROHIBITED AT SPORTING AND INTERSCHOLASTIC EVENTS
TEX. PENAL CODE § 46.03(a)(8)

(a) A person commits an offense if the person intentionally, knowingly, or recklessly possesses or goes with a firearm, location-restricted knife, club, or prohibited weapon listed in Section 46.05(a):

(8) on the premises where a high school, collegiate, or professional sporting event or interscholastic event is taking place, unless the person is a participant in the event and a firearm, location-restricted knife, club, or prohibited weapon listed in Section 46.05(a) is used in the event; ...

The issue of sporting events causes much confusion. Texas law prohibits the carrying of a handgun on the premises of a high school, collegiate, and professional sporting or interscholastic event. This means, quite obviously, that a person cannot carry his or her open or concealed handgun at a high school soccer game, a professional football game, a professional baseball game, or similar event.

1. Collegiate sporting events

With regard to collegiate sporting events, a person generally may not carry a firearm because of Texas Penal Code Section 46.03(a)(8). However, for a license holder, there is an exception. Texas Penal Code Section 46.15(q) (the Non-Applicability Statute) explains that Section 46.03(a)(8) does not apply if the person carries a concealed handgun on a premises where a collegiate sporting event is taking place, holds a Texas LTC, and was not given effective notice under Texas Penal Code Section 30.06.

If you plan on attending a collegiate sporting event, you may lawfully carry a concealed handgun (not open carry) into the event as long as there is no effective notice pursuant to Texas Penal Code Section 30.06. But what about some events that are not so obvious? Some of the confusion comes from the fact that the Texas Penal Code does not define a "professional" sporting event. Pro football, baseball, basketball, and so forth are easy sports to identify, but what about all the flavors of rodeo in Texas?

2. Professional rodeos

Some rodeos are considered professional sporting events where the carrying of handguns and weapons is prohibited. This means that a person is prohibited from carrying a handgun in the arena where the rodeo is taking place. Remember, because "premises" includes only the building or structure where the event is taking place, and not the parking lots, sidewalks, fairways, or other similar areas, a person would only be prohibited from carrying in the arena. Be careful, however: at many rodeos, high school students from the local FFA or 4H club may have booths or exhibits set up in areas outside of the arena. At those locations, it would be unlawful for a person to carry a firearm since those areas are hosting "interscholastic" events, which are also prohibited by this statute. It can get legally murky.

3. Private golf tournaments, sporting events, or rodeos

What about the scenario where a person decides to "host" a rodeo, golf tournament, or other sporting event on his or her private property? Is such an event prohibited to handgun carriers under the statute? It depends on the manner in which the event takes place. If the hosted rodeo, golf tournament, or other sporting event is one of an amateur nature (and not interscholastic), rather than of a professional nature, then the event likely falls outside the definition of Texas Penal Code Section 46.03. On the other hand, if participants are persons who regularly compete in professional competitions, if there is a significant prize or purse associated with the rodeo, or if the event is sponsored completely or in part by outside organizations and companies, then the event begins to look a lot more like a professional sporting event—even though it may not take place at a prominent public venue. It is worth pointing out that there is no case law on this subject, and it falls squarely within some of the legal "gray area" we see all too often in firearms law.

As a general reminder, keep in mind that the statutory definition of the word "premises" makes carrying a weapon in parking lots, sidewalks, and similar areas permissible under the law. This would include events outside the actual venues themselves of high school, collegiate, and professional sporting events, such as a tailgate party in the parking lot. As always, however, watch for effectively posted Texas Penal Code Section 30.05, 30.06, 30.07, or other applicable signs in areas where you wish to carry.

I. Correctional facilities

> **WEAPONS PROHIBITED AT CORRECTIONAL FACILITIES**
> **TEX. PENAL CODE § 46.03(a)(9)**
>
> (a) A person commits an offense if the person intentionally, knowingly, or recklessly possesses or goes with a firearm, location-restricted knife, club, or prohibited weapon listed in Section 46.05(a):
>
> (9) on the premises of a correctional facility; ...

A person is not permitted to carry an open or concealed handgun into a correctional facility (the statute makes no distinction between public/private correctional facilities, state prisons, municipal jails, *etc.*) under Texas law. A person is not prohibited, however, from carrying the handgun in the parking lot or other area not considered the "premises" of the facility. Note: Texas Department of Criminal Justice facilities have specific rules about securing a gun in your car when you visit an inmate. *See* Texas Dep't of Criminal Justice, "Offender Rules and Regulations for Visitation" Reference BP-03.85 — "Offender Visitation," Revised: November 2015.

J. Civil commitment facilities

> **WEAPONS PROHIBITED AT CIVIL COMMITMENT FACILITIES**
> **TEX. PENAL CODE § 46.03(a)(10)**
>
> (a) A person commits an offense if the person intentionally, knowingly, or recklessly possesses or goes with a firearm, location-restricted knife, club, or prohibited weapon listed in Section 46.05(a):
>
> > (10) on the premises of a civil commitment facility; ...

A civil commitment facility houses people who have been found to be sexually violent predators under Texas Health and Safety Code Chapter 841. These are people who have served a prison sentence, but a court has found they are a continued danger to society. Deadly weapons are prohibited in correctional facilities and civil commitment facilities under Texas Penal Code Section 38.11, and people are specially prohibited from bringing their handguns into these facilities by Texas Penal Code Section 46.03(a)(10).

K. Mental hospitals

> **WEAPONS PROHIBITED AT MENTAL HOSPITALS**
> **TEX. PENAL CODE § 46.03(a)(12)**
>
> (a) A person commits an offense if the person intentionally, knowingly, or recklessly possesses or goes with a firearm, location-restricted knife, club, or prohibited weapon listed in Section 46.05(a):
>
> > (12) on the premises of a mental hospital, as defined by Section 571.003, Health and Safety Code, unless the person has written authorization of the mental hospital administration; ...

Weapons are prohibited at mental hospitals. Section 571.003 of the Health and Safety Code defines "mental hospital" as "a hospital: (A) operated primarily to provide inpatient care and treatment for persons with mental illness; or (B) operated by a federal agency that is equipped to provide inpatient care and treatment for persons with mental illness."

L. Hospitals, nursing facilities, and amusement parks

WEAPONS PROHIBITED AT HOSPITALS AND NURSING FACILITIES
TEX. PENAL CODE § 46.03(a)(11)

(a) A person commits an offense if the person intentionally, knowingly, or recklessly possesses or goes with a firearm, location-restricted knife, club, or prohibited weapon listed in Section 46.05(a):

> (11) on the premises of a hospital licensed under Chapter 241, Health and Safety Code, or on the premises of a nursing facility licensed under Chapter 242, Health and Safety Code, unless the person has written authorization of the hospital or nursing facility administration, as appropriate; ...

WEAPONS PROHIBITED AT AMUSEMENT PARKS
TEX. PENAL CODE § 46.03(a)(13)

(a) A person commits an offense if the person intentionally, knowingly, or recklessly possesses or goes with a firearm, location-restricted knife, club, or prohibited weapon listed in Section 46.05(a):

> (13) in an amusement park; or ...

An LTC holder may legally carry on the premises of a hospital, nursing home, or amusement park if effective Texas Penal Code Section 30.06 or 30.07 notice has not been provided. Because of the manner in which the law is written, this area of the law causes confusion. It is because Texas Penal Code Section 46.03 states that these areas are prohibited places, only to be trumped by a later section that says an LTC holder may carry unless they are given effective notice under Section 30.06 or 30.07. This exception comes from Texas Penal Code Section 46.15(p), which reads:

(p) Sections 46.03(a)(7), (11), and (13) do not apply if the actor:
   (1) carries a handgun on the premises or other property, as applicable;
   (2) holds a license to carry a handgun issued under Subchapter H, Chapter 411, Government Code; and
   (3) was not given effective notice under Section 30.06 or 30.07 of this code or Section 411.204, Government Code, as applicable.

So, although a hospital, nursing home, and amusement park are generally prohibited places, an LTC holder may carry into those locations as long as he or she is not given notice under Section 30.06 and 30.07. For non-LTC holders, these areas are strictly prohibited.

M. Open government meetings

> **WEAPONS PROHIBITED AT ROOMS OF AN OPEN GOVERNMENT MEETING**
> **TEX. PENAL CODE § 46.03(a)(14)**
>
> (a) A person commits an offense if the person intentionally, knowingly, or recklessly possesses or goes with a firearm, location-restricted knife, club, or prohibited weapon listed in Section 46.05(a):
>
> > (14) in the room or rooms where a meeting of a governmental entity is held, if the meeting is an open meeting subject to Chapter 551, Government Code, and if the entity provided notice as required by that chapter; ...

Just like the prohibition on carrying in hospitals, nursing facilities, and amusement parks, a non-license holder may not carry into a governmental meeting subject to the open meetings law. This same prohibition does not apply to LTC holders even if the governmental entity attempts to exclude the license holder with Texas Penal Code Sections 30.06 and/or 30.07 notice. This means that an LTC holder is permitted to carry at a city council meeting or other meetings of governmental entities in locations that are not otherwise prohibited (*e.g.*, school, office utilized by court, *etc.*).

This law applies only to "open meetings" where the government has complied with all notices required by the Texas open meetings law. In other words, the state agency could not claim every meeting was an open meeting in order to prohibit handguns carried by non-LTC holders from all governmental meetings.

Previously, Texas law allowed the governmental entity to give notice to prevent handguns carried openly or concealed, by requiring the governmental entity to provide notice to LTC holders that handguns were not permitted in the room or rooms where their meeting is actually held. With the passage of the Firearm Carry Act of 2021, this is no longer the case. LTC holders cannot be prohibited from carrying a concealed handgun or visibly holstered handgun in an open meeting, assuming the place is not otherwise prohibited. *See* Tex. Penal Code § 46.15(b)(6); *see also* Government Code Chapter 551. This stands in stark contrast to the person who carries under the authority of Texas Constitutional Carry, who commits a felony by carrying into the open meeting.

N. General defenses and certain classifications

As mentioned above, there are, of course, certain exceptions to possessing firearms and other weapons in the places listed in Texas Penal Code Section 46.03. Most of these defenses pertain to LTC holders, but others are in line with a person acting within the scope of their employment or duties.

1. Volunteer emergency services personnel and first responders

In 2021, the 87th Legislature enacted a law pertaining to first responders and handguns. It seems that the Legislature meant to strike (or at least combine) the previous law relating to voluntary emergency services personnel, but the old law was not repealed or seamlessly transitioned into the new law. As a result, Texas law provides exceptions to Texas Penal Code Section 46.03 for both volunteer emergency personnel and first responders. However, it is important to note that the law is more permissive for volunteer emergency personnel than first responders, as volunteer emergency personnel have more opportunities for defenses to prosecution.

First responders

Texas Penal Code Section 46.01 defines a "first responder" as "a public safety employee whose duties include responding rapidly to an emergency." The term includes fire protection personnel and emergency medical services personnel but does not include volunteers. To become a first responder, a person must take a training course, meet all requirements, and receive a certification of completion. *See* Tex. Gov't Code § 411.184.

As a starting point for where LTC holders who are first responders may carry, Chapter 179 of the Local Government Code explains that the primary benefits under the first responder law only apply to cities with a population of less than 30,000 and counties with a population less than 250,000. In such areas, those municipalities and counties can adopt a policy to allow first responders who have an LTC and additional training to carry concealed or openly while on duty and store handguns on the premises of or in a vehicle owned or leased by the municipality or county. Additionally, in these counties, it is a defense to prosecution under Texas Penal Code Sections 30.06 and 30.07 if the license holder is a first responder and has an unexpired certificate of completion at the time of engaging in the applicable conduct and was engaged in the actual discharge of the first responder's duties while carrying. So, if a qualifying LTC first responder carries past effectively posted Section 30.06 or 30.07 notice, that person may have a defense to prosecution.

When it comes to prohibited places, directors must approve devices to enable a first responder to secure and store a handgun if the first responder, while on duty, is required to enter a location where carrying the handgun is prohibited by federal law or otherwise. Still, for prohibited places, Texas Penal Code Section

46.15 explains that Sections 46.02 and 46.03 do not apply to a first responder who: was carrying a handgun in a concealed manner or in a holster; holds an unexpired certificate of completion under Section 411.184 of the Texas Government Code at the time of engaging in the applicable conduct; was engaged in the actual discharge of the first responder's duties while carrying the handgun; and was employed or supervised by a municipality or county to which Chapter 179 of the Local Government Code applies.

Volunteer emergency services personnel

Under Texas Penal Code Sections 30.06 and 30.07, it is a defense to prosecution that the license holder is a volunteer emergency services personnel. Meaning, LTC holders who are also volunteer emergency services personnel have a defense to prosecution under Sections 30.06 or 30.07, even when not engaging in rendering emergency services. Therefore, while first responders only receive the defense in areas with a certain population number, volunteer emergency services personnel who have an LTC have the defense to prosecution at all times, even when not engaging in rendering emergency services. This is most likely an error in the Texas Legislature's drafting, but it remains the law nonetheless.

If a person has an LTC and they are a volunteer firefighter, a volunteer emergency service provider pursuant to Texas Health & Safety Code Section 773.003, or a person who is rendering services for the general public during emergencies, Texas Penal Code Section 46.03 (prohibited places) does not apply to them.

2. Peace officers

The prohibitions in Texas Penal Code Section 46.03 do not apply to police officers, regardless of whether they are on or off duty.

Further, these prohibitions do not apply to honorably retired peace officers or other qualified retired law enforcement officers under 18 U.S.C. § 926C, federal criminal investigators or former reserve law enforcement officers who have served at least 15 years as a reserve and who maintain a certificate of proficiency issued under Texas Occupations Code Section 1701.357. *See* Tex. Penal Code § 46.15(a)(1) and (5).

V. TEXAS PENAL CODE SECTION 46.15: THE NON-APPLICABILITY STATUTE

Under Section 46.03(a) of the Texas Penal Code, "a person commits an offense if the person intentionally, knowingly, or recklessly possesses or goes with a firearm, location-restricted knife, club, or prohibited weapon listed in Section 46.05(a)" on to certain premises. However, beyond the specific defenses mentioned in the prior sections, there is another general defense to prosecution listed in Texas Penal Code Section 46.15:

> (m) It is a defense to prosecution under Section 46.03 that the actor:
> (1) carries a handgun on a premises or other property on which the carrying of a weapon is prohibited under that section;
> (2) personally received from the owner of the property, or from another person with apparent authority to act for the owner, notice that carrying a firearm or other weapon on the premises or other property, as applicable, was prohibited; and
> (3) promptly departed from the premises or other property.

In short, it is a defense to prosecution if a person carries a handgun into an otherwise prohibited location under Section 46.03, personally received notice that carrying a firearm or other weapon on the premises was prohibited, and then promptly departed from the premises or other property.

For instance, if you accidentally walk into a building, open a door, and find yourself (to your surprise) in a courtroom, you may have a defense under Section 46.15 if you depart immediately upon receiving personal notice that carrying the weapon was prohibited.

However, the defense provided above does not apply if a sign (as described in Section 46.03(o)) was posted prominently at each entrance to the premises or other property, as applicable; or at the time of the offense, the actor knew that carrying a firearm or other weapon on the premises or other property was prohibited. *See* Tex. Penal Code § 46.15(o) and Chapter 13 for a discussion on Texas Penal Code Section 46.03 signage.

LAW CHANGE

Note on repealed Texas Penal Code Section 46.035:

Texas Constitutional Carry (87(R) HB 1927) repealed Texas Penal Code Section 46.035. However, just before the repeal, amendments to Section 46.035 were made, creating what appears to be a conflict. But there is good news, since this conflict is easily resolved. Because the repeal of Section 46.035 took place after it was amended, the repeal trumps the amendment under the Code Construction Act. Therefore, amended Section 46.035, in light of Texas Constitutional Carry, is irreconcilable, making it ineffective. We expect lawmakers to clean this provision up in a future legislative session. *See* Tex. Gov't Code §§ 311.025(b) and 311.026(b).

VI. GENERALLY NON-PROHIBITED PLACES A NON-PROHIBITED PERSON MAY CARRY WITHOUT NOTICE

Throughout this section, you will see the term "constitutional carrier." This term refers to a person who is: at least 21 years old; is not prohibited under state or federal law to possess firearms and ammunition; and is carrying a handgun concealed or openly in a holster on their person, generally in public. *See* Chapter 12 for the full explanation of who may or may not qualify under the Firearm Carry Act of 2021 to carry a handgun without an LTC.

The following places and locations do not generally prohibit the lawful carry of long guns or a handgun by either a constitutional carrier or an LTC holder. However, as previously discussed, if a gun owner is provided notice by the owner or a person with apparent authority over a place or premises that carrying a firearm is not allowed, the person should not proceed into that location with their gun. If the handgun carrier ignores these warnings, criminal penalties including potential jail time and fines would likely follow them.

A. Person's premises or premises under their control

A person who may legally possess a handgun may do so on their premises or premises under their control. The handgun may be loaded or unloaded, concealed or unconcealed in any manner, whether holstered or not. How does the law define the term "premises" in this context? Texas Penal Code Section 46.02(a-2) states: "For purposes of this section, 'premises' includes real property and a recreational vehicle that is being used as living quarters, regardless of whether that use is temporary or permanent. In this subsection, 'recreational vehicle' means a motor vehicle primarily designed as temporary living quarters or a vehicle that contains temporary living quarters and is designed to be towed by a motor vehicle. The term includes a travel trailer, camping trailer, truck camper, motor home, and horse trailer with living quarters." This definition means that "premises" is more than just a person's habitation; it also includes the land surrounding a habitation and extends to all property which is either owned by a person or is under a person's control. This is a much broader definition than when the term "premises" is used to describe public locations where an LTC holder or constitutional carrier may or may not carry their handgun, concealed or visible in a holster. *See* Chapter 13 for more information on where an LTC holder or constitutional carrier can legally carry a handgun.

What does "premises under the person's control" mean?

In 1913, the Texas Court of Criminal Appeals held in *Gibbs v. State* that premises under a person's control means "to exercise restraint or deciding influence over; to dominate; regulate; to hold from action; to curb; subject or overpower." *Gibbs v. State*, 156 S.W. 687 (1913). The Court held in that case that the location of "premises" will mean real property or the building upon it, and the property or building is owned by the person or the person's employer. If the property is not owned by the person or his employer, then the property should be subject to the control of the person or his employer in some capacity.

> **EXAMPLE:**
> Joe, an 18-year-old, legally carries a handgun in his car for protection. One day Joe goes to visit his old friend Sam, at Sam's jewelry store. During this visit, Sam has to go take care of an emergency at home, and instead of closing the store, he asks Joe to watch his store. Sam leaves, and Joe goes out to get his gun and take it into Sam's store for protection in case it gets robbed.

While Joe is not carrying under the authority of Texas Constitutional Carry or an LTC, Joe is in legal possession of his handgun while in Sam's store. Sam has explicitly left Joe with the authority to control who can come into his store; therefore, it is now a premises under his control. Issues involving "premises under a person's control" have been scarcely litigated in the history of Texas jurisprudence. Since the *Gibbs* case in 1913, there has been little commentary on what it means to have premises under a person's control.

In 1973, the Texas Attorney General issued an opinion in an attempt to clarify further what this term really means: "While control need not be exclusive of others, it must be a real right to exercise some dominion over the premises... The person in question must actually have the right to exercise some control over the conduct of other persons upon the premises although his control need not be exclusive." Op. Tex. Att'y Gen. No. H-185 (1973). Of course, since 1913, and even since 1973, what can be considered a premises has evolved, and today the term also includes recreational vehicles.

In September of 2014, the Texas Court of Criminal Appeals held that this includes the common area of condominiums (not apartments) where a person has an undivided ownership interest in the common areas. *See Chiarini v. State*, 442 S.W.3d 318 (Tex. Crim. App. 2014).

The Second Amendment rights of renters (and their guests) are protected thanks to Texas Penal Code Sections 30.05(f-1)-(f-3). These sections of Texas law prohibit "no firearms" clauses by building owners in lease agreements or amendments entered into after September 1, 2019. This protects tenants' rights to possess lawfully owned firearms and ammunition in dwelling units (condos and apartments) and to transport their guns directly between their personal vehicles and their homes. Additionally, this same law provides that there is a defense to prosecution for an alleged violation of Texas Penal Code Sections 30.06 and 30.07 (criminal trespass), if the notice was posted in an area needed to access the rental unit or vehicle of the tenant or guest.

Whether carrying under the authority of an LTC or Texas Constitutional Carry, a non-prohibited person facing prosecution for an alleged violation in this situation would have the legal argument they were lawfully carrying their handgun into a location protected by Texas's version of the Castle Doctrine if they moved directly *en route* to or from their vehicle to their (or the leaseholder's) rental unit or vehicle.

It is important to note that this change in the law does not infringe on the right of landlords or building owners to prohibit the possession or carrying of firearms or ammunition in common areas not used to travel directly *en route* to a dwelling unit. Therefore, firearms and ammunition can still be prohibited in leasing offices, swimming pool areas, workout facilities, mailbox areas, community rooms, *etc.* with proper notice. *See* Tex. Penal Code §§ 30.05(f-1)-(f-3); *see also* Tex. Prop. Code §§ 82.002, 82.121, 92.026, 94.257.

Additionally, Texas Property Code Section 202.021 prohibits a property owners' association from including or enforcing any provision in a document or instrument that would allow a home owners' association to prohibit, restrict, or has the effect of prohibiting or restricting any person, who is otherwise authorized, from lawfully possessing, transporting, or storing firearms or ammunition on their property.

B. Recreational vehicles or motorhomes
When is an RV considered a "premises"?
A recreational vehicle ("RV") is defined in the Texas Penal Code as a premises whenever it is being used as a home (living quarters). *See* Tex. Penal Code § 46.02(a-2). Conversely, when an RV is being used as a vehicle, it is a vehicle, and it is not a premises, *i.e.*, when it is actively being driven or towed. This is also an important distinction in whether a handgun must be concealed or not when not being transported in a holster.

Carrying of handguns on own premises
Texas law does not make it a crime for a non-prohibited person to openly or concealed carry a handgun on their own premises; therefore, it is legal. However, as a practical legal matter, a person may not carry the firearm "in a manner calculated to alarm," if the particular area could be argued to be a public place. For example, a crazy man waving a gun around in his own front yard could arguably be violating Texas Penal Code Section 46.02 because he can be observed from the street, which is a public place. If a person carries in this manner, the person could be charged with the crime of disorderly conduct under Texas Penal Code Section 42.01(a)(8). Remember, if a person intentionally and knowingly displays a firearm in a public place in a manner he knows is likely, under an objective standard

of reasonableness, to frighten the average, ordinary person, they could be found guilty of disorderly conduct. *See State v. Ross*, 573 S.W.3d 817, 825 (Tex. Crim. App. 2019).

C. Motor vehicles
Inside of or directly en route to a motor vehicle or watercraft owned by the person or under the person's control

Carrying a handgun in a motor vehicle or watercraft is not generally referred to as "constitutional carry." However, we will continue to use the term "constitutional carrier" below to refer to someone who is 21 years old and not otherwise prohibited by law from carrying a handgun under the Firearm Carry Act of 2021.

What is the legal definition of a "motor vehicle"? A motor vehicle is defined in Texas Penal Code Section 32.34(a)(2) and means "a device in, on, or by which a person or property is or may be transported or drawn on a highway, except a device used exclusively on stationary rails or tracks." This definition is very broad and includes (but is not limited to) vehicles that are not cars or trucks, such as:
- Motorcycles;
- Golf carts;
- Motorized scooters;
- ATVs; and
- Riding lawnmowers.

One question that is often asked is whether or not a personal mobility scooter (like a Rascal) or some other personal mobility device qualifies as a motor vehicle? Under Texas Transportation Code Section 552A.0101, a personal mobility device is not a motor vehicle as long as it is not capable of speeds exceeding 8 miles per hour and a person operating one is considered to be a pedestrian. Before the Firearm Carry Act of 2021, a person was not able to legally carry a handgun while traveling in public on such a device without an LTC.

However, thanks to the 87th Legislature, both LTC holders and constitutional carriers operating their personal mobility devices may lawfully carry concealed or openly in a holster publicly as long as they are not in a prohibited place or provided notice by a person with apparent authority that handguns are not allowed on the premises of a non-prohibited location.

The term "watercraft" is defined in Texas Penal Code Section 46.02(a-3) and means "any boat, motorboat, vessel, or personal watercraft, other than a seaplane on water, used or capable of being used for transportation on water." Where watercraft are concerned, the general understanding is that if you can float it, you can boat it.

When is a vehicle under a person's control so as to allow them to possess a handgun legally?

For those persons under 21 years of age, a motor vehicle or watercraft must be "under the person's control" for that individual to lawfully possess a concealed handgun. A person does not have to be the owner of the vehicle or watercraft to carry. For instance, a rental car is the property of the company that rents the car. However, a person who rents the car from a company and takes possession of the car is the person who has control over the vehicle. Where vehicles are concerned, the person "in control" of a vehicle is generally understood to be the driver, as that is the singular individual who has the ability to move the automobile. For that reason, a person may lawfully possess a handgun in a rental vehicle, the same way they can legally possess a handgun in their own vehicle. The same principles would apply to watercraft: whoever drives the boat is the person that has control of the boat. However, there are no appellate cases directly clarifying this issue.

Beginning September 1, 2021, a passenger in a vehicle or watercraft who is a legal constitutional carrier may have a handgun concealed or open in a holster as long as they have not been provided specific notice firearms are prohibited by the owner or person in control of the vehicle or watercraft. *See* Tex. Penal Code § 30.05(a)(d-3).

> **PRACTICAL LEGAL TIP**
>
> If you carry a handgun in your vehicle, don't allow yourself to be drawn in to a road rage incident, no matter how minor. Someone who calls 911 to report that you pointed a gun at them, even though it was really just your middle finger, may get you arrested and charged with a crime. So, if you carry a gun in the car, forget how to flip the bird! –Emily

How can a person legally carry a handgun in a commercial vehicle?

One question that is often asked is whether a person who operates a commercial shipping vehicle (such as a semi-truck or similar) is entitled to follow the same rules and regulations governing ordinary LTC holders and constitutional carriers in Texas.

The answer to this question is simple: Yes, they are. This is because there are no specific Texas or federal regulations regarding carrying in a commercial shipping vehicle beyond those regulations which may be imposed by the operator's employer. This may be a breach of company policy, but not the law and is not a crime. A breach of company policy may lead to a person being terminated from their employment. It is important to remember, however, when you are in another state, you are subject to their laws—check the law ahead of time if you are trucking across the nation.

May the handgun be loaded?
Yes. The law allows the handgun to be loaded and accessible—it may be transported concealed or openly in a holster by an LTC holder or constitutional carrier. If you are a non-prohibited person between the ages of 18 and 20 carrying in a vehicle you own or are operating, the handgun must remain concealed.

What does it mean to be "en route" to a motor vehicle or watercraft?
Traveling *en route* means to travel directly to a motor vehicle or watercraft. The more a person strays from a direct route to their vehicle, the less likely it will look like they are in *en route*. There is, however, no case law drawing bright lines in determining this issue.

A warning on unholstered handguns in vehicles
It is not uncommon to find an unholstered handgun tucked away or obscured in a vehicle. While this practice may be legal for qualifying individuals, it may not be advisable. What if a person is required to exit the vehicle and the handgun is visible and not holstered (such as during a traffic stop)? Of course, in addition to the potential problem of a handgun becoming unconcealed, there's

also the matter of safety; just because something is legal does not mean that it's smart!

May I keep a handgun in my vehicle if there are children in the car?
Yes, having children in the car does not change the law on whether a person is able to possess a handgun in the vehicle legally. However, it is a violation of the law under Texas Penal Code Section 46.13 if a person allows a child to gain access to a readily dischargeable firearm and with criminal negligence:
1) fails to secure the firearm; or
2) leaves the firearm in a place in which the person knew or should have known the child would gain access.

See Chapters 5 and 6 for more information on children and firearms.

LIMITATIONS ON HANDGUNS FOR THOSE UNDER 21
TEX. PENAL CODE § 46.02(a)

(a) A person commits an offense if the person:
   (1) intentionally, knowingly, or recklessly carries on or about his or her person a handgun; [and]
   (2) at the time of the offense:
      (A) is younger than 21 years of age; or
      (B) has been convicted of an offense under Section 22.01(a)(1), 22.05, 22.07, or 42.01(a)(7) or (8) committed in the five-year period preceding the date the instant offense was committed; and
   (3) is not:
      (A) on the person's own premises or premises under the person's control; or
      (B) inside of or directly *en route* to a motor vehicle or watercraft that is owned by the person or under the person's control.

Gun owners younger than 21 years old generally may not carry in public

Legal gun owners between the ages of 18 and 20 do not qualify as a constitutional carrier under Texas's new laws. The 87th Legislature amended Texas Penal Code Section 46.02(a) to include a new offense for 18-to-20-year-olds who attempt to illegally carry a handgun in a public place. A violation of this section is a Class A misdemeanor. *See* Tex. Penal Code § 46.02(b).

Keep in mind, active or honorably discharged members of the military and persons protected under certain protective orders, between the ages of 18 to 20, may qualify for an LTC and lawfully carry in public pursuant to that license. *See* Chapter 12 for LTC qualifications and rules.

LIMITATIONS ON HANDGUNS IN VEHICLES
TEX. PENAL CODE § 46.02(a-1)(2)

A person commits an offense if the person intentionally, knowingly, or recklessly carries on or about his or her person a handgun in a motor vehicle or watercraft that is owned by the person or under the person's control at any time in which the person is:

(A) engaged in criminal activity, other than a Class C misdemeanor that is a violation of a law or ordinance regulating traffic or boating; or

(B) prohibited by law from possessing a firearm.

No criminal activity or criminal street gangs

Individuals who are engaged in criminal activity, other than a Class C misdemeanor regulating traffic or boating or who are prohibited from possessing a firearm by law, are not allowed to have a handgun in their vehicle or watercraft. *See* Tex. Penal Code § 46.02(a-1)(2).

If a person is engaged in any crime other than minor traffic or boating offenses, the person will lose the right to possess a handgun in their vehicle or watercraft under Texas law. Similarly, the law generally does not allow individuals who are prohibited from possessing firearms to have a handgun in their vehicle.

It should be noted, however, that not all traffic violations are Class C misdemeanors. A person who is stopped by law enforcement for changing lanes erratically or running other drivers off the road, for instance, may be charged with reckless driving, which is a crime where jail time is a possible punishment. In that case, possession of a handgun in the vehicle would be illegal.

> **LIMITATIONS ON HANDGUNS IN VEHICLES**
> **TEX. PENAL CODE § 46.04(a-1)**
>
> A person who is a member of a criminal street gang, as defined by Section 71.01, commits an offense if the person intentionally, knowingly, or recklessly carries on or about his or her person a handgun in a motor vehicle or watercraft.

How does the law define "criminal street gang"? Texas Penal Code Section 71.01(d) states that a criminal street gang "means three or more persons having a common identifying sign or symbol or an identifiable leadership who continuously or regularly associate in the commission of criminal activities." An offense under this provision is a Class A misdemeanor. *See* Tex. Penal Code § 46.04(e).

An important exception lives in Texas Penal Code Section 46.15(b)(6), which provides criminal street gang members a means of avoiding prosecution under Texas Penal Code Section 46.04(a-1) for having a handgun in a vehicle or watercraft as long as they were carrying pursuant to a valid LTC.

Members of criminal street gangs are prohibited from possessing a handgun in their vehicle or watercraft even though they may not be otherwise committing a crime. Strangely enough, this prohibition does not extend to an otherwise legal constitutional carrier who is a criminal street gang member from carrying a handgun concealed or openly in a holster outside of their motor vehicle or watercraft (*e.g.*, on a public sidewalk).

Is it legal for an owner of a vehicle to possess a handgun when a passenger in the vehicle is a felon or is otherwise disqualified from possessing firearms?

Yes, so long as the felon (or person disqualified) never possesses the firearm. The law focuses on who has possession, defined as "actual care, custody, control, and management." *See* Tex. Penal Code § 1.07(39).

EXAMPLE:
> Charles arrives at the McDonald's in Huntsville to pick up his brother Jamie, who is being released from prison. Charles always keeps a handgun under the driver seat of his vehicle. When Jamie gets in the car, he sits in the front passenger seat.

Has Charles violated the law? No, Charles still has possession of the handgun. It is a crime to affirmatively give a handgun to a disqualified individual—like a felon—but it is not a crime to possess a handgun around such an individual.

The law here revolves around whether the prohibited person possesses the firearm, not whether a firearm is nearby. *See* Tex. Penal Code § 46.04(a). For instance, if we change the example to a person who hands a recently released felon a handgun in the car and asks the felon to "put it under the seat," then the person has committed a crime. *See* Tex. Penal Code § 46.06.

What if Charles kept the handgun in the center console? Charles certainly has not committed a crime, but could Jamie be considered to be in "possession"? Here, the answer is less clear. In the real world, the legal fight will be over who was actually in possession of the firearm (or joint possession in this case). This issue may ultimately be for the jury to decide.

> **GIVING A GUN TO DISQUALIFIED INDIVIDUALS**
> **TEX. PENAL CODE § 46.06(a)(1)**
>
> A person commits an offense if the person: sells, rents, leases, loans, or gives a handgun to any person knowing that the person to whom the handgun is to be delivered intends to use it unlawfully or in the commission of an unlawful act.

Cannot "give" a handgun to someone who intends to break the law

This one is simple: if someone asks you for your gun in order to rob a bank or knock off a liquor store, it is a crime for you to give them the gun. A violation of this law is typically punishable as a Class A misdemeanor, but a person could be charged with a state jail felony in some instances! *See* Tex. Penal Code § 46.06(d).

> **NONAPPLICABILITY OF SECTION 46.02**
> **TEX. PENAL CODE § 46.15(b)(2) AND (3)**
>
> Sections 46.02, 46.03(a)(14), and 46.04(a-1) do not apply to a person who:
>
> (2) is traveling;
>
> (3) is engaging in lawful hunting, fishing, or other sporting activity on the immediate premises where the activity is conducted, or is *en route* between the premises and the actor's residence, motor vehicle, or watercraft, if the weapon is a type commonly used in the activity.

Handguns are allowed if traveling or engaged in sporting activities
The criminal provisions for possession of a weapon under Texas Penal Code Sections 46.02 (including firearms), 46.03(a)(14), and 46.04(a-1) are not applicable if a person is traveling or engaged in sporting activities.

Unfortunately, there is no statutory definition of the term "traveling." In fact, much of the case law on matters addressing traveling is contradictory as to what does and does not qualify as traveling. Of note, however, is one case that declares definitively what traveling is not: it is not traveling from a person's place of business to the person's home. *Bergman v. State*, 90 S.W.3d 855 (Tex. App.— San Antonio 2002 no pet.). Who, then, determines whether a person was traveling or not? Ultimately, a jury will make the determination. In *Illingworth v. State*, the Fort Worth Court of Appeals held that "the question of whether one is a traveler is a fact question to be resolved by the trier of fact." *Illingworth v. State*, 156 S.W.3d 662 (Tex. App.—Ft. Worth 2005 no pet.).

Although much was made over this "traveling exception" for many years, the 2007 passage of the Texas Motorist Protection Act (creating Texas Penal Code 46.02(a)(3)(B)) essentially put an end to the questions and uncertainty surrounding this law. As long as a person complies with the minimum legal restrictions regarding carrying a handgun in a motor vehicle or watercraft discussed earlier in this Chapter, what constitutes "traveling" is no longer a concern.

Hunting and sporting activities

Any non-prohibited person may legally engage in hunting, fishing, or other lawful sporting activities with a handgun. However, the handgun must be a type commonly used in whatever sporting activity the person engages.

D. Public places not otherwise prohibited by law

Generally, public locations (owned by private companies or individuals) and their premises that are not otherwise prohibited by law are fair ground for constitutional carriers and LTC holders to carry their handguns. This would include grocery, convenience, and retail stores that do not otherwise provide a constitutional carrier or LTC holder proper notice that handguns are not allowed inside their premises. Conversely, as previously discussed in Chapter 13, a store owner or person with apparent authority over a premises may provide notice by posting compliant signage, individualized oral notice, or by handing a would-be patron an index card with the appropriate legal warnings that firearms are not allowed inside. *See* Tex. Penal Code §§ 30.05, 30.06, 30.07.

The good news for property owners is that it's not an all-or-nothing proposition. There may be private property owners who have grown comfortable with license holders carrying openly or concealed in their places of business but are uneasy with the thought of unlicensed individuals carrying on their property. Unlicensed people can be prevented with effective notice under the general criminal trespass statute, Texas Penal Code Section 30.05. However, this Section does not apply to license holders carrying handguns. If a property owner wants to prevent license holders from carrying, they are still required to provide effective criminal trespass notices under Texas Penal Code Sections 30.06 (for concealed carry) and 30.07 (for open carry in a holster).

Stores selling alcohol without notice prohibiting firearms

As discussed in Chapter 13, businesses selling alcohol (not 51% locations) previously posted TABC "blue signs" to warn unlicensed handgun carriers that carrying into their premises was a third degree felony. However, thanks to the 87th Texas Legislature, all "blue signs" are repealed and no longer have legal meaning because it is no longer a felony for the unlicensed carrying of a handgun in one of these locations. After September 1, 2021, "blue signs" may be ignored by LTC holders and constitutional carriers alike.

Constitutional carriers and LTC holders may carry into grocery stores, liquor stores, convenience stores, and restaurants selling alcohol if they have not received proper notice the establishment prohibits handguns inside. However, if an establishment has 30.05 notice that's reasonably likely to come to the attention of persons entering the premises, constitutional carriers should not carry inside as it would be treated as a trespass. Alternatively, if a liquor store has 30.06 and 30.07 signs properly posted, an LTC holder should not carry their handgun inside or they could be prosecuted for criminal trespass. Finally, just like any other private location accessible to the public (other than prohibited locations under Texas Penal Code Section 46.03), a business owner can exclude all handgun carriers by effective 30.05, 30.06, and 30.07 notices. *See* Chapter 13 to learn more about proper signage and notice requirements.

May a person carry in a restaurant?

Restaurants are establishments that are subject to the same restrictions discussed earlier in Chapter 13 governing the use of 51%, 30.06, 30.07, and 30.05 notice. If a restaurant derives more than 51% of its income from the sales and service of alcohol, then the carrying of a handgun is prohibited by both constitutional carriers and LTC holders. Likewise, if a restaurant has posted an effective 30.06 sign, the carrying of a concealed handgun by a license holder is prohibited, and if it has posted an effective 30.07 sign, the carrying of a handgun openly carried in a holster is prohibited. Furthermore, if the restaurant has posted a proper 30.05 sign, a constitutional carrier should neither carry concealed nor openly into the premises. However, if none of these signs are present, then a constitutional carrier or license holder is legally able to carry their handgun in a restaurant, unless they are given an alternative form notice. Under most circumstances, the bar area of a restaurant is not a separate location for TABC licensing purposes. So, as a general rule, if you can carry in the restaurant, you can carry in the bar.

E. Employer/employee parking lot rules

What about an employee with an LTC or a legal constitutional carrier who wants to store a firearm in their private vehicle while at work? Under Texas Labor Code Section 52.061, those lawfully carrying are allowed to conceal their handgun within their locked, privately owned motor vehicle in an employee parking lot, garage, or other parking area provided by an employer. However, some employers are lawfully allowed to exclude all firearms. Texas Labor Code Section 52.062 lists the employers allowed to exclude firearms legally in the parking lot, including:

1) in a vehicle owned or leased by a public or private employer and used by an employee in the course and scope of the employee's employment, unless the employee is required to transport or store a firearm in the official discharge of the employee's duties;
2) a school district;
3) an open-enrollment charter school, as defined by Section 5.001, Education Code;
4) a private school, as defined by Section 22.081, Education Code;
5) on property owned or controlled by a person, other than the employer, that is subject to a valid, unexpired oil, gas, or other mineral lease that contains a provision prohibiting the possession of firearms on the property; or
6) on property owned or leased by a chemical manufacturer or oil and gas refiner with an air authorization under Chapter 382, Health and Safety Code, and on which the primary business conducted is the manufacture, use, storage, or transportation of hazardous, combustible, or explosive materials, except in regard to an employee who holds a license to carry a handgun under Subchapter H, Chapter 411, Government Code, and who stores a firearm or ammunition that the employee is authorized by law to possess in a locked, privately owned motor vehicle in a parking lot, parking garage, or other parking area the employer provides for employees that is outside of a secured and restricted area:
    a. that contains the physical plant;
    b. that is not open to the public; and

    c. the ingress into which is constantly monitored by security personnel.

The law on employer/employee handgun relations is very interesting, not because of the rights provided and/or restricted, but because of the fact that there is no penalty for either party who violates this law. Thus, an employer who disciplines an employee for having a firearm in the employee's personal vehicle is not subject to any criminal responsibility or civil liability for doing so. In fact, an employee can be fired for violating company policy in the employee handbook and have no legal recourse against the employer, but the employee does not need to fear criminal prosecution.

The 85th Texas Legislature created an interesting wrinkle to a school district's exemption from the employer parking lot law. The Texas Education Code was amended to state that a school district could not prohibit employees who are also LTC holders from keeping firearms and ammunition concealed in their locked private motor vehicles while parked in school parking lots. School districts irrationally reacted to this new law and began imposing unreasonable storage and notice conditions on their employees, undermining the legislative intent. In response in 2019, the Texas Legislature further amended the Texas Education Code to add that schools may not regulate the manner in which the handgun, firearm, or ammunition is stored in a private vehicle. This closed the loophole that school districts had been using to thwart the restrictions. *See* Tex. Educ. Code § 37.0815(a).

The 87th Texas Legislature in 2021 did not further amend the Texas Education Code to explicitly allow constitutional carrier employees the ability to store their firearm and ammunition in their private vehicle parked in school parking lots. The law applies only to LTC holders;

therefore, school districts can still prohibit firearms or ammunition in the private motor vehicles of non-LTC holder employees. This is another example of why it is beneficial to obtain a Texas LTC.

F. Houses of religious worship

When the original CHL (now LTC) law was created in 1995, it included a list of places where a license holder could not carry under the now-defunct Texas Penal Code Section 46.035. This list forbade carrying in churches, synagogues, and other places of religious worship. In 1997, the law changed so that these places were only prohibited if effective 30.06, and later 30.07, criminal trespass notice was provided. However, over the decades, this created an incredible amount of confusion about whether or not an LTC holder could carry into a church. While the law provided that an LTC holder could carry into a place of religious worship so long as they were not provided effective 30.06 or 30.07 criminal trespass notice, many were unsure about carrying a handgun.

In 2019, the Texas Legislature amended the law to clear up the confusing language regarding an LTC holder's ability to carry a handgun into places of religious worship by striking "churches, synagogues, or other places of religious worship" from the list of prohibited locations. This change in the law clarified these places were to be treated the same as other private property premises.

As previously discussed throughout this book, the 87th Texas Legislature repealed Texas Penal Code Section 46.035 and relocated its prohibited places list to Texas Penal Code Section 46.03. Places of religious worship are not located within the newly formed list under Section 46.03, and therefore, are still to be treated as any other private property. This means if a place of religious worship does not provide effective 30.05 notice to a constitutional carrier or 30.06 and/or 30.07 notice to an LTC holder, a person may carry within the premises of the house of religious worship. However, religious entities are free to post these signs if they choose to prohibit handguns within their premises.

G. College campuses

As of September 1, 2021, under the Firearm Carry Act of 2021, an unlicensed, constitutional carrier is allowed to walk the parking lots, parking garages, streets, sidewalks, and walkways of a college campus, as well as grounds where a school-sponsored activity is not taking place, with a concealed or openly holstered handgun. However, once that constitutional carrier reaches the threshold of a building, school-sponsored activity, or sporting event of that college or university, they cannot carry.

LTC holders may also carry a concealed handgun in the parking lots, parking garages, streets, sidewalks, walkways, and into the buildings on the campus of a public or private institution of higher learning (including junior colleges) if the specific building does not have effective Texas Penal Code Section 30.06 notice prohibiting concealed carry of handguns. *See* Tex. Penal Code § 46.03(a)(1)(B). Additionally, LTC carriers without effective 30.06 notice may carry concealed onto the premises, grounds, and buildings where a sponsored activity is taking place as well as a passenger transportation vehicle of an institution of higher learning. Disregarding a 30.06 notice in these locations is punishable as a Class A misdemeanor. *See* Tex. Penal Code § 46.03(g-2).

An LTC holder who does not keep their handgun concealed on the premises, grounds, and buildings of a private institution of higher learning where a sponsored activity is taking place, in addition to a passenger transportation vehicle of the private institution of higher learning, may commit the Class A misdemeanor of Unlawful Carry of a Weapon. *See* Tex. Penal Code §§ 46.03(a-2), (g-2).

An interesting quirk arising out of the Firearm Carry Act of 2021 is the confusion surrounding campus carry when not inside of buildings. Because the campus carry language was essentially copied and pasted out of Texas Penal Code Section 46.035 (now repealed) and contains the phrase "under the authority of Subchapter H, Chapter 411, Government Code," it raises the question as to whether constitutional carriers are limited by the campus carry provisions that previously only existed for LTC holders (*i.e.*, must carry concealed). Only time will tell how the courts will interpret these provisions, but on the plain reading of the law, it appears that LTC holders and constitutional carriers carrying in these areas are not limited to concealed carry.

Remember, gun owners between the ages of 18 and 20 do not qualify as a constitutional carrier under Texas's new laws, so unless a college student qualifies under an exception for an LTC, they may not carry a handgun on a college campus!

Can a college or university have a general prohibition on handguns on campus?

A public college or university cannot establish a general prohibition against carrying concealed by license holders. However, the president of an institution of higher education may adopt reasonable rules and restrictions for carrying a concealed handgun after consulting with students, faculty, and staff. This means that certain areas may be off-limits to handguns as long as effective notice is given pursuant to

Texas Penal Code Section 30.06, but the institution cannot make a universal prohibition on handguns being carried on campus. *See* Tex. Gov't Code § 411.2031(d) and (d-1).

If the president adopts an anti-handgun policy that results in a general prohibition, they may be violating Texas Government Code 411.209 when they prohibit LTC holders from carrying. What is a person to do if they find themselves at a public university campus that has a general prohibition for LTC holders? A rule that acts as an unreasonable ban on an LTC holder carrying into the buildings may open the door to an official complaint followed by a lawsuit from the attorney general of the State of Texas.

In contrast to a public institution, a private institution of higher learning retains the right to create a universal prohibition against LTC holders carrying concealed handguns into buildings where a sponsored activity is taking place as well as a passenger transportation vehicle of an institution of higher learning. If a private institution chooses to prevent LTC holders from carrying concealed handguns, it must provide proper trespassing notice under Texas Penal Code Section 30.06. *See* Tex. Gov't Code § 411.2031(e).

What kind of restrictions can a college or university adopt?

After consulting with students, faculty, and staff, the president of the public or private institution of higher learning may establish "reasonable rules, regulations, or other provisions regarding the carrying of concealed handguns by license holders…" while on campus. *See* Tex. Gov't Code §§ 411.2031 (d-1), (e). The rules may prohibit LTC holders from carrying into specific areas of campuses, or any grounds or buildings where an institution sponsored activity is held, or in a passenger transportation vehicle owned by the institution. For any areas that are designated off-limits to concealed handguns, whether they be indoors or outdoors, the institution must comply with the notice rules of Texas Penal Code Section 30.06. Therefore, if a university wants to keep an LTC holder with a concealed handgun out of the student center, it must post an effective 30.06 sign, give personal, verbal notice, or provide written notice. *See* Chapter 13 for a detailed discussion of effective section 30.06 notice.

An institution must widely distribute its rules and restrictions concerning concealed handguns to students, faculty, and staff, including prominently posting them on the institution's website. Colleges and universities cannot hide the ball here. It must make these rules and restrictions easy to find, read, and understand. *See* Tex. Gov't Code § 411.2031(d-3).

Do I have to store my handgun in a particular way?
An institution of higher learning may establish rules for the storage of handguns in dorms or other residential facilities that are operated by the institution and located on the campus. *See* Tex. Gov't Code § 411.2031(d). If a college or university requires that a specific type of safe or locking device be used in storing a handgun, a gun owner must comply.

Is a person legally permitted to possess a firearm in their vehicle in the parking lot of a college or university?
Yes, all individuals may possess a firearm in a vehicle the person owns or is under their control in a college or university parking lot, as the parking lot does not constitute the "premises" of the institution. Some colleges and universities passed their own rules and regulations to prevent employees, visitors, and students from

having firearms in their cars. Texas Government Code Section 411.2032 prevents an institution of higher learning from creating a disciplinary policy preventing LTC holders from storing firearms and ammunition in their locked motor vehicles on campus parking lots. While this law was not amended by the 87th Texas Legislature to reflect constitutional carriers directly, a student constitutional carrier safely and securely storing their handgun in their vehicle parked in the parking lot of a public institute of higher learning would have a strong legal argument against a disciplinary policy. However, this area of the law is brand-new, and thus, there have yet to be any court cases tackling the issue at the time of this book's printing.

Carrying into a collegiate sporting event

When it comes to collegiate sporting events, an LTC holder may carry a concealed handgun while in attendance so long as they are not provided effective Texas Penal Code Section 30.06 notice. *See* Tex. Penal Code § 46.15(q). If an effective 30.06 sign is present at the sporting event, or a person does not have an LTC and carries a handgun unlawfully into a collegiate sporting event, it is a Class A misdemeanor to be in possession of a concealed handgun. *See* Tex. Penal Code § 46.03(g-2).

As previously discussed in this Chapter, Texas law also makes it unlawful to carry a firearm at an interscholastic sporting event (elementary, middle, or high school) or at a professional sporting event.

H. State and municipal parks

Local municipalities are preempted by state law from prohibiting the carrying of a handgun concealed or openly carried in a holster by either an LTC holder or a constitutional carrier and are therefore not authorized to prevent the legal carrying thereof. *See* Tex. Loc. Gov't Code § 229.001.

It is also permissible for an LTC holder or constitutional carrier to possess a concealed or visibly holstered handgun in a state park.

I. Hotels

> **APPLICABILITY OF FIREARMS POLICY TO HANDGUNS**
> **TEX. OCC. CODE § 2155.1025**
>
> (a) Unless possession of a handgun or handgun ammunition on hotel property is prohibited by state or federal law, a hotel may not adopt a firearms policy described by Section 2155.102 prohibiting a hotel guest from:
> (1) carrying or storing a handgun or handgun ammunition in the guest's hotel room;
> (2) carrying a handgun or handgun ammunition directly *en route* to or from the hotel or the guest's hotel room;
> (3) carrying a handgun or handgun ammunition directly *en route* to or from the guest's vehicle located on the hotel property, including a vehicle in a parking area provided for hotel guests; or
> (4) carrying or storing a handgun or handgun ammunition in the guest's vehicle located on the hotel property, including a vehicle in a parking area provided for hotel guests.

> (b) A hotel may adopt a firearms policy requiring a hotel guest carrying a handgun or handgun ammunition in a common area on the hotel property to:
>
> (1) carry a handgun in a concealed manner; or
>
> (2) carry handgun ammunition in a case or bag.

Prior to the 87th Texas Legislature, hotels were permitted to follow the same guidelines for other businesses in that they could post a 30.06 sign or a 30.07 sign to effectively prohibit LTC holders from carrying concealed or openly visible holstered handguns in certain areas. However, a hotel room is considered premises, or premises under a person's control, and the law already allowed for the transport to and carry of a firearm in such places under Texas Penal Code Section 46.02. In addition to the prohibitions in certain public areas by LTC holders, hotels were also allowed to provide notice under Texas Penal Code Section 30.05 for unlicensed gun owners that firearm possession was prohibited in or on their property.

However, sweeping changes were made to the laws affecting hotel guests and their rights to carry in 2021. "'Hotel' means a hotel, motel, inn, or similar business entity that offers more than 10 rooms to the public for temporary lodging for a fee." *See* Tex. Occ. Code § 2155.101.

DEFENSES TO PROSECUTION FOR HOTEL GUEST CONSTITUTIONAL CARRIERS AND LTC HOLDERS TEX. PENAL CODE §§ 30.05, 30.06, AND 30.07:

Section 30.05(f-4) It is a defense to prosecution under this section that:

    (1) the conduct occurred on hotel property, and the basis on which entry on that property was forbidden is that entry with a firearm or firearm ammunition was forbidden;

    (2) the actor is a guest of a hotel, as defined by Section 2155.101, Occupations Code; and

    (3) the actor:

        (A) carries or stores a firearm or firearm ammunition in the actor's hotel room;

        (B) carries a firearm or firearm ammunition directly *en route* to or from the hotel or the actor's hotel room;

        (C) carries a firearm or firearm ammunition directly *en route* to or from the actor's vehicle located on the hotel property, including a vehicle in a parking area provided for hotel guests; or

        (D) carries or stores a firearm or firearm ammunition in the actor's vehicle located on the hotel property, including a vehicle in a parking area provided for hotel guests.

Section 30.06(e-4) It is a defense to prosecution under this section that the license holder is a guest of a hotel, as defined by Section 2155.101, Occupations Code, and the license holder:

    (1) carries or stores a handgun in the license holder's hotel room;

> (2) carries a handgun directly *en route* to or from the hotel or the license holder's hotel room;
> (3) carries a handgun directly *en route* to or from the license holder's vehicle located on the hotel property, including a vehicle in a parking area provided for hotel guests; or
> (4) carries or stores a handgun in the license holder's vehicle located on the hotel property, including a vehicle in a parking area provided for hotel guests.
>
> Section 30.07(e-4) It is a defense to prosecution under this section that the license holder is a guest of a hotel, as defined by Section 2155.101, Occupations Code, and the license holder:
> (1) carries or stores a handgun in the license holder's hotel room;
> (2) carries a handgun directly *en route* to or from the hotel or the license holder's hotel room;
> (3) carries a handgun directly *en route* to or from the license holder's vehicle located on the hotel property, including a vehicle in a parking area provided for hotel guests; or
> (4) carries or stores a handgun in the license holder's vehicle located on the hotel property, including a vehicle in a parking area provided for hotel guests.

Beginning September 1, 2021, hotels may no longer prohibit a guest who is a lawful constitutional carrier or LTC holder from carrying or storing a firearm or firearm ammunition: in the guest's hotel room; while the guest is directly *en route* to or from the hotel or the guest's hotel room; directly *en route* to or from the guest's vehicle located on the hotel property, including a vehicle in a parking area provided for hotel guests; or in the guest's vehicle located on the hotel property, including a vehicle in a parking area provided for hotel guests.

Strangely, the 87th Texas Legislature left language for hotels (which violate this new provision of the law) requiring them to provide notice on their Internet reservation website of their policy regarding the possession, storage, and transportation of firearms. If a hotel owner or operator fails to follow these laws, the hotel owner or keeper commits a misdemeanor offense punishable by a fine of not more than $100. *See* Tex. Occ. Code § 2155.103(c).

J. Lower Colorado River Authority areas

Tucked away in an obscure section of the Texas Parks and Wildlife Code is Section 62.081, which states "no person may hunt with, possess, or shoot a firearm, bow, crossbow, slingshot, or any other weapon on or across the land of the Lower Colorado River Authority." This strange law was passed in 1975 and was left apparently unnoticed until 2013, when the legislature amended Section 62.082 to exclude LTC holders from the application of this law. Thus, an LTC holder is allowed to possess a handgun concealed or visibly carried in a holster on the land of the Lower Colorado River Authority. It is important to note, however, this law went unchanged in 2021. This means if a constitutional carrier is not otherwise authorized by law to possess a firearm (or one of the other aforementioned weapons) within Lower Colorado River Authority lands, they could be prosecuted for a Class C misdemeanor. *See* Tex. Parks & Wild. Code § 62.084.

K. Carrying during a declared disaster

In 2019, Texas Penal Code Section 46.15 was amended to add subsections which address carrying a handgun during a declared disaster. With the substantial changes made to handgun carry laws in the 87th Texas Legislature, the legality of carrying during a declared disaster was also modified.

Previously, Texas Penal Code Section 46.15(k) provided a blanket protection from prosecution for unlawful carrying of a weapon to a person who was carrying a handgun if they were: evacuating from an area following the declaration of a state disaster or local state of disaster or reentering that area following the person's evacuation; not more than 168 hours had elapsed since the state of disaster or local state of disaster was declared, or the governor extended the period during which a person could carry a handgun under this subsection; and the person was not prohibited by state or federal law from possessing a firearm.

With the passing of the Firearm Carry Act of 2021, a constitutional carrier would have little need for this non-applicability protection in most scenarios. However, if a person is 18 to 20 years old, this protection will serve them well should they find themselves evacuating from a declared disaster and the rest of the provisions of Texas Penal Code Section 46.15(k) apply.

When it comes to emergency shelters, Texas Penal Code Sections 46.02; 46.03(a)(1), (a)(2), (a)(3), and (a)(4) do not apply to a person who carries a handgun if: (1) the person carries the handgun on the premises of a location operating as an emergency shelter during a declared state of disaster or a declared local state of disaster; (2) the owner, controller, or operator of the premises or a person acting with the apparent authority of the owner, controller, or operator authorized the carrying of the handgun; (3) the person carrying the handgun complies with any rules and regulations of the owner, controller, or operator of the premises that govern the carrying of a handgun on the premises; and (4) the person is not prohibited by state or federal law from possessing a firearm. *See* Tex. Penal Code § 46.15(l).

This means a person may be able to legally carry their handguns during a disaster and on the premises of an emergency shelter if they abide by the shelter's rules.

VII. UNDERSTANDING GUN-FREE SCHOOL ZONES LAWS

The discussion of Gun-Free School Zones is one that covers many different areas of the law and affects both persons who hold an LTC as well as persons who do not. That is because "Gun-Free School Zones" laws and their meanings cause a lot of confusion. Signs warning about being in a "Gun-Free School Zone" are common around schools, but what does this mean to people lawfully in possession of firearms? There are actually both Texas and federal "Gun-Free School Zones" laws, each with very different meanings and consequences. For this reason, we will explain the applicable rules for individuals who possess and do not possess an LTC in this Chapter, even though it has been dedicated to possessing or carrying a firearm without a license.

A. Texas "Gun-Free School Zone" law: enhancement statute

The Texas Gun-Free School Zone law is part of Texas Penal Code Section 46.11. This statute does not create any new crimes or make any rights under other statutes inapplicable, but it is what is legally known as an enhancement statute. This means that if a person is already committing a weapons crime in violation of Chapter 46 of the Texas Penal Code, and if it is shown at the trial of the defendant that the crime occurred within 300 feet of a school or a school function, then the range of punishment for that crime is increased.

Since LTC holders, as well as other lawful individuals, are allowed to carry handguns in their motor vehicles under Texas Penal Code Chapter 46, this law does not prohibit them from carrying a handgun, visible in a holster or concealed, within 300 feet of the premises of a school. The law only applies to people who are committing, or who have committed, a weapons crime near a school.

B. Federal "Gun-Free School Zone" law: 18 U.S.C. § 922(q)

The text of the federal Gun-Free School Zone law is found in 18 U.S.C. § 922(q)(2)(A), and, in contrast to Texas law, creates its own independent criminal offense. This law states that it is a federal crime for a person to possess a firearm that has moved through interstate commerce (this includes virtually all firearms) on the grounds of or within 1,000 feet of a public, parochial, or private school. As surprising as it may seem, under this federal law, the mere possession of a firearm by the occupant of a motor vehicle while driving past a school or dropping off a child is a federal crime.

However, 18 U.S.C. § 922(q)(2)(B) provides seven exceptions:
1) Exception one: if the possession is on private property which is not part of the school grounds. This means that a person living within 1,000 feet of a school can keep a firearm in their house.
2) Exception two: if the individual possessing the firearm is licensed to do so by the state in which the school zone is located or a political subdivision of the state, and the law of the state or political subdivision requires that, before an individual obtains such a license, the law enforcement authorities of the state or political subdivision verify that the individual is qualified under law to receive the license. This means that an LTC holder may legally carry a firearm into a Gun-Free School Zone in Texas. However, there is one important note about the statute:

a person can only lawfully carry in a school zone located in the state that issued the firearms license. Therefore, if a person has a Texas LTC, they can only carry through Texas school zones. If that Texas LTC holder is traveling through another state, this exception under federal law does not apply, and they may be in violation of this law. It also means that a Texas resident who holds a non-resident, non-Texas handgun carry license or permit does not benefit from this exception and is in violation of the law if they take a firearm into a school zone and he or she does not meet another exception. Likewise, an individual carrying a firearm under the authority of Texas Constitutional Carry would be in violation of this law if they did not meet another exception.

3) Exception three: if the firearm is not loaded, and is in a locked container, or a locked firearms rack that is on a motor vehicle. This means that if a firearm is unloaded and carried in a locked case, or other type of locked container such as a glove box or trunk, there is no violation of the federal law.
4) Exception four: if the firearm is carried by an individual for use in a program approved by a school in the school zone. This exception covers school-sponsored shooting activities, such as an ROTC program.
5) Exception five: if the firearm is carried by an individual in accordance with a contract entered into between a school in the school zone and the individual or an employer of the individual. This means that school security guards can carry firearms while on the job.
6) Exception six: if the firearm is carried by a law enforcement officer acting in his or her official capacity. This exception covers police officers while on-duty only. It does not appear to cover them while they are off-duty, even if they are required by state law to carry while off-duty.

7) Exception seven: if the firearm is unloaded and is in the possession of an individual while traversing school property for the purpose of gaining access to public or private lands open to hunting, if the entry on school premises is authorized by school authorities. This means that if a hunter must cross school property to get to a lawful hunting ground, they must have the permission of the school, and the firearm must be unloaded.

C. Reconciling Texas and federal laws on Gun-Free School Zones

The law puts a vast number of unknowing and unsuspecting people in conflict with federal law while being in full compliance with state law. As a result, it is likely that this law is violated thousands of times a day. However, while this has been federal law since 1996 and its predecessor was the law since 1990, there does not appear to be a wave of federal prosecutions for the mere possession of a firearm by a person who is only driving through a school zone or picking up or dropping off their child. Nevertheless, even though it appears that the Feds are not inclined to enforce some of the provisions of this statute today, the law is on the books right now.

D. "School Marshals" teachers with guns

Generally, while a teacher or administrator is not permitted to possess a handgun inside an elementary, middle, or high school building, schools can allow it through a written regulation or with written authorization. In 2013, Texas enacted a law creating a new type of licensee in the form of a school marshal. *See* Texas Code Crim. Proc. Art. 2.127. In order for an individual to become a school marshal, the person must:

1) be appointed by the board of trustees or the governing body of the school;

2) complete an 80-hour training course conducted by a law enforcement academy administering the school marshal curriculum;
3) complete a psychological examination; and
4) possess a valid license to carry a handgun.

In 2021, the 87th Legislature amended Texas Education Code Sections 37.0811, 37.0813, 51.220, and expanded the ability of school marshals to carry. Previously, a school marshal was not permitted to carry a concealed handgun on their person if their job required regular, direct contact with students. As of September 1, 2021, school marshals can carry a concealed handgun on their person even if they have regular, direct contact with students (*e.g.*, teacher). If a school marshal chooses not to keep the handgun on their person, the handgun must be kept in a locked and secured safe or in another secured location on the physical premises of the school.

The Commission on Law Enforcement Officer Standards and Education ("TCOLE") states that a school marshal's "sole purpose is to prevent the act of murder or serious bodily injury on the school premises" and that school marshals are "not peace officers."

Upon a written inquiry by a parent or guardian of a student enrolled at a school, the school district or charter school must provide written notice indicating the existence of an employee appointed as a school marshal. However, the actual identity of the school marshal is confidential and will not be made available to an inquiring parent or guardian.

Any handgun carried by a school marshal on a school or junior college's campus must be loaded with frangible ammunition in an effort to minimize unintended collateral damage.

VIII. HOW LTC HOLDERS AND CONSTITUTIONAL CARRIERS SHOULD INTERACT WITH LAW ENFORCEMENT WHILE CARRYING

A. Do I legally have to present my LTC to a police officer if they ask for my identification and I am carrying my gun?

> **REQUIREMENT TO DISPLAY LICENSE**
> **TEX. GOV'T CODE § 411.205**
>
> If a license holder is carrying a handgun on or about the license holder's person when a magistrate or a peace officer demands that the license holder display identification, the license holder shall display:
> (1) both the license holder's driver's license or identification certificate issued by the department and the license holder's handgun license; and
> (2) if the license holder's handgun license bears a protective order designation, a copy of the applicable court order under which the license holder is protected.

Yes, but there is no legal penalty if you fail to present the LTC. Texas LTC law has always required that a person present their LTC along with their driver's license or other state-issued identification anytime they are carrying a concealed handgun, or a handgun visible in a holster, and they have been asked for identification by a law enforcement officer or a magistrate. *See* Tex. Gov't Code § 411.205.

While this is and always has been the law, there is no penalty for a person who fails to present their LTC to law enforcement upon request for identification. However, the law requires that a person be in possession of their LTC at all times that they are carrying pursuant to their LTC. There is no benefit to concealing one's status as an LTC holder. Every LTC holder can be identified in the personal data search a police officer runs when they check an LTC holder's driver's license. Even if you do not present your LTC, the officer will know that you have an LTC. If you have failed to identify yourself as an LTC holder who is carrying a handgun, this may alarm the police officer and cause an already stressful situation to become more stressful. In short, you are not gaining anything by not telling the police that you are an LTC holder who is carrying a handgun.

Under the Firearm Carry Act of 2021, if an LTC holder is not carrying their license, and instead claims constitutional carrier status, they may be subject to prosecution if they are found trespassing where effective 30.05 notice is provided.

The legalization of an LTC holder's ability to open carry a handgun in a holster caused a bit of controversy as to whether or not a police officer could lawfully stop and ask to see the LTC of a person he observes openly carrying a handgun.

Prior to the Firearm Carry Act of 2021, it appeared that if a police officer had reasonable suspicion (*see* Chapter 2 for a description of reasonable suspicion) that a person was violating the previous version of the law by being in possession of a handgun while not on his own property, in his motor vehicle, or in his watercraft, the officer could stop and investigate further to see if that person was exempt because they possess an LTC. *See* Tex. Penal Code § 46.15(b)(6). Once the officer confirmed the person was a lawful LTC holder, he should have had no other reasonable suspicion that a violation of Texas Penal Code Section 46.02 (as it existed before September 1, 2021) was occurring and allow the person to be on his way.

However, with Texas Constitutional Carry, it is unlikely a court would side with an officer who, without reasonable suspicion, detained someone to check on their LTC status based solely on an observation the person was carrying a handgun concealed or open in a holster in a non-prohibited public place. Appellate courts have yet to consider a case involving this type of police interaction.

B. How should constitutional carriers interact with law enforcement?

Police encounters with constitutional carriers were a hotly contested topic during the house and senate floor debates on Texas Constitutional Carry. There was a proposed amendment that would not allow a police officer to stop anyone he or she sees carrying a firearm to inquire as to whether or not that person can legally possess a firearm. This was the most highly debated amendment to the bill, and though the house adopted this amendment, it did not make it into the final version.

The Legislature left the decision to the courts as to whether or not a police officer, during the lawful discharge of duties, may stop someone simply because they are carrying a firearm. No court has had an opportunity to rule on this topic yet, but it will surely reach the bench in the coming years. In contrast to an LTC holder's obligations, there is nothing in the law that states that if you are constitutionally carrying that you must disclose that information to a law enforcement officer.

C. Can a police officer legally take an LTC holder's handgun away?

Yes, police are allowed to disarm LTC holders in the interest of officer safety. Texas Government Code Section 411.206 states that a police officer can disarm an LTC holder and confiscate the LTC of a person he or she has arrested for a criminal offense. In addition, under Section 411.207 of the Texas Government Code, a police officer may disarm an LTC holder during an encounter with the LTC holder if the officer reasonably believes it is necessary to disarm for the protection of the LTC holder, the police officer, or any other individual.

At the conclusion of the encounter with the officer, if the officer determines that the LTC holder is not a threat and has not committed any violation of the law that results in the person's arrest, then the police officer shall return the firearm to the LTC holder. *See* Tex. Gov't Code § 411.207. Keep in mind, however, that the statutes do not dictate the way the officer must return the firearm, which means a person may receive their firearm back unloaded, disassembled, or placed in an area of the automobile where it was not originally found.

D. Can a police officer legally take a constitutional carrier's handgun away?

AUTHORITY OF PEACE OFFICERS
TEX. CODE OF CRIM. PROC. ART. 14.03

(h)(1) A peace officer who is acting in the lawful discharge of the officer's official duties may disarm a person at any time the officer reasonably believes it is necessary for the protection of the person, officer, or another individual. The peace officer shall return the handgun to the person before discharging the person from the scene if the officer determines that the person is not a threat to the officer, person, or another individual and if the person has not committed a violation that results in the arrest of the person.

> (2) A peace officer who is acting in the lawful discharge of the officer's official duties may temporarily disarm a person when the person enters a nonpublic, secure portion of a law enforcement facility, if the law enforcement agency provides a gun locker or other secure area where the peace officer can secure the person's handgun. The peace officer shall secure the handgun in the locker or other secure area and shall return the handgun to the person immediately after the person leaves the nonpublic, secure portion of the law enforcement facility.
> (3) For purposes of this subsection, "law enforcement facility" and "nonpublic, secure portion of a law enforcement facility" have the meanings assigned by Section 411.207, Government Code.

Yes, police are allowed to disarm constitutional carriers in a manner similar to how they treat LTC holders as explained above. This is because the Firearm Carry Act of 2021 essentially imported the language found in Texas Government Code Section 411.207(a)-(b), removed the term "license holder," replaced it with "person," and implanted it into the new Texas Code of Criminal Procedure Article 14.03(h)(1). A strict reading of this new statute implies any person with a handgun can be disarmed by the police temporarily—constitutional carriers and LTC holders alike.

It could be argued police already may temporarily disarm anyone of any dangerous weapon if safety is an issue during a detention or arrest. As with many of the new law changes concerning carrying handguns in Texas, it will be interesting to see how the courts interpret the temporary disarming of constitutional carriers and how that intersects with the traditional police powers of search, seizure, and arrest. At least one court has held that the police already have the authority to disarm anyone of a deadly weapon to protect themselves. *See Lovett v. State*, 523 S.W.3d 342 (Tex. App.—Fort Worth. 2017, pet. ref'd).

E. What are a passenger's obligations when the driver is stopped by law enforcement?

Sometimes police will ask passengers in the vehicle for identification to run a check for outstanding warrants, but passengers are generally not legally required to present identification. However, pursuant to Texas Government Code Section 411.205, passengers who are LTC holders who are carrying a handgun and are asked for identification are required to present their LTC (even though, as discussed earlier, there is no penalty for failure to do so) and may be disarmed by police in the interest of safety as described earlier. *See* police interactions discussed at length in Chapters 2, 3, and 4.

On the other hand, if a passenger is constitutionally carrying a handgun pursuant to the Firearm Carry Act of 2021, there is no legal obligation to tell the officer they have a firearm or otherwise identify themselves. *See* Tex. Penal Code § 38.02. However, every situation is different. If the police are investigating a crime which could potentially implicate the passenger or they are lawfully ordered out of the vehicle and detained themselves, the constitutional carrying passenger will likely be identified as such and disarmed.

IX. LAW CONCERNING LONG GUNS
A. May be carried openly in public
Texas law does not require a person to have a permit to carry a long gun, nor does the law require that a long gun be concealed when in public. Texas Penal Code Section 46.02 only addresses handguns. There is no statute that addresses the manner in which a long gun may be carried other than that it may not be displayed in a public place in a manner calculated to alarm.

B. Manner in which long guns may not be displayed in public
A person may legally display a long gun in public but not intentionally or knowingly in a "manner calculated to alarm," in violation of the Texas disorderly conduct statute.

> **DISORDERLY CONDUCT**
> **TEX. PENAL CODE § 42.01(a)(8)**
>
> A person commits an offense if he intentionally or knowingly displays a firearm or other deadly weapon in a public place in a manner calculated to alarm.

The intention of this statute is to prevent individuals from displaying firearms in a way which would cause some type of panic or scare to others. However, the statute also requires that the person who displays the firearm publicly, do so intentionally or knowingly in a manner calculated to alarm in order to be charged with a crime.

> **EXAMPLE:**
>
> Tim has a store in a shopping mall that sells firearm accessories but not firearms. However, Tim takes his rifle to his store every day

> because he uses it for demonstration purposes. One day after work, instead of going straight to his car, Tim decides to do a little shopping while carrying his AR-15 on a sling pointed down to the ground on his back, coffee in one hand and fast food bag in the other. Tim is stopped by a police officer.

Has Tim engaged in disorderly conduct? No. Tim legally carried his rifle in public in a safe, non-threatening manner. He certainly did not knowingly or intentionally calculate alarm to anyone. The law focuses on Tim's intent and the manner in which the firearm is displayed. However, if Tim (in our example) was engaging in threatening behavior, his conduct might constitute an act of disorderly conduct. A word of caution: Tim's conduct is open to interpretation by third parties and law enforcement, which could land a person in legal hot water. *See State v. Ross*, 573 S.W.3d 817 (Tex. Crim. App. 2019).

C. May I keep a long gun in my vehicle under Texas law?
Yes, and the long gun does not have to be concealed or locked in a gun rack. However, openly displaying a long gun in one's vehicle may attract thieves—particularly when it is parked and unattended!

D. May I possess a long gun while riding in another person's vehicle?
Yes. Texas does not have any restrictions on a person carrying a long gun in an automobile, regardless of who owns the vehicle.

E. May I have a long gun on a boat or other watercraft?
Yes, the same rules which allow the possession and carrying of a long gun in a vehicle also apply to boats and other watercraft.

X. TRAVELING ACROSS STATE LINES WITH FIREARMS

Many people vacation and travel outside of Texas. Naturally, no Texan wants to travel unarmed if they can help it, but, unfortunately, not every state shares the same views on gun ownership and gun rights as we do in the Lone Star State. This is especially true in the northeast corner and west coast of the United States. How then does a person pass through states that have restrictive firearms laws or those that are different from Texas? For example, how does a person legally pass through a state that prohibits the possession of a handgun without a license from that state? The answer: Safe Passage.

A. Federal law: qualifying for firearms "Safe Passage"

Traveling across state lines with a firearm means that a person may need to use the provisions of the federal law known as the "Safe Passage" provision. Federal law allows individuals who are legally in possession of firearms in their state (the starting point of traveling) to travel through states that are not as gun-friendly. This protection is only available under federal law to transport such firearms across state lines for lawful purposes, as long as they comply with the requirements of the Firearm Owners' Protection Act, 18 U.S.C. § 926A, nicknamed the "Safe Passage" provision. The first requirement to qualify for the federal Safe Passage provision is that throughout the duration of the trip through the anti-firearm state, the firearm must be unloaded and locked in the trunk, or locked in a container that is out of reach or not readily accessible from the passenger compartment. The ammunition also must be locked in the trunk or a container. Note that for the storage of both firearms and ammunition, the glove box and center console compartment are specifically not allowed under the statute.

B. Safe Passage requires legal start to legal finish

To get protection under federal law, a gun owner's journey must start and end in states where the traveler's possession of the firearm is legal; for example, a person traveling with their Glock 17 starting in Texas and ending in Vermont. Even though a person must drive through New York or Massachusetts to get to Vermont, as long as the person qualifies under the Safe Passage provision, then they may legally pass through. However, if the starting point was Texas and the ending point was New York (a place where the handgun would be illegal), there is no protection under the federal law. Safe Passage requires legal start and legal finish.

Although traveling across state lines naturally invokes federal law, it is important to remember that whenever a person finally completes their journey and reaches their destination state, the laws of that state control the possession, carrying, and use of the firearm. Federal law does not make it legal or provide any protection for possession of a firearm that is illegal under the laws of the destination state *(i.e.,* the "end" state of your travels).

C. What qualifies as "traveling" under Safe Passage?

The final requirement for protection under the federal law is that individuals MUST be "traveling" while in the firearm-hostile state. The legal definition of "traveling" is both murky and narrow. The Safe Passage provision protection has been held in courts to be limited to situations that strictly relate to traveling and nothing more. Traveling is a term that is not defined in the federal statute; however, it has received treatment in the courts that is indicative of what one can expect. Generally speaking, if a person stops somewhere for too long, they cease to be traveling and, therefore, lose their protection under the Safe Passage provision. How long this time limit is has not been determined either statutorily or by case law with any definitiveness.

While stopping for gas or restroom breaks may not disqualify a person from the traveling protection, any stop for an activity not directly related to traveling could be considered a destination, and thus you would lose the legal protection. For example, in Chicago, anyone in the city for more than 24 hours is not considered to be traveling under local policy. In an actual case, stopping for a brief nap in a bank parking lot in New Jersey caused a Texan driving back home from Maine to lose the traveling protection. *See Reininger v. Attorney General of New Jersey*, No. 14—5486—BRM, 2018 WL 3617962 (D.N.J. July 30, 2018). He received five years in prison for possession of weapons that are illegal under New Jersey law. Of course, if the driver would have made it to Allentown, Pennsylvania, he would have been safe. The moral of the story is to travel through these gun-unfriendly states as fast as you can—without breaking the speed limit, of course!

D. Protection under federal law does not mean protection from prosecution in gun-unfriendly states

To make matters even worse for firearms travelers, even if a person qualifies for protection under the federal Safe Passage provision, New Jersey and New York seem quite proud to treat this protection as an affirmative defense. This means that someone can be arrested even though he or she met all of the requirements of the federal statute. Then, they would have to go to court to assert this defense. In other words, while a person could beat the rap, they will not beat the ride! This becomes even more troublesome in the instance of someone who is legally flying with their firearm, and then due to flight complications, must land in New Jersey or New York, as travelers in this position have been arrested or threatened with arrest. Once again, the Safe Passage provision only applies while a person is traveling; as soon as they arrive at their destination and cease their travels, the laws of that state control a person's actions. Remember: check all applicable state firearms laws before you leave for your destination!

XI. AIR TRAVEL WITH A FIREARM

A. How do I legally travel with a firearm as a passenger on a commercial airline?

It is legal to travel with firearms on commercial airlines so long as the firearms transported are unloaded and in a locked, hard-sided container as checked baggage. Under federal law, the container must be completely inaccessible to passengers. *See* 49 U.S.C. § 46505(b)(1). Further, under Transportation Security Administration ("TSA") rules, firearms, ammunition, and firearm parts, including firearm frames, receivers, clips, and magazines, are prohibited in carry-on baggage. Finally, "realistic replicas of firearms are also prohibited in carry-on bags and must be packed in checked baggage. Rifle scopes are permitted in carry-on and checked bags."

1. Firearms must be inaccessible

Federal law makes it a crime subject to fine, imprisonment for up to 10 years, or both, if a person "when on, or attempting to get on, an aircraft in, or intended for operation in, air transportation or intrastate air transportation, has on or about the individual or the property of the individual a concealed dangerous weapon that is or would be accessible to the individual in flight." *See* 49 U.S.C.

§ 46505(b)(1). Additionally, under 49 U.S.C. § 46303(a) "[a]n individual who, when on, or attempting to board, an aircraft in, or intended for operation in, air transportation or intrastate air transportation, has on or about the individual or the property of the individual a concealed dangerous weapon that is or would be accessible to the individual in flight is liable to the United States Government for a civil penalty of not more than $10,000 for each violation."

2. Firearms must be checked in baggage

The following guidelines are provided by the TSA for traveling with firearms on airlines: You may transport unloaded firearms in a locked hard-sided container as checked baggage only. Declare the firearm and/or ammunition to the airline when checking your bag at the ticket counter. The container must completely secure the firearm from being accessed. Locked cases that can be easily opened are not permitted. Be aware that the container the firearm was in when purchased may not adequately secure the firearm when it is transported in checked baggage.

Firearms

- When traveling, comply with the laws concerning possession of firearms as they vary by local, state and international governments.
- If you are traveling internationally with a firearm in checked baggage, please check the U.S. Customs and Border Protection website for information and requirements prior to travel.
- Declare each firearm each time you present it for transport as checked baggage. Ask your airline about limitations or fees that may apply.

- Firearms must be unloaded and locked in a hard-sided container and transported as checked baggage only. As defined by 49 CFR 1540.5 a loaded firearm has a live round of ammunition, or any component thereof, in the chamber or cylinder or in a magazine inserted in the firearm. Only the passenger should retain the key or combination to the lock unless TSA personnel request the key to open the firearm container to ensure compliance with TSA regulations. You may use any brand or type of lock to secure your firearm case, including TSA-recognized locks.
- Bringing an unloaded firearm with accessible ammunition to the security checkpoint carries the same civil penalty/fine as bringing a loaded firearm to the checkpoint. You may find information on civil penalties at the Civil Enforcement page.
- Firearm parts, including magazines, clips, bolts and firing pins, are prohibited in carry-on baggage, but may be transported in checked baggage.
- Replica firearms, including firearm replicas that are toys, may be transported in checked baggage only.
- Rifle scopes are permitted in carry-on and checked baggage.

Warning: United States Code, Title 18, Part 1, Chapter 44, firearm definition includes: any weapon (including a starter gun) which will, or is designed to, or may readily be converted to expel a projectile by the action of an explosive; the frame or receiver of any such weapon; any firearm muffler or firearm silencer; and any destructive device. As defined by 49 CFR 1540.5, a loaded firearm has a live round of ammunition, or any component thereof, in the chamber or cylinder or in a magazine inserted in the firearm.

Ammunition
- Ammunition is prohibited in carry-on baggage, but may be transported in checked baggage.
- Firearm magazines and ammunition clips, whether loaded or empty, must be securely boxed or included within a hard-sided case containing an unloaded firearm. Read the requirements governing the transport of ammunition in checked baggage as defined by 49 CFR 175.10 (a)(8).
- Small arms ammunition, including ammunition not exceeding .75 caliber and shotgun shells of any gauge, may be carried in the same hard-sided case as the firearm.

Transportation Security Administration. (2021). Transporting Firearms and Ammunition. [online] Available at: https://www.tsa.gov/travel/transporting-firearms-and-ammunition [Accessed 19 July 2021].

B. May I have a firearm while operating or as a passenger in a private aircraft flying just in Texas?

Generally, yes. For purposes of Texas state law, a private aircraft is treated like any other motorized vehicle. For more information concerning firearms in vehicles. *See* our earlier discussion in this Chapter under Sections II and III.

C. May I have a firearm in a private aircraft that takes off from Texas and lands in another state?

In situations where a private aircraft is taking off from one state and landing in another, the law will simply view this as traveling interstate with firearms. Where no other statutes apply to the person's flight, the person will be subject to the provisions of 18

U.S.C. § 926A. This statute allows a person to transport firearms between states subject to the following conditions: the person can lawfully possess the firearm at his or her points of departure and arrival, and the firearm remains unloaded and inaccessible during the trip. However, what if the person is an LTC holder and wants to carry a handgun between states? Fortunately, 18 U.S.C. § 927 states that Section 926A does not preempt applicable state law. Thus, if a person can lawfully carry a weapon in the state in which he or she boards the aircraft and in the state in which he or she lands, the LTC holder is not subject to the unloaded and inaccessible restrictions of Section 926A, unless, of course, there are stops in more restrictive states.

For operations of private aircraft within one state, a person will only be subject to the laws of the state within which he or she is operating. The person will need to review their state's statutes to determine whether they impose any restrictions on possession of firearms within non-secure areas of airports. The person will also need to be familiar with the airports he or she will be visiting to determine whether each airport has any restrictions (*e.g.*, posting to prohibit carrying a firearm, *etc.*).

PRACTICAL LEGAL TIP

Most people say that the reason they forgot to remove a firearm from their baggage at the airport is because they were in such a hurry to not miss their flight. But, if you do accidentally leave it in your carry-on bag, you can be assured that you *will* miss your flight! At a very minimum, if TSA finds a gun in your baggage, you will not only cause a scene and miss your flight, but you will also incur a fine from the TSA and possibly be subjected to prosecution by local law enforcement if you are not in possession of your handgun license.
—Emily

CHAPTER FIFTEEN

RESTORATION OF FIREARMS RIGHTS: THE LAW OF PARDONS AND EXPUNCTIONS

I. IS IT POSSIBLE TO RESTORE A PERSON'S RIGHT TO BEAR ARMS?

What happens after a person has been convicted of a crime? Is it possible to later clear their name and/or criminal record? If possible, then what is the process for removing a conviction and restoring a person's right to purchase and possess firearms? This Chapter will explain how, under very limited circumstances, a person can have arrest records, criminal charges, and even criminal convictions removed or nullified.

But a word of caution: success in this arena may be rare. Further, each state has different rules concerning these issues, as well as a completely different set of rules under federal law. Before we begin a meaningful discussion, it is important to explain two terms and concepts: clemency and expunction. A small point about terminology: Texas law uses the word "expunction" and federal law uses the word "expungement" to refer to the same process; therefore, these words are usually used interchangeably.

A. What is clemency?

Clemency is the action the government, usually the chief executive (*e.g.,* the President on the federal level or a governor on the state level), takes in forgiving or pardoning a crime or canceling the penalty of a crime, either wholly or in part. Clemency can include full pardons after a conviction, full pardons after completion of deferred adjudication community supervision, conditional pardons, pardons based on innocence, commutations of a sentence, emergency medical reprieves, and family medical reprieves. Clemency can be granted at both the federal and state level.

B. What is an expunction?

An expunction is the physical act of destroying or purging government criminal records, unlike sealing, which is simply hiding the records from the public. Under certain circumstances, a person may have their criminal record either expunged or sealed. If a record is expunged, the record is destroyed and no longer exits. If a record is sealed, a governmental agency can still access the record but the general public cannot.

> **PRACTICAL LEGAL TIP**
>
> While our intention is to provide you with as much information as possible as to how you can have your firearms rights restored if you are convicted of a crime, it's also important to make sure you are aware of how rarely pardons, expunctions, and restorations of firearms rights are granted. While it's certainly worth the effort to apply for a pardon, be careful not to get your hopes up, because they are seldom granted.
> –Edwin

II. FEDERAL LAW

A. Presidential pardon

Under Article II, Section 2, Clause 1 of the United States Constitution, the President of the United States has the power "to grant reprieves and pardons for offenses against the United States, except in cases of impeachment." The President's power to pardon offenses has also been interpreted to include the power to grant conditional pardons, commutations of sentence, conditional commutations of sentence, remission of fines and forfeitures, respites, and amnesties. However, the President's clemency authority only extends to federal offenses; the President cannot grant clemency for a state crime.

1. How does a person petition for federal clemency or a pardon?

Under federal law, a person requesting executive clemency must petition the President of the United States and submit the petition to the Department of Justice. The Pardon Attorney for the Department of Justice can provide petitions and other required forms necessary to complete the application for clemency. "Petition forms for commutation of sentence may also be obtained from the wardens of federal penal institutions. A petitioner applying for executive clemency with respect to military offenses should submit his or her petition directly to the Secretary of the military branch that had original jurisdiction over the court-martial trial and conviction of the petitioner." *See* 28 CFR § 1.1.

The Code of Federal Regulations requires an applicant to wait five years after the date of the release of the petitioner from confinement, or in a case where no prison sentence was imposed, an applicant is required to wait five years after the date of conviction prior to submitting a petition for clemency. The regulation further states that "generally, no petition should be submitted by a person who is on probation, parole, or supervised release." *See* 28 CFR § 1.2. With that in mind, the President can grant clemency at any time, whether an individual has made a formal petition or not. For example, President Gerald Ford granted a full and unconditional pardon to former President Richard Nixon prior to any indictment or charges being filed related to his involvement in Watergate.

2. What should a petition for clemency include?

Petitions for executive clemency should include the following information:

1) that the person requesting clemency must state specifically the purpose for which clemency is sought, as well as attach any and all relevant documentary evidence that will support how clemency will support that purpose;
2) that discloses any arrests or convictions subsequent to the federal crime for which clemency is sought;

3) that discloses all delinquent credit obligations (whether disputed or not), all civil lawsuits to which the applicant is a party (whether plaintiff or defendant), and all unpaid tax obligations (whether local, state, or federal); and

4) that includes three character affidavits from persons not related to the applicant by blood or marriage.

In addition, acceptance of a Presidential pardon generally carries with it an admission of guilt. For that reason, a petitioner should include in his or her petition a statement of the petitioner's acceptance of responsibility, an expression of remorse, and atonement for the offense. The forms and required information can be found on the United States Department of Justice website.

3. What happens after a petition for executive clemency is submitted?

The Attorney General reviews each petition and makes a non-binding recommendation on an application to the President. Federal regulations also provide for guidelines and requirements to notify victims of the crimes, if any, for which clemency is sought. *See* 28 CFR § 1.6. The President will either grant or deny a pardon. There are no hearings held on the petition, and there is no appeal of the President's decision. *See* 28 CFR § 1.8.

4. What is the effect of a Presidential pardon?

A pardon is the forgiveness of a crime and the cancellation of the penalty associated with that crime. While a Presidential pardon will restore various rights lost as a result of the pardoned offense, it will not expunge the record of your conviction. This means that even if a person is granted a pardon, the person must still disclose their conviction on any form where such information is required, although the person may also disclose the fact that the offense for which they were convicted was pardoned.

B. Expungement of federal convictions

1. No law exists for general federal expungement

Congress has not provided federal legislation that offers any comprehensive authority or procedure for expunging criminal offenses. There exist only statutes that allow expungement in certain cases for possession of small amounts of controlled substances and, interestingly, a procedure to expunge DNA samples of certain members of the military who were wrongfully convicted. *See* 18 U.S.C. § 3607(c) and 10 U.S.C. § 1565(e). Because there is no statutory guidance, federal courts have literally made up the rules and procedures themselves, often coming to different conclusions. Some federal court circuits have stated they have no power to expunge records. However, other federal courts have indicated that they do have the power to expunge. The federal Fifth Circuit, which includes Texas, has held that under certain limited circumstances, federal courts may order expungement both of records held by other branches of the government (*e.g.*, executive branch) and its own court records. *See Sealed Appellant v. Sealed Appellee*, 130 F.3d 695 (5th Cir. 1997). The Supreme Court has passed on hearing cases that would have resolved the split between the circuits. This issue remains legally murky.

2. Possible procedure for federal expungement

There are no statutory guidelines for how to seek an expungement under federal law; however, the place to start would be to file a motion with the federal court that issued the conviction that a person wants to have expunged. However, federal judges very rarely grant these types of motions. Some circuits, including the Fifth Circuit, have adopted a balancing test to decide if a record held by the court may be expunged. The court weighs the interests of the government in keeping open, unredacted records, against the injury to the individual of maintaining a criminal record. The Fifth Circuit, however, has acknowledged that "expungement is 'exceedingly narrow' and is granted only in exceptional circumstances." The court explained "the government cannot and should not be forced to rewrite history" every time a wrongfully accused wants his record expunged. *Sealed Appellant v. Sealed Appellee,* 130 F.3d 695 (5th Cir. 1997). Some of the areas where expungement has worked are in incidents of extreme police misconduct, or where the conviction is being misused against the person. Unless there exist compelling reasons, a federal judge is highly unlikely to grant expungement.

3. Expungement for drug possession: statutory authority

Under a federal law entitled "special probation and expungement procedures for drug possessors," certain persons are allowed to request a federal court to issue an expungement order from all public records. Congress intended this order to restore the person to the status he or she "occupied before such arrest or institution of criminal proceedings." *See* 18 U.S.C. § 3607(c).

In order to qualify for the expungement, you must have been under the age of 21 when you were convicted, you must have no prior drug offenses, and your conviction must have been for simple possession of a small amount of a controlled substance.

4. How does a person have firearms rights restored under federal law?

Under the Gun Control Act of 1968 ("GCA"), a person who has received a Presidential pardon is not considered convicted of a crime preventing the purchase and possession of firearms subject to all other federal laws. *See* 18 U.S.C. §§ 921(a)(20)(B) and (a)(33)(B)(ii). In addition, persons who had a conviction expunged or set aside or who have had their civil rights restored are not considered to have been convicted for purposes of the GCA "unless the pardon, expungement, or restoration of civil rights expressly provides the person may not ship, transport, possess, or receive firearms." *See* 18 U.S.C. §§ 921(a)(20)(B) and (a)(33)(B)(ii).

The GCA also provides the United States Attorney General with the authority to grant relief from firearms disabilities where the Attorney General determines that the person is not likely to act in a manner dangerous to the public safety and where granting relief would not be contrary to the public interest. *See* 18 U.S.C. § 925(c). The Attorney General has delegated this authority to the ATF. Unfortunately, the ATF reports that it has been prohibited from spending any funds in order to investigate or act upon applications from individuals seeking relief from federal firearms disabilities. This means that until the ATF's prohibition has been lifted, a person's best—and most likely—option to have their firearms rights restored is through a Presidential pardon. *See* www.atf.gov.

III. TEXAS LAW

A. Clemency by the Governor and the Board of Pardons and Paroles

The Governor of Texas possesses the authority to grant executive clemency under Article IV, Section 11 of the Texas Constitution except in cases of treason and impeachment. Unlike federal clemency where the President is free to pardon whomever the President chooses, the Governor of Texas can only grant clemency if a majority of the members of the Texas Board of Pardons and Paroles makes such a recommendation. *See* Tex. Code of Crim. Proc. Art. 48.01. However, the Board is required to consider any request of the Governor for clemency under Section 508.050 of the Texas Government Code.

1. Who is eligible for executive clemency in Texas?

Under Texas Administrative Code, a full pardon can be granted to any person who has been convicted of a felony or misdemeanor, or any person who has successfully completed a term of deferred adjudication community supervision for a criminal offense. In addition, a full pardon may be granted to a person based on "innocence." A pardon for innocence requires: "1) a written recommendation of at least two of the current trial officials of the sentencing court, with one trial official submitting documentary evidence of actual innocence; or 2) a certified order or judgment of a court having jurisdiction accompanied by a certified copy of the findings of fact and conclusions of law where the court recommends that the Court of Criminal Appeals grant state habeas relief on the grounds of actual innocence." *See* 37 Tex. Admin. Code §§ 143.1 and 143.2(a).

2. How does a person seek executive clemency in Texas?

A person seeking executive clemency in Texas is required to complete an application which is available from the Texas Board of Pardons and Paroles. www.tdcj.texas.gov/bpp/forms/forms.html. Once properly submitted, the file of any applicant eligible for clemency will be reviewed by the Board of Pardons and Paroles ("Board").

The Board will review the application in a public hearing; however, the hearing is actually a review of the applicant's file rather than a formal hearing. The Board members vote on case files individually, and an applicant must obtain a majority number of votes of the Board before the application will be sent to the Governor for a final determination. Applicants are not able to appeal the decision of the Board, if denied, but applicants may re-apply for clemency after two years. *See* Tex. Admin. Code § 143.14(b). If the majority of the Board recommends clemency be extended to an applicant, the file is sent to the Governor, who may either accept the Board's recommendation and grant clemency or reject the recommendation. For more information on the process, please visit www.tdcj.state.tx.us/bpp/faq/ClemencyProcess.html.

3. What is the effect of executive clemency in Texas?

Similar to federal clemency, unless the person receiving clemency has their records expunged, the records of the original conviction continue to exist. A person granted clemency must still disclose the conviction on any relevant form seeking such information; however, the person may also state the nature of the clemency received. The result of executive clemency in Texas depends on the type of clemency granted by the Governor.

B. Texas expunction

Chapter 55 of the Texas Code of Criminal Procedure controls expunction under Texas law and provides for when a person is entitled to an expunction. Chapter 55 allows an expunction for persons who: were acquitted or pardoned; had charges dismissed or were no-billed by a grand jury; were convicted as a juvenile for being delinquent or for an alcohol-related offense; or were victims of identity theft (where a criminal gave the innocent person's name as their own to law enforcement). *See* Tex. Code Crim. Proc. Art. 55.01. In 2021, the Texas Legislature passed a first-of-its-kind law that allows for an expunction of a final adult conviction. Under this new law, if you were finally convicted of the crime of Unlawful Carry of a Weapon under Texas Penal Code Section 46.02(a) as it existed before September 1, 2021, then you can have that conviction expunged from your record. *See* Tex. Code Crim. Proc. Art. 55.01(a)(1)(C).

However, not all individuals are entitled to an expunction of their record. For instance, if a person was acquitted of one offense, but was convicted or remains subject to prosecution for another offense relating to or arising out of the charge for which they were acquitted, that person is not entitled to an expunction of their record. *See* Tex. Code Crim. Proc. Art. 55.01(c).

Expunction petitions under Chapter 55 can become adversarial proceedings involving one or more parties, including the state, which may object to the court granting an order of expunction. Under Texas law, prosecutors and law enforcement officers may object to the expunction of arrest records if the statute of limitations has not expired for a charge that was previously dismissed and they plan on re-filing, or if they wish to reserve the right to re-file charges against that person in the future.

To obtain an expunction, a petitioner is required to file a petition for expunction in a state civil district court. Even though expunction proceedings are governed by the Code of Criminal Procedure, an expunction itself is a civil matter and, therefore, is a matter addressed by civil courts. Individuals who apply for an expunction within 30 days of an acquittal are not required to pay the filing fees associated with the expunction petition. If an individual was acquitted and files a petition for expunction more than 30 days after the date of acquittal, the normal fees for filing in the civil district court will apply. *See* Tex. Code Crim. Proc. Art. 55.02.

C. How does a person have firearms rights restored under Texas law?

After five years, some rights are automatically restored. Texas Penal Code Section 46.04(a) allows a convicted felon to possess a firearm in their residence after "the fifth anniversary of the person's release from confinement following conviction of the felony or the person's release from supervision under community supervision, parole, or mandatory supervision, whichever date is later."

Further, for a person seeking executive clemency, the person or the Governor may petition the Board of Pardons and Paroles to grant a "Pardon with Restoration of Firearms Rights." *See* 37 Tex. Admin. Code § 143.12. In addition to qualifying for a pardon, in order to also have the Board recommend that one's firearms rights be restored, the provisions of Section 143.12 must be met:

> The board will consider recommending restoration of the right to receive, possess, bear, and transport in commerce a firearm only in extreme and unusual circumstances which prevent the applicant from gaining a livelihood, and only if the applicant: (1) provides either proof of clearance by a previously granted full pardon or a request for such express restoration in a pending application for a full pardon from jurisdiction(s) of the relevant conviction(s) or successful completion of a punishment similar to a term of deferred adjudication community supervision; and (2) provides proof of application under the United States Code, Title 18, Section 925(c), for exemption, relief from disabilities to the Director of Alcohol, Tobacco, Firearms, and Explosives, and furnishes copies of all relevant applications and responses thereto by the Director of Alcohol, Tobacco, Firearms, and Explosives including any final actions by said Director...

The process for obtaining a restoration of firearms rights is essentially the same as receiving a grant of executive clemency in Texas and is subject to the non-appealable decisions of the Governor and the Board of Pardons and Paroles.

➤ CHAPTER SIXTEEN ◄

I'M BEING SUED FOR WHAT?
CIVIL LIABILITY IF YOU HAVE USED YOUR GUN

I. WHAT DOES IT MEAN TO BE SUED?

The term "lawsuit" refers to one party's assertion in a written filing with a court that another party has violated the law. In the context of firearms, typically the party suing has been injured and wants a ruling or judgment from the court stating that the party was injured and entitling the party to money.

A. What is a civil claim or lawsuit?

A civil "lawsuit" or "suit" refers to the actual filing of written paperwork with a court asserting that another party violated the law, and seeking some type of redress. A "claim" can exist without the filing of a lawsuit. A claim is simply the belief or assertion that another party has violated the law. Many parties have claims they never assert, or sometimes parties informally assert the claim in hopes of resolving the disputes without the filing of a lawsuit. Also, another term commonly used is "tort" or "tort claim." A tort is a civil claim arising out of a wrongful act, not including a breach of contract or trust that results in injury to another's person, property, reputation, or the like. This Chapter reviews some common tort claims with regard to firearms.

B. Difference between "civil claims" and "criminal charges"

To start with the basics, there are two different aspects of the legal system that gun owners may face after the use of a firearm: criminal and civil. There are several names and descriptive terms used for each (*e.g.,* civil lawsuit, criminal actions, civil claims, criminal proceedings, *etc.*), but regardless of the terms, the same breakdown applies; most cases are either criminal or civil. There is another subgroup of proceedings called administrative actions. Those actions are not covered by this Chapter but can sometimes impact LTC holders. For example, appealing the denial, suspension, or revocation of an LTC is an administrative act. *See* Chapters 12 and 13 for more information.

With that said, the three primary differences between a criminal action and a civil proceeding are: 1) who or what is bringing the action or lawsuit; 2) what they are seeking; and 3) the burden of proof. These differences are fairly straightforward.

1. State versus individual bringing claims

In a criminal case, the party bringing the action is the "sovereign," meaning the United States, state, municipality, county, *etc.* that believes a person violated their laws. Even if an individual calls the police, fills out a criminal complaint, or even asks the district attorney to file charges, the party that actually brings a criminal action is the state, county, *etc.,* not the individual.

However, a civil action may be filed by any individual, business, or other entity (partnership, LLC, trust, *etc.*). The entity bringing the claim is called the "plaintiff." Even governmental entities can bring civil claims; *i.e.*, if you negligently shoot a county propane tank, causing a fire, the county can sue you civilly for those damages. The typical gun case, though, will involve an individual filing a lawsuit against another individual for damages caused by the firearm. If the incident occurs at a place of business, the plaintiff may also sue the business, claiming that it is in some way at fault for the incident. The party being sued is typically called the "defendant."

2. Relief sought/awarded

In a criminal case, the governmental entity prosecuting the case is usually seeking to imprison or fine you. Most crimes are punishable by "X" number of days/months/years in prison or jail, and a fine not to exceed "X" amount of dollars.

By contrast, the plaintiff in the civil case is almost always seeking a monetary award. Several other types of relief are available (declaratory, injunctive, specific performance), but for the most part, gun cases will involve the plaintiff seeking monetary damages.

3. Burden of proof

In a criminal case, the amount of evidence to convict is "beyond a reasonable doubt." In civil cases, however, a plaintiff must prove a person is liable for damages by a "preponderance of the evidence" standard. A preponderance of the evidence is a much lower standard than the criminal standard of beyond a reasonable doubt. It generally means that the party with the greater weight of credible evidence wins that issue. The preponderance of the evidence has been described as more than half, that is, if the evidence demonstrates that something more likely occurred than not, this meets the burden of proof. Whereas in a criminal case, if there exists any "reasonable doubt," the burden of proof is not met. It does not mean the party with the most exhibits or greater number of witnesses will prevail. One highly credible witness can prevail over the testimony of a dozen biased, shady witnesses.

> **EXAMPLE:**
>
> John mistakes a utility meter reader for a burglar due to his disheveled appearance, tool bag, and because he looks to be snooping around John's house. John fires a shot without warning and injures the meter reader.

Possible criminal liability: the State of Texas could bring criminal charges against John for a number of crimes (aggravated assault, attempted murder, deadly conduct, discharge of a firearm inside the city limits, and so forth). The state would be seeking to imprison and/or fine John for his conduct, and would be required to prove that John committed the crime at issue "beyond a reasonable doubt."

Possible civil liability: the meter reader could also file a civil lawsuit against John alleging that John was negligent or committed the tort of assault. The meter reader would seek monetary damages and be required to prove his claims by a "preponderance of the evidence."

C. Impact of result in one court upon the other
1. Can a result in a criminal trial be used in a civil trial?

Yes, because of the legal doctrines of *res judicata* and collateral estoppel. These two legal doctrines govern the impact of a ruling or judgment in one case, upon a separate case involving the same set of facts and circumstances. For the present discussion, if a person is found guilty of a crime in a criminal proceeding, because that court uses a higher standard of "beyond a reasonable doubt" than the civil requirement of "preponderance of the evidence," the finding of the criminal court may be used for purposes of establishing civil liability. Entire chapters in law books have been written on these topics, so, suffice to say, this section is a brief overview of these laws.

The criminal concept of *nolo contendere* or "no contest" often generates confusion in this area. In a criminal case, a plea of *nolo contendere* or no contest means that the defendant does not admit guilt. The plea, however, still results in a judgment that the defendant is guilty of the crime, and that judgment can be used to help establish the defendant's liability in a separate civil case.

EXAMPLE:

Patrick and Joseph are at a BBQ when they start arguing about which team is better, the Cowboys or the Texans. Patrick shoots Joseph for supporting the wrong team. Not only is Patrick charged and convicted of aggravated assault, Joseph sues him because of his injuries.

Joseph's lawsuit against Patrick for medical bills, physical impairment, pain, and suffering is a civil action. Joseph will very likely be allowed to use the finding of Patrick's guilt in the criminal case (because it used the higher standard of beyond a reasonable doubt) to help establish his burden in the civil case that Patrick owes him monetary damages. This is an example of collateral estoppel; Patrick will not be permitted to re-litigate his guilt in the civil case because the criminal court already found him guilty beyond a reasonable doubt.

Both collateral estoppel and *res judicata* are based on the concept that a party to a legal proceeding should not be able to endlessly litigate issues that have already been decided by the legal system. At its most basic level, it means that a party to a legal proceeding who receives a final ruling on a particular issue, win or lose, cannot attempt to have another trial court or even the same court decide the same issue.

Note about appeals: collateral estoppel and *res judicata* are different concepts than an appeal, or asking the court in the first proceeding to reconsider its ruling or grant a new trial. An appeal is a request to a higher court to review the decision of a lower court. Likewise, in any given case, the parties will have numerous opportunities to ask the current court to reconsider its rulings, or even ask for a new trial after a trial is completed. Collateral estoppel and *res judicata* come into play after a final judgment or ruling that is no longer subject to appeal or revision by the trial court.

EXAMPLE:

Emily is sued for accidentally shooting Nancy. Nancy wins a judgment of $350 against Emily, much less than Nancy believed she was damaged.

In that case, Nancy can appeal the decision, or even ask the trial court for a new trial. However, Nancy cannot file another, or new, lawsuit regarding the same incident and attempt to recover more in the second case because of the doctrine of *res judicata*. In order for the doctrine to apply, the parties, facts, circumstances, and issues must be the same.

> **EXAMPLE:**
> Enrique fires his hunting rifle from his deer blind, hitting Phillip with one round. Phillip files a civil suit against Enrique and loses at trial. The court awards Phillip no damages. Phillip appeals and loses the appeal also.

Phillip is legally barred from recovering in another lawsuit against Enrique involving the same incident. However, Phillip is not barred from filing suit against Enrique for damages arising out of another set of facts and circumstances, for example, if the two are involved in a car wreck on a different day.

2. Civil case result impact on criminal case

Suppose you lose a civil suit and a judgment is entered against you arising out of a shooting incident. Can that judgment be used to establish that you committed a crime? No. The burden of proof is much higher in the criminal case than the civil case. The plaintiff proved his civil case by a "preponderance of the evidence." This does not mean that he proved his case "beyond a reasonable doubt," meaning a separate criminal trial is required to make that determination.

The one area where a civil case can impact a criminal case is the potential overlapping use of evidence and testimony. Your admission in one case can almost always be used against you in another case. Meaning, your sworn testimony in the civil case ("yes, I shot the guy") can almost always be used against you in the criminal case, and vice versa.

> **PRACTICAL LEGAL TIP**
>
> Unlike criminal cases where a unanimous jury verdict is required to convict someone, to prevail in a civil suit in Texas, only 10 of the 12 jurors (or five out of six, depending upon the court where your case is pending) must agree to render a verdict. In a criminal case, many times the goal of the defendant is to avoid conviction by convincing a single juror that the State cannot prove its case at the higher "beyond a reasonable doubt" standard. By contrast, in a civil lawsuit, in a district court, a plaintiff can prevail and recover damages, even if two of the jurors vehemently believe the defendant should prevail, as long as the remaining 10 jurors believe that the plaintiff has proven his case by the lower "preponderance of the evidence" standard. –Kirk

II. WHAT MIGHT YOU BE SUED FOR? GUN-RELATED CLAIMS IN CIVIL COURTS

A. Liability for unintentional discharge

This section deals with accidental or unintentional discharges of your firearm. Common unintentional discharges are associated with hunting and cleaning accidents or the mishandling of a weapon. Intentional shootings are addressed in the following section.

With that said, the following are the types of civil claims that may be asserted in connection with an unintentional discharge.

1. Negligence/gross negligence

Most civil cases for damages resulting from an accidental discharge will include a negligence or gross negligence claim. What does this mean, and what does a plaintiff have to prove before they can win? Under Texas law, negligence is defined "as the failure to use ordinary care, that is, failing to do that which a person of ordinary prudence would have done under the same or similar circumstances, or doing that which a person of ordinary prudence would not have done under the same or similar circumstances." *Thota v. Young*, 366 S.W.3d 678, 683 (Tex. 2021). If a person fails to use ordinary care, then they have acted negligently and will be liable for damages resulting from their conduct. "Ordinary care" means the degree of care that would be used by a person of ordinary prudence under the same or similar circumstances. This is an "objective standard," meaning, the test is not whether you believed you acted prudently, but whether the judge or jury believes you acted as a person of ordinary prudence would have acted. Of course, this is the definition of negligence in the civil context. There is actually a different definition of criminal negligence, which is beyond the scope of this book's discussion.

What is "gross negligence," and how is it different than "regular" negligence? Many gun cases will include a claim for gross negligence by the plaintiff. The primary reason for this is that if a plaintiff establishes gross negligence by a defendant, the plaintiff may be entitled to additional types of damages or amounts of money that are legally not available if mere negligence is established. Texas Civil Practice and Remedies Code Section 41.001(11) defines gross negligence as follows:

> **"GROSS NEGLIGENCE" MEANS AN ACT OR OMISSION:**
> (A) which when viewed objectively from the standpoint of the actor at the time of its occurrence involves an extreme degree of risk, considering the probability and magnitude of the potential harm to others; and
> (B) of which the actor has actual, subjective awareness of the risk involved, but nevertheless proceeds with conscious indifference to the rights, safety, or welfare of the others.

The defendant's state of mind is also a key difference between negligence and gross negligence. Negligence involves an objective standard—how would a reasonable person have acted? Gross negligence applies a subjective component—was this particular person actually aware of the risk involved?

EXAMPLE:
Caitlyn has practiced shooting at a private range on her country property for 20 years, without incident. She shoots toward an area where she has never seen another person, and she believes the range of her guns cannot reach her property line. One day, a neighbor is hit by a shot as he is strolling through the woods just off of Caitlyn's property.

Caitlyn might be liable for negligence if a jury determines, for example, that a reasonably prudent person would have acted differently, tested the range of her guns, or built a different type of backstop or berm, *etc.* However, Caitlyn was not subjectively aware of an extreme degree of risk, so there would be no evidence of gross negligence. However, change Caitlyn's awareness and it changes the result.

> **EXAMPLE:**
>
> Caitlyn has received several complaints over the years about bullets leaving her property and hitting her neighbor's property. Nevertheless, she ignores the complaints and continues shooting in the same direction. One day while practicing, her bullet leaves her property and hits her neighbor. Caitlyn is later sued by the neighbor for gross negligence.

In this example, Caitlyn may very well be liable for gross negligence because she was subjectively aware that her shots were reaching the neighbor's property and that there were people in the same area (*i.e.*, the folks who reported the shots). Despite that knowledge, she continued to shoot without changing direction or building a backstop or berm, and someone was injured as a result.

2. Negligent entrustment of a firearm

Some Texas Courts recognize a claim for entrusting (*e.g.*, giving, lending, transferring) a firearm to another person. To prove that a person or entity negligently entrusted a firearm, the plaintiff must show that:

1) the owner entrusted the gun;
2) to a person who was incompetent or reckless;
3) whom the owner knew or should have known was incompetent or reckless;

4) the person with the gun was negligent; and
5) the person's negligence proximately caused the incident and the plaintiff's injuries.

The courts that have recognized the claim of Negligent Entrustment of a Firearm use the elements of Negligent Entrustment of an Automobile as well as the Restatement Second of Torts Section 390. The Restatement Second of Torts states "A person who gives a chattel to another, knowing the other person, due to youth, inexperience, or other factors, is likely to use the chattel in a manner involving unreasonable risk of harm to himself or others, may be held liable for harm caused by the use of the chattel." There are only a few courts that have actually upheld this claim. This type of tort was created entirely by case law, and does not exist in a statute, and does not apply to the sale of a firearm. *See Prather v. Brandt*, 981 S.W.2d 801 (Tex. App. 1998); *In re Academy, Ltd.,* ___ S.W.3d ___ (Tex. June 25, 2021) (No. 19-0497).

> **EXAMPLE:**
> Stephen lets his adult grandson Gene borrow a shotgun to take on a fishing trip because he knows there are water moccasins in the spot where they plan to fish. Gene has never been in trouble with the law, has repeatedly been trained in firearms safety, and has never had an incident with a gun. However, while on the trip, Gene accidentally shoots a fellow fishing buddy with Stephen's shotgun. The fishing buddy, now turned plaintiff, sues Gene for negligence and Stephen for negligent entrustment of a firearm.

Can the plaintiff win his claim for negligent entrustment? Probably not. Stephen might get sued for giving the shotgun to his grandson, but the facts described do not meet the elements necessary to establish negligent entrustment under Texas law. Stephen should prevail in any lawsuit. First, there are no facts that suggest Gene was incompetent or reckless. Further, there are no facts showing Stephen's knowledge that Gene was either incompetent or reckless. Thus, the negligent entrustment claim would legally fail.

Many plaintiffs have urged Texas appellate courts to adopt a "strict liability" standard when looking at gun cases. In other words, if you give someone your gun, you are automatically liable for whatever happens. Texas appellate courts have, to-date, uniformly rejected a strict liability standard.

3. Is negligent storage of a firearm recognized in Texas?

A question commonly asked by gun owners is, "if someone steals my gun, am I liable if they shoot someone?" In other words, if I store my gun and a criminal or another less-than-responsible person gets the gun, am I liable if they shoot someone? As of the date of this publication, the answer in Texas is "probably not." A Texas appellate court has affirmatively stated that the claim of negligent storage of a firearm is not recognized in Texas. *Richardson, et al. v. Crawford,* No. 10-11-00089-CV, 2011 LEXIS 6578 (Tex. App.—Waco 2011). What does this mean? If someone accesses your gun and you did not intend for them to access your gun, since Texas does not currently recognize this claim, a plaintiff should not be able to recover if the person who accesses your gun injures himself or others.

Several caveats to this exist:
1) many other states do recognize this claim;
2) until the Texas Supreme Court rules on this issue, it is possible that another appellate court in Texas could decide differently; and

3) there are severe criminal consequences for storing your gun where it can be accessed by a minor. *See* Tex. Penal Code § 46.13.

As a result, while no civil claim exists in Texas today, it remains extraordinarily important to exercise care in the storage of your firearms.

B. Intentional discharge: a person intended to shoot
1. Negligence/gross negligence

Just because you intend to shoot someone, or otherwise "use" your gun, does not necessarily mean that the plaintiff will not assert negligence or gross negligence claims. In other words, you may have fully intended to pull the trigger, but the plaintiff may claim you were negligent for any number of reasons; for example, you mistook the mailman for a burglar, or you were negligent in shooting at a criminal. The negligence and gross negligence claims, as defined above, can be brought even if you intended to pull the trigger.

2. Assault and battery

If a person has shot at or shot someone, if they are sued, it may include a claim for assault and battery. This is an intentional act, not an accident or a claim based on a deviation from a standard of care. An assault occurs if a person:
1) intentionally, knowingly, or recklessly causes bodily injury to another, including the person's spouse;
2) intentionally or knowingly threatens another with imminent bodily injury, including the person's spouse; or
3) intentionally or knowingly causes physical contact with another when the person knows or should reasonably believe that the other will regard the contact as offensive or provocative.

Tex. Penal Code § 22.01(a); *Loaisiga v. Cerda,* 379 S.W.3d 248, (Tex. 2012) (recognizing civil assault elements mirror criminal assault).

> **EXAMPLE:**
>
> Bernice is startled while driving. Mark is standing next to her passenger window at a light, screaming that she cut him off in traffic, but taking no action to indicate he intends to harm Bernice or do anything besides verbally lodge his complaints. In response, Bernice fires a shot at Mark to make him go away, and hits him in the leg.

Bernice has committed an assault, which is also a civil cause of action referred to as a battery in the common law. She intended to and did cause serious bodily injury to Mark without a legal justification. Therefore, a civil jury would likely find Bernice liable and award damages to Mark.

> **EXAMPLE:**
>
> Bernice is startled while driving. Mark is standing next to her passenger window at a light, screaming that she cut him off in traffic, but taking no action to indicate he intends to harm Bernice or do anything besides verbally lodge his complaints. In response, Bernice points her gun at Mark and says "You're dead!" She fires her gun but misses.

Bernice has committed an assault. She knowingly threatened Mark with imminent bodily injury without any legal justification.

3. False imprisonment: being sued for detaining people

What if a gun owner detains someone at gunpoint? If the person who was detained later decides to sue, they will likely include a claim

for "false imprisonment." Texas recognizes a civil claim for false imprisonment. This claim can arise when someone detains a person while waiting for the police (*e.g.*, homeowners detaining burglars, *etc.*). However, it can also come up commonly in shoplifting cases (*see* Chapter 10). The elements of false imprisonment are:
 1) a willful detention;
 2) without consent; and
 3) without justification or authority of law. *Dangerfield v. Ormsby*, 264 S.W.3d 904 (Tex. App.—Fort Worth 2008, no pet).

EXAMPLE:

> Elizabeth fears she is about to be attacked in a grocery store parking lot by Richard. Richard follows her step-by-step through the parking lot and stops right next to Elizabeth's car. Elizabeth draws her .380 and tells Richard to "stay right there while I call the police." Richard complies, and Elizabeth holds him at gunpoint until the police arrive. When the police arrive, they determine that Richard was an out-of-uniform store employee tasked with rounding up the grocery carts in the parking lot and was no threat to Elizabeth.

If a jury determines that Elizabeth acted without justification (*i.e.*, she was not reasonably in fear of bodily injury or death), Elizabeth could be civilly liable for falsely imprisoning Richard and may owe him damages.

4. Wrongful death

If a person is in the unfortunate position of having shot and killed another individual and a civil suit occurs because of the shooting, it likely will include a claim for wrongful death. In Texas, "[a] person is liable for damages arising from an injury that causes an individual's death if the injury was caused by the person's or his agent's or servant's wrongful act, neglect, carelessness, unskillfulness, or default." Tex. Civ. Prac. & Rem. Code § 71.002. A wrongful death claim can be proven by establishing that one of the other claims described in this Chapter caused the death of another person. In other words, the "wrongful act, neglect, carelessness, unskillfulness, or default" that is needed to establish a wrongful death claim, can be established by proving that the defendant was liable for a tort such as battery or negligence and that the tort caused the death of a person.

III. WHAT CAN THE PLAINTIFF RECOVER?

If a person is sued in civil court and the plaintiff convinces a jury that the defendant was liable for damages, what and how much can a plaintiff get? There are scores of cases discussing the details of each category of damages that a plaintiff can recover in a civil lawsuit. The following is a brief description of two very important concepts: "proximate cause," which is essential to recover damages in most circumstances; and the basic types of damages that a plaintiff may typically seek in a gun case.

A. Proximate cause

One basic concept that is important to most civil claims, and is usually required to recover damages, is "proximate cause." Virtually every tort claim will require the plaintiff to prove that their damages were proximately caused by the defendant. "Proximate cause" is defined as cause that was a substantial factor in bringing about an event and without which the event would not have occurred. This concept is much discussed and has few bright-line tests.

For a gun owner, the most obvious cases of proximate cause are pulling the trigger on a firearm and hitting the aimed-at person or thing. The law will hold that your action proximately caused whatever physical damage the bullet did to persons or property. But what about those circumstances where the use of the gun is so far removed from the damages claimed? This is where the doctrine of proximate cause will cut off liability. If the damage is too far removed from the act of firing the gun, then it cannot be a proximate cause of the damage.

> **EXAMPLE:**
>
> James is cleaning his AR-15 one night in his apartment and is negligent in his handling of the rifle. He has an accidental discharge and the bullet goes through the wall of his apartment and strikes his neighbor, Donny, in the leg. Donny, although in massive pain, received prompt medical care from his wife, Catherine, and made a speedy recovery.

If James is later sued by Donny and his wife Catherine, James' negligence undoubtedly "proximately caused" damages for things like Donny's medical bills, hospital stay, and perhaps even lost wages. But what if Catherine claims that because of her having to treat Donny's wounds that she missed a big job interview and lost out on a big raise in pay? The law would hold that Catherine likely could not recover damages for her lost raise in pay because the loss would not be "proximately caused" by the sued-upon action. To put it another way, it is reasonably foreseeable that the negligent discharge of a firearm will cause medical bills for someone struck by a bullet. Therefore, this is recoverable. However, the law would say that the loss of a possible job opportunity for the wife who treated the person who was actually shot is not a reasonably foreseeable consequence of negligently discharging a firearm and, therefore, was not proximately caused by the act of negligence. In that case, there will be no recovery for the plaintiff, Catherine. Proximate cause must be established in every case and may appear to be arbitrary legal-line drawing, because it is.

As discussed later in this Chapter, Texas law also recognizes a doctrine that unforeseen criminal conduct breaks the causal link between an action and a third party's injuries.

B. What types of damages can a plaintiff recover?

The following is merely a brief snapshot of the types of damages recoverable in a firearms case. To recover any of the damages below, the plaintiff must first prove one of the claims above by a preponderance of the evidence. For example, if the jury determines a defendant was not negligent, a plaintiff cannot recover his or her medical costs, no matter how severe the plaintiff's injuries. Some of the damages a plaintiff can try to recover include:

- Lost wages;
- Medical costs;
- Disability;
- Pain and suffering (physical, mental, and emotional);
- Funeral and burial costs;
- Disfigurement;
- Loss of companionship;
- Loss of household services;
- Lost future wages;
- Past and future mental anguish;
- Loss of inheritance;
- Future medical costs; and
- Punitive or exemplary damages (Note: the standard of proof for punitive/exemplary damages is "clear and convincing

evidence," which is higher than a "preponderance of the evidence." Punitive damages are also only available in cases of intentional or reckless conduct, or gross negligence.)

A court can find the defendant 100% at fault, but award no damages because the plaintiff failed to prove damages by a preponderance of the evidence. For example, a plaintiff who seeks reimbursement for medical expenses but has no evidence that they ever went to a doctor or hospital, will very unlikely be able to recover for medical expenses.

> **PRACTICAL LEGAL TIP**
>
> Most people don't know that civil courts in Texas have no independent means of sifting through the thousands of lawsuits filed every year to determine which are frivolous and which are meritorious and should go forward. The civil justice system is "user driven," meaning that unless one side or the other asks the judge to rule on a particular issue (usually called a "motion"), no one at the courthouse, including the judge, is going to take any action to examine the merit, or lack thereof, of a lawsuit. –Kirk

IV. HOW GOOD ARE TEXAS CIVIL IMMUNITY LAWS FOR GUN OWNERS?

A. No immunity from lawsuits

There is a common misconception that there exists a law stating if you are legally justified in using your gun, you can't be sued.

This is just not the case. First, if a person has the filing fee, anyone can sue anyone in the State of Texas. There is no procedure to stop someone from filing a lawsuit. Winning a lawsuit is a different issue entirely. If someone files the lawsuit, no matter how frivolous, it still must be shown to the court that a defense bars this lawsuit. This process can take significant time, money, and legal energy even for the most frivolous of cases. In short, lawyers get paid, and even if you beat the "rap," you still have to take the civil "ride." So, if there is no immunity to lawsuits for gun owners, what protection is there?

B. Immunity for certain claims

The most important statute for gun owners who find themselves included in a civil suit after a justified use of force is Texas Civil Practice and Remedies Code Section 83.001.

> **IMMUNITY FROM DAMAGES**
> **TEX. CIVIL PRACTICE AND REMEDIES CODE § 83.001**
>
> A defendant who uses force or deadly force that is justified under Chapter 9, Penal Code, is immune from civil liability for personal injury or death that results from the defendant's use of force or deadly force, as applicable.

This section provides that a person who uses force or deadly force that is justified under Chapter 9 of the Texas Penal Code is immune from civil liability for personal injury or death that results from the defendant's use of force or deadly force. This statute does not prevent lawsuits; it just makes one that is filed harder to win. Immunity from liability is an affirmative defense, and, as such, will only be considered after a plaintiff is well into the pain a civil suit may cause an innocent defendant. Texas courts have ruled that immunity from suit would be a violation of the "Open Courts Doctrine" of Article 1, § 13 of the Texas Constitution. A Texas intermediate appellate court ruled in *In re Smith* that Section 83.001 does not mean immunity from suit; it means immunity from damages if the defense is proven during the litigation of the case. *In re Smith,* 262 S.W.3d 463 (Tex. App.—Beaumont 2008).

Also, note the language in Section 83.001 is "liability for personal injury or death." While it has not yet been interpreted by the appellate courts, this language likely means that property damage is not covered. What could that mean?

EXAMPLE:

Brooke is the victim of a home invasion. She fires several shots at the intruder. The intruder is hit and stopped. One shot, however, misses the intruder and hits a propane tank at the house across the street. The propane tank explodes and burns down the neighbor's home. Luckily, the neighbor was not home at the time.

The resulting damage is neither personal injury nor death. It is very unlikely that the immunity statute will provide Brooke with any protection from a civil suit by the neighbor for the damages to the house.

C. Justification

All of the justifications under Chapter 9 of the Texas Penal Code can also be asserted as affirmative defenses in a civil action. This means, for example, if you shoot someone in defense of yourself, others, or your property and are sued as a result, you may assert the applicable sections of the Penal Code as a defense to the civil claims. If the judge or jury agrees that you acted in self-defense, or properly used force to defend others or property, the plaintiff will be barred from recovery. *See* Chapters 7 through 10.

D. Statute of limitations for civil claims

The statute of limitations is a doctrine in Texas (and almost every other jurisdiction) that requires civil claims to be brought within a certain period of time after the incident. If the claim is not brought within the statute of limitations period, it is barred. There are a number of issues relating to when the statute of limitations starts to run in many cases, but for the most part, limitations will start to run immediately after a shooting incident. The statute of limitations can vary from claim to claim; most, however, are between one and four years. In Texas, the limitations period most likely to apply to gun cases is going to be two years. Assault, negligence, wrongful death, and false imprisonment claims all provide two-year limitations periods. *See* Tex. Civ. Prac. & Rem. Code § 16.003.

What does this mean for gun owners? If you use your gun, the plaintiff must bring a civil suit against you within two years of the incident in almost all cases or else the claim will be barred.

E. Superseding or intervening criminal conduct

Texas law recognizes a doctrine that absolves someone from responsibility for conduct that might otherwise be a tort (*e.g.*, negligence) if a criminal act breaks the causal connection between the tort and the injury. Generally, a third party's criminal conduct is a superseding cause which relieves the negligent actor from liability. However, the actor's negligence will not be excused where the criminal conduct is a foreseeable result of the actor's negligence. *Byrd v. Woodruff,* 891 S.W.2d 689 (Tex. App.—Dallas 1994); *Nixon v. Mr. Prop. Mgmt. Co.,* 690 S.W.2d 546 (Tex. 1985).

> **EXAMPLE:**
> Jonathan allows his nephew Andrew to use his handgun for protection. Jonathan knows Andrew has been in trouble with the law repeatedly and has been accused of armed robbery. While Andrew has the handgun, his apartment is burglarized, and the gun is stolen and used in a crime spree. During the crime spree, Melanie is shot and injured.

Melanie would not be able to recover from Jonathan, even though he may have been negligent in giving his gun to Andrew, because the criminal act of burglarizing Andrew's apartment and subsequent crime spree were superseding causes that broke the link between Jonathan's actions and the resulting injuries.

F. Contributory negligence/proportionate responsibility

Texas has a doctrine called proportionate responsibility. If this defense is applicable and properly raised, either the judge or the jury will be asked to determine the percentage of fault or responsibility of the parties involved in the incident. The damages are then apportioned based upon the percentages assigned by the judge or jury. *Kroger Co. v. Keng,* 23 S.W.3d 347 (Tex. 2000).

> **EXAMPLE:**
> Ronny is a young adult trick-or-treater. He uses a fake gun as a part of his costume and knocks loudly on Carol's door at 11:30 p.m. on October 31. Carol, having forgotten about Halloween, is

frightened by the knock, the fake gun, and the late hour of Ronny's arrival. She fires through the door, injuring Ronny.

In the civil suit that follows by Ronny against Carol, the jury will be permitted to consider whether Ronny's negligence, if any, contributed to cause the resulting injuries. The jury could determine that Ronny was 0% at fault, 100%, or anything in between. This will reduce the amount of damages that Ronny can recover. By way of example only, if the jury awarded Ronny $100,000 in damages, but found he was 30% at fault and Carol 70%, Ronny would only be able to recover $70,000 of his damages.

In Texas, this rule applies only where the damaged party is 50% or less at fault. In other words, if the plaintiff bringing the lawsuit is determined to be more than 50% responsible for the injuries, he or she cannot recover any damages. This can be important for the average gun owner in that a carjacker/home invader who is the overwhelming cause of an incident cannot recover just because the judge or jury finds you made a slight misstep in defending yourself or your home.

V. WHAT ABOUT THIRD PARTIES?

Texas law provides a different standard when it comes to injuries to third parties. In this section, a third party generally means someone who is not a party to the encounter with the firearm (*e.g.*, bystanders, witnesses, folks nearby who were not the intended target, *etc.*).

"Acts of self-defense or in defense of one's property have always been in accord with the public policy of Texas, and those persons having sufficient courage to so act legally enjoy the privilege. It is only when acts in self-defense or in defense of one's property are committed under circumstances where the actor should realize that such acts create an unreasonable risk of causing harm to innocent third parties that such third parties may subject the actor to liability." *Helms v. Harris,* 281 S.W.2d 770, 771 (Tex. Civ. App. 1955). Likewise, the Texas Penal Code also provides in Sections 9.05 and 9.06 that a person cannot use justification as a defense where they injure a third party by their reckless acts. This means that even if you defend yourself, others, or property, but you create an unreasonable risk to others in doing so, you can be liable if one of those third parties is injured.

> **EXAMPLE:**
> Heather shoots at Calvin as he unlawfully breaks into Heather's occupied home at night. She fires a single shot with her .22 that narrowly misses Calvin but hits a man washing his car down the street.

Heather is probably not liable to the man down the street, because her conduct did not unreasonably place third parties at risk.

> **EXAMPLE:**
> Rick shoots at Calvin as he unlawfully breaks into Rick's occupied home at night. Rick fires 30 shots with his fully-automatic M-16, missing with the initial burst. Calvin turns and runs. Rick continues to fire haphazardly at Calvin as he runs down the street. One shot hits a man washing his car four houses away.

Rick could very likely be liable to the man washing his car because he unreasonably placed third parties at risk by recklessly firing a fully automatic weapon down a neighborhood street.

VI. WILL INSURANCE COVER IT IF I SHOOT SOMEONE?

A. Homeowners insurance

With few exceptions, almost every homeowners insurance policy excludes coverage for intentional acts. The act of using your firearm in self-defense is almost always an intentional act. You intended to stop the threat. Plaintiffs' attorneys will very likely assert a negligence claim against a homeowner in an attempt to fall within the coverage and negotiate a settlement with the insurance carrier. However, at the end of the day, if the only evidence is that you intentionally shot the plaintiff because you intended to stop a threat, it is likely that any policy with an intentional act exclusion will not provide coverage for any damages awarded.

B. Auto insurance

Scores of cases around the country exist where the parties allege that a gun incident is covered by automobile insurance merely because the use of the firearm occurs in the auto or involves an auto. Almost universally, courts have held that these incidents are not covered under insurance policies merely because the discharge occurs in a car or involves a car.

In order for automobile insurance coverage to apply, the injury must arise from the "use" of a motor vehicle as a motor vehicle. There must be a causal connection between the use of the motor vehicle and the injury. This connection is shown if the injury is the natural and reasonable consequence of the motor vehicle's use. There is no coverage if the injury results from something wholly disassociated from, independent of, and remote from the motor vehicle's normal use.

> **EXAMPLE:**
> Jeff is cleaning his 9mm handgun in the car. It accidentally discharges, causing his passenger, Connie, severe injuries.

This event will almost certainly not be covered by auto insurance.

> **EXAMPLE:**
> Jeff discharges his 9mm handgun in the car at Connie during an attempted carjacking, causing Connie severe injuries and also hitting a bystander.

This event will almost certainly not be covered by auto insurance.

For an injury to fall within the "use" coverage of an automobile policy:
1) the accident must have arisen out of the inherent nature of the automobile;
2) the accident must have arisen within the natural territorial limits of an automobile;
3) the actual use must not have terminated; and
4) the automobile must not merely contribute to cause the condition which produces the injury, but must itself produce injury.

Two Texas courts of appeals have used these factors to conclude that a drive-by shooting does not arise out of the use of a vehicle. Also, if the injury occurs when purposefully handling a gun (*e.g.*, playing with it or intentionally shooting it), not in order to place or remove the gun from the vehicle, there is no causal connection between the injury and the use of the vehicle; the vehicle is merely the place of the injury and its use incidental to the injury-producing act. *See Texas Farm Bureau Mut. Ins. Co. v. Sturrock,* 65 S.W.3d 763 (Tex. App.—Beaumont 2001).

Texas recognizes one minor exception. While a gun is resting in or being removed from a gun rack permanently attached to a vehicle, the presence of the permanently attached gun rack in the vehicle establishes a significant causal connection between the accident and the "use" of the vehicle. In other words, if a gun discharges while resting on or being removed from a gun rack attached to a vehicle, auto insurance will likely cover the event under existing Texas law. *See Mid-Century Ins. Co. v. Lindsey,* 997 S.W.2d 153 (Tex. 1999).

VII. WHAT CIVIL LIABILITY DOES A PERSON FACE IF THEIR CHILDREN ACCESS THEIR FIREARMS?

A. Parents are not responsible for minor children's actions merely because they are parents!

As a general rule, minors are civilly liable for their own torts (that is, their wrongful actions such as negligence, gross negligence, assault, *etc.*). The mere fact of paternity or maternity does not make a parent liable to third parties for the torts of his or her minor children. Under this general rule, parents are not responsible for their minor children's tortious actions when the minor child commits a tort and the parent had no direct relationship to the child's action, such as providing a firearm in a negligent manner, failing to supervise the child, or allowing the child to engage in behavior the parent knows is dangerous or risky. *See Sanders v. Herold* 217 S.W.3d 11 (Tex. App. 2006).

B. Parents who fail to "parent" may become responsible for minor children's actions

While a parent who has no direct relationship to a minor child's tortious actions is generally not liable for that child's actions, if the parent negligently allows their child to act in a manner likely to harm another, if they give their child a dangerous instrumentality, or if they do not restrain a child known to have dangerous tendencies, the parent may be liable.

Another potential situation where a parent may be held civilly liable arises with the negligent storage of a firearm in violation of Texas Penal Code Section 46.13. Under this code section, a parent can be held criminally liable if a child gains access to a readily dischargeable firearm, but can the parent be held civilly liable? There is no published authority on the issue of *per se* liability as of this writing. However, one appellate judge in a dissenting opinion (dissenting opinions are not binding on other courts) has suggested that a claim for negligence *per se* might exist for violations of Section 46.13. *See Perez v. Lopez,* 74 S.W.3d 60 (Tex. App.—El Paso 2002) (dissenting opinion). Negligence *per se* means that liability is automatically established due to the violation of the statute, while damages and proximate cause must still be proven. Regardless, all gun owners should exercise great care to avoid unintended access to guns by minors.

> **EXAMPLE:**
> Johnny's 17-year-old son Connor has been hunting since he was 11 and has taken several firearms training courses.

If Johnny takes Connor hunting and for some reason Connor accidentally discharges his shotgun, injuring another person, it is highly unlikely that Johnny, the parent, will be civilly liable for an accident that occurs while hunting.

> **EXAMPLE:**
> Johnny's 12-year-old son Curtis has never handled a gun or taken a firearms training course. Johnny decides to take him to the range

for the first time, but they are both asked to leave the range after Curtis repeatedly fires into the ceiling and the floor. Not to be deterred, Johnny takes Curtis to another range with no additional instruction or training.

If Curtis shoots and injures someone at the second range, it is likely that Johnny will be liable, because Johnny allowed Curtis to act in a manner likely to harm another, and Johnny did not restrain Curtis despite his dangerous conduct.

C. Parents have a duty to control and discipline children

In addition to the situations described in the preceding section where parents may become liable for a minor child's actions when the parent's own actions (or lack thereof) played a role, Texas has a statute that also provides limited parental liability. Texas Family Code Section 41.001 provides that a parent or other person who has the duty of control and reasonable discipline of a child is liable for any property damage proximately caused by:

1) the negligent conduct of the child if the conduct is reasonably attributable to the negligent failure of the parent or other person to exercise that duty; or
2) the willful and malicious conduct of a child who is at least 10 years of age but under 18 years of age (recovery for damage caused by willful and malicious conduct is limited to actual damages, not to exceed $25,000 per occurrence, plus court costs and reasonable attorney's fees).

The first subsection mirrors the standard for parental liability in Texas, meaning a parent is liable for the negligence of a child, if the parent was negligent in failing to control or discipline the child. For example, if your child has previously injured someone in a gun incident, and you fail to better supervise, discipline, or take control of their shooting, you will almost certainly be liable for subsequent shooting incidents.

> **EXAMPLE:**
>
> In preparation for the annual family hunting trip, Larry took his 16-year-old son Robert to the outdoor shooting range. As happens every year, while at the range, Robert was haphazard and intentionally unsafe in his handling of his firearm. Robert, who refuses to take anything seriously, repeatedly pointed his firearm in the direction of other persons, and even discharged his gun into the air three times while ululating. Larry scolded Robert by telling him that it is "not nice" to point guns at other people. During the hunting trip, Robert randomly fired his shotgun for no apparent reason into the trees. Robert's last shot hit a fellow hunter standing among the trees.

Is Larry liable for his minor son Robert's acts? Probably yes. Larry was well aware of the fact that Robert handles firearms in a dangerous manner, and Larry failed to take any reasonable measures to prevent Robert from injuring another person. The law would very likely find that Larry's failure to reasonably discipline and supervise his child proximately caused the injury to the other hunter.

The second subsection provides *per se* (*i.e.*, automatic), but limited, liability for willful and malicious damages caused by a child aged 10-17. This will commonly cover incidents of vandalism but could also encompass intentional (but not negligent) shootings. The damages under this subsection are capped at $25,000.

EXAMPLE:

Kevin, a 14-year-old boy, does not like his neighbor. One day, he retrieves the family 12-gauge shotgun and decides to shoot the neighbor's fence. Kevin's parents know nothing about this behavior, and Kevin has never had trouble with a firearm in the past. As a result of the shooting, a number of pickets from the fence were destroyed, three windows were broken, and numerous pockmarks were left in the brick façade of the home.

Under the second subsection of Texas Family Code Section 41.001, Kevin's parents would be liable for the damage Kevin caused to his neighbor's property, up to $25,000 plus court costs and reasonable attorneys' fees, because Kevin's actions were willful and malicious.

> CHAPTER SEVENTEEN ◁

BEYOND FIREARMS: KNIVES, CLUBS, AND TASERS

I. INTRODUCTION AND OVERVIEW

In addition to Texas's many firearms laws, there also exist state laws governing the possession and use of other weapons. This includes any object that is not a firearm, but could be used as a weapon. This Chapter will briefly discuss the laws governing these other weapons, including weapons that are absolutely illegal under the law, weapons that are illegal to carry, and exceptions to the laws prohibiting the carrying of illegal weapons.

A. There are no longer illegal knives

The 2017 Texas Legislature worked to fully deregulate knives. This included the 2013 legislature's action to decriminalize switchblades and the 2015 legislature's prohibition on local knife laws. As of 2017, the only types of knives that are restricted are "location-restricted" knives. A location-restricted knife is a knife with a blade length over 5½ inches. *See* Tex. Penal Code § 46.01(6). These types of knives are prohibited in certain prohibited places. As long as you are 21 years of age or older and not carrying one of these knives in a prohibited place, they are perfectly legal to own and carry anywhere else. *See* Chapter 14 for a list of the prohibited places under Texas Penal Code Section 46.03.

B. "Knuckles" no longer prohibited

With all knives decriminalized and legal to carry, the 86th Texas Legislature turned its attention to knuckles and clubs. For over a century, knuckles were illegal to purchase, possess, or carry. For just as long, people had been trying to find a way around the law. This issue finally got the attention of the Texas Legislature when a self-defense tool specifically marketed to women got an unsuspecting and otherwise law-abiding citizen arrested. The "knuckles" in this instance was a cat-shaped keychain where the user's fingers held the keychain through the cat's eyes, and the cat's ears were shaped into sharp lancets. Since far more lethal weapons can be lawfully purchased, possessed, and carried, it seemed illogical that a woman's self-defense keychain should put a person at risk of punishment with a year in the county jail and a $4,000 fine. In response, the Texas Legislature eliminated the statutory prohibition and definition of "knuckles." Therefore, as of September 1, 2019, the Texas Penal Code contains no references or restrictions on the previously forbidden knuckles.

Traditional "Brass Knuckles"

Other objects which may be held in the hand are used to augment the strength of a punch as an offensive weapon, such as a "fist filler" (pictured below). Fist fillers are not regulated under Texas law and are not considered prohibited weapons.

Commercial "Fist Filler"   *Roll of Coins*

II. ABSOLUTELY PROHIBITED WEAPONS
A. What is an absolutely prohibited weapon?
Texas Penal Code Section 46.05, entitled "Prohibited Weapons," states that it is a crime if a person "intentionally or knowingly possesses, manufactures, transports, repairs, or sells" certain prohibited weapons. As opposed to many laws which merely prohibit the carrying of a weapon in a public place, this section of the Penal Code prohibits a person from even possessing such a weapon—including in their home or on any property under their control or influence.

B. What weapons are absolutely prohibited under Texas law?

The list of absolutely prohibited weapons is found in Texas Penal Code Section 46.05. This section prohibits the possession, manufacturing, transporting, repair, or sale of several different weapons or classes of weapons. Possession of most of these weapons is a third degree felony.

1. Chemical dispensing devices are prohibited with an exception

A chemical dispensing device means a "device, other than a small chemical dispenser sold commercially for personal protection, which is designed, made, or adapted for the purpose of dispensing a substance capable of causing an adverse psychological or physiological effect on a human being." *See* Tex. Penal Code § 46.01(14). Because this definition of chemical dispensing device specifically excludes "small chemical dispenser[s] sold commercially for personal protection," items such as personal mace or pepper-spray, as well as bear or wasp spray, are not prohibited. Instead, a chemical dispensing device includes items that cause "adverse psychological or physiological effect[s]" on people such as tear gas, including items available to the military or law enforcement, and not the general public.

2. Zip guns

A zip gun is defined as "a device or combination of devices that was not originally a firearm and is adapted to expel a projectile through a smooth-bore or rifled-bore barrel by using the energy generated by an explosion or burning substance." *See* Tex. Penal Code § 46.01(16). Essentially, this definition prevents individuals from building a firearm with spare parts lying around that are not firearm parts or parts originally from a firearm. In other words, a potato gun could potentially land you in trouble.

Formerly, Texas law allowed individuals to possess zip guns with proper registration under the National Firearms Act. However, the 84th Texas Legislature in 2015 removed this exception. It is now illegal to possess a zip gun, and there is no defense or way to make the zip gun legal for possession. If you are caught with a zip gun, your legal defense is limited to arguing that it isn't a zip gun!

3. Improvised Explosive Devices

In response to the increased threat of attacks using an Improvised Explosive Device ("IED") as was demonstrated in tragic events like the Boston Marathon bombing, the Texas Legislature has made it a felony to possess, manufacture, transport, repair, or sell these weapons. An IED is defined as "a completed and operational bomb designed to cause serious bodily injury, death, or substantial property damage that is fabricated in an improvised manner using nonmilitary components." *See* Tex. Penal Code § 46.01(19). The law specifically excludes the unassembled components and exploding targets used for firearms practice (*i.e.*, Tannerite).

4. Tire deflation devices

Texas law prohibits tire deflation devices, which are defined as "a device, including a caltrop or spike strip, that when driven over, impedes or stops the movement of a wheeled vehicle by puncturing one or more of the vehicle's tires." *See* Tex. Penal Code § 46.01(17). What is a caltrop? A caltrop is a weapon made up of two or more sharp nails arranged in a way that one always points up from a stable base. Anciently, caltrops were used as a way to slow the advance of horses, war elephants, camels, and human troops and were used as early as 331 BC. Today, caltrops (pictured below) are used to deflate automobile tires.

Caltrops

Personal-use, mobile spike strips are also prohibited. These strips should not be confused with permanent traffic control devices that are "designed to puncture one or more of a vehicle's tires when driven over in a specific direction; and [have] a clearly visible sign posted in close proximity to the traffic control device that prohibits entry or warns motor vehicle operators of the traffic control device." *See* Tex. Penal Code § 46.01(17). These types of traffic control devices are often seen at airports and other secured facilities to prevent the unauthorized entry or exit from the facility, such as the one pictured below.

C. Additional weapons prohibited by Texas Penal Code Section 46.05 unless NFA compliance is met

Section 46.05 also prohibits the following weapons and devices which are discussed in greater detail in Chapter 18, "National Firearms Act." These weapons include:
- Explosive weapons;
- Machine guns; and
- Short-barreled firearms.

Possession of these weapons and devices remains prohibited unless the weapon is registered "in the National Firearms Registration and Transfer Record maintained by the Bureau of Alcohol, Tobacco, Firearms and Explosives or classified as a curio or relic by the United States Department of Justice." *See* Tex. Penal Code § 46.05(a).

In 2021, the Texas Legislature passed a law which legalized the possession of "Texas-made suppressors." The law itself is discussed in further detail later in Chapter 18. However, interestingly, the change in the law also removed "firearm silencers" of any type from the list of prohibited weapons in Texas Penal Code Section 46.05. This does not mean that an individual will not be arrested if in possession of a silencer that is not registered with the NFA. The Supremacy Clause, Article VI, Paragraph 2 of the U.S. Constitution, makes it clear that if federal law and state law are in conflict with each other, then federal law generally prevails. This means that under federal law, a firearm silencer is required to be registered with the NFA and a tax be paid. *See* 26 U.S.C. § 5861. But how does this work in reality? If an individual is in possession of an unregistered silencer and encounters a Texas law enforcement officer, that individual cannot be arrested for possessing the silencer by the Texas law enforcement officer under state law. However, Texas law enforcement may contact the ATF, who will investigate the potential violation under federal law. Bottom line: if an individual wants to legally possess a firearm silencer or suppressor, they need to apply for a tax stamp. *See* Chapter 18 for discussion on applying for a tax stamp.

D. Defense for members of the military or law enforcement
Under Texas Penal Code Section 46.05(b), persons who are members of the armed forces or national guard, a governmental

law enforcement agency, or a correctional facility who use one of these prohibited weapons in the course of their official duties are provided a defense to prosecution. This explains why, most commonly, one would see a police officer use a spike strip in the course of a high-speed chase down the highway but not be charged with a crime for breaking the law regarding prohibited weapons.

E. Affirmative defenses for antique weapons, and use of or sales of tire deflation devices to military or law enforcement agencies

In addition, Texas law provides an affirmative defense to prosecution available to individuals whose conduct was incidental to dealing with a tire deflation device solely as an antique or curio. This means that persons who possess ancient caltrops, such as those described earlier, are subject to the affirmative defense. *See* Tex. Penal Code § 46.05(d)(1).

Moreover, individuals whose conduct was incidental to dealing with a tire deflation device solely for the purpose of making them available to an organization, agency, or institution within the armed forces or national guard, a governmental law enforcement agency, or a correctional facility are also provided with an affirmative defense. *See* Tex. Penal Code § 46.05(d)(3).

III. GENERALLY PROHIBITED WEAPONS

As opposed to Texas Penal Code Section 46.05, which strictly prohibits the possession, manufacture, transport, or sale of certain weapons, Section 46.02 prohibits the carrying of handguns and location-restricted knives. Section 46.02(a), as amended by the Firearm Carry Act of 2021, prohibits the carrying of a handgun on or about one's person either intentionally, knowingly, or recklessly and, at the time, the person:

1) is younger than 21 years of age;
2) has been convicted in the last five years of Assault Causes Bodily Injury; Deadly Conduct; Terroristic Threat; or Disorderly Conduct (for either discharging or displaying a firearm); and
3) is not on the person's own premises, a premises under their control, or inside of or directly *en route* to a motor vehicle or watercraft owned by that person or under their control.

See Chapter 13 for a further discussion on Texas Constitutional Carry.

Section 46.02(a-4) makes it a crime for a person younger than 18 years of age to intentionally, knowingly, or recklessly carry on or about their person a location-restricted knife, and they are not on their own premises, a premises under their control, or inside of or directly *en route* to a motor vehicle or watercraft owned by that person or under their control, or under the direct supervision of a parent or legal guardian.

Note, however, this Section does not prohibit the possession, manufacture, or sale of such weapons—merely the carrying and transport of them at any place other than the person's premises, motor vehicle, or watercraft (if certain requirements are not met).

A. Location-restricted knives

Texas no longer criminalizes "illegal knives." This was a welcome change to the law because prior to September 1, 2017, Texas Penal Code Section 46.01(6), had an extensive list of "illegal knives" that included:
- A knife with a blade over 5½ inches;
- A hand instrument designed to cut or stab another by being thrown;

- A dagger, including but not limited to a dirk, stiletto, and poniard;
- A Bowie knife;
- A sword; or
- A spear.

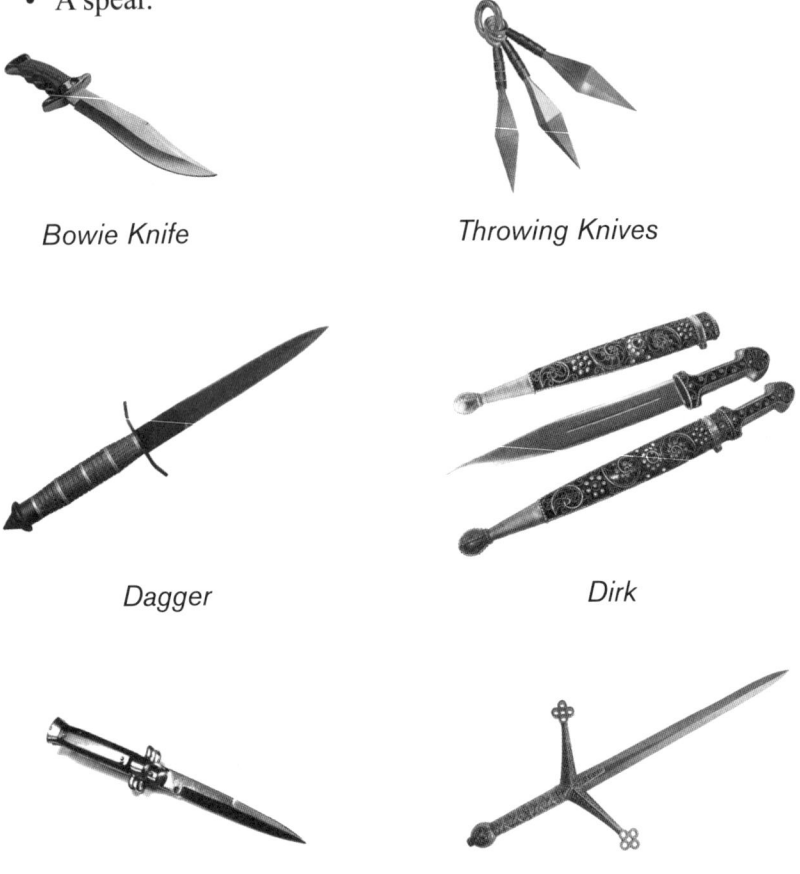

Bowie Knife

Throwing Knives

Dagger

Dirk

Stiletto

Poniard

A particularly aggravating facet of the prior law was the fact that none of these specifically named knives were actually defined in the statute. Therefore, there was much debate as to whether a particular knife was or was not illegal. Fortunately, these debates will now be left to the knife collectors and enthusiasts, and not police, prosecutors, and criminal defense lawyers.

While knives are still present in Texas Penal Code Section 46.02, the restriction now only applies to persons under the age of 18 carrying a knife with a blade longer than 5½ inches. These persons can still legally carry a location-restricted knife on their own property, in their motor vehicle, or watercraft. It is also legal for them to carry a location-restricted knife while under the supervision of their parent or guardian. The penalty for violating this general prohibition is a Class C misdemeanor, which is an arrestable offense.

1. Prohibited places

The general restriction on carrying an "illegal knife" any place other than a person's property, motor vehicle, or watercraft has now been replaced with a list of specific places where "location-restricted knives" cannot be carried. These places should be well known to Texas gun owners, in particular LTC holders. This is because the locations are the same ones listed in Texas Penal Code Section 46.03. It is a third degree felony to carry a location-restricted knife into a school or educational institution (including colleges and universities) or at a school-sponsored activity. It is a Class C misdemeanor to carry a location-restricted knife into the following premises:
- Polling places;
- Courts or offices used by the courts;
- Racetracks used for pari-mutuel betting;
- Secured areas of airports;
- Within 1,000 feet of a place used for executions on execution day;

- Establishments that receive 51% of their income from the sale of alcohol for on-premises consumption;
- High school, collegiate, or professional sporting events;
- Interscholastic events;
- Correctional facilities;
- Civil commitment facilities;
- Hospitals;
- Nursing facilities;
- Mental hospitals;
- Amusement parks; and
- Room where an open meeting of a governmental entity is being held.

Additionally, private property owners retain the ability to exclude knives from their property with a general "no trespassing," "no knives," or "no weapons" warning. The Texas Legislature did not create a specific criminal trespassing statute to cover location-restricted knives in the way that Texas Penal Code Sections 30.05, 30.06, and 30.07 do for constitutional carriers and LTC holders carrying a handgun.

2. Exception for location-restricted knives

Texas Penal Code Section 46.15(e) provides a specific exception to the law prohibiting the carrying of location-restricted knives if the weapon is used in a historical demonstration or in a ceremony in which, the knife is significant to the performance of the ceremony. This exception exists because the Texas Legislature recognizes that some location-restricted knives are necessary in historical reenactments and ceremonies.

> **EXCEPTION FOR LOCATION-RESTRICTED KNIVES**
> **TEX. PENAL CODE § 46.15(e)**
>
> Section 46.02(a-4) does not apply to an individual carrying a location-restricted knife used in a historical demonstration or in a ceremony in which the knife is significant to the performance of the ceremony.

Under this exception, individuals who are historical reenactors under the age of 18 who are demonstrating a historical battle where a sword is a part of the reenactment are not guilty of the crime of carrying a location-restricted knife. Likewise, persons under the age of 18 who are participating in a ceremony, such as a wedding where the bride and groom walk under a steeple of swords, would also not be guilty of carrying a location-restricted knife since this exception states that the provisions of Texas Penal Code Section 46.02(a-4) do not apply in such a situation.

3. Switchblades are no longer illegal!

Once listed as a prohibited weapon that was illegal to possess in any place, switchblades were removed from the list in 2013. In 2017, the legislature removed Texas Penal Code Section 46.01(11), which defined switchblade. The continued presence of this definition after 2013 had caused some confusion as to whether or not there continued to be some regulations specific to switchblades, but rest assured, it did not. This definition was a statutory relic of a bygone era, that is no more.

However, all switchblades and automatic knives that possess a blade longer than 5½ inches are regulated as any other location-restricted knife.

4. Municipalities may not impose their own regulations regarding knives!

In 2015, the Texas Legislature added knives to the list of weapons covered by the Texas preemption law. *See* Tex. Loc. Gov't Code § 229.001, discussed in Chapter 1. Local municipalities, government agencies, and other regulatory bodies cannot enact laws, ordinances, and rules regulating knives that are more restrictive than state law, which, thanks to the Texas Legislature, is now very little.

B. Clubs

In 2019, the Texas Legislature, while considering decriminalizing knuckles, noticed that the prohibition on carrying clubs made little sense and was no longer necessary. Therefore, at the same time it eliminated knuckles from the entire Texas Penal Code, it removed the unlawful carrying of clubs, generally in public. However, since Section 46.03 of the Texas Penal Code continues to prohibit the carrying of clubs into specific secure locations *(i.e.,* schools, polling places, *etc.*), a discussion of clubs therefore continues to be enlightening.

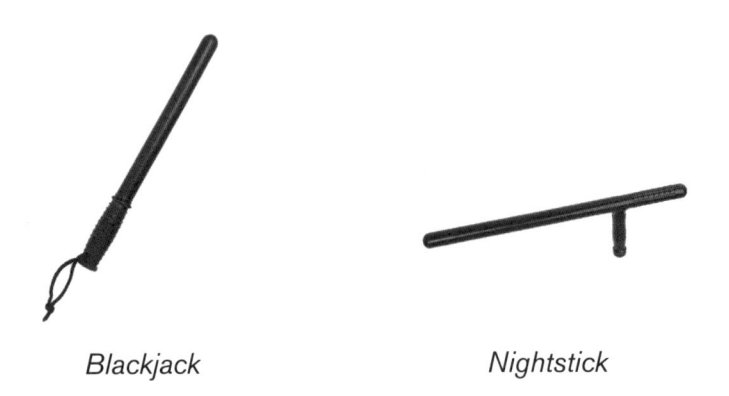

Blackjack

Nightstick

Mace

Tomahawk

1. When do ordinary items become clubs?

The legal definition of a club includes any instrument "adapted for the purpose of inflicting serious bodily injury or death by striking the person with the instrument." *See* Tex. Penal Code § 46.01(1). This means that many ordinary items that a person may find in their home or vehicle may be considered to be a club if the item has been adapted to serve a different purpose than originally intended.

For instance, a baseball bat is designed to be used for playing baseball. However, if a person takes a baseball bat and hammers a few nails through the end of the bat, the baseball bat has been adapted to become a mace.

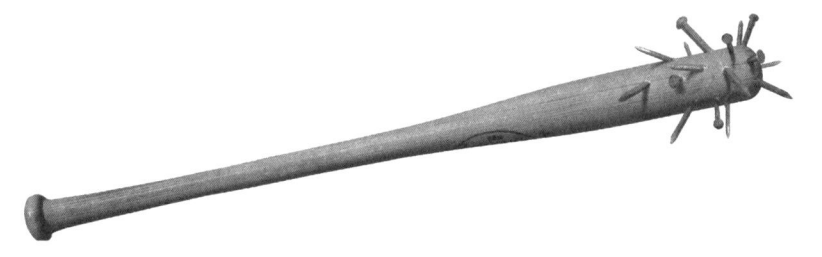

Baseball Bat Adapted as a Mace

2. Specific exceptions to the law prohibiting the carrying of a club

Texas Penal Code Section 46.15 also contains a number of exceptions for persons who, as a result of their employment, need to carry a club in a prohibited place under Texas Penal Code Section 46.03.

Members of the armed forces and employees of penal institutions

EXCEPTION FOR MEMBERS OF THE ARMED FORCES AND EMPLOYEES OF PENAL INSTITUTIONS AT PLACES OF EXECUTION
TEX. PENAL CODE § 46.15(f)

Section 46.03(a)(6) does not apply to a person who possesses a firearm or club while in the actual discharge of official duties as:
(1) a member of the armed forces or state military forces, as defined by Section 437.001, Government Code; or
(2) an employee of a penal institution.

The exception provided in this portion of the statute is specific to places of execution and those members of the armed forces or employees of a penal institution who are present at or within 1,000 feet of the place of execution in an official capacity as they carry out their duties.

Animal control officers

EXCEPTION FOR ANIMAL CONTROL OFFICERS
TEX. PENAL CODE § 46.15(g)

The provisions of Section 46.03 prohibiting the possession or carrying of a club do not apply to an animal control officer who holds a certificate issued under Section 829.006, Health and Safety Code, and who possesses or carries an instrument used specifically for deterring the bite of an animal while the officer is in the performance of official duties under the Health and Safety Code or is traveling to or from a place of duty.

The exception for animal control officers may be slightly misleading. First, it is important to point out that this only provides an exception for licensed animal control officers. Second, and more importantly, the exception is also only for the use of a club that is specific to the catching of an animal, such as a "catcher's pole" or snare. Animal control officers who attempt to use a mace, for instance, are unlikely to avail themselves of this exception.

Code enforcement officers

> **EXCEPTION FOR CODE ENFORCEMENT OFFICERS**
> **TEX. PENAL CODE § 46.15(h)**
>
> Sections 46.02 and 46.03 prohibiting the possession or carrying of a club do not apply to a code enforcement officer who:
> (1) holds a certificate of registration issued under Chapter 1952, Occupations Code; and
> (2) possesses or carries an instrument used specifically for deterring an animal bite while the officer is:
>   (A) performing official duties; or
>   (B) traveling to or from a place of duty.

Code enforcement officers who are employed under Chapter 1952 of the Occupations Code are protected as well.

Note on First Responders

In 2021, the Texas Legislature amended Texas Penal Code Section 46.15 to include First Responders to the list of individuals who Section 46.03 does not apply to. Interestingly, the new language is specific to First Responders carrying a handgun only; it does not create an exception to First Responders carrying a club or location-restricted knife. *See* Chapter 14 for full discussion of First Responders.

IV. TASERS

There is no Texas statutory law governing the carrying or use of tasers. As such, it is perfectly legal for persons to purchase, sell, carry, and use tasers under Texas law. Of course, the use of tasers is not without controversy. Most frequently, tasers are used by law enforcement officers as a method of subduing a suspect without the use of a firearm. Unfortunately, in some instances, the use of a taser has amounted to deadly force.

The Texas Penal Code does not provide a definition for a taser. In fact, the term taser is not used anywhere in the Penal Code. The term "stun gun" is defined, however, in Texas Penal Code Section 38.14(a)(2) as "a device designed to propel darts or other projectiles attached to wires that, on contact, will deliver an electrical pulse capable of incapacitating a person." Unfortunately, this definition applies specifically to a law that prohibits a criminal or suspect from taking or attempting to take the device from a peace officer. The statute does not define any other type of taser beyond the kind that expels darts.

Handheld "Stun Gun"   *Cartridge Taser*

In addition, there are no appellate court cases specifically addressing any particular situations as to when or how a taser may be used. For that reason, it is important to be aware that the use of a taser will subject a person to the same standards of self-defense as outlined in Chapters 7 through 10 of this book, in that a person will likely need to be justified in using either force or deadly force before the use of a taser will also be justified. Because the law does not clearly classify or define a taser in any way, and because there are no cases on this subject, how a prosecutor, judge, or jury will view a person's use of a taser as being either mere force or deadly force is unknown. Although a taser is not designed to kill, you should be aware that under certain circumstances, and when used in a manner other than designed (such as prolonged use), a taser may play a part in a person's cause of death.

V. TRAPS AND SPRING GUNS

Texas Penal Code Section 9.44 governs the use of "devices" to protect land or tangible movable property. Non-lethal devices are completely permissible in Texas as long as they are not designed to cause death or serious bodily injury and must be reasonable under all circumstances at the time installed.

However, a "trap" or "spring gun" that discharges a firearm may cause death or serious bodily injury and is illegal. Basically, any "device" with a loaded firearm capable of discharging will be prohibited by Section 9.44.

EXAMPLES:
1) Barbed wire around a business in the warehouse district of town: likely permitted. Barbed wire is typically a reasonable security measure and usually not capable of, or designed to, cause death or serious bodily injury.
2) Razor wire around a playground across from an elementary school: likely unlawful. While probably not designed to cause death, it is arguably unreasonable to install such a "device"

near an elementary school, particularly around a playground likely to attract children.

Also, note that warnings, notices, and the like are not included in the wording of the statute, meaning that using a warning sign is unlikely to shield you from liability. Notice, warning, or knowledge of the maintenance of a spring gun or similar device has been held not to constitute a defense to a criminal prosecution and is unlikely to shield a person from liability for such a device. In the criminal context, courts around the country have held that even if the deceased person knew of the spring gun, this alone did not justify his killing.

A. Drones for self-defense

Can an individual arm a drone to shoot bullets at someone? In 2021, the Texas Legislature passed a law removing the availability of justification for civilians who use force or deadly force with a drone. This means that you cannot arm a drone to use in self-defense. This law does allow for law enforcement agencies to use force-utilizing drones in self-defense, but only under limited circumstances. *See* Tex. Penal Code § 9.54.

> CHAPTER EIGHTEEN <

WHAT IS THE
NATIONAL FIREARMS ACT?
SILENCERS, SHORT-BARRELED WEAPONS, AND MACHINE GUNS

Can an individual in Texas legally own a silencer or suppressor, short-barreled shotgun, short-barreled rifle, machine gun, or destructive device? Yes, if all National Firearms Act regulations are satisfied. This Chapter deals with the laws regarding the possession and use of firearms that are subject to the provisions of the National Firearms Act ("NFA") codified in 26 U.S.C. Chapter 53, specifically, silencers, short-barreled firearms, machine guns, and firearms that are otherwise illegal. These firearms are illegal to purchase or possess without possessing the proper paperwork and a tax stamp. In this Chapter, we will discuss the purpose behind the NFA, what firearms are regulated by the Act, as well as the process and procedure for legally possessing weapons that are subject to the Act's provisions.

I. INTRODUCTION AND OVERVIEW

The National Firearms Act was enacted in 1934 in response to gangster crimes. Prior to the Act's passage, any person could go to the local hardware store and purchase a Thompson Submachine Gun or shorten the barrel on their rifle or shotgun. President Roosevelt pushed for the passage of the NFA in an attempt to diminish a gangster's ability to possess and carry dangerous and/or easily concealable firearms, such as machine guns and short-barreled rifles and shotguns.

A. The NFA is firearms regulation using a registration and tax requirement

The NFA requires both the registration and tax on the manufacture and transfer of certain firearms. The law created a tax of $200 on the transfer of the following firearms: short-barreled shotguns, short-barreled rifles, machine guns, silencers, and destructive devices. The tax is only $5 for transferring firearms that are classified as "Any Other Weapons" or AOWs. Back in 1934, a $200 tax was the approximate equivalent of about $4,000 today!

Five years after the NFA's passage, the Supreme Court held in *United States v. Miller* that the right to bear arms can be subject to federal regulation. Miller defended himself against the government arguing that the NFA infringed upon his Constitutional right to bear arms under the Second Amendment. While the Court agreed that the Constitution does guarantee a right to bear arms, it held that the right does not extend to every firearm. *See United States v. Miller*, 307 U.S. 174 (1939).

II. WHAT FIREARMS DOES THE NFA REGULATE?
A. Short-barreled rifles and shotguns

In order to be legal, short-barreled shotguns and rifles must be registered, and a tax must be paid on the firearm. What is a short-barreled shotgun? Under both federal and Texas law, short-barreled shotguns have one or more barrels less than 18 inches in length, and the overall length of the shotgun is less than 26 inches. What is a short-barreled rifle? It is any rifle with one or more barrels less than 16 inches in length, and the overall length of the rifle is less than 26 inches. *See* 27 CFR § 478.11 and Tex. Penal Code § 46.01(10).

Short-barreled shotguns and rifles may be purchased from an FFL that deals in NFA items. Also, short-barreled firearms are very popular for individuals to build and/or modify on their own. This is legal if the person has properly registered the firearm to be modified into a short-barreled firearm with the ATF and paid the tax before it is modified. Once approved, a person may alter or produce a short-barreled firearm and must engrave legally required information on the receiver of the firearm such as manufacturer, location, *etc. See* discussion later in this Chapter for detailed requirements.

B. Stabilizing braces

The most common type of rifle that is manufactured or modified into a short-barreled rifle ("SBR") is the AR-style sporting rifle. The AR can also be manufactured as a pistol. An AR-style SBR and an AR-style pistol appear very similar. The key difference between the two is that the SBR has a shoulder stock and the pistol does not. However, the AR pistol will have a "buffer tube" extending from the back of the receiver to compensate for the firearm's recoil. In recent years it has become a trend that some manufacturers and DIY firearm hobbyists will attach a device to this buffer tube, called an "arm brace" or "stabilizing brace." This is an accessory, typically made of plastic and Velcro that wraps around the shooter's forearm, enabling him or her to have better aim and recoil control. When the arm brace was first developed, it had the appearance of a telescoping shoulder stock. Attaching a shoulder stock to a traditional handgun or AR-style pistol with a barrel length under 16 inches turns the handgun into an NFA weapon, which is only allowed upon the approval of an ATF Form 1. Many manufacturers of these stabilizing braces have sought pre-approval from the ATF's Firearms Technology Industry Services Branch to confirm that their devices did not turn AR pistols into SBRs. In a somewhat confusing series of letters and statements, the ATF has historically taken the position that the stabilizing brace, when used as manufactured and intended, does not make an AR pistol into an SBR or AOW. However, as of the publishing of this book, the ATF has floated the idea of regulating arm braces under the NFA; stay tuned.

If an individual installing and using a brace made any alterations with the intent to use it as a shoulder stock, such as adding padding or taping the sides of the brace together, and they did not get approval with a Form 1 and pay the $200 tax, they could be subject to prosecution for illegally making an NFA weapon. Further, if a person does affix a stabilizing brace to a pistol, a vertical foregrip cannot be added because the ATF has determined that this addition alters the character of the firearm so that it is no longer a pistol (since it is not designed to be fired with one hand).

C. Personal defense firearms

A new category of weapon came onto the market in 2017 designed as a personal defense firearm utilizing shotgun rounds. Mossberg was the first manufacturer to produce such a weapon, the Shockwave. This market now includes the Remington TAC-14 and the Black Aces Tactical Pro Series S Semiautomatic, to name a few. These firearms have barrels that are shorter than the 18 inches required for a non-NFA shotgun. However, the ATF has determined that these firearms are not short-barreled shotguns (because of their "bird's head" stocks, which are not designed to be fired from the shoulder). As such, these firearms fall outside the NFA regulations. *See* Chapter 5.

D. Machine guns

Machine guns are illegal under federal and state law. However, if the requirements of the NFA are satisfied, machine guns may be legally owned by individuals. First, what is a machine gun? Federal law defines a machine gun as "any weapon which shoots, is designed to shoot, or can be readily restored to shoot, automatically more than one shot, without manual reloading, by a single function of the trigger. The term shall also include the frame or receiver of any such weapon, any part designed and intended solely and exclusively, or combination of parts designed and intended, for use in converting a weapon into a machine gun, and any combination of parts from which a machine gun can be assembled if such parts are in the possession or under the control of a person." *See* 27 CFR § 478.11. As a result of this definition, the individual metal components that make up a whole machine gun, such as a full-auto sear, individually meet the federal definition of a machine gun. The parts for the machine gun do not have to be assembled in order to be illegal.

Similarly, under Texas law, a machine gun is defined as "any firearm that is capable of shooting more than two shots automatically, without manual reloading, by a single function of the trigger." Tex. Penal Code § 46.01(9). Texas law lists machine guns as prohibited weapons under Section 46.05 of the Texas Penal Code unless the item is registered pursuant to the NFA. In other words, if more than two bullets come out of a firearm with only one pull of the trigger, the firearm is a machine gun.

There is no new manufacturing of machine guns for private ownership. Because of a federal law that effectively disallows private ownership of any machine gun manufactured after May 19, 1986, machine guns available for private ownership are limited to the legally registered machine guns that existed prior to May 19, 1986. Thus, the private market is very limited and prices, as a result, are very high.

Bump stocks

Bump stocks are a rifle accessory that harness the energy of the recoil to assist the shooter in pulling the trigger as soon as it resets. This device does not alter the mechanical operation of the rifle; it still fires only one round for each trigger pull. The bump stock became controversial after the October 1, 2017, shooting at an outdoor concert in Las Vegas. Politicians and the media immediately declared that these devices allow a semi-automatic rifle to fire as rapidly as a machine gun. Many of them erroneously stated that a bump stock "turns a rifle into a machine gun." Bills were filed in Congress which did not pass, but ultimately in 2018, the Department of Justice, through the ATF, issued a final rule banning bump stocks by way of regulation. This was done in spite of an ATF determination in 2010 that bump stocks did not modify a semi-automatic rifle to make it an NFA-regulated machine gun. This new rule specifically defined bump stocks as "machine guns" under federal law. This effectively renders all such devices illegal to possess under federal law, since any lawful machine gun must have been in existence and properly registered under the National Firearms Act as of May 19, 1986, decades before the bump stock was invented. In crafting the new rule, the ATF reasoned that bump stocks allow the shooter to produce fully automatic fire while continuously applying pressure to the trigger. The new rule mandated that all bump stocks must be destroyed or surrendered to the ATF by March 26, 2019. Afterward, it became a federal felony to possess a bump stock. This crime is classified as a violation of 18 U.S.C. § 922(o)—illegal possession of a machine gun. If convicted of such a crime, you could face up to 10 years in federal prison and up to a $250,000 fine for each bump stock in your possession. Immediately following the passage of this rule, Second Amendment advocacy groups and individuals across the United States began litigation. As these cases work their way through various federal circuit courts of appeal, this issue has a high likelihood of ultimately being resolved by the United States Supreme Court.

E. Federal firearm suppressor law

What is a suppressor? It is just a muffler for a firearm and is legal if all NFA requirements are met. In legal terms, a firearm suppressor is defined in 27 CFR § 478.11 as "any device for silencing, muffling, or diminishing the report of a portable firearm, including any combination of parts, designed or redesigned, and intended for use in assembling or fabricating a firearm silencer or firearm muffler, and any part intended only for use in such assembly or fabrication."

Firearm suppressors are very practical instruments. They are great for hunting and recreational shooting not only because they suppress gunshots in a way so as to not alarm other animals being hunted nearby, but also because they lessen the impact on the shooter's ears. However, firearm owners should be carefully aware that the definition of a suppressor is very broad. Suppressors do not need to be items manufactured specifically for use as a suppressor. There are some ordinary, everyday items that could be easily converted into a suppressor, such as a water bottle or an automotive oil filter. Possession of otherwise legal items when used or modified to be used as a suppressor is illegal. In 2017, and in the years since, the Hearing Protection Act (among others bills) sought to remove silencers from regulation under the NFA and treat them as common firearms. Unfortunately, efforts to deregulate firearm suppressors have been unsuccessful on the federal level. To further complicate matters, in 2019, in response to a mass shooting where a suppressor was used, a bill banning them was introduced in Congress.

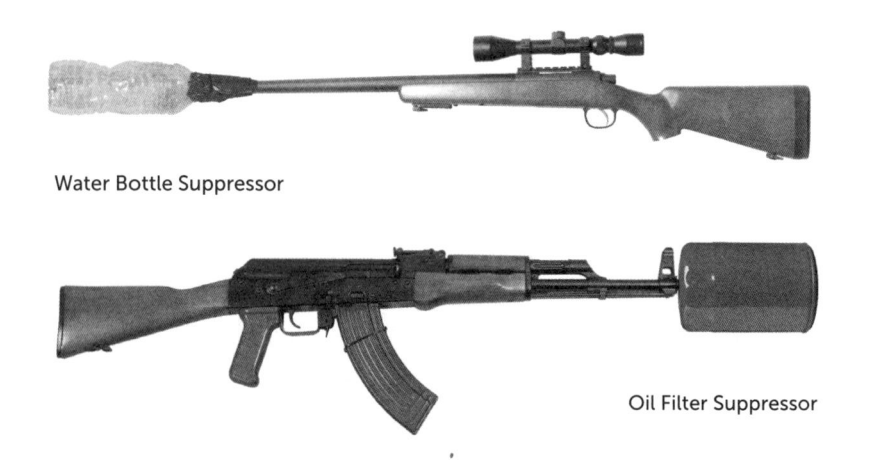

Water Bottle Suppressor

Oil Filter Suppressor

F. Texas Firearm Suppressor Law

In 2021, the Texas Legislature acted to legalize suppressors and silencers that are solely made in Texas by adding Chapter 2 to Title 1 to the Texas Government Code. In short, the law states if an individual has a silencer or suppressor that was "Made in Texas," then this silencer or suppressor would not be subject to federal law. Theoretically, this would mean a tax stamp would not be needed to own and possess the item as it would not be subject to the federal requirements under the NFA.

Under the "Made in Texas" suppressor law, the item would essentially have to be made in Texas from basic materials or insignificant parts. Additionally, a suppressor manufactured and sold in Texas must have the words "Made in Texas" clearly stamped on it. The law goes on to say that a person interested in manufacturing a suppressor under the "Made in Texas" statute must write the Texas Attorney General expressing their intent. At that point, the Texas Attorney General's office will seek a declaratory judgment from a federal district court stating that this law is valid and consistent with the United States Constitution. We are hopeful, but similar attempts in Kansas and Montana have been unsuccessful.

End of story, right? Wrong! As we all know, federal law trumps state law. Article VI, Paragraph 2 of the United States Constitution, the Supremacy Clause, states that the Constitution takes precedence over state law. If there is a state law that is in conflict with federal law, then the federal generally prevails. In this case, silencers and suppressors are governed by federal law. Therefore, an individual would be required to get a tax stamp and pay a tax to the federal government to own or possess a silencer or suppressor.

So, if a person manufactures or possesses one of these "Made in Texas" suppressors, it is very likely that the ATF could come knocking on their door; this could result in an arrest and prosecution for a serious federal felony. It will take some time before one of these cases makes it before a court to see if the law is upheld. In the meantime, if you do not want to be a test case under this law, go through the ATF process.

It is worth noting that at the same time the "Made in Texas" law was passed, Texas Penal Code Section 46.05 was amended. "Firearm silencers" have been removed from the Texas Penal Code and are no longer on the list of prohibited weapons. Keep in mind, however, while Texas won't arrest someone for possessing a suppressor under state law, that doesn't mean an individual cannot be prosecuted under federal law. The requirement to register a silencer or suppressor and pay the $200 tax stamp still exists under 26 U.S.C. § 5861.

G. Destructive devices

The term "destructive device" is a legal term given to certain firearms, objects, and munitions that are illegal under the NFA.

DESTRUCTIVE DEVICES – PART A
27 CFR § 478.11

Any explosive, incendiary, or poison gas (1) bomb, (2) grenade, (3) rocket having a propellant charge of more than 4 ounces, (4) missile having an explosive or incendiary charge of more than one-quarter ounce, (5) mine, or (6) device similar to any of the devices described in the preceding paragraphs of this definition.

DESTRUCTIVE DEVICES – PART B
27 CFR § 478.11

Any type of weapon (other than a shotgun or shotgun shell which the Director finds is generally recognized as particularly suitable for sporting purposes) by whatever name known which will, or which may be readily converted to, expel a projectile by the action of an explosive or other propellant, and which has any barrel with a bore of more than one-half inch in diameter.

> **DESTRUCTIVE DEVICES – PART C**
> **27 CFR § 478.11**
> Any combination of parts either designed or intended for use in converting any destructive device described in [part] (A) and (B) of this section and from which a destructive device may be readily assembled.

The "destructive devices" as defined in the statute are effectively broken down into three categories: explosive devices, large caliber weapons, and parts easily convertible into a destructive device.

The first portion of the definition of a destructive device deals with explosive, incendiary, and poison gas munitions. The definition specifies that any explosive, incendiary, or poison gas bomb, grenade, mine, or similar device is a destructive device. In addition, the definition includes a rocket having a propellant charge of more than four ounces and a missile (projectile) having an explosive or incendiary charge of more than one-quarter ounce. These topics and the regulations thereof are beyond the scope of this book's discussion.

The second section of the definition addresses large caliber weapons and states that any type of weapon that has a bore of more than one-half inch in diameter is a destructive device with the exception of shotguns (and shotgun shells) that are suitable for sporting purposes. Thus, any caliber in a rifle or handgun more than .50 inches or 50 caliber is classified as a destructive device. Shotguns are exempt from this prohibition on size unless the ATF rules it is not for sporting purposes. How do you know if a shotgun is suitable for sporting purposes? The ATF keeps a list, and has issued rulings classifying specific shotguns as destructive devices because they are not considered to be particularly "suitable for sporting purposes" including the USAS-12, Striker-12, Streetsweeper, and 37/38mm Beanbags. The ATF does not provide any specific definition of what constitutes being "suitable for sporting purposes" nor does it specify the methodology in which it determines what makes a particular shotgun suitable for sporting purposes. Ultimately, one will have to check with the ATF lists to see whether a particular shotgun with a larger bore-diameter is classified as a destructive device or not.

Finally, a destructive device does not need to be a completed and assembled product to fall under the federal definition and regulation under the NFA. Much like machine guns, if a person possesses parts that can be readily assembled into a destructive device, whether or not the device has actually been constructed is irrelevant—by law it's already a destructive device.

Although these firearms, munitions, and devices are prohibited by the law on its face pursuant to the National Firearms Act, a person may nevertheless receive permission to possess them so long as they possess the correct legal authorization.

H. "Any Other Weapons" or AOWs

The AOW category under the NFA pertains to firearms and weapons that may not fit the traditional definition of some of the firearms discussed elsewhere in this book due to the way in which they are manufactured or modified. Under federal law, an AOW is "any weapon or device capable of being concealed on the person from which a shot can be discharged through the energy of an explosive, a pistol or revolver having a barrel with a smooth bore designed or redesigned to fire a fixed shotgun shell, weapons with combination shotgun and rifle barrels 12 inches or more, less than 18 inches in length, from which only a single discharge can be made from either barrel without manual reloading, and shall include any such weapon which may be readily restored to fire. Such term shall not include a pistol or a revolver having a rifled bore, or rifled bores, or weapons designed, made, or intended to be fired from the shoulder and not capable of firing fixed ammunition." *See* 26 U.S.C. § 5845(e).

1. Concealable weapons and devices

Weapons that are capable of being concealed from which a shot can be discharged are AOWs. This includes such weapons as a pen gun, knife gun, or umbrella gun. Texas law does not use the term AOW but rather makes "zip guns" illegal. A "zip gun" is "a device or combination of devices that was not originally a firearm and is adapted to expel a projectile through a smooth-bore or rifled-bore barrel by using the energy generated by an explosion or burning substance." *See* Tex. Penal Code § 46.01(16).

AOWs can be registered legally with the ATF; therefore, they are legal to possess in Texas. On the other hand, zip guns are illegal, regardless of registration. Due to a 2015 amendment, the wording of Section 46.05 was changed. Instead of making NFA registration a defense to crimes under Section 46.05, the Texas Legislature criminalized only the possession of unregistered silencers, machine guns, short-barreled rifles, and short-barreled shotguns. In doing this, the Texas Legislature removed the NFA tax stamp as a defense to possessing a zip gun. However, Texas law does not specifically criminalize possession of an AOW. What is the difference between AOWs and zip guns? While not the clearest line, the definition of zip guns lends itself more readily to something that is not originally created as a firearm, but is adapted to be a firearm, whereas an

AOW is a firearm capable of being concealed from which a shot can be discharged. In other words, making a potato gun would be a zip gun, but putting a gun inside of an umbrella would be an AOW.

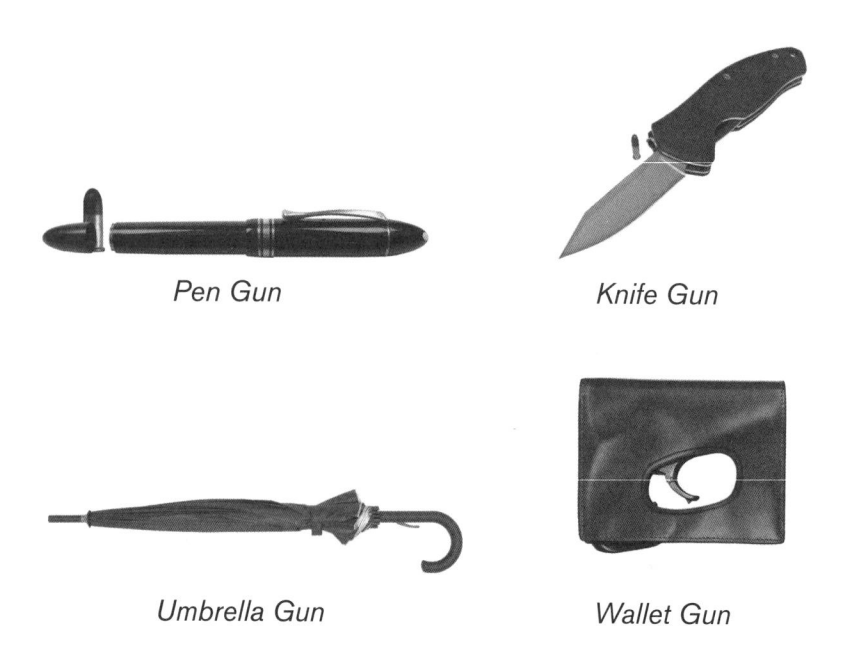

Pen Gun

Knife Gun

Umbrella Gun

Wallet Gun

2. Pistols and revolvers having a smooth-bore barrel for firing shotgun shells

Pistols and revolvers which have a smooth bore (no rifling) that are designed to shoot shotgun ammunition are defined as AOWs. The ATF cites firearms such as the H&R Handy Gun or the Ithaca Auto & Burglar Gun as firearms that fall under the AOW category. Note: handguns with partially rifled barrels, such as The Judge, do not fall under this category due to the rifling of the barrel.

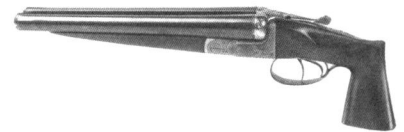

H&R Handy Gun *Ithaca Auto & Burglar Gun*

3. Weapons with barrels 12 inches or longer and lengths 18 inches or shorter

The definition of AOW also includes any weapon which has a shotgun or rifle barrel of 12 inches or more but is 18 inches or less in overall length from which only a single discharge can be made from either barrel without manual reloading. The ATF identifies the "Marble Game Getter" as the firearm most commonly associated with this definition (excluding the model with an 18-inch barrel and folding shoulder stock).

4. Pistols and revolvers with vertical handgrips

If a pistol is modified with a vertical grip on the front, it will now be legally classified as an AOW and require registration and a paid tax. Note: vertical grips are readily available and are legal to own as long as they are not placed on a handgun. The definition of a handgun is a firearm intended to be fired by one hand; the addition of the vertical foregrip makes it so the weapon now is intended to be used with two hands to fire. *See* 18 U.S.C. § 921(a)(29). This modification changes the weapon from a handgun to an AOW and is now a prohibited weapon without the proper documentation. It is not an SBR or SBS because it is not designed to be fired from the shoulder. *See* 26 U.S.C. § 5845(e).

AOW

I. Antique firearms

Firearms that are defined by the NFA as "antique firearms" are not regulated by the NFA. The NFA defines antique firearm in 26 U.S.C. § 5845(g) as "any firearm not designed or redesigned for using rimfire or conventional center fire ignition with fixed ammunition and manufactured in or before 1898 (including any matchlock, flintlock, percussion cap, or similar type of ignition system or replica thereof, whether actually manufactured before or after the year 1898) and also any firearm using fixed ammunition manufactured in or before 1898, for which ammunition is no longer manufactured in the United States and is not readily available in the ordinary channels of commercial trade." Under this statute, and for NFA purposes, the only firearms that are antiques are firearms that were both actually manufactured in or before 1898 and ones for which fixed ammunition is no longer manufactured in the United States and is not readily available in the ordinary channels of commercial trade.

With this in mind, the ATF states in its NFA handbook that "it is important to note that a specific type of fixed ammunition that has been out of production for many years may again become available due to increasing interest in older firearms. Therefore, the classification of a specific NFA firearm as an antique can change if ammunition for the weapon becomes readily available in the ordinary channels of commerce." The ATF National Firearms Act Handbook is available on their website at www.atf.gov/firearms/national-firearms-act-handbook [Accessed 3 August 2021].

J. NFA curio firearms and relics

Under federal law, curios or relics are defined in 27 CFR § 478.11 as "firearms which are of special interest to collectors by reason of some quality other than is associated with firearms intended for sporting use or as offensive or defensive weapons." Persons who collect curios or relics may do so with a special collector's license, although one is not required. The impact of an NFA item being classified as a curio or relic, however, is that it allows the item to be transferred interstate to persons possessing a collector's license. The collector's license does not allow the individual to deal in curios or relics, nor does it allow the collector to obtain other firearms interstate as those transactions still require an FFL. *See* 27 CFR § 478.93.

> **PRACTICAL LEGAL TIP**
>
> Some of the items regulated by the NFA simply don't make as much sense as the other things it regulates. Suppressors are really nothing more than mufflers for your firearm—they aren't really firearms themselves (notwithstanding the legal definition). Thinking about the utility of the suppressor, if the firearm was invented today, you can be sure that not only would the government not prohibit them, OSHA would probably require them for safety purposes! —Emily

To be classified as a curio or relic, federal law states that the firearm must fall into one of the following three categories:

1) firearms which were manufactured at least 50 years prior to the current date, but not including replicas thereof;
2) firearms which are certified by the curator of a municipal, state, or federal museum which exhibits firearms to be curios or relics of museum interest; or
3) any other firearms which derive a substantial part of their monetary value from the fact that they are novel, rare, bizarre, or because of their association with some historical figure, period, or event.

See 27 CFR § 478.11.

The ATF maintains a list of firearms classified as curios or relics, available on their website: www.atf.gov/firearms/curios-relics.

K. How can some after-market gun parts make your firearm illegal?

A number of companies manufacture and sell gun products or parts that alter the appearance or utility of a fircarm (*i.e.,* shoulder stocks, forward hand grips, *etc.*). However, some of these after-market products can actually change the firearm you possess from one type of a weapon to another for legal purposes, whether you realize it or not. As a result, many individuals make modifications to their firearms thinking that because there was no special process for purchasing the accessory, any modification would be in compliance with the law. Unfortunately, this is not always the case. Consider the example of short-barreled uppers for AR-15s: selling, buying, or possessing AR-15 "uppers" with barrels less than 16 inches is legal. However, it is illegal to put the upper on a receiver of an AR-15 because this would be the act of manufacturing a short-barreled rifle and is legally prohibited. This is equally true of vertical foregrips on a handgun. Vertical foregrips are legal to buy or possess; however, if you actually install one on a handgun, you have manufactured an AOW, and it is illegal, unless registered and a tax paid.

III. PROCESS AND PROCEDURE FOR OBTAINING NFA FIREARMS
A. Who can own and possess an NFA firearm?

Any person may own and possess an NFA firearm as long as they are legally not disqualified to own or possess firearms and live in a state that allows possession of NFA items. *See* Chapters 5 and 6. The ATF also allows for a non-person legal entity to own these items, such as corporations, partnerships, and trusts, *etc.* On July 13, 2016, ATF Final Rule 41F went into effect and modified the process for filing for a transfer or manufacture of an NFA weapon. *See* 27 CFR §§ 479.61-479.71; 479.81-479.93.

B. What are the usual steps for buying or manufacturing NFA items?

Whether a person is buying or making (manufacturing) an NFA firearm, there are several steps in the process. The transfer or manufacture of an NFA firearm requires the filing of an appropriate form with the ATF, payment of any federally mandated tax, approval of the transfer or making by the ATF, and registration of the firearm to the transferee or maker. Only after these steps have occurred may a buyer legally take possession of the NFA item, or may a person legally assemble or manufacture the NFA item. In this section, we will walk through the process, step by step, of: (1) purchasing an NFA item that already exists; and (2) manufacturing an NFA firearm.

> **PRACTICAL LEGAL TIP**
>
> Even if you don't own a machine gun today, that doesn't mean you won't be the intended owner of one later. A person could always leave you their NFA items in a will. If this happens, you must file the appropriate paperwork with the ATF as soon as possible, or at least before probate is closed. –Emily

Steps for buying an existing NFA item (for example, a suppressor):
1) select and purchase the item (suppressor) from a transferor who is usually an FFL dealer who is authorized to sell NFA weapons;
2) assemble appropriate paperwork: ATF Form 4 (*see* Appendix C), fingerprints on an FBI Form FD-258, a passport-size photograph, and a payment for the tax of $200

a. if the buyer is an individual, they must notify the Chief Law Enforcement Officer of their city or county of residence by delivering the CLEO a copy of ATF Form 4;
   b. if the buyer is a corporation or trust, each "responsible person" of the corporation or trust must complete an ATF Form 5320.23 (*see* Appendix C), including fingerprints and a passport photograph, and must notify the Chief Law Enforcement Officer of their city or county of residence by delivering to them the CLEO copy of ATF Form 5320.23;
3) submit paperwork, fingerprints, and tax to the ATF for review and approval;
4) ATF sends approval (tax stamp affixed to Form 4) to the transferor; and then
5) transferor notifies the buyer to pick up the suppressor.

Steps for manufacturing an NFA item (such as a short-barreled rifle):
1) select the item to manufacture or modify, *i.e.*, short-barreled AR-15;
2) assemble appropriate paperwork: ATF Form 1 (*see* Appendix C), fingerprints on an FBI Form FD-258, a passport-size photograph, and a payment for the tax ($200):
   a. if the maker is an individual, they must notify the Chief Law Enforcement Officer of the city or county of their residence by delivering the CLEO copy of ATF Form 1;
   b. if the maker is a corporation or trust, each "responsible person" of the corporation or trust must complete an ATF Form 5320.23 (*see* Appendix C), including fingerprints and a passport photograph, and must notify the Chief Law Enforcement Officer of their city or county of residence by delivering to them the CLEO copy of ATF Form 5320.23;

3) the "Applicant" submits paperwork and tax to the ATF for review and approval;
4) ATF sends approval (tax stamp affixed to Form 1); and then
5) the short-barreled AR-15 may be legally assembled, *i.e.*, put upper with a barrel length of less than 16 inches on a lower receiver, *etc.* The item must now be engraved and identified.

When purchasing an NFA firearm from a dealer, the dealer is required to have the purchaser fill out ATF Form 4473 when the purchaser goes to pick up the item from the dealer.

C. How must an NFA item be engraved and identified if I make it myself?

Once you receive ATF approval to manufacture your own NFA item (such as the short-barreled AR-15 in the previous section), federal law requires that you engrave, cast, stamp, or otherwise conspicuously place or cause to be engraved, cast, stamped, or placed on the frame, receiver, or barrel of the NFA item the following information:

1) the item's serial number;
2) the item's model (if so designated);
3) caliber or gauge;
4) the name of the owner, whether individual, corporation, or trust; and
5) the city and state where the item was made.

This information must be placed on the item with a minimum depth of .003 inch and in a print size no smaller than 1/16 inch. *See* 27 CFR § 479.102.

D. Which way should I own my NFA item? Paperwork requirements for individuals, trusts, or business entities to own NFA items

Form 4 and Form 1 are the appropriate paperwork that must be assembled and submitted to the ATF under the NFA and varies depending on whether an individual or a legal entity such as a trust, corporation, or partnership is purchasing or manufacturing the NFA item. The paperwork generally starts either with an ATF Form 4 used for purchasing an existing item, or an ATF Form 1 which is used if a person wishes to manufacture a new NFA item. All relevant portions of the forms must be completed. Both Form 4 and Form 1 have a requirement that a Chief Law Enforcement Officer for the city or county where the applicant lives must be given their copy of the ATF Form.

Who is a Chief Law Enforcement Officer who must be notified? For the purposes of ATF Form 4 or Form 1 and the responsible person questionnaire, ATF Form 5320.23, the Chief Law Enforcement Officer is considered to be the chief law enforcement officer who has jurisdiction where the transferor, the applicant, and any "responsible persons" are located. These persons include "the Chief of Police; the Sheriff; the Head of the State Police; or a State or local district attorney or prosecutor."

Photograph and fingerprints are required for individual applicants and "responsible persons." If an individual is purchasing or manufacturing an NFA item, the applicant must submit an appropriate photograph and their fingerprints. An entity such as a trust or corporation must designate "responsible persons" who are allowed to have access to use and possess an NFA weapon. Additionally, corporations and trusts must submit the appropriate documents showing their existence, such as the trust or corporate formation documents, the ATF responsible person questionnaire, fingerprints, and passport photographs of these persons.

"Responsible persons" of trusts, partnerships, associations, companies, or corporations, are defined as "any individual who possesses, directly or indirectly, the power or authority to direct the management and policies of the trust or entity to receive, possess, ship, transport, deliver, transfer or otherwise dispose of a firearm for, or on behalf of, the trust or legal entity." *See* ATF Form 1, Instructions. Further, with regard to NFA trusts, responsible persons are defined in the following way: "those persons with the power or authority to direct the management and policies of the trust includes any person who has the capability to exercise such power and possesses, directly or indirectly, the power or authority under any trust instrument, or under State law, to receive, possess, ship, transport, deliver, transfer, or otherwise dispose of a firearm for, or on behalf of, the trust." The ATF Form 5320.23 provides examples of responsible persons, including "settlors/grantors, trustees, partners, members, officers, directors, board members, or owners." Persons who are not "responsible persons" are "the beneficiary of a trust, if the beneficiary does not have the capability to exercise the enumerated powers or authorities."

E. Why are trusts so popular to own NFA items?

There are three major reasons trusts are very popular to own NFA items: paperwork, control, and ease of ownership. A trust is a legal entity that can hold property.

A major reason for having a trust own an NFA item is that it makes owning and using the NFA item easier if more than one person wishes to use the item. If an individual owns the item, then only the individual can possess it. On the other hand, if the item is owned by a trust, all trustees, including co-trustees, are able to possess and use the items contained in the trust. Therefore, co-trustees may be added or removed as necessary.

Further, unlike other entities such as corporations, LLCs, *etc.*, a trust requires no filings with the government to create, which saves expenses. Further, these expense savings continue because there are no continuing government fees or compliance requirements. Thus, trusts are one of the best ways currently to own an NFA item.

F. The tax stamp

Once the ATF has an applicant's materials in hand, they will be reviewed and checked by NFA researchers and an examiner. The application will then either be approved or denied. A denial will be accompanied by an explanation of why the application was denied and how to remedy it, if possible. If the application is approved, the examiner will affix a tax stamp on either the submitted Form 1 or Form 4 and send the newly stamped form to the applicant.

This tax stamp on the appropriate form is a person's evidence of compliance with the NFA's requirements and is a very important document. A copy should always be kept with the NFA item.

G. What documents should I have with me when I am in actual possession of my suppressor, short-barreled firearm, or other NFA item?

If you have an NFA item, it is a good idea to have the proper documentation with you to prove that you legally possess the item. Texas law states it is a crime to be in possession of an unregistered NFA item (except a legal suppressor/silencer), which means the police officer will need reasonable suspicion of your failure to register in order to detain you to determine the status of your item. Reasonable suspicion is a very low standard to meet. While Texas law regarding suppressor possession changed in 2021, federal law still requires suppressors (and all other NFA items) to be registered under the NFA. As previously discussed in this Chapter, federal law generally trumps state law. While Texas law enforcement officers may not enforce the federal law regarding NFA registration of "Made in Texas" suppressors, our friends at the ATF will continue to prosecute anyone who is in possession of an unregistered suppressor or silencer. Therefore, those who do not wish to become a "test case" for the new Texas suppressor law should continue to register their suppressors or silencers with the ATF.

It is good advice that if you are in possession of your suppressor, short-barreled firearm, destructive device, or, if you are lucky enough, your machine gun—have your paperwork showing you are legal, or it may be a long day with law enforcement. To show you are legal, always keep a copy of your ATF Form 4 or Form 1 (as applicable) with the tax stamp affixed for every NFA item in your possession, personal identification, and if the item is held in a trust or corporation, a copy of the trust or articles of incorporation, along with the authorization for your possession. Care should be given to make sure these documents name the individual so as to show legal ownership, *i.e.*, trust and/or amendments showing the person is a co-trustee or an officer of the corporation.

Practically, individuals should not carry around the original documents, as they could be destroyed by wear and tear, rain, or be misplaced, effectively destroying the required evidence of compliance. Photocopies of the stamp and any other pertinent documents are generally enough to satisfy inquisitive law enforcement officials. The more technologically advanced may take pictures on their phone or other mobile device, or even upload them to a cloud database. Keep in mind that if the phone dies or the cloud cannot be reached, and you have no way to access the documents, your proof is gone and you may have a very bad day ahead of you! We recommend keeping photocopies of the ATF Form with the tax stamp affixed and appropriate documents with the NFA weapon to avoid any problems with technology.

H. Is the paperwork necessary?

According to Texas Penal Code Section 46.05, explosive weapons, machine guns, and short-barreled firearms are illegal to possess without the item being registered. Until 2021, firearm silencers were also included in the list of items requiring NFA registration for lawful possession. As previously mentioned, if a suppressor or silencer meets the requirements of the "Made in Texas" suppressor law, state law does not require NFA registration for these items. However, if after September 1, 2021, a person is caught with an unregistered suppressor or silencer that does not comply with the "Made in Texas" law, even though it may no longer be listed as an offense in the Texas Penal Code, local law enforcement would likely report that person to federal authorities. Again, federal agents will continue to enforce federal laws and likely prosecute folks who try to circumvent the NFA registration requirements for suppressors.

Law enforcement officials are required to have reasonable suspicion to detain you to inquire about your item's ATF registration status. If you do not have your paperwork with you, an officer could very easily develop probable cause the NFA item is unregistered because most state law enforcement officials cannot access the ATF's database of registered items. Once probable cause has been developed, the officer has enough evidence to arrest you and see if the district attorney will accept charges.

This is a long way of saying that it is a good idea to keep your paperwork with you to prove compliance!

> APPENDICES <

APPENDIX A:
Selected Texas Statutes

This Appendix utilizes Quick Response ("QR") codes to link the reader to the exact law as published by the State of Texas.

HOW TO USE A QR CODE

1. Open the camera app on your iPhone, Android device, or Google phone; or open your Bixby-enabled camera app.
2. Focus the camera on the QR code.
3. Follow the instructions on the screen to complete the action (*e.g.*, tap the command prompt, tap the code, *etc.*).

TEXAS PENAL CODE CHAPTER 9:
JUSTIFICATION EXCLUDING CRIMINAL RESPONSIBILITY

statutes.capitol.texas.gov/docs/pe/htm/pe.9.htm

TEXAS PENAL CODE CHAPTER 9 CONTENTS

SUBCHAPTER A. GENERAL PROVISIONS
Sec. 9.01. DEFINITIONS.
Sec. 9.02. JUSTIFICATION AS A DEFENSE.
Sec. 9.03. CONFINEMENT AS JUSTIFIABLE FORCE.
Sec. 9.04. THREATS AS JUSTIFIABLE FORCE.
Sec. 9.05. RECKLESS INJURY OF INNOCENT THIRD PERSON.
Sec. 9.06. CIVIL REMEDIES UNAFFECTED.

SUBCHAPTER B. JUSTIFICATION GENERALLY
Sec. 9.21. PUBLIC DUTY.
Sec. 9.22. NECESSITY.

SUBCHAPTER C. PROTECTION OF PERSONS
Sec. 9.31. SELF-DEFENSE.
Sec. 9.32. DEADLY FORCE IN DEFENSE OF PERSON.
Sec. 9.33. DEFENSE OF THIRD PERSON.
Sec. 9.34. PROTECTION OF LIFE OR HEALTH.

SUBCHAPTER D. PROTECTION OF PROPERTY
Sec. 9.41. PROTECTION OF ONE'S OWN PROPERTY.
Sec. 9.42. DEADLY FORCE TO PROTECT PROPERTY.
Sec. 9.43. PROTECTION OF THIRD PERSON'S PROPERTY.
Sec. 9.44. USE OF DEVICE TO PROTECT PROPERTY.

SUBCHAPTER E. LAW ENFORCEMENT
Sec. 9.51. ARREST AND SEARCH.
Sec. 9.52. PREVENTION OF ESCAPE FROM CUSTODY.
Sec. 9.53. MAINTAINING SECURITY IN CORRECTIONAL FACILITY.
Sec. 9.54. LIMITATION ON USE OF FORCE BY DRONE.

SUBCHAPTER F. SPECIAL RELATIONSHIPS
Sec. 9.61. PARENT-CHILD.
Sec. 9.62. EDUCATOR-STUDENT.
Sec. 9.63. GUARDIAN-INCOMPETENT.

TEXAS PENAL CODE CHAPTER 30: BURGLARY AND CRIMINAL TRESPASS

statutes.capitol.texas.gov/docs/pe/htm/pe.30.htm

TEXAS PENAL CODE CHAPTER 30 CONTENTS

Sec. 30.01. DEFINITIONS.
Sec. 30.02. BURGLARY.
Sec. 30.03. BURGLARY OF COIN-OPERATED OR COIN COLLECTION MACHINES.
Sec. 30.04. BURGLARY OF VEHICLES.
Sec. 30.05. CRIMINAL TRESPASS.
Sec. 30.06. TRESPASS BY LICENSE HOLDER WITH A CONCEALED HANDGUN.
Sec. 30.07. TRESPASS BY LICENSE HOLDER WITH AN OPENLY CARRIED HANDGUN.

TEXAS PENAL CODE CHAPTER 46:
WEAPONS

statutes.capitol.texas.gov/docs/pe/htm/pe.46.htm

TEXAS PENAL CODE CHAPTER 46 CONTENTS

- Sec. 46.01.   DEFINITIONS.
- Sec. 46.02.   UNLAWFUL CARRYING WEAPONS.
- Sec. 46.03.   PLACES WEAPONS PROHIBITED.
- Sec. 46.035. UNLAWFUL CARRYING OF HANDGUN BY LICENSE HOLDER.
- Sec. 46.04.   UNLAWFUL POSSESSION OF FIREARM.
- Sec. 46.041. UNLAWFUL POSSESSION OF METAL OR BODY ARMOR BY FELON.
- Sec. 46.05.   PROHIBITED WEAPONS.
- Sec. 46.06.   UNLAWFUL TRANSFER OF CERTAIN WEAPONS.
- Sec. 46.07.   INTERSTATE PURCHASE.
- Sec. 46.08.   HOAX BOMBS.
- Sec. 46.09.   COMPONENTS OF EXPLOSIVES.
- Sec. 46.10.   DEADLY WEAPON IN PENAL INSTITUTION.
- Sec. 46.11.   PENALTY IF OFFENSE COMMITTED WITHIN WEAPON-FREE SCHOOL ZONE.
- Sec. 46.12.   MAPS AS EVIDENCE OF LOCATION OR AREA.

Sec. 46.13.   MAKING A FIREARM ACCESSIBLE TO A CHILD.
Sec. 46.14.   FIREARM SMUGGLING.
Sec. 46.15.   NONAPPLICABILITY.

> APPENDICES <

APPENDIX B:
Selected Federal Forms

This Appendix utilizes Quick Response ("QR") codes to link the reader to the exact Forms as published by the ATF.

HOW TO USE A QR CODE
1. Open the camera app on your iPhone, Android device, or Google phone; or open your Bixby-enabled camera app.
2. Focus the camera on the QR code.
3. Follow the instructions on the screen to complete the action (*e.g.*, tap the command prompt, tap the code, *etc.*).

ATF FORM 4473
FIREARMS TRANSACTION RECORD

atf.gov/firearms/docs/4473-part-1-firearms-transaction-record-over-counter-atf-form-53009/download

ATF FORM 1
APPLICATION TO MAKE AND REGISTER A FIREARM

atf.gov/file/11281/download

ATF FORM 4
APPLICATION FOR TAX PAID TRANSFER AND REGISTRATION OF FIREARM

atf.gov/firearms/docs/form/form-4-application-tax-paid-transfer-and-registration-firearm-atf-form-53204/download

ATF FORM 5320.23
NATIONAL FIREARMS ACT (NFA)
RESPONSIBLE PERSON QUESTIONNAIRE

atf.gov/firearms/docs/form/national-firearms-act-nfa-responsible-person-questionnaire-atf-form-532023/download

➢ ABOUT THE ◁
ATTORNEY AUTHORS

KIRK EVANS
CO-AUTHOR

Kirk is the President of U.S. & Texas LawShield and has practiced law in Texas for nearly 30 years, concentrating most of his work on litigation including constitutional issues and complex civil litigation. He has advised gun owners, instructors, ranges, and law enforcement. He is an ardent supporter of each of our rights to keep and bear arms and is a proud gun owner.

Kirk is a graduate with honors from Texas A&M University and attended law school at the University of Houston, where he graduated as editor of the Law Review. Kirk was recognized as a "Rising Star" in the legal profession by the Texas Monthly publication *Super Lawyers*.

Kirk is a frequent speaker on civil liability associated with gun ownership and has been a presenter at events across the United States, including the FBI Dallas CAAA Active Shooter Seminar, the national NRA Foundation Banquet, and multiple civic and community organizations. In addition, Kirk has served as a media source for firearms law, including appearances on Fox News, KXAN in Austin, KSAT television in San Antonio, and a national interview with Yahoo Sports, along with more than 50 radio interviews with stations across the country. Kirk has also authored a number of legal publications on firearms topics such as "Tribal Law and Your Firearms."

EDWIN WALKER
CO-AUTHOR

Edwin Walker is an Independent Program Attorney for U.S. & Texas LawShield and a partner with Walker & Taylor, PLLC. A native Texan, Edwin earned his bachelor's and law degree at the University of Houston and has been practicing law in Texas since 1993. Edwin's legal career has been focused primarily on criminal law, and he is a proud member of the State Bar of Texas, Texas Criminal Defense Lawyer's Association, and the Harris County Defense Lawyers Association. Edwin continues to make numerous appearances as a speaker to large crowds, small groups, radio programs, internet podcasts, and television shows. He is currently living in La Porte, Texas, and will enthusiastically share his views on our Constitutional rights, and anything concerning music, politics, and Texas history to anyone who will listen.

EMILY TAYLOR
CO-AUTHOR

Emily Taylor is an Independent Program Attorney for U.S. & Texas LawShield and a partner with the law firm of Walker & Taylor, PLLC. Emily received her bachelor's degree and her J.D. from Vanderbilt University in Nashville, Tennessee. A proud Texan by birth, Emily returned from Nashville to be sworn in as an Assistant District Attorney for Galveston County, Texas, before moving her career into the world of gun law with Walker & Taylor. Emily prides herself on providing aggressive, attentive criminal defense for her clients all over the State of Texas who have been charged with offenses related to firearms and self-defense.

Emily is a frequent lecturer and instructor to both law enforcement officials and civilians on firearm-carry laws and the use of force and deadly force. She is a frequent contributor to Fox News affiliates and other media outlets on issues of firearms law, and has been cited as an authority on firearms law in national publications.

RICHARD D. HAYES, II
CO-AUTHOR

Richard D. Hayes, II is an Independent Program Attorney for U.S. & Texas LawShield and a partner with the law firm of Walker & Taylor, PLLC. As a former senior felony prosecutor with extensive criminal trial experience, Richard has combined his law enforcement experience with his passion for individual rights and government accountability and is a zealous advocate for his clients.

Richard is also known in the firearms and Second Amendment community as a Texas gun and weapons law authority. To that end, Richard regularly travels around the state and country and presents on self-defense, weapons law, and the legal aftermath following a defensive incident. Additionally, Richard regularly consults with lawmakers and industry experts on firearms law and best practices.

Richard earned his J.D. from St. Mary's University School of Law in San Antonio, Texas, in 2013 and was admitted to the Texas Bar the same year. Before law school, he received his B.S. in Maritime Administration with a minor in Economics from Texas A&M University. Richard is also a native Texan, parliamentarian, outdoorsman, pistol instructor, and Eagle Scout.

The U.S. & Texas LawShield® Legal Defense for Self Defense® Program is dedicated to preserving its members' fundamental and Constitutional right to self-defense through zealous legal representation by Independent Program Attorneys experienced in self-defense and gun laws. A cornerstone of the U.S. & Texas LawShield program is legal education.

U.S. & Texas LawShield boasts hundreds of thousands of members, including civilians, law enforcement and security officers, and military personnel. U.S. & Texas LawShield is honored to be affiliated with thousands of gun ranges, gun stores, FFL dealers, instructors, educators, and other firearms experts and professionals. U.S. & Texas LawShield is one of the largest civilian repositories of state-specific self-defense and gun law legal information available anywhere.

For more information about the U.S. & Texas LawShield Legal Defense for Self Defense Program, visit www.uslawshield.com.

Edwin Walker, Emily Taylor, and Richard Hayes are Independent Program Attorneys for U.S. & Texas LawShield with the law firm of Walker & Taylor, PLLC. This publication is not an endorsement or solicitation for any product or service. The content in *Texas Gun Law: Armed And Educated* was produced for educational purposes only as a general legal overview of the law in Texas. No legal advice is being provided and no attorney-client relationship is being created. This publication is not a substitute for legal advice. You should contact an attorney regarding your specific legal circumstances.